EUREKA

Published by Little m Press
Colchester, England
www.littlempress.co.uk

Front cover concept by Paddy Tyson
Jacket design by Naked Creative and Jo MacDonald
Printed in Poland

For more copies of the book, please email:
graham@grahamfield.co.uk

www.grahamfield.co.uk

EUREKA

Finding the Line between Desire and Contentment, then Riding It

by

Graham Field

Publisher
Little m Press, England

For Mum
Please stop climbing ladders or you will compromise both our lifestyles.

FOREWORD

I can always remember where I was and what the weather was like at significant moments in my life, so I remember that the sun had just come out, and I was seated on the terrace overlooking my vegetable garden, with a large gin and tonic by my side waiting to be tasted, when I first opened Graham Field's book.

I wasn't expecting much.

At the time *Jupiter's Travels* was first published, thirty-eight years ago, I don't remember there being a lot of competition. Of course there was *Zen and the Art of . . .* , that improbable blockbuster which came out just before mine and opened the door for books related to motorcycles, but people had only just begun to use bikes to make interesting journeys rather than for joy-riding.

All that changed dramatically during the last decades. More and more people began to take off on ever more ambitious trips, and inevitably, large numbers of them felt impelled to write a book. And now of course there's a deluge of blogs as well. I'm all in favour of it. Some of them keep friends and family entertained. Some reach out to an ever-growing community of motorcycle travellers, but they all start with the same premise: "If you like bikes you will like this book or blog or whatever." In other words, they don't really stand up on their own any more than a bike does.

That's why Graham's book was such a joy. I wrote to him almost immediately.

"Even though you put me down in the first paragraph of your introduction, I think your writing is bloody marvellous. I've only read four chapters, but I wanted you to know that I am really glad to have met you."

Graham is a dancer. He moves like one and writes like one, dancing through his experiences with a light and lovely touch. He is effortlessly amusing, and I know how much work goes into that. His writing comes out of nowhere, and I am sure it will just get better. He has his own idiosyncratic view of life as he wanders around the world like a pied piper taking us along for the ride and . . . you don't even have to like bikes.

—Ted Simon

Ted is the author of *Jupiter's Travels* and *Riding High* (about his 1973 round-the-world ride on a Triumph Tiger), *Dreaming of Jupiter* (a 2001 ride of 59,000 miles through 47 countries on a BMW R80 GS), and *Jupiter's Travels in Camera*. Ted's books have been the inspiration for many adventure riders and travelers seeking to understand the world they pass through on their journeys. Ted is founder of the Ted Simon Foundation, that supports and promotes travelers and whose " . . . ultimate aim is to promote understanding, reduce tension and to favour the chances of peace between our many cultures."

About the Author

Author and travel writer Graham Field was "born at a very early age, and independent travel begun shortly after he learned to crawl." During obligatory but inadequate schooling, he spent the majority of his time looking out of the window and escaping into his favourite daydream—the freedom of the road. Making restless dreams become a reality has been his single-minded talent.

Graham's life of travel really started with his first motorbike, obtained way before he was old enough to have a licence. By the age of eighteen he was living in the US, working in construction, in strip clubs, and riding a 1960 Harley-Davidson. In 1990, he set off around the world with a backpack, and this was followed by challenging solo cycling trips in India and China.

For over a quarter of a century, Graham has had three constants in his life: motorcycles, travel, and diary keeping. He appeared on a national TV game show, where he announced he would use his modest winnings to ride to Mongolia. This was when all three of his obsessions came together. On a thousand-dollar KLR 650, he rode 15,000 miles east from his home in the UK—105 days on a $7,500 budget. This journey, the people met, the challenges, and the startling contrasts of both the cultures and landscapes became the subject of his hugely popular and inspirational diary-format book, *In Search of Greener Grass*.

A few years later, his KLR, with the same budget, distance, and time-frame, took him to Iraq and Azerbaijan. A "eureka moment" occurred during this journey, and that epiphany became the topic of his enthralling second book, *Ureka* [*Eureka* in the North American Edition]. His third book, *Different Natures*, takes the reader on earlier motorcycle trips from the Alaskan Arctic Circle to southern Mexico. Delving into diaries packed with tales of naivety, and at times eyebrow-raising debauchery, the reader soon discovers that Graham's mantra is "You never lie to your diary."

Graham writes regularly for *Overland Magazine*. His articles and columns are published in British national papers and motorcycle publications in both Europe and North America. His presentations are widely regarded as some of the funniest in the genre, and in radio interviews he is well known for his passion for travel and his off-the-cuff comments, which both challenge and amuse. He makes regular contributions to *Adventure Bike TV*, where he was nominated as "most inspirational adventurer." Graham has a residency on *Adventure Rider Radio*, alongside travel writers Brian and Shirley Hardy-Rix, Grant Johnson of Horizons Unlimited, and myself. He currently lives in Bulgaria, with a variety of iconic motorcycles, a cluster of KLRs, and some gold-digging cats.

—Sam Manicom

Sam is the author of a four-book series (*Into Africa*, *Under Asian Skies*, *Distant Suns*, and *Tortillas to Totems*) about his eight-year journey around the world by motorcycle.

ACKNOWLEDGEMENTS

Who to thank? Well the last book which was also the first book, changed my life, but not beyond all recognition, in a springboard to fame—overnight success—dark glasses in public kind of way. However the bike shows and the signings introduced me to a new group of people, the readers, people who have an insatiable zest for life, who don't just turn pages but also turn their dreams into realities.

People with a passion regardless of age, means or abilities, they know life is to be lived and do their best to live it to the full. I have met independent struggling authors, artists, film makers and photographers, designers and fabricators most of whom, like myself, have a day job but who believe in their product and are driven not by profit but a desire to encourage and inspire, to share their view of the world through their chosen medium.

Every activity has a pyramid of successful participants. At the top are a few household names, as you move further down the names are only recognised in smaller circles of enthusiasts. More hardcore but less marketable, these are the people who create cult followings, in underground movements they are the back street heroes, all doing what they love regardless of where it leads. Short of being mentioned in a tweet by Lady Ga Ga, they progress one sale at a time, standing proudly behind their products knowing it is real, genuine, and in the right hands with the right frame of mind, it might just enhance a life.

I'm not sponsored, I don't drop names for favours but if a product or person performs outstandingly well or if it pisses me off, I can't help but mention it. Gabe at Zen Overland went above and beyond any definition of customer service to create my beautifully manufactured, aluminium tank box, designed to keep my camera dust-, shock- and waterproof as well as instantly accessible. It turned out to be a bit of a naysayer magnet, particularly on the forums, but on the road, not in front of the computer, is where it turned from a controversial concept into a fully functioning reality.

Who else to thank? You of course, I hope you read on.

TABLE OF CONTENTS

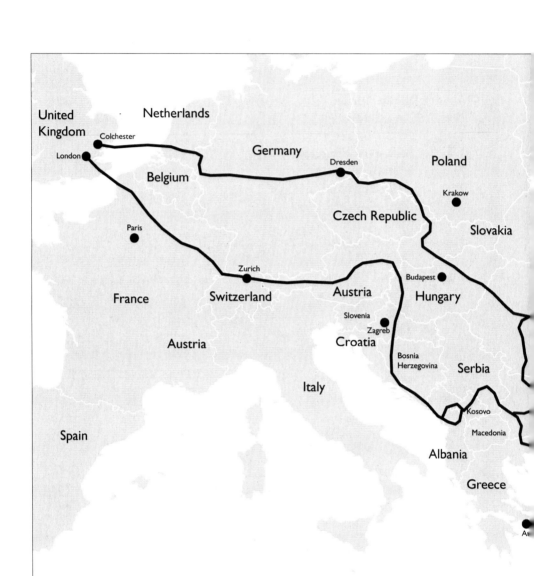

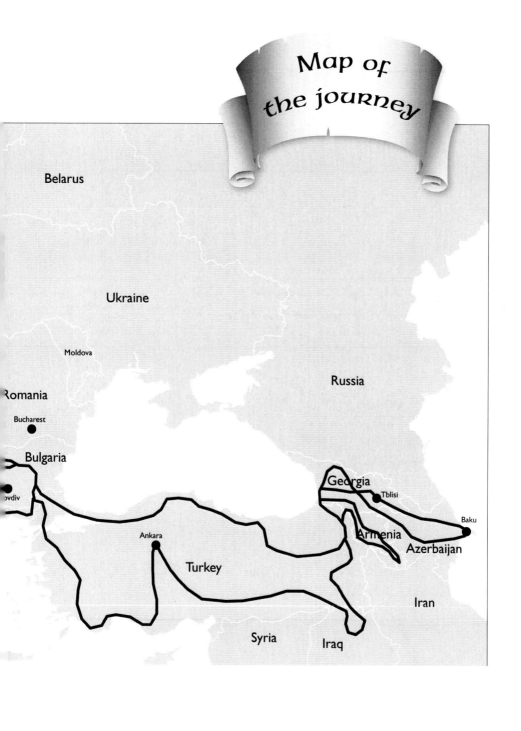

Map of the journey

Belarus

Ukraine

Moldova

Russia

Romania

Bucharest

Bulgaria

ovdiv

Georgia

Tblisi

Baku

Armenia

Azerbaijan

Ankara

Turkey

Iran

Syria

Iraq

How often I found where I should be going only by setting out for somewhere else.

—R. Buckminster Fuller

Experience is simply the name we give to our mistakes.

—Oscar Wilde

On Iron Horse he flies
On Iron Horse he gladly dies
Iron Horse his wife
Iron Horse his life.

—Motorhead

If I'm free it's 'cus I'm always running.

—Jimi Hendrix

INTRODUCTION

You know those travel books that start with the big drama; the love scene, the life-threatening confrontation, the horrific accident, or indeed, a single event that encompasses all three? An attention-seeking paragraph to hook the reader and drag them to the next page? Well I don't do that.

There are many reasons to leave the place you call home and head into the unknown: different agendas, different objectives. Whether on a quest for it or not, the traveller will inevitably discover a truth. That's why travel is so pure and appealing. Truth about people, culture, religions and oneself, all witnessed first-hand. An undistorted vision of a country, vulnerable, exposed. Not impressions tainted by TV, but the day-to-day functioning of life; lives of the traveller and those encountered.

And nowhere is truth and honesty more abundant than in a diary, hence the format of this book; it is my diary. Lying in a diary is as pointless as trying to change the world by clicking "like" on Facebook. I've been keeping a diary for over a quarter of a century. It's the one discipline in my life, and like anything that's done repeatedly, you get better at it. But not so good I can actually predict the day to come, so I don't know at this stage any more than you do what is around the corner.

However, judging by the size if this book, it is unlikely that I'm hit by the 7:35 to London as I cross a malfunctioning level crossing on my way to the ferry terminal.

So this is less a book about a journey, just a journey in a book.

No TV game show winnings this time, I had to actually go out and earn the bloody stuff to pay for this trip. Still it keeps me in the real world. I'm still on the same KLR 650, which is now 17 years old with about 40,000 miles on the clock. I've still got Monklet, my left-hand man, my ever-smiling mascot, sitting between the clutch lever and the Bark Buster; always happy, regardless of the weather, dutifully breaking ice in the most dire of situations.

The only big thing about my budget is the impact it has on the way I travel.

My journey to Iran and the "'Stans" started with a more local Stan; Stanstead Airport. I flew to Vienna; well technically I flew to Bratislava and then got a bus to Vienna, but that's Ryan Air. Then I walked several miles to the Iranian embassy. It was Monday, and I had allowed six days to get my passport stamped with an Iranian entry visa. I arrived at the embassy at 12.20PM, and thankfully, there was no queue. Annoyingly, it was because they'd closed at noon. That's not what the website said. I asked an Iranian woman the other side of the locked steel gates if I could come in. I asked in English, of course, my German and Farsi are equally inadequate. She wandered off and came back with a key, a good sign I thought, as I was ushered into the typically beautiful Viennese building with excessively high ceilings. I was beckoned to a desk and spoke to a very genteel Iranian gentleman.

"I've come to apply for my visa."

He fingered through his file and found my pre-applied for letter of invitation. I gave him the paperwork I had, which all appeared to be in order.

"Yes, you will be able to pick up your visa tomorrow."

"Tomorrow?"

"Yes, if you had come earlier you could have got it today, but we have closed now. You will get a 30-day visa starting from tomorrow."

"Wait, um, I'm not ready yet, can it not start in a month?"

"Then you must come back in a month."

"I have just flown here from the UK to get this visa."

"I understand, but due to our elections we can only offer you a 30-day visa starting today." I knew of the pending elections and the trouble it may cause; not only could the wrong result reignite earlier protests, but also the authorities wanted to avoid any foreigner getting involved by limiting visits during this time. "But tell me," he continued, "why did you fly here? Why did you not just send us your passport?"

"Because I didn't know I could just send you my passport. You never answer your phone or respond to emails."

He apologised and gave me his direct number. I left him my passport and said I would be back tomorrow.

Sitting by a fountain in the almost adequate warmth of the Viennese early spring sun, I considered my options. I hadn't even got my bike ready yet. I'd have to fly home and then hurtle through central Europe, Romania, Bulgaria, and right across Turkey. If I rode like a demon I might just get a week in Iran before the visa expired. On top of all that, I hadn't even applied for my Carnet de Passage, and the processing time for that is a month. This wasn't going to work at all. Shit. I'd told everyone I was going to Iran.

So there I was, looking at a tranquil and relaxing fountain with a week to kill in Vienna and I'd just given away my passport. What was I going to do now? Look up an old girlfriend?

By morning I knew what I was going to do, or at least what I wasn't going to do: I wasn't going to Iran. I could still go east to Azerbaijan then across the Caspian Sea on the notoriously unreliable ferry to Turkmenistan. Assuming it arrived on time, I would still only have a three-day allowance to transit on to Uzbekistan, where I could catch my breath before it is taken away again on the legendary high-altitude Pamir Highway in Tajikistan. Then, finally, the visa-exempt Kyrgyzstan and from there into Kazakhstan, and Russia, just because it's on the way home.

Day 1

Into Mainland Europe, 172 Miles

Where does the journey start? When does the adventure start? At what point does the plan become reality? When the visas are obtained and the panniers are loaded? Maybe when the engine is started and first gear selected? With the clutch released, the left hand rises to wave goodbye and then flips down the visor in a futile attempt to stop the chill wind from making the eyes water. This is it. I'm off.

The bike may suggest adventure, but the location does not; I'm waiting outside the local sorting office at 7AM on a Monday morning, trying to get the situation into perspective. How much do I really need this last minute eBay purchase? Isn't it more important not to miss the pre-booked ferry? A van arrives and is enthusiastically unloaded with the buzz and banter of postal colleagues who really don't seem to mind that once again it's Monday morning.

"What size is it, Graham?"

"Imagine a grapefruit in a box, about that size."

"Where are you going this time?"

"Turkey." That will be an adequate answer for now.

At 7.32AM, with a box bungeed hastily on a pannier lid, I'm on my way, the first uninterrupted mile of the journey.

I've been travelling this road since I was nine. So many emotions, preoccupations and forms of transport. School bus oblivion, rowdy and smoking fags on the back seat, big trucks with fiddled tacos, paid for a night out on the road but slept in my bed, riding to a girlfriend's house, driving to a job interview. Today it's more significant but not really scary. I'm only going to the ferry, having opted for seven dull hours sailing to the Hook of Holland over the equally dull route to Dover and then through France and Belgium to Holland. Western Europe is, regardless of the way I enter, only an area of transit. It's expensive, it's cold, and it's on the way, or more accurately, in the way of where I am heading.

And so the mind is free to wander; the lists are left behind. From now on, the road beneath my tyres will be the only thing my days consist of. Where it takes me, the temperature, condition, what lies next to it, and beyond it. What tempts me to pull off it and encourages me to stay on it. Excited by the prospect of what distractions I will get from it and hoping to keep enough attention to stop from hitting it. Providing nothing more than a complacent commute for a local, will for me, be as complex as the country it carries me through.

However, before I reach that sea of excitement and romance, I have to leave this island I call home. I ride a stream of monotony that takes me to Harwich, and apart from the night I discovered the 500hp truck I was driving had a broken speed limiter, this journey has never been either romantic or exciting.

Straight down the ferry boarding ramp, the only bike on board. That's OK; I don't need company. I have plenty to occupy myself. I find a comfy chair and head for the canteen for a not quite full-English breakfast and try to eat it without being distracted. Just relax and bask in the glory of the completion of six weeks of lists and chores: from bike restoration and preparation to obtaining visas and so many other necessities and obligations that occupied my every waking second and continued to occupy my restless mind when I wanted to be asleep. The satisfaction of everything done, everything that mattered anyway. Highlighted, crossed off or forgotten, it's all left behind. I'm moving away from that.

This year spring seems to be reluctant to bloom, spread its fragrances, and sound its morning chorus. Crocuses crept into late April, and tulips are yet to show their colours. I can't wait any longer for my favourite time of year to arrive, I'm going south to meet it, to be fatigued by heat, heat I can't imagine as I sit on a ferry with my boots off to caress my cold feet. I keep wriggling my toes in my clean but inadequate socks to circulate the blood. What little warmth this action generates is stolen from the soles of my feet, through the worn carpet that lies over a steel floor.

I think I'll take another trip to the buffet, circulate the blood. Got to feed myself up, got to kill time, got to use up the rest of my sterling; chips are easily justified.

The next event to pass the time is hard to justify. I open the box I picked up from the sorting office and take out my . . . well, it's not a grapefruit.

I don't find it a huge challenge to summon the courage to set off on a 15,000 mile trip alone, into the unknown with no language and little research. It's not that I don't appreciate it, but I'm lucky enough to have experienced this a few times before. It sounds like a brag, but it's not; it's just something I have conditioned myself to do. So this box, I have to 'fess up to, is a digital box of pure hypocrisy. Against all my principles and ideals, I've gone and brought a sat nav. I would like to use this ferry crossing to try to understand how this thing works. Like a pensioner with an iPhone, I have no experience or understanding of its capabilities. The instruction book is fat, but as I thumb through the German pages, I assume it's written in many languages. But the German goes on, in fact, from cover to cover. There are no instructions in English, and the on-screen language is German too. I stab my finger on the virgin touch screen and bring up a menu I can't read. Well great. So begins and ends my first attempt to understand a sat nav. On top of that, I've run out of chips and phone reception. What am I going to do now? Shake from Facebook withdrawal?

I have two inadequate excuses for buying into the sat nav generation. This particular cheap, unknown brand came with a European map that included Turkey, a place where I will be trying to procure my onward visas. Not only do I have to find the individual embassies, I also have to find the embassies' designated banks to pay for said visas. There will be bureaucracy and limited opening hours, combined with a processing time that can only be guessed at. So, if I can at least ride straight to the address, I will have all the more time for standing in queues.

That was one reason to get the thing; the other is my sight. I love maps; the satisfaction and knowledge gained from spreading them out on the floor, plotting a route, or just getting perspective and distance, discovering the landscape, familiarising myself with place names, which I find easier to remember when I have actually read them. These are all wonderful by-products that come from looking at a road map. However, I now no longer have the ability to glance away from the road ahead and instantly focus on a map to read a road number or village name. My eyes have done what they do to so many people of my age; the muscle that focuses has lost some of its strength and elasticity. My arms aren't long enough to hold text at a distance I can focus on. So the glancing down to the map on the tank bag is as futile as trying to check the oil level as I ride. It's a pain in the arse, especially trying to locate that elusive cheap hotel on a page ripped from an out-of-date *Lonely Planet*, a skill I once got great pleasure from. So, instead of burying my long-sighted head in the sand, I decide to accept that this sat nav technology might help with this degenerative sight problem. And that's all I can come up with. Like Facebook, I hate the thought of it, but that's just the way things are, and reluctantly I have to accept it.

I am not recreating an historic journey undertaken in a past century, plotting a course by the stars, or eating meats preserved in salt. I'm just going for a ride.

The ferry docks, I ride up the ramp; maybe the trip starts here. The Dutch customs lady seems to think so.

As I lift the lid on the tank box to retrieve my passport, she asks where I'm going.

"Russia," I hear myself say.

"Alone?"

"Yes."

My sat nav is in German; I don't understand it, I'll just ask.

"It's that way, right?"

"Yes, straight ahead," she says with an uneasy laugh.

At the first junction, I come to the road I think I may want, but it's closed. That's OK; I don't really know which way I'm going anyway. Towards Rotterdam, I suppose, the signs correspond with the notes I made. Holland is a constant criss-cross of motorways, I pay no attention to anything much other than direction. I come down a slip road and am battered by the turbulence of a coach doing the same speed as me. The KLR is not a fun bike like a Ducati, it's fun because of where it can take you, but on a Dutch motorway it's really not in its element.

I pass a signpost for a place called "Best," but that won't do, I'm looking for better, and I'm looking for it tonight. The sky is clear, the air cool and fresh, and I'm looking forward; I have a little rendezvous planned.

It could have been easy to find the meeting point. Could have been, but it isn't, and it takes a few calls until I am met and follow a car to the hotel. Pizza and beer, drink too little, and talk too much, she says she has never met anyone who leads such an uncompromising lifestyle as me. I'm not sure if that's a compliment or not, probably just a fact. A big bottle of Jagermeister is produced, but that isn't going to improve anything tonight. It may take away the inhibitions, but it erases the memory too. I know she only wants to use me, I want to use her too. I want something from her, something I can't get from an English girl.

"Can you change the language on my sat nav?"

Day 2

Sittard, Holland, 172 Miles

A text in the night informs me a dying friend in the States has taken her last breath; this is my third bereavement this year, and its only April. This is further confirmation I'm doing the right thing; if I'm to be next it's going to be without a job or pension, but with a full tank and empty wallet, heading into the unknown. My motorcycle boots on my feet, sleeping bag in the top box and no room anywhere for regret. I'm not going to sit at home and wait for the end to come. If death wants me it will have to come and chase after me. I'm not being morbid, it's just that as you get older you really can't help but notice that life is, as you are constantly told, actually quite short. I know of a guy who lived in the Australian outback. He had a metal bathtub in his yard; he would fill it with water and pass his days laying in it, shooting passing rodents and spiders. He admitted it was boring, but that was the point of the exercise, it made the time go slow, and therefore, his life seemed longer. You're only middle-aged once; I've got a life to live, and I'm not sure how much is left.

I'm woken by hacking, coughing, violent guttural evacuation of deep-seated phlegm; it penetrates the thin hotel walls. Blimey, this was only my first night. If I was in India I would expect this dawn delight, where it is part of the culture, here it's just bloody annoying. It wakens me fully as it continues, now amplified and eased by the steam from the shower I hear running.

I have low expectations for breakfast. The benefit of the negative online reviews of this place is that the standard is higher than I expected, but only just. At this stage in the journey, I have little to compare it to. I enter my room to a ringing phone. She will be round in ten minutes, she's coming early as she has to leave earlier than expected. I barely have time to shower.

She has to leave by midday, so what am I supposed to do after that? I'm only here for her pleasurable company.

The atmosphere, the encounter, feels forced, it was always going to be a clandestine meeting, but this is so unnatural. We go for a walk. Spring is yet to grace the wooded surroundings of this lake, and even if it did, the sound from the motorway makes this environment as unnatural as this meeting.

Back in the room for some temperate Jagermeister, it doesn't hit the spot, but its warm, sickly taste does break the ice a little. Nothing screams affair like morning sunlight streaming through the netted windows of a sordid hotel.

Some people said the last book should have been called *In Search of a Shag*, but in my defence, it's basically my diary. I share a lot; some things are just personal. There are countless publications, magazines, chicklit, etc. where you can read about sex. I write about not having sex, as failed attempts and romantic disasters are something everyone can relate to. If someone wants to use my platform of self-deprecation to promote their own carnal success, then I think that says far more about them than about me.

It's not even lunch time, and all I'm left with is the bitter taste of deceit, combined with the sickly denial of Jagermeister.

I have a day to kill in a place I don't want to be. This encounter was not based solely on consummation of the relationship. I was really hoping for a day with someone whose company I actually quite enjoy, however, now I'm just a used up piece of meat. Right, that's the sex out the way, now I just need drugs and rock 'n' roll. Has the journey started yet?

I text a friend who, in the context of this long trip, lives quite close. He is in and has no plans. I pack up, and although like a gigolo I have had my accommodation paid for (we didn't go Dutch), I won't be getting another visit, so I won't be staying another night. I want to leave this soulless room behind and indulge in something far more wholesome, like the Dutch coronation. The queen has given up her throne to her son, a reckless lad who married an Argentine beauty that won the hearts of the country and so the acceptance of the new king. Behind every great man is a great woman. What I left behind just grates.

The sat nav is now operating in English, and I set the controls for the heart of Holland. So begins the directional dictation, and I follow with utter dependence straight to my friend's house, but in entirely the wrong direction for Asia.

"No. 6" is not having his identity protected due to any extra marital activity; he has nothing to hide. He is as single and is as honest as I am, or at least as I was until lunchtime. He just has an unpronounceable name. I met him in a guest house in Mongolia; he stayed in room number 6. Since then, he has ridden his KTM from here to South Africa. There is plenty of common ground. For eight hours we talk bikes, travel, encounters, and all the subjects that sprout from them. We drink in a continuous but responsibly Dutch way. Other than the fact it's a Tuesday night and the bars are alive, there is no other evidence of the day's Coronation events. Whether dressed in orange, national costume, or simply "out-for-the-night" clothing, people seem well-dressed; no baggy sweat-suits or rolls of fat exposed beneath crop tops, no obnoxious ranting or singing. Children play in the cobble-stoned town square until late, and from students to parents or overlanders, there is a feeling of calm, respectful celebration. I have to be on my guard not to change this atmosphere. We don't need the token Brit on all fours puking on the pavement or bloodied and being comforted by the hoop ear-ringed girlfriend saying, "Leave it Gram 'e's not worf it." Why is our British drinking culture so reckless? An evening is not over until bodily fluids are spilt. Given the choice, I suppose I would opt for the morning's sound of hacking if I have to choose a fluid to flow and an orifice for it to exit from.

DAY 3

ERFURT, GERMANY, 301 MILES

It's sunny and clear, and so is my head. No. 6 has to go to work and without question leaves me the keys to his domain. I can pack and prepare without time pressure or distraction, at least there is little excuse for distraction. But as soon as I hit the road, I realise I'm in a muddled and distracted state. The only cure I know for this is to ride. With miles comes routine and organization. Camping tonight will help this transition. I can walk around my bike and fettle. I've had too much company in the last two days. It relieves the anxiety and daunting thoughts of what lies ahead, but it's delaying the appropriate mindset from developing.

It doesn't just happen, this "road mode"; the transition is a gradual thing. Just because I can't read the signs and have to consider which side of the road to ride on doesn't automatically mean I'm in the travel zone. Far from it, the traffic I have to assume will look out for me at this stage, as I weave round tiny roundabouts and make last minute lane changes. There is too much to take in; not scenery, just the all-consuming thoughts of bike, location, and direction. On the plus side, my bike, although heavy, is quite manageable. It's not exactly nimble, but I do have confidence in my ability to control it. Apart from spare tyres, some other things I am not taking this trip are waterproofs and spare brake pads, therefore at this early stage, hard braking due to lack of concentration irritates me. These pads have to get me an estimated 13,000 miles, and No. 6 said that his actual trip from here to Cape Town was double his estimated mileage. Still, that won't be an issue if I don't pay attention to the road now. The sat nav comes unstuck, and I ride one-handed until I find a place to stop and remoisten the suction cup.

I am heading south down the narrowest strip of Holland; 1 km to my left is Germany and 2 kms to my right is Belgium. If I lose my balance and wobble I could very well end up in another country. It's a tightrope, this little strip of the Netherlands.

I see signs for places I've come from, and I have a desire to revisit the familiar. Forging forward into the unknown has, at this point, no attraction at all. I could call, send a text, but although this trip is for no one but me, what would I achieve if I just stuck around the familiar.

Soon enough the *autosnelweg* turns to *autobahn* and another language I can't read. I do know that German fuel is slightly cheaper than Dutch, so I fill up and then buy an extortionately priced breakfast bun.

Something has changed in my approach. All my life I have had little confidence in my requests in English as I try to convey my desires to the natives, always humiliated and embarrassed at my mono-linguistic skills. OK, I can use the appropriate Americanisms to avoid confusion when I'm in the US, but until recently, that was the extent of my bilingual ability. But now I have Spanish. It's not good. I can't have conversations, but I can use the odd right word, if not always in the correct context. I, at least, have enough of a vocabulary to express myself.

As I eat my bun, standing by my bike, a trucker approaches and says something in neither English nor Spanish.

"Nein Deutsch," I reply, as he points at my loaded bike. "Holiday?" No, lifestyle choice, actually.

"Yes, Turkey." I get the thumbs up, and he goes.

Slowly and discreetly the sun disappears, the shadows lose definition, and the sat nav screen is easier to see, if not read. The denial went on for about 18 months. I couldn't see what the reduced price said on the sticky label at the supermarket, couldn't read the menu in a mood-lit restaurant or the smaller kph figures on my speedo. It's now at the stage where I simply have to add glasses to the list of things to take before I leave the house; wallet, phone, keys, and bloody glasses. The addition of which does not fully solve the problem. I have just discovered that when I look up and away into the distance with them on everything is blurry, so in circumstances like important navigation, I have the glasses perched on the end of my nose with my visor down to stop them falling off completely. It's not a good look, not one you ever see on those biker posters depicting freedom, power, and strong handsome riders, but this is real life. I'm still alive and I'm still riding, it's better than any alternatives I can think of.

As the dull autobahn miles pass, my head sorts through the bombardment of issues that were buffeting my thoughts like the violent and turbulent wind does to my less than aerodynamic windshield when a truck passes me. Most things pass me, which is just fine; I'm happy to have a clear road ahead and no need to judge the speed of a distant German driver before leaving the slow lane.

I seem to have to keep stopping. With more focused concentration and clarity, little adjustments need to be made. Also, now the temperature is dropping, I notice that the tank box seems to have the effect of pushing a downdraft of cold air onto the tops of my legs. This may be a benefit in the heat, but at this point it's a chill I don't need.

Despite the perception we have of rigid German regulations, one of the things I like is that the autobahns have, unlike our UK motorways, an abundance of parking places. You don't have to wait for a corporate service area, so my frequent stops don't involve a tour of an ill-planed labyrinth of bollards and concrete dividers, dodging e-number fuelled kids, aimless wandering coach parties, and blinkered caravaners. I simply drift into a lay-by (using engine braking—thereby saving my pads) and deal with whatever nagging little distraction is delaying my progress. On one such stop I've barely come to a halt when a loaded GS pulls up in front of me. He has a patch on his back but it's not threatening, even though I can't read it, I can tell it indicates a union alliance, rather than a territorial membership.

When he eventually finishes his post pull-over practices, he catches what is about my third nod of acknowledgement and comes over.

"Holiday?"

"Yes, I'm off to Turkey."

"You're going the wrong way."

"Not directly, I'm going to visit friends in the Czech Republic."

"It's still the wrong way."

I'm not 100% confident in my direction, not enough to argue it. That's a sat nav for you; I am already relying on it, even though I have, as a backup, scribbled down the numbers of the highways I will be taking. Said sat nav is being uncharacteristically quiet. It usually babbles away in lay-bys; perhaps it does it all the time, but I only hear it when I slow the pace. However, it is now making no effort to defend itself, so I'm left with no reply option but a rather ineffectual "I have plenty of time."

"How long?"

"Four months; I have no job."

"I've never seen a metal tank bag before; it is dangerous," he continues, looking round my bike. He points at my fork brace. "You need this? If the police see it, they will make you take it off, and you can't have a headlight cover like that. They don't like homemade things here."

"Well, I don't have a lot of money; I do what I can on a budget."

"What do you want to do?" What, apart from getting away from you?

"What do you mean?"

"For work."

"I was a truck driver."

"You should work here in Germany. There are many jobs. You just have to learn to drive on this side of the road." Oh right, sounds a bit tricky.

"This is not a Touratech rack your panniers are on."

"No, it came with the bike."

"Your panniers are not secure. Touratech is the best."

I know some Austrians I'm sure you'd really like.

My internationally understood body language is now screaming "fuck off ," and Mr. Negativity finally picks up on it. Having sorted out my destination, equipment and employment, he leaves me to digest his advice and get myself back on track, which I will, but not until he is well down the road so our paths never cross again.

My 12-volt auxiliary charger has stopped working, so the sat nav battery is flat, which would explain its lack of contribution to the one-sided conversation. And Monklet went unnoticed too. I'm sure there would have been a cautionary tale about quarantine laws and mistaken identity.

This little electrical job can be done two ways, so I practice the Zen option. It's rewarding and satisfying; the charger is dismantled, reassembled, and all connections made secure. My voltmeter confirms it now has a 12-volt feed and then that the fuse in the sat nav charger has blown, so the previous hour's maintenance was, in fact, unnecessary. Well, the positive thing is my earth wire is clean and secure now, and achieved without the help of Mr. Negative.

However, our conversation replays in my mind as I ride, and I get more and more annoyed as I mull it over. There is a line in Shakespeare's *King Lear*, which says: "Have more than you show, speak less than you know." He went off thinking I was an unemployed truck driver, which is a truth, but a tiny part of a story he will never know. I don't have a destination today, and with the dropping temperature, this morning's desire to camp is fading into the dismal grey sky. I'm in the former East Germany now. Although there is no evidence of the cold war era, there isn't any evidence of anything much from this autobahn. Occasionally the road crosses a valley. Beyond the barely visible spring growth on the trees are images of pleasantly located villages sitting on green slopes. Not worth a photo, but the only pleasurable sight as I pass down this concrete corridor. I suppose I shall try and find a room. I stab at buttons on the sat nav, but I can't make it understand I want to stop here, now and not on the outskirts of some German town 400 kms away. I open my eyes and wake up my common sense.

I find a town, head for the centre, and see a sign for a hotel. See, this is OK; it sends me down a country lane. I anticipate a posh and expensive golf club annex accommodation but keep riding, just in case I'm wrong, into a tiny village, and there it is, a small but obvious hotel in keeping with the other local accommodation.

The door is locked. I speak English into the intercom, and I'm greeted by an English speaking landlady. Yes, they have a room. I seem to be the only guest, but I'm not even a guest yet.

"How much?" She says a big number in German and then shows me outside again to the board on the wall and points. Cool, 39. I had 35 in my head, but it includes breakfast and Wi-Fi, so that's fine. I think it's safe to say the journey has definitely started now; it's just not much fun yet.

I'm really hungry. I walk the village; there's not even a bar, and the place is dead. I walk the other way. A sign and arrow with 400m written underneath it takes me down a single lane, through rapeseed oil fields that are yet to blossom and it's 1st May today, a national holiday, which explains the lack of activity. I count my steps, 400 of them. This can't be right; it's a dead end.

There in the distance is a single house with a massive glass lean-to. There is movement inside, and as I approach, I see it is heaving, there is a car park, and it's full. Just what I wanted. I stand inside the door, trying to be seen by a waitress but only being stared at by diners. "One person," I say when I'm finally noticed.

After sitting, an elderly waiter approaches and says, "I hear you are English."

"Yes, I am."

"Would you like help with the menu?"

"No, I think I can manage. Can I have a glass of red wine please."

I watch him pour it, and as he offers it to me, I say, "Dankeschön."

"Don't speak to me in German. I am not German," he says.

Pizza, spaghetti, lasagne, oh wait, I'm in an Italian restaurant. It all makes sense now.

My bike is covered and safe, my room is warm, and my tummy is getting bigger every day. Today's expenses were significant, but that's Western Europe for you—luxuries I don't need at this stage, and money I would rather save for later. But I have to transit this western wealth; it's where I live. It's just an inevitability of leaving from my home, independently overland.

Day 4

Kobierzyce, Poland, 307 Miles

I feel a little rushed. Breakfast is at eight, and this being Germany, I expect means it will be on the table on the dot punctually. There is plenty to eat and to take away. I have a Spinal Tap moment as large slices of ham overlap the miniature bread, but I'll rise above it, I won't let it affect my day. I fill my tummy and then my pockets. It's a nondescript restaurant in a featureless hotel in an unremarkable village off a dull autobahn. Yesterday, at least, started with sunshine. Today is grey, but through the window there is some faint green, early evidence of a late spring. However, there is not a shadow in sight. Today there isn't much hope for anything better. So it's quite a dismal start, and I can't say I'm full of zest.

Today I'm heading towards Dresden; not a name that does anything to lift my spirit. It hasn't the ring to conjure excitement like Rio, San Francisco, or even Vienna, unless you're a World War 2 enthusiast, and I'm not. But Dresden is not my destination. For the third time in this fledgling trip I intend to stay with company, some Czech people I met in Mongolia. We have had occasional contact since we met and parted, but there has been more communication in the last three weeks than in the whole of the last three years.

It's not an early start. I know my direction today, and there is no need for the sat nav. Yesterday its location interfered with the opening of my tank box, the day before it obscured the speedometer, today it sits higher on the screen, and with the constant buffeting of passing traffic, I'm not sure it is going to stay put. If it hits the road, I'm not sure how bad that would be.

I do 100 miles and then stop and boil some water at the kerb side. I put the liner in my riding trousers; I have a chill and little to drive me on. Come on transition, where's the buzz, the excitement, the enthusiasm?

Unceremoniously I cross into Poland. The only evidence from the road is a sign with the word *Poland* written in a circle of gold European stars. The motorway is new and concrete, and the traffic has decreased but passes me with less respect and space.

Petrol is cheaper here; life is cheaper here. At the petrol station kiosk a group of large Polish men stand around being loud and smelling of vodka, and as I walk back to my bike, a peroxide woman exits her car and spits. I'm sure this is not a true representation of Poland, but it's my first image, and it sticks. What blossom there is, is wasted against a drab grey backdrop. It starts to rain and the sat nav is getting wet, I'm getting wet. I go past Wroclaw and off the motorway. The rain and road speed continues; the spray increases as does the misery factor. However, I am granted variety in my soaking.

The speed and spray stop. The traffic is backed up waiting for a train to cross this busy road. The rain taps on my helmet and drips from my lifted visor. I'm seriously questioning the wisdom of leaving my waterproofs at home. There is no sign of this letting up. When I see a hotel with a price on the signpost I do some currency calculations in my head. Eight pounds? Surely that can't be right? I'm right, it isn't, it's sixteen, but that does include breakfast. I'll take it, it's 5:30PM. I'm very damp, my feet are soaked, and at this price at this time of day, being inside is preferable to out.

Just as I've finished locking and covering the bike, I am advised to move it from the car park to the side of the hotel. I try and persuade myself that the appropriate response to this recommendation should be gratitude and not annoyance but only manage something in between. The delayed gratification of getting out of these clothes is another ten minutes away. The room is tiny and dark, and I decorate it from TV to curtain rail with my hanging moist clothing as I peel off the layers.

In the UK I make a point of never listening to the weather forecast. I find it inaccurate and deliberately pessimistic. I'm convinced it's a national conspiracy to keep us all at home and off the overcrowded roads. If you listen to the way the forecast is reported, the sentences always have a negative slant "mainly sunny with the possibility of rain later" or "expect rain for most of the day." The same report could be expressed as "sunshine for most of the day" or "possibility of sunshine later." But no, I'm sure the pessimistic weather forecast is partly responsible for the national psyche, and I would much rather look out of the window and decide for myself what the day will bring than wait for the predicted doom. Like football fans who want to avoid hearing the score of a match, they have recorded but not yet seen. I happily take my bike out under a blue sky only to be told, "It's not going to last." Of course, it's not going to last, nothing ever does. When I used to paint house exteriors the instructions on the can would say, "Don't use if rain is imminent." It's England, rain is always bloody imminent, and if it wasn't I wouldn't need to use this product of protection in the first place. Having said all that, this isn't England, it's Poland, so I watch the weather report. Apparently, it's going to rain all day tomorrow. Bollocks.

DAY 5

KOBIERZYCE, POLAND, 0 MILES

It's pissing down, and just to make it worse I'm being well informed just how lovely the weather it is at home. There are three bike events I could attend this weekend in sunny England, but I'm here in wet Poland sitting in my room trying to enjoy my adventure.

I go down for my breakfast; the restaurant is underneath the flat roof my room looks out over, and it has leaked. The staff are busy moving chairs and mopping the floor. The leaking ceiling is covered by a mural of ancient Polish history; wolves and bearded men, rulers, hunters and gods, primitive settlements, and harsh winter snows. It's all most impressive, certainly labour intensive, and the figures and stories depicted have my eyes wandering around the entire interior until they come to rest on the scrambled egg brought to my table. There is some Euro pop playing with an annoyingly happy beat, and somehow I seem to know the words. I silently sing the lyrics, trying to recall the song. As I reach the chorus, I realise with horror I'm singing along to a disco version of Metallica's *Enter Sandman*. Oh dear.

I make an emergency snack from the supplies on the table and go out to my bike to stash it. The cover has kept the worst of the rain off, but the sheepskin seat cover has become a sponge, a wet bottom-rash inducing sponge. I have no desire to sit on it at all. I make a decision, unsure of whether the journey I'm about to pause has really even started yet.

With my Wi-Fi connection I can occupy myself all day, not useful research of routes or handy Polish phrases such as "I would like to purchase a bottle of your cheapest red wine." Instead, I just watch YouTube videos and find other distractions that stop me considering my location. There are some men working on the flat roof outside that makes me feel a little on display, but not enough to close the curtains. With nothing better to think about, I try to decide if closing them looks like I've something to hide or leaving them open on this dark day with the light on makes me seem like an exhibitionist. It's a dilemma I am giving way too much thought to.

When the breakfast has digested and my tummy brings itself back to my attention, I wander back to the bike to retrieve my secret roll. The tables it would seem were not being moved out the way of the dripping roof; they have been arranged in a large circle and are covered with tablecloths, adorned with candles and brimming champagne glasses. There are plates of delicious appetisers and enough cutlery to suggest there is much more to come. It's suddenly all very fancy and decadent in here.

"Are you having a party?"

"Yes, 47 guests are coming." It sounded like he said "for a bar mitzvah," but I definitely caught the fact there will be no food tonight for uninvited guests. That's me, I suppose.

"Then may I purchase that bottle of red wine," I say in near-perfect English, and as I hand over my credit card there is the sound of horns as a soggy convoy of cars trailing ribbons and balloons pulls into the car park. I retreat to my room. In different company, in a different mood, I might see if I could crash this party, but the solitude of my tiny room seems more inviting, and that's where I stay.

There is a lot of laughing and excited voices, and after a few glasses of wine, intrigue gets the better of me. I go down through the throng on the pretence of going out to fetch something from my bike. The look I'm trying to convey is pretty vacant, available for any invitation that might be offered, but none are. A few girls are dancing, not to Metallica and it's not any kind of pole dancing I've ever seen before. I withdraw to my room and keep my wine bottle company. The bass pounds until 4AM and is then replaced by door banging; maybe I shouldn't have stayed a second night.

DAY 6

JESENIK, CZECH REPUBLIC, 74 MILES

Outside my window the grey is lighter, inside my room my mood is too. Time for a different country I think. I'm two days later than planned for my little stay in the Czech Republic, but today is Saturday and probably a better day to turn up. Although I'm informed by text that my friend, Michal, is running a market stall today, it sounds OK; I can get behind that.

The motorways are behind me and the scenery has improved, it couldn't have got much blander. Now there are hills, and a castle sits on one of them. It's not screaming orgasm brilliant, but it helps to sever that tie that was holding me back. Going forward is more pleasurable today. It's also a little bit embarrassing when I realise just how close I was to the Czech border and that in just over an hour I'm in Michal's village. I could really have managed that journey in the rain I think. I'm sure I will become more road-hardened as the journey progresses and the time passes. I am so early that I ride round the village to try and find his house. I ride up dirt tracks that take me through forests that are just beginning to cover their winter bleakness with a new green coat. There isn't much about, no houses, people, cars, or any real signs of life and certainly not the slightest indication as to where Michal's house might be. So I go back to the main road through the village towards the next one, over bridges that cross fast running rivers and past long established stone-built houses. It's just so good to finally be off the motorways. They are very good at getting you to places fast, but a motorway is like an aisle seat on a plane, easy access at the loss of a view, and on these back roads I have the window seat and am not disturbed by the food trolley. I don't expect to win any awards with this analogy.

Some people remember faces, others can recall a name. I can do neither, and it has made for a lifetime of social embarrassment, from tagging someone who wasn't even included in a game of playground touch, to the noncommittal pub conversation with someone who clearly knows who I am; "Keeping busy then?" However, due to the fact I have kept a diary for over a quarter of a century, I'm quite good with dates. I met Michal and his five friends when they were driving Ladas across Mongolia in early August 2010. I spent less than 24 pleasurable hours in their company. I've not seen any of them since, but I have a single photograph of them, proudly standing by their cars. Michal stood tall, skin and bones in a pair of boxers. He emanated such an enthusiastic, gregarious zest for life it was almost exhausting. Multilingual, he displayed his talent in a restaurant, telling us in Czech, German, and English what was on offer and then confirming the order in a sort of Russian/Mongolian language to the owner. If that wasn't enough, he then picked up the bill because "it was his birthday." So that was my brief encounter with Michal, and why would you not want to revisit such a positive experience?

As I ride out the other side of the village, I see a log-cabin-community-village-hall type thing. There are some cars in the car park, and as I pass I see there are quite a few people setting up tables and stalls. "That must be it," I think as I brake and turn around, "That must be him," they think and come out to meet me. I'm glad I'm recognisable; the man I have to assume is Michal bears no resemblance to the person in the three year old photo. He's filled out, grown his hair, a beard, and to add to his girth, he has a baby in a sling on his chest; apparently it's his.

I'm introduced to his partner (who he met in a Mongolian airport). How romantic. I also meet the array of stall holders; it's a very close and bohemian community. Everyone seems to have a child under four, and most of the girls are pregnant again. What a great environment to grow up in; safe and natural, wild and unspoilt countryside, organic and clean, rich in provisions, if not in possessions. I'm welcomed and spoken to in English by everyone. I don't feel like I'm intruding, but Michal has a lot to do today, and I'm happy to come along for the ride.

The ride is more like a guided tour; he is a mine of information. I get a history of the country and culture from invasion to immigration, national traditions to opinions. He explains the architecture and geology, castles and quarries, invasions, ownership, exoduses, and borders. He explains how it all ties in locally, nationally, internationally, historically, and recently. I am becoming so informed; it's so interesting, insightful. It's not blind patriotism, it's a genuine pride in knowing where he and his people have come from and what they have been through. An expansive general knowledge, like people had before Google, when stories of old were told around campfires by elders, stories that the young and inquisitive couldn't help but absorb. That's how I imagine it anyway. It is riveting and if I try really hard to stir my dormant brain into life, I can occasionally add a piece of semi-precious fact to this mosaic of explanation. Sadly, I store information like this in the same deficient mental file as name and face recognition. However, there's one thing I recall; on the village green is a tall phallic pole, erected for the month of May. It depicts new life. Every village has one, and it is the job of the men of the village to guard this pole all month from any potential invaders who will try to burn the pole down, thus symbolizing the impotence of the protectors of the smouldering pole. The victorious arsonists would then take this opportunity to breed their strategy, strength, and stamina into the next generation with the recently humiliated local lovelies. Sounds like fun to me; where's me lighter?

What a wonderful life he has, it's not hippy dippy idealistic, it's genuine, functional, and simplistic. There seems to be an appreciation, rather than a yearning; there are plans and explanations, not failed efforts and excuses. The journey has definitely started now, I can tell this because I've found somewhere I want to stop.

We drive through valleys into fields and up a muddy track to a large dilapidated stone house where Michal and his small but growing family live. They occupy a single room in the empty house. A large, light, airy, homely room with an Aga-style stove, big dining table, and beds placed long ways against the walls. The entire area is bigger than many flats, and with its white walls and views of green rolling hills, it feels anything but claustrophobic.

No time for making myself at home, though, we are moving on from here. He explains that houses are numbered chronologically, so the new builds have the highest numbers and the lower numbered houses are scattered all over the village. I wouldn't want to be a temporary postman here.

We have to go and meet a Polish family who have also come across the border today. In a lay-by waiting for us are three generations in one car. The driver has come to see Michal about the location and organization of an adventure activity course for his youth group. He is accompanied by his youthful Canadian born and raised son and his elderly but fit and healthy father.

We drive to the edge of a forest. The land is elevated and looking over the plains of Poland. The sky has cleared now to reveal the first really spring-like day. It's glorious. Michal has a gypsy caravan here; a genuine, authentic wooden caravan. A chimney protruding from the roof invites all year occupancy. Underneath, a winter's worth of logs are stacked up between perished tires to validate the invite. It's more permanent than parked and too adored to be abandoned. It is situated by a river with nothing else around but views. He says I could have stayed here if his friends were not using it this weekend. Damn, I want to live in a gypsy caravan, live by a river, boil my kettle outside over a log fire. I want to get up in the night and, under the light of the moon, go and burn down maypoles in neighbouring villages. I want to impregnate impressed local Czech girls with my adventurous and nomadic genes, then contentedly ride back to fix the punctures on the flat and perished caravan tyres, load up the wood, and tow it to the next village. It's the perfect existence. Actually, it sounds quite exhausting; perhaps I'll just have a cup of this herbal tea instead. It must be this unspoilt environment that provokes such a self-indulgent daydream, which I'm thoroughly enjoying as the others talk outdoor activities, zip lines, and obstacle courses. Their plans are far more realistic than mine but equally exhausting I think. I feel like a bit of a contradiction in this situation, this hippy lifestyle of minimalism and respect for nature. Whilst my new friends wear holey jumpers, sandals, and cloth baby slings, toddlers play on the steep steps of the caravan, and no one bats an eye. And here I sit on a mossy log by the smoking camp fire, with my designer shades, logo T-shirt and Gore-Tex trainers, acknowledged, accepted, maybe even integrating but somehow feeling a little disconnected from it all, but enjoying it none the less. I help fetch water from the river, and although I would love to capture this scene, I'm quite glad I don't have my outrageously large camera with me. That is sitting unattended in a tank box of a petrol burning, air polluting motorcycle, left in the car park of a jumble sale. I'm sure it will be fine.

The day continues with traditional Czech food in a village pub. This time my host speaks Polish, English, and Czech to establish the order. It's quite cabbage orientated, very tasty, but I hope I won't be sharing a room later. On we go, round the grounds of an imposing fort overlooking the village. The Poles are most knowledge about the landscape and trees, and when they get stuck they ask me what variety this one might be. "The daffodils are late this year; umm, can we talk about geography soon?" I'm beginning to feel I have little to offer the conversations they are having.

On to an ancient building deep in a valley at the side of a noisy river. It once was the archbishop's dance hall and is now in the process of being restored. The reshaping of oak beams with hand tools is financed with the help of a grant from an ancestor with a personal interest. On we go, past an abandoned and boarded-up uranium mine and through another valley past hills of granite and quartz with crystal clear lakes at the summit where once were mines. It's all enhanced by an evening light that says summer is on the way. In a half hour I could have ridden past everything I've seen today, oblivious to it all. Motorways are the blinkered corridor to a destination; back roads are the open doors that lead into rooms that educate the traveller about the journey. Better?

The day ends at a little guest-house of self-contained suites. The landlady and I click immediately; some people you can just be yourself around. Even though we have only just met, somehow there is something honest, genuine, and stimulating about our conversation. She says I am my own man and for her this season in her life has passed. It's not said with sadness or envy, it's just a statement. My lifestyle has been getting this reaction a lot lately. I really don't see it that way myself, like anorexics won't believe they are not fat.

DAY 7

OSWIECIM, POLAND, 210 MILES

The couch I slept on was about 6 inches too short, but as the landlady pointed out, "The couch is not for sleeping on, it's only permitted as you're special." Which was a lovely way of saying, "The Poles got the three beds in the bedroom, and I didn't want you messing-up another room."

Once my sleeping bag is rolled up, we all drink coffee in my "bedroom." The conversation turns from travel to motorcycle travel, to the dangers of motorcycle travel. It's beginning to piss me off a bit; you don't talk about plane crashes on the way to the airport do you?

"Well at least I'm living now, better than dying of boredom," I say with a clear "end of subject" emphasis that cuts through the language barrier.

It's raining again. I could stay here another night, but I will never get out of Europe if I don't ride in the rain, so I follow the Poles in their car back to Michal's village.

The first thing I do whenever I arrive in a new country is observe and copy: customs, dress-code, dining, and driving habits. Well, maybe not copy, but at least I'm aware and try not to blatantly offend. Having a bit of decorum saves embarrassment at best and confrontation at worst. I've seen topless Russian girls screaming at local "pervs" on an Indian beach, but it's pretty obvious who's at fault. There is Western European consideration in the Czech driving techniques. They don't have an insatiable and senseless need to overtake every car in front of them. The car I'm following does. It causes unnecessary fatigue on a wet and quiet country Sunday morning road. I stay behind; overtaking in these conditions at this time of morning involves too much effort and a needless soaking from spray. Predictably, I catch up at the junction; now it's my turn to lead across the fields and muddy tracks—the ones I was driven down yesterday as I looked at cloud

24

formations, and paid little attention to the terrain. The Poles get stuck on the slippery grass, but my KLR effortlessly takes me to the door, and I lean it against the stone wall and follow the smell of coffee through the back door.

We all sit around the large dining table. The conversation starts with history from the 1300s, moves forwards, and stops at World War 2. It appears to be quite a popular subject. In fact, it seems to be making a comeback. When I backpacked in the '90s, the Germans I would meet barely mentioned it; now it seems they are embarrassed and apologetic for it all over again. It wasn't our generation, nor our parents. I think blame died with the perpetrators. There is one awkward moment though; my first intended site to see on my vague itinerary is Auschwitz. It's a bit of a conversation stopper. I knew I would be in the vicinity, and it's just something I want to see. Anyway, I think I will go outside now and photograph the blossom that's falling from the trees like confetti.

I could easily spend a week, a season, a whole year here, but I've got the urge to press on, and I'm going to obey it. I say my goodbyes, and for the first time this trip, I get to wear my fingerless gloves. I ride across the dew-soaked, slick grassy fields and head out of the village and through the valley. This area has possibly the greenest grass I have ever seen. In a flash of realisation it occurs to me that moisture is the cause of it. I don't want any more wetness, I want warmth and I want dryness, so I think I'm going to search for something else now.

The altitude increases, and the bike splutters. It feels like the choke is on, running too rich. It won't accept any throttle. It's never done this before, not that I take it up to 3,000 feet very often in Essex.

I had some last minute mechanical trauma before I left home. In an almighty backfire I blew the end out of my SuperTrapp exhaust, making the bike excessively loud. In desperation, I bought a silencer off eBay that was equally as loud and another one from a local breakers, the diameter of which was so wide it interfered with the pannier. Out of time, I reluctantly put the original exhaust on, which weighs at least twenty pounds. I started the bike to discover the joint along the length of the silencer was split, but it was too late to do anything about it. The exhaust pops a bit when I throttle back or go down hills, but I can live with that. Maybe it's this damp air that is now causing the misfire. With a drop in altitude the bike runs fine again, and soon I forget about it, distracted by waving. The Czech biker is an enthusiastic waver, but then it is Sunday, and any ride today is for pleasure. Back in Poland the motorways are clear and new. Gone are the castles, replaced by Burger Kings, the pastures of grazing horses, replaced by Tescos. This dull mileage is not totally without value; all the time I'm getting more used to my machine. When I reach the town of Oświęcimia, I realise I'm negotiating tram lines and traffic with absolute control and can once again ride with confidence.

I find a dormitory hotel not far from Auschwitz. I'm the only guest. I get some supplies and make appalling spaghetti bolognaise. The times I most frequently long for company on the road is when it's time to cook. My meal is basically fried onions sitting in tomato puree on top of boiled spaghetti. It's bloody awful, but the perspective gained from being on the outskirts of Auschwitz makes complaining seem ludicrous.

DAY 8

NOVA LESNA, SLOVAKIA, 185 MILES

Not just a dorm to myself but an entire building, I stash my valuables and ride the short distance to Auschwitz. I've just locked and covered my bike when I'm approached and told to move it; still a place of uniformed authority then?

I'm early and have the place to myself; I like to do this in popular places, especially when I want to be alone with my thoughts. I'm sure there is nothing I can say about this place that hasn't already been written. I go through the gates, above which once hung the sign "work makes you free." It was recently stolen, and I have worked for several firms who could be suspects.

I walk to the holding huts, where the first thing that hits me is the smell. They are wooden and far from weatherproof, but it's like nothing I've smelt before, wood or otherwise, and I've been in a lot of damp sheds. If I ever smell that smell again I'm pretty sure it will bring me back here. Some still have the bunks in them, stacked three high from floor to ceiling, end to end. The beds look of an adequate size, until I see the photos and realise people slept in them width wise, not along them.

As I walk from one to the other I notice that on the road beyond the fence and watchtowers someone is rollerblading to work. It seems such a paradox, not disrespectful, just unlikely.

One point the Poles I had been with made very clear was that although Auschwitz is in Poland it was within the borders of Nazi Germany during the war. Not only were the Poles not responsible for the atrocities, but the first murders at this camp were of Jewish Poles. This is the very beginning of a long list of shudder-inducing facts.

For me the children's holding shed was by far the most moving. There were two large pictures on the wall. One drawing depicts a line of kids parading with

27

hobbyhorse, drum, and doll. I wonder if this brought comfort, joy, or escapism to the inhabitants. I walk the length of the deathly silent hut. A few notes and toys have been left on some of the bunks; it brings the past into the present with a consciousness that numbs. I try to focus my camera on a dying red rose someone has placed by a headboard. The dim light and dark ceiling make for a slower shutter speed, larger aperture, and higher ISO numbers. I deliberately let this technicality distract me from displaying an overwhelming sadness. In my limited experience, children will accept any situation as being normal, due to so few comparisons in their new lives, but what did these little innocents make of this environment?

Well, I wanted to see it. I never expected it to be fun. It's all about variety of experiences; not every song can be danced to. Everybody takes something away from this, I'm sure.

When the road straightens and the signposts confirm direction, my concentration lapses and my thoughts return to this morning's sightseeing and education. I don't need more confirmation that there is no god. No all seeing, all powerful being would ever have let this continue year after year, millions of innocent deaths. This is the doing of man, and all the praying in the world won't change that, only taking responsibility for our actions will. Religious hatred is still a major motivator of violence. Do the instigators really wish the horrors of Auschwitz on their enemies? If they do, then four million people were murdered in vain.

When I've exorcised my anger, I'm able to take a look around me. Finally I find some beauty in Poland, it's almost Swiss-like. I ride along a mountain ridge looking down onto a patchwork of fields, clusters of pine trees, flowery meadows. Some well-positioned properties have spectacular views of sunset and sunrise valleys; shame they are so close to the road.

I don't exactly know what my next destination is, but the sat nav doesn't seem to want me to ride this scenic road. I'm not paying much attention to it, and when I arrive in Nowy Sacz instead of Nowy Targ I can see the point it was trying to make, but it's the best mistake I've made in a while. No wonder I was seeing signposts for Ukraine; it all makes sense now. If this gadget could display emotions, then right now it would be smug. It does nothing to endear itself to me; in fact, I find most of its habits annoying.

I spend the last of my Polish zloty on fuel and cross into Slovakia. Here they have the Euro, which is convenient because so do I, and it saves me the strain of mental calculations. What shall I do now I'm free of this preoccupation?

The hills and valleys continue with picturesque churches and then the real bonus. It just occurred to me, although I've been seeing signs of spring, what's been missing is the fragrances, and now they are here along with rivers and good roads that are twisty, and then a big snowy mountain, spectacular. This is the benefit of not knowing where you are going or what to expect. This is my favourite aspect of travel. It's a good way to end the day. The temperature still doesn't encourage camping, but neither does the price of a room. For ten euros I get a little annex with a view.

I walk the town in search of food, but all I find is a bar with a restaurant that is closed. Three silly teenage girls are cooing over the bartender, and all giggle when I leave. It docsn't bother me. Yes it does, but not as much as hunger. The town seems to be void of a café or, indeed, any shops. I look at the craggy mountain view from my window and eat the last of my bread. Rock 'n' Roll.

DAY 9

MIKEPERCS, HUNGARY, 291 MILES

I've got three choices today and am incapable of making a decision. The timing is not working out, and nothing is on the way. I planned to start the trip by visiting some European friends. The theory was that it would put perspective on the journey, instead of leaving home wondering how the hell I was going to get to Turkmenistan. But it's not having that effect. It's delaying me and certainly not comforting me. Living on an island, Europe is not a spontaneous ride away, so while I'm here I thought catching up with some friends would be a good idea. Scotland, I suppose, is a spontaneous ride, but I've never actually bothered to do it. One of the Czech girls from the Mongolian Lada crew has invited me over, but I'm 300 km south of there now. The other rendezvous I was hoping to make west of here is not looking promising. To help raise my enthusiasm a little, I look up the Transfăgărășan in Romania, the legendary military-constructed highway, which consists of 90 kilometres of winding roads across the Carpathian Mountains. It's my second intended site this trip. I discover a website I haven't seen before that informs me that, due to the altitude and snow, it is rarely open before June. What? So still without direction, I do a little check over the bike, hoping my phone will ring and everything will fall into place. Typically, when I'm dithering around waiting for someone or something to occur it never does. However, independently go forth with a strong plan, keeping mind and spirit occupied, and opportunities just seem to materialize. Annoyingly, I'm very far from having a strong independent plan; in fact, this state of being would better be likened to a puppy waiting to be let out of the back door—completely dependent and helpless. It's not a good frame of mind, particularly for continuing a long overland journey that still doesn't really feel like it's started properly; in fact it's pathetic.

Come on, sex or scenery? Sex or scenery? Make a fucking decision. I got laid last week, and there is loads more scenery to come. Aarrggghh, what's it gonna be?

If only changing frame of mind was as easy as changing tyres, but it's not, particularly when you travel alone. The highs are higher and the lows are lower. There is no-one to give me a slap and tell me get on with it. Plus, while I'm out here on the bike living the dream, no-one really has much time to listen to me whinge.

Scuba divers know that underwater everything appears 20% bigger. Lone travellers know that on the road all decisions are at least 50% bigger, because we don't have to worry about the basic necessities of a conventional lifestyle. The MOT is due on the car, the lawn needs mowing, got to pick up some toilet roll on the way home: all the endless tasks that happen as life passes by. On the road, these are left behind and replaced with one enormous, all-consuming deliberation after another. When shall I get fuel? Is it going to rain? Shall I change my gloves? It's not necessarily a bad thing, but keeping things in perspective can be a bit tricky alone inside the helmet.

I once had a job working for an interior design company; a lot of the clients were super rich. They would never have any financial shortcomings in their lives, so they found other things to worry about. Most were neurotic about their physical health when, in fact, it was their mental health that should have caused them concern. The point is daily distractions are quite healthy, and not having any is making this relatively easy decision torturous.

I get on the bike, head for the motorway, and ride west, slowly, hoping for a call. It's actually quite scenic, lakes and mountains; I'm pleasantly surprised. Unfortunately, the lakes reflect the dark storm clouds and the mountains are obscured by them. Prior to this trip, my only experience of Slovakia was Bratislava airport. It really wasn't an accurate representation of the country.

I take a winding road that follows a river. No traffic, but all I'm doing is fiddling with a sat nav that won't charge and looking at my phone, which I've now put in the transparent map holder so I will see it light up with a call under this dismal sky. I'm still waiting for a call because an unanswered voicemail left on a switched-off phone leaves me with optimism. I can't honestly say I'm living in the moment. This behaviour is really annoying me; it's a total waste of everything. I stop at a wet and horrid service station. I can't waste any more time; this is the last junction, and I have to make a decision. I turn to the east and head for Romania. I try consoling myself by saying that heading east will mean less wear on my tyres, but I'm not listening. I ride through a grey industrial town and stop for lunch at a place with a sign that says, "bikes welcome." Really? If that was a welcome I'm glad I didn't go where I wasn't. The plate has meat on it, accompanied by something with a consistency between pasta and potato.

I'm making no progress today, and when I do get back on the road I'm nearly pushed off it by a 4x4 that cuts me up on a corner, as I glance over I see pink nails and white knuckles rapped round a steering wheel. Reminds me of a poem I once wrote. I'm still thinking I could turn round if I get a call. At 3PM she calls. We try all options, but it's not going to work out. Thunder rumbles in the distance as she says this. We are both disappointed, but at least I know.

Do I feel better now? Actually yes, I must; I'm stopping to take photos. I'm seeing what's around me, noticing the wet and empty villages under dark and stormy skies. It reflects my mood perfectly. There is a canopy over the road where once was the border control between Slovakia and Hungary. I shelter underneath it as the heavens open and the lightening cracks. It's a little ghost town of immigration and customs buildings. It feels naughty to be wandering around an area that was once so controlled. Grass grows between cracks in the road, but no windows or doors are boarded or broken—the Marie Céleste of border crossings.

The storm passes, and unceremoniously I head into Hungary. The spray decreases, the road dries, the sun shines, the wind is warm, and I dry out. I have no currency, and I'm feeling good. Perhaps I will just pass right through.

To continue today's indecision, I decide to stay, in a shitty little motel. A strip light in my dismal room only helps show a ceiling insulated with spray-on expanding foam. I think I'd rather be where my bike is garaged. A dog barks all night, and when it stops I hear snoring from a neighbouring room. Living the dream?

Day 10

Alba, Romania, 211 Miles

Farmyard noises and sunshine, I hope today will be better. I get up to go and check the bike is where I left it; its absence could certainly have a bearing on the day. A tattooed guy assumes I'm the owner; he speaks some English and shows me his DR650. Then he helps me get my bike out of the garage area, where they seem to service ice-cream vans, and I have to negotiate my way round them. He admires my bike. Don't say it, please don't say it; don't mention the money and how lucky I am. I can feel it coming.

"You are so rich; you are very lucky."

Yep that's why I stayed in this shit hole last night and ride a 17 year old, £700 bike, and you know why you didn't see me here last year? Because I was working that's why. But yes, I am lucky, and I am rich, by the way. "Can I get some breakfast at that café?"

He sees me and the bike and assumes the rest. It's OK, just human nature, I suppose. It's how marketing works: see desirable packaging and want the contents. The bike does look cool; any bike geared-up for a long journey would stop me in my tracks. It's got romance, independence, desire, but the price paid is often far more than financial. My house is rented, I have places to go but nowhere to stay, the sun is shining and unknown destinations are just a throttle twist away. But look at yesterday, it ain't all *Easy Rider* Mardi Gras. Although, without days like yesterday I wouldn't have the glowing appreciation that I woke up with this morning. Helped along by his envy and admiration, it's his dream and he thinks I'm living it.

He helps me order an omelette and coffee. I think perhaps I could have managed that myself, but he wants to be a part of my journey, and he is. I would do the same at home. "Do you need a hand getting it on the centre stand? You

33

want to use my tyre pressure gauge?" If it's the high point of his day, I'm honoured to be the provider. Anyway, maybe this interaction will be the high point of mine, second only to a surprisingly good omelette.

Out onto the road, and before I have time to consider anything much, a bug comes over the top of my screen, under my lifted visor, and manages to hit me just above the bridge of my nose. A bindi couldn't be better placed. It was an excellent shot, and said bug should be proud of its terminal flight.

In less than an hour I'm in Romania, and now things are beginning to feel more foreign; horses and carts trundle down the road, labourers in the fields use scythes. Life is probably harder this way but aesthetically more pleasing for us rich and lucky adventurers.

I head straight into a city. I'm not sure I needed to be right in the centre, but I am now and stuck in stationary traffic. The bikers' thin line between comfort and discomfort is crossed. Pedestrians walk the streets in shorts and loose shirts, and I'm sitting over a hot engine in direct sunlight in black heavily armoured clothing. I don't care if it is breathable, I'm suffocating. As the hooting, shimmering traffic crawls to a junction, the cause of the queue become visible; police with whistles who have us stopping on green and going on red. Once I'm past their traffic flow techniques, the choked up traffic again has room to breathe and moves freely. Builders are browning their beer bellies with rolled up T-shirts. I suspect I haven't ridden into summer, this is just the first hot day of the year. This heat doesn't change the dressing habits of the elderly, though; women wear head scarves and house coats, and the old men dressed in black sit on benches in the shade beside their walking sticks, playing backgammon or cards. Ancient community past-times that seem to have got lost as our society advances to a point where we no longer have time to pass. Community is a hall with a locked door, which lacks the spontaneity of a bench on the pavement.

I'm utilizing my tank box, flipping it open for photos of horse-drawn transport and storks nesting on top of telegraph poles. I feel I've got my mojo back; I've missed it so much. There are two ways to find your mojo on the road. One is if you've travelled too much to stop, the other, is when you've stopped too much to travel. The trick is to know which one has been in excess and which one is lacking.

The road conditions are not good but made worse by sloppy maintenance; a shovel full of tarmac appears to have been thrown off the side of a passing truck without any kind of compression or levelling, so it just adds to the irregularity of the road surface. I stop for a lunch break and try to find the source of an annoying rattle. The oil level is fine, and the fasteners all seem tight, so now that I know nothing is about to seize or fall off, psychologically the bike will feel better. As I remove the liners from my jacket and trousers, a truck pulls into the lay-by, the driver gets out to check the security of his load, indicating this road shakes everything. Yeah, I know, I would like to be able to tell the trucker that I used to do what he does for a job, 20 years on and off behind the wheel wondering what I wanted to do with my life, the answer was this.

Much as I love this warm weather I have ridden into, I seem to have totally bypassed spring. I had one day of yellow rapeseed fields in Hungary, and now everything is green and summery. I missed my favourite season. I suppose I'm going the wrong direction for a prolonged spring. I should be going from south to north, much like flying east to west will prolong a sunset.

I once flew from Denver to a wedding in Baltimore. The day after the festivities, I was driven back to the airport the wrong way, round three quarters of the outer ring road. I was stressing that I was going to miss my flight and be late for my pizza delivery job. As we pulled into the passenger drop-off area and I was about to jump from the car, the driver said, "Hey, smoke this," and I took a lung full of potent weed. The sunset from the window seat seemed to last the entire three-hour flight. Flying over an orange sky, chasing a sun that is sinking behind the planet, pressing my foam-covered Walkman headphones to my ears, and having a momentary lapse of reason. I wasn't stressed anymore but was really looking forward to a pizza.

As I pass through a town, I see a homeless man settle down on a bench. He methodically gets his meagre possessions out of his bag to have lunch. He has so little but seems to have appreciation for what he does have. In my own way, I too am homeless, carrying all I own with me, apart from my other bikes and my CDs . . . but the point is, taking the time to find pleasure from little things is a satisfying source of happiness.

There are a lot of truck-stop whores on the sides of the road, mostly dead-eyed and hard-faced, but at one service area there are three very attractive girls, dressed in stockings and sexy underwear. They are happily flirting, waving, giggling, and bouncing off each other. I really wish I had stopped for a photo of them by my bike. I would have happily paid them a modelling fee. But if you don't brake as the thought occurs, the moment passes, and all I have is the image in my head.

I've crossed a time zone, and there is a sign for a campsite with a Dutch flag. If they are Dutch, I think they will speak English, and sure enough, they do. I erect my tent for the first time this trip and dig out my shorts, but when I open the pannier I find it has leaked. All my maps are sodden, as are the guidebooks and photocopies of important documents, camera instructions, and phrase book. Although they were all wrapped in plastic bags, they have sat in water for days. I spend an hour carefully unpeeling maps, from Iraq to Azerbaijan, and spread them out across the grass. I think I have saved them, although their volume has increased three-fold. The Canon handbook is now the thickness of a guidebook, and the guidebook has fanned out to *Yellow Pages* proportions. On the plus side, I discover my Russia map covers the area I'm in now, if I could just compress it enough to get it in my map holder. The evening's entertainment consists of me totally unpacking and repacking my panniers, reminding myself that minimalistic travel is something I'm incapable of. My possessions may not be that meagre, but I'm getting pleasure from the moment, and that's good enough for me.

DAY 11

BECHET, ROMANIA, 274 MILES

I wake with the theme from *Cheers* in my head, which is strange because the last place I want to be is where "everybody knows my name."

Apparently, summer is not here yet; it's cloudy again, and I have to dig to the bottom of my drybag to find my fleece. I ask Mrs. Owner if the Transfăgărășan is open, and she says it is, not that she looks like the type who rides it regularly, in fact, this is just a caravan site. It's only because I happened to be here pre-season that the place is bearable, however, there is an underlying militant caravan-site mentality waiting to blossom as the season approaches. I can tell she is just itching to cover the site with signs of instruction and command. "The size of maps to be dried on washing lines is limited to 1.4m x 1m and only during the hours of daylight."

Back on the road snowy mountains are visible; they will be the Carpathians then. A 4x4 inconsiderately weaves past me and then cuts up other cars. Later, the traffic slows due to flashing blue lights, and we bask in the indulgence of seeing him pulled by the police. I'm sure every one of us that passes feels the self-righteous satisfaction of seeing justice being done, and then we all speed up again once we are round the corner.

I stop for some fuel, not a total fill-up, just enough to see me over the pass without excess weight. The nozzle leaks, but it's not a big deal; I just wasn't expecting it. Us British don't expect the unexpected any more, health and safety has bred that instinct out of us, which makes us all the more vulnerable when we go abroad, it will be the death of us, it will.

I see a turn-off for road 7C, the one I want. As I go down it, I see a sign in red which says no entry but also a sign in green which could mean it's open, so optimistically I continue. The mountain range ahead of me looks as impenetrable as the Auschwitz fence did. I'm soon back up at 3,000 feet, and the bike is not sputtering today. A German-plated van comes the other way. So has he come over the pass or is he turning back? The altitude increases; the snow gets closer. There is a waterfall on a hairpin and then concrete barriers across the road. Bollocks. I sit on the barrier and have some lunch, watch the waterfall, and contemplate taking off my panniers and squeezing the bike between the edge of the concrete block and the precipice. It would really fuck things up if I dropped it. And I could very well end up having to come back through; this is beyond naughty, it borders on really stupid. As stupid as riding 1,800 miles to come here? I'm not sure. Some of my bike has done this road before. Definitely the frame, engine, and back wheel have, unfortunately, this owner and his eclectic mix of eBay purchases have not had the pleasure.

Once again, disproportionate disappointment. It's only a mountain pass, but it's pretty bloody legendary. It's the failure it represents more than the opportunity that is denied. Riding back the way I came I'm just not enjoying this. I see the journey as a trip of two halves; the easy run through to Turkey and then the tricky visa-restricted Stans, and I can't even get the Romanian bit right. I ride with a frown and gritted teeth and a negative spiral of thoughts.

I take an alternative road; a busy, noisy, dirty, truck route through a shallow valley in the Carpathians. The road shares the valley with a river and railway track. It could be pretty but it isn't, just industrial. The whores are more scenic than the view. To replicate the way I'm feeling, my air-filled seat mat has gone flat too, then a bird shits on my hand as I ride. It splats across my jacket. I can see it in the mirror. I'm not feeling the love of the journey, it has to be said.

I don't want to go into Bucharest, so I stop to look at the map and find a road away from this busy artery of cholesterol traffic. A hand comes into my field of vision, a begging gypsy; you've picked the wrong moment love. I take my place back in the restricted flow. I find my alternative road and instant tranquillity, but with it comes another annoyance. The land is flat and farmed, the gypsy population is high, there is a lot of time here and not much to spend it on it would appear. Young and old stand around, alone or hunched down in groups against fences, and everybody stares. Waves are not forthcoming. The feeling is not good, and there is absolutely nowhere to wild camp; in fact, it's hard to even find a spot where I can take a piss. Every field is tended to diligently; irrigated, hoed, protected. There is a grid-work of tiny roads; inevitably I take some wrong ones. They take me past even more secluded settlements, and the stares penetrate all the deeper. Bicycle and horse are the main forms of transport, and my engine noise precedes my arrival and prepares the audience. The sat nav only tells me there is water nearby, and then I'm at the port; the river that separates me from Bulgaria. It's 7PM, and the sun is going down. I turn back. There is a building that could be a hotel, but which has no signs to confirm this. Desperate, I ask. It is a hotel. The room has a heavy choking pungent smell, I can't trace its source, maybe it's just impregnated into greasy walls and sticky carpet; it will be fine. The little bonus is the cook-hostess-barmaid-housekeeper speaks some Spanish, and so do I. Embarrassingly, I'm completely stumped when she says the word for fifteen. I should know that. But I thought we were talking about food and was trying to equate the sound of that word with something I could eat. But, nevertheless, when she ushers me into the empty dining hall, on the plate is what I actually expected to see. I just didn't expect to see the other fourteen plates.

Day 12

Motocamp, Idilevo, Bulgaria, 135 Miles

The stench in the room was certainly sleep-inducing, much like carbon monoxide. Thankfully only 12 hours passed, not what's left of my life. I can't smell it now, of course, I've been immersed it in all night, but I'm sure it's still there. It was here first, and it will remain long after I've gone.

I'm being watched by a multi-generation family dining at an outside table as I pack my bike. I handle this intrusive scrutiny by making no eye contact at all. It wasn't necessarily the right tactic to apply, as the hotel is at the end of the road. They are clean and fresh, and there is the most enticing aroma on the air, surely coming from one of the girls. I've either become super sensitive to scent or this delicate choice of perfume she is wearing was specifically selected not to go unnoticed and to harmonise with this sunny morning. Inciting it may be, but I leave without it affecting my solitude.

Out on the bike, I'm hoping something good will happen today. Am I really enjoying this? Am I whinging too much? Why paint a picture of permanent pleasure? It's just life, albeit a transient style. Inevitably there are hardships. I'm not going to lie to my diary. What exactly would make it better? Do I want something eventful to happen? Careful what I wish for. It's a long talk I have with myself on the short ride to the port. What if I had come this far with company? Then the looming parting of ways would be playing on my mind. What if I was in a relationship? Arrgghhh, the torture of being me. Always wondering if it could be better must be better than assuming it will get worse, though; I never do that.

It's not much of a port—it's only one docking ramp and a customs post away from being a river bank. I'm told the ferry is free for motorcycles, but after I've showed my passport, I'm informed I still have to pay taxes. The ferry company giveth and the authorities taketh away. Then they tell me I've just missed the ferry, but it will be back in 45 minutes. I go past the trucks to the front; the fresh and sweet-smelling family are there. Now I've broken the morning vow of silence, I'm more open to social interaction. Which would have been less awkward if I had acknowledged them this morning, although I'm the only one who seems to be phased by that. The father is a general manager of a pastry company, and they proudly give me some samples. The boot is full of food, not for export but personal consumption; they are going to Bulgaria for the weekend. It's his pregnant daughter-in-law who smells so good. I tell her this, because it's so much easier to tell someone they smell good than it is to tell them they smell bad. In fact, it seems to be an unwritten universal law that body odour and bad breath are discussed with everyone but the person it emanates from. Mentioning smelly feet is just about acceptable; socks can be scapegoats, the excuse is simple. However, a direct remark on bad hygiene has to stay below the ankle.

Daughters, mothers, brothers, and in-laws all are friendly and inquisitive; they ask if I have friends or family in Bulgaria. "Once knew of a Great Uncle." They seem to have an insatiable hunger. Food is constantly taken from the extensive provisions, and I'm given eggs, fruit, juice, rolls, and finally a cup of Syrian coffee to wash it all down. We take each other's photos on the short crossing and swap Facebook details. Friends for life we'll be now then.

My knowledge of this new country was zero; if it wasn't for the Wombles I would never have heard of it at all. Before I left the UK, I publicly asked the question "Is there anything in the country I would be a fool to miss?" The most appealing suggestion was "Motocamp," a motorcycle haven. And that is where I am heading.

First impressions of Bulgaria are "once was better," judging by the poor condition of the roads, the state of the houses, and the dress of the people. The men all have shaven heads, and the Cyrillic alphabet is used here, so I can't read anything at all. Then again, this is just the first impression, and although I like to think I'm a pretty good judge of character, summing up an entire country by whatever place you happen to enter it from can be very unfair. Imagine flying into Clacton airport? You'd want to leave immediately, and your instincts in this case would be absolutely right. I seem to have crossed the river into a poor and underemployed farming community, however, the road soon brings variety. My map is a scale so small only with my magnifying glass can I see town names, and they are only significant ones, so I have total dependency on my sat nav, and frankly, I wouldn't trust it to take me to the driveway from the garage.

First I smell it, then I get bug splats on my visor, then through the trees I see it; the rapeseed oil fields are back. Big, bright, and yellow, it's been the most intermittent of springs. The conker trees too have their little white pyramids of blossom along with early lavender and poppies. The timing may be wrong, but the colours complement each other, all this against a blue sky with a warm breeze. Despite the frequent photo stops, I just can't seem to capture it; one of those rides that just have to be ridden, in the moment, senses simultaneously satisfied.

A road is closed. The sat nav can't handle this, but I can with common sense and an inherent sense of direction. I must wipe this bird shit off my jacket; it keeps catching my eye in the mirror. It's one of those things I only notice when I ride and forget about when I'm able to do something about it. Somehow its 3PM already; whether I'm awake or asleep the hours are just flying past. Again I can see snowy mountains; my moodometer has swung back up to happy levels. Is this still the transitory part of the trip? If I really want eventful I will have to stop to find it; there is no real time pressure. I'm not solely focused on a destination, but Europe was never a place to dither through. Then again, Europe has many definitions; as a continent it reaches into Russia and Turkey. As a Union it takes in here and Romania. As a song contest apparently Israel and Azerbaijan are included. As an undocumented traveller you won't get out of a British airport.

Anyway, the spring ride comes to a sudden end; my sat nav has flown its chequered flag and left me in a rubbish dump. I don't think this is Motocamp. I go back to a town, find an Irish pub with Internet and re-Google the location. I have my first beer in a week, draw a little map, and then look up from my pink laptop and realize I'm much too scruffy for these plush surroundings, finish my drink, and get back on the bike. I feel more excited and exhilarated than I have all week. I'm sure it's because I'm nearly at this anticipated Motocamp, not because I've just had a beer. I'm not dependent on alcohol; it's only my happiness that is.

Motocamp is everything a caravan site isn't. It's tasteful, unrestricted, and relaxing. It assumes the guests are trustworthy and keep count of the beer they help themselves to. That they have the common sense and consideration to keep bathrooms and eating areas clean after use without the need for a sign. There is an extensive workshop you are given access to; it's proof there is an honour among bikers that evidently must not exist in the caravan community. The hosts are welcoming but not overpowering; it's the best of both worlds. When you stay with friends you always have to be on your best behaviour, double-think your habits, and adjust to their schedule. When you stay in a hotel you can wake, sleep, eat, and watch TV as you please but only within the confines of your walls. Here you have company should you want it, privacy, facilities, advice, and recommendations; ride out or sit around, as you please. Beer served on the honour system gives me an immense feeling of joy. I feel a bit of a prolonged stay coming on.

DAY 13

MOTOCAMP, BULGARIA, 3 MILES

The hospitality may not have been overpowering, but the home brewed plum brandy was. Thankfully my tent is pitched in the shade, so I don't wake up as shrivelled as the aforementioned fermented plums. I unzip the tent, and the camp dog, Harley, comes straight in. Not camp as in effeminate; he appears perfectly secure in his masculinity. He just likes to check on the campers, which is lovely and everything, but he's really big and hairy and . . .

"Hey, did you wipe your feet?"

There is a first floor clubhouse-cum-recreational-area-cum-restaurant, and inside there is enough memorabilia on the walls to pass several hangovers. I do a double-take at one of the photos on the wall. I thought it was me. Doug, the owner, an American who isn't here, bears more than a passing resemblance to me. In his absence the place is managed by his other half, Polly, a very switched-on girl who runs Motocamp with an absolute passion. Then there is Ivo, a long-haired Bulgarian who speaks English with the most aggressive of accents, completely unlike his personality; he is the epitome of a lovely bloke. And that is why, before your engine has cooled and before you've chosen between tent or guest room, the pressures of the road have left you quicker than a £20 note in a London pub. I chat to some Lithuanians who are off to Iran and Pakistan. That's where I wanted to go. It appears the criteria for issuing an Iranian visa is based more on nationality than by the merits of the applicant or the requested time of transit. I know that an American citizen has to have a permanent in-car guide to travel independently. I'm envious of their planned journey, but I worry for their bike and lack of mechanical knowledge. They have a Plan B, which basically entails abandoning the bike, which is quite prudent I think. Still, they are young, good looking, and multilingual; I'm sure they will go far.

There are a lot of British expats here, attracted by low property prices and a general lack of pedantic laws, rules, and regulations. I take a walk with Polly through the village, and she points out the houses that are either empty or foreigner owned. We visit some Brits I met last night who are renovating a place. The location, price, space, views, and peace are all desirable. I can see the appeal.

Later, I ride helmetless over to their place. We use some silicon to try and seal my leaking panniers. Then we ride off road to some lakes; it's like *Little House on the Prairie*, on bikes—just dirt tracks through meadows and woods; no one around, no stupid signs, no signs of anything much, just nature.

Back at Motocamp the day passes, chatting, dozing, reading, surfing, researching, bike maintenance, and to end the day, a barbeque. It takes considerable skill to create an environment like this. Committees and suggestions boxes would never manage it. It takes passion, observation, trust, and patience. It's one of those rare places that you know if you ever revisit will not have changed for the worse like so many places do. It's a site with vision.

Day 14

Koprivshtitsa, Bulgaria, 240 Miles

Sunrises and early starts seem to be a thing of the past, along with solitude, at least for the moment. The Lithuanians are packing up; in the clubhouse over breakfast we all discuss their route. There is no formal invitation to join them, and I know they are in a hurry to get to Iran due to visa entry dates. Not only do I ride slowly, but I rarely ride in a straight line either. That aside, I'm just not ready to leave yet. I am, however, formulating a bit of a plan. Firstly, I'm only a border away from Turkey, and that's quite exciting in itself, because Turkey has some very exotic borders: Syria, Iran, Iraq, and Georgia. It also has Greece, and that is the indirect route I've decide to take.

There is this flying saucer type monument called Buzludzha, and I want to have a look. It's an abandoned but recent relic from the time of Bulgaria's Soviet occupation, perched on top of a mountain, 4,700 feet above sea level. Apparently it's rated in the top 10 of abandoned monuments in the world. I wasn't even aware there was a chart for such things, but now I am and that this one rates high. I want to go and see it. Abandoned generally means no tourists, which equates to no entry fee and more atmosphere, all enticing ingredients. It's good to have an urge, and even though it's been a shorter than intended stay here, there is no doubt in my mind that it is not going to be my only visit to Motocamp.

Before I leave, I have another abandoned relic to look at. A dilapidated house on the outskirts of the village I could purchase if I wanted, for the price of one of my unused bikes. I can usually see the potential in a property, but through the heaps of discarded and filthy clothing, the rooms of defecation, rotten wood, holey roof, and glassless windows I think I would rather buy some road tax and go for a fast ride than invest in this particularly uninhabitable hovel, which is nothing more than vertical hardcore.

So good-bye, Idilevo. I didn't even know my batteries needed recharging, but now that they are, I'm off to see the world . . . again.

And then I'm back, because I forgot my gloves; always a little embarrassing to have two good-byes. I have put my route into my sat nav. I'm not going to do a lot of touring in Bulgaria, and I don't want to invest in a readable map. It seems like a straight forward enough country to navigate, so off I go. Up into the hills the road is windy, and it is all looking quite promising. I don't see any signposts announcing the place, but then would an abandoned building actually have any signposts?

As I reach the summit, there it is, the Shipka Monument, but I don't want the Shipka monument. I'm sure it's all very important in its own symbolic way, but that's not what I came to see. It doesn't look anything like a flying saucer, and it's certainly not abandoned. I'm sure Buzludzha is supposed to be round here somewhere. I find another mountain pass; there are more trucks on this one. I manage to miss the snowy mountains I could see from a distance, and I certainly can't see any flying saucers. In fact, it's quite hard to stay within the mountains at this point in the Balkans. This is the perfect range for the vertigo sufferer; no sooner have you gained a little elevation than you are quite literally over the hill and looking down at the plains on the other side. I'm beginning to think this bloody flying saucer has flown off to a dilapidated part of Galactic Sector Z99 where it isn't considered such an eyesore. I turn off down smaller twisting mountain roads of blossom and aromas until I find myself within ten miles of Motocamp, which I left four hours ago. I can't go back; I just can't.

Bloody sat nav, bloody monument, bloody plan. See, that's the problem of having a plan; when I expect to see something, even though I know what it's going to look like, I do expect to see it. Stumbling across the unexpected and unknown is so much more satisfying. You can't miss the unknown; it's just there, it occurs. And even if you did miss it, by definition you wouldn't know you had. This would be an OK ride; country roads, no traffic, pleasant temperature, sunny evening, but it wasn't meant to be a ride out and back, it was goodbye. I'd even said it twice.

So back over the mountain on yet another road to yet another summit and another bloody monument, this one a tall concrete arch; the mountains are littered with them. I've given up the search. I'm off to the other site I wanted to see, but now if any wild camp possibilities arise I will be pulling off the road. There was one, a flat grassy elevated ledge overlooking the valley. Although with broken glass and condoms strewn around it's somewhere I don't even want to put my foot down, let alone my tent.

I decide to just head for the next place. Storm clouds are gathering, and it's getting late. Through Sunday evening, villages where old Bulgarian babas gather to discuss the day's events, possibly embellishing the truth or just plain lying due to a lack of anything worth mentioning. Maybe that is how history is held in the heads of the village elders, because although it sounds unfeasible to have a half millennia of recountable stories, in reality I'm sure a decade could pass with nothing more than a couple of significant births, deaths, and marriages; and to be honest, remembering a few social gatherings has got to be way easier than trying to grasp the Cyrillic alphabet.

These worthless thoughts occupy my mind until I weave through the dark grey heavy outcrops of rock that the village of Koprivshtitsa hides behind. The shallow gorge eases away to reveal a wide sky of similar dark colours but sliced by streaks of lightning, which brings a little more urgency to my search for accommodation. There is no shortage; I just have to choose. The first one has a raging fire in the large but empty restaurant, and two old men are sitting by a table. Reluctantly, one lifts himself up. He is paralytic, can barely walk or communicate in any language, "No ya alright, never mind."

On to the next one. The landlady sighs heavily upon opening the door. "TA DARRR," I sarcastically say inside, although it does not seem like an appropriate greeting. "I'm here because the sign outside suggests you are in the hospitality trade" probably wouldn't do me any favours either. Grudgingly she shows me a room in a self-contained annex that's reasonably priced, the bike is off the road, and unfortunately for her I've decided I will stay.

I walk the streets and find a restaurant with just the right amount of people in it. The menu is in English, and I order a beef casserole. When it arrives, it's in a jug. I pick at the salad and look around the restaurant in hope of a clue of how to eat it. The only option seems to be lift it up and put it to my mouth. I'm not even sure what's inside, but I'm hungry, and something has to be done. I go to pick it up by the loop handle, and the top half comes off in my hand. Oh right, I get it now. I have an earthenware bowl of easily accessible meaty stew, steaming in front of me. Perfect. I've just completed the last challenge of the day.

DAY 15

LIDIA, GREECE, 229 MILES

In cheap accommodation sleep deprivation is often caused by banging doors, blaring televisions, and barking dogs, although it's more preferable when caused by excitement and anticipation of the day to come. In my twee little room there is silence and no excitement, therefore no sleep deprivation; where is the bloody mojo? Two weeks ago I left home, and predictably, there was some apprehension, but that's long gone. I hoped I would not spend the first half of the journey considering the visa complications involved for the second half, and I'm not. I've put those niggles in a mental file and closed it. The only thing I can think that's causing this sporadic loss of mojo is the dilemma between transit and tour. Where am I saving time and where am I spending it? Another thing I consider is, with freely available Wi-Fi in most places these days and a device that connects so effortlessly, it's hard to sever the connections with home. How many are really necessary? Before the ferry left the port, I spoke to a knowledgeable traveller who said, "Stay off Facebook," and I have. Other than a few photos, I've maintained social media silence. When I backpacked round India alone for six months in the '90s I called home once every six weeks, and that was fine. Now with all this instant communication there is an expectation of prompt response, and if it's not forthcoming it's considered rude but turns to worry in about 24 hours. So no more Skype and only one line email responses. How can you immerse yourself in the moment, in the culture, in the country, if you're off escaping into cyberspace every time there is a connection? I'm not that bad; I know of plenty who are worse. Any Facebook status that begins "morning all" pretty much says where any spare time is spent. But just because I know people who are worse doesn't make my habits any better. It's always reassuring to visit my little group of debauched friends, just to reassure myself that my lifestyle is actually quite healthy in comparison. And today it's going to start with a nice cup of tea on the porch overlooking the oh-so neat garden. Carefully stacked logs, weeded flower beds, and a manicured lawn with just the slight impression of motorcycle tyres across it. I suppose I better go have a look around before the coach loads I saw last night spew from their quarters.

There are old solid stone houses with barns of weathered wood all standing on the edge of narrow cobbled streets. The windows have shutters and the chimneys are immense. There are authentic craft shops with spinning wheels and other hand-operated machinery. It's all very lovely I'm sure, but I have little knowledge of what I'm looking at and no real urge to find out. I head back to the jug of stew restaurant and have an omelette; it is presented with far less challenge than yesterday's dinner. The best bit of this town for me is the accommodation and the food. That means I'm seriously lacking the appreciation of a place which is clearly quite significant, judging by the tour parties and school outings that have converged here.

Well I won't take up any more precious space. I'm off; I'm going to a national park. The weather has not improved; a day on the road has to be pretty dismal for Monday morning at home to have more appeal. When I realise the alternative to what I'm doing, the morning improves dramatically. I stop to take photos of poppies in derelict railway sidings. Maybe I didn't want to see a quaint old village; what do I want to see? I want to see the unexpected; I want to be wowed by the spectacular. I want to be in awe of might and scale, and I want to apprehensively explore the unvisited. I want to push my limits and scare myself. I want unease and concern in volatile territory. Yeah, that's what I want; no wonder a twee little village left me cold and taking photos for the hell of it. Horses tethered to wooden stakes by stone bridges over little rivers all looks great on greeting cards. However, I'm not here for Hallmark or even landmarks. I want benchmarks, high ones, well not too high, I don't mind breaking new ground, but I don't want to break anything else really. Well it certainly won't be speed limits. Whilst I'm considering all this I've found I've widden onto a windy woad next to a waging wiver in weally wovely valley. I make myself smile, come on Flid, chin up mate.

At the next town I stop for supplies at a supermarket. The building next door, whatever it is, requires four security guards to securely guard it. They are typically big beefy guys and are pushing each other round on a tiny moped trying to bump start it. My little KLR with is voluptuous load is monstrous next to their skinny little moped. The fact I manage it unaccompanied does not go unnoticed, and we all laugh without saying a word at the absurdity of our proportions. That's all it takes, just that and the day smiles again. The introspective thoughts disperse, replaced by gladness. I swear I'm not lonely, I'm not; I know what loneliness feels like. In fact, I'm generally quite aware of my feelings and why I feel the way I do. I just can't figure out why this repeated agonizing over destination is occurring.

The road takes me through farmland, and despite the fact it's started to rain, the crops are still tended, mainly by old women bent over in an "L", a posture that seems permanent as they walk the roadside seeing only the ground in front of their feet. Maybe they just don't wanna be straight.

It's pissing down now, I stop in a lay-by. I stab at the sat nav, but it just won't show me to the national park anymore. I'm getting really aggravated with it; it takes all my self control not to throw the fuckin' thing in a ditch. I ride on, into an over-developed ski area full of large hotels, all closed as it's summer. The bike is cutting out. The sat nav is bleeping and displaying big arrows defying all logic. Does it derive pleasure from getting me so close to my intended destination and then denying me the arrival? Because I'm certainly not getting anything out if it. This ski town of urban misery is nowhere I want to stay. I'm really wet now; the rain won't relent; it's altogether a miserable experience. Fuck it; I don't even want to go to the national park now. Bollocks to it, I'm going to Greece.

In less than half an hour I'm on a dry sunny mountain road. I stop and spread some wet clothes out in the sun as I eat my fresh food supplies. I relax and look at the snowy mountains that rise above the cloud. They are grand but not inviting enough to put myself back through that awful bloody corporate hotel hell. That really was a horrendous little ball of stress, pissing rain, cutting out bike, numerous dead ends, and one way streets in a soulless modern concrete resort. Even though I'm at the side of a busy road, I feel relief. There is warmth in the sun, birds are singing, and there are flowery meadows.

I ride through a tunnel and pop out at the Greek border sooner than I expected; I still have Bulgarian currency left. I had wanted to fill up to avoid the expensive Greek fuel prices.

The heavens open, and I stop under a canopy. Déjà vu, just like my entry into Hungary, except this border's manned. Driving rain is just not what I associate with Greece; this isn't a tropical downpour or an April shower, it's just a wet and dismal soaking.

First impression of Greece? Friendly but expensive with better signposts. The first hotel I try is beyond my budget, so I ride on, in and out of rain. There is a Kawasaki shop, annoyingly I don't know the Greek word for "jets." I look round the workshop, find a dismantled carburettor, and show him my needs; "Naar sorry mate, we'd 'af ta order it in special like" is the impression I get. It was always a long shot, but there was just a chance there was an abandoned KLR out the back. I splutter off down the road, through a place called "Drama." I can't let this one go. I have to text an ex; "You'd love it here; you could be queen!" We still get on fine; she'll text me if she stays in a place called "Miserable Git" or "Balding Hippy."

I see a sign. I find a place. It's super friendly; I'm the only guest. Again I have a self-contained apartment to myself. My laptop won't connect to their Wi-Fi; it says it is but won't display anything. The bike is still cutting out, and the sat nav is beneath contempt. Electronics have been the bane of my day.

DAY 16

ZAGORA, BULGARIA, 296 MILES

Right better have a look at the bike, it's not happy, the air filter is filthy. The whole area is, it's where the exhaust blows. I take out the petrol filter to see if it's blocked and clean the air filter with petrol. Brilliant how I wait until I get to the most expensive fuel of the trip before I start using the stuff for cleaning. I've been brought some breakfast which was thoughtful, it's not included in the price but it's little gestures like this when you've not been in a country for 24 hours that endear you to it. I haven't waved goodbye when leaving a guest house for a while.

The bike is running a little better. I go down to the coast, where the Mediterranean is dark and inky, peppered with darker islands that float like oil slicks. It's still cloudy. It's neither the clear blue ocean I expected nor the omnipresent heat. I didn't associate Greece with the low grey sky either. I'm still wearing my fleece as I plod down the motorway. Contrary to what I have heard it does seem to be toll free. I'm heading east, directly east, towards the Turkish border and that is quite an exciting prospect. This may be a dull flat concrete motorway but it's only a few hundred kilometres away from a significant change in culture and I like how that makes me feel. To the north of me somewhere in the mountains is the Bulgarian border, I contemplate crossing back over just to use my currency on cheap fuel, and although there appears to be a mountain road, the sat nav says naaa.

I manage to find a really expensive petrol station to fill my tank and then discover they don't take credit cards. I do however get given a sweety, as consolation for exhausting my supply of euros.

I embark on the daily stabbing of the sat nav, it wants to send me north to go east, but this motorway has to go to the Turkish border, it's too busy not to. At every junction I defy its commands. As I reach the international crossing the clouds seem to lift a little. I'm not sure if it's just excitement or a genuine lightening of the skies.

50

I pass through the Greek customs and then I see the red Turkish flag flying, with its crescent moon and single star; Islam and intrigue lay ahead. There are armed military guards on the bridge that separates the countries, coiled barbed-wire runs along the sides of the guard rails to deter me from any urge I may have of riding over the edge into a marshy river. The road turns a corner and reveals an expansive border control area. Before I get to that, there is a single booth with a barrier. I pull up level, helmet flipped up, bandanna pulled down, engine off and smile fixed.

"Vehicle passport" says the uniformed man.

"Yes hang on." I look through my waterproof folder of all things crucial. Immunization certificates, international driving permits, medical and bike insurance, bank and credit card details, including that stupid little calculator thing I need to access my online account, clearly devised by someone who has never been away longer than a two week holiday to the Canaries. But I'm not seeing my log book. I do seem to have accumulated and kept quite a lot of paperwork so far. I see the green and red of a document with DVLA on it and hand it to him.

"What is this?"

"Actually it's the paper half of my driving licence."

"Vehicle document."

"Yeah I know, hang on."

The traffic is building up behind me now, never good for stress levels. I push my bike forward to let the next, more organized, vehicle get processed. I'm pointed to a quiet area and get off the bike to look properly. It's not in my document wallet, so I dig to the bottom of the pannier where there are photocopies of everything. I even have a list of my medical kit contents and what potion to use for what ailment, but there is no registration document and no photo-copy. I go through my folder again. I cannot accept that it's just not there, it has to be. My first thought is theft; my second is recalling when I last saw it. I have no recollection of seeing it or indeed packing it. My next reaction is denial. I call my mother, who's storing all my important stuff.

"Look in the red folder that says KLR on it, is there a brown envelope in it containing the log book?"

"Yes dear, it's here."

FUCKKKKKKKKKKKKKKK. "Is everything OK?"

"I'll call you later." How the hell did I leave it behind? I turn to a loitering officer with a feeling of utter hopelessness. "I haven't got it."

He wants me to take my bike for "inspection" and leads me over to a higher ranking man who is already very busy. There are several officials standing around a box van with twenty Muslim men in the back, along with sleeping bags and an array of food and empty wrappers. It looks like people smuggling to me. There is a lot of confusion, agitation and several alert customs dogs straining at leads. It's a brief distraction in this dazed nightmare.

I try to get a grip and decide thinking for myself might be better than having someone think for me. Having focused my mind and applied some thought to the situation it isn't difficult to see what the next move is. A U-turn, I have to go back because from this point on I will need it. I know this is the first thing they ask for at any international frontier, not to mention random police and military checkpoints. I should know, I've been through enough of them. There is no point in trying to negotiate my way into Turkey without it.

Trying to leave a country I haven't even entered yet is not so easy. The exit is not accessible from the entrance, U-turns are not commonplace. The authorities, although not sympathetic, are at least understanding as to what a complete and utter idiot I am.

I go back across the bridge that was, 15 minutes ago, a bridge of anticipation. Now it's a bridge of sighs. I sit in a line to be processed back into Greece. I'm in a state of bewilderment, total shock I can't even focus my eyes. If everything happens for a reason, what could possibly be the reason behind this? I cannot see how, with all my preparation, my pedantic packing, all those check lists, the photo-copies, visa applications, all this paperwork, I managed to forget the second most important travel document of them all. I lived by lists, I always live by lists. I had the thing out to scan it for my Russian visa. Mr World traveller has forgotten his fucking motorcycle ownership document. How embarrassing.

Car by car I move forward to the customs post, my mind is in turmoil.

"Destination?" the officer asks.

"Home." Am I lying? Where am I going to go now? I head north, towards Bulgaria, I'm not really sure why, now the signs for Turkey don't excite they just taunt me.

It's less than two hours to the Bulgarian border and the miles pass in a haze of disbelief. Every aspect of this is negative; from unnecessary wear on the tyres to the humiliation of having to admit what happened. And as for destination? Has this journey even really started yet? What the fuck? I'm not sure I'm progressing through the five stages of grief in order but this is definitely the anger part. The bike is running fine now so there is nothing to distract me from this persecution.

At the frontier there is a particularly happy border guard. He seems much happier to see me than I am to be here. He thinks Monklet is hilarious, he can't stop laughing.

A "Mr. Bean" character he keeps saying "teddy" and his colleague comes over to see what fun he is missing, I'm glad I made someone's day. Poor Monklet, he may be at his usual place on the handguard, but metaphorically he seems to have taken a back seat for this trip. I don't need his company so much now; I have a sat nav to scream at daily. I am without a clue as to where I'm going, the only plan I have come up with is to get drunk. I can't even find a town to get alcohol, let alone a place to drink it. On and on I go, heading further from Turkey all the time. The villages are small, one generation away from abandonment. What inhabitants there are, appear to be elderly; out in the street staring from benches or sitting at tables watching this whirl of confusion ride through their village. I have half a mind to stop and the other half is still numb.

Finally I come to a decent sized town, find a hotel that looks expensive but seems to be the only option. However they appear to have no other guests and are happy to accommodate and feed me for a very reasonable fee. Now I can start drinking, it seems to be the only thing I am doing well today. I have two philosophies I live my life by, one is karma and the other is "everything happens for a reason." What on earth could be the reason behind me forgetting my log book? As I sit on my balcony overlooking the main road I see a yellow DHL truck go past and some logic breaks into my thoughts. The log book is only an express courier away.

DAYS 17-19

MOTOCAMP, BULGARIA, 206 MILES

In the light of a new day the solution is pretty obvious—get the log book sent over. Today being Wednesday, I decide that having it sent directly to the DHL office in the capital, Sofia, could avoid a weekend of waiting. But regardless of the length of time I'm going to be here, it will be spent in my new found haven, Motocamp. I have better perspective today and the situation has been downgraded from utterly infuriating to mildly frustrating, while my mood has also changed from self-inflicted misery to cringing humiliation.

As the miles to Motocamp pass, I'm occupied with the creation of feasible excuses, telling of half-truths, and the possibility of belief in a blatant lie to spare me from the shame and ridicule. In spite of this I can't even come up with a good lie. How can I justify a U-turn so early in the trip? I consider other destinations. Despite Russian and Kazakh visas already being in my passport I still feel a little directionless, goal-less. In a round trip it's hard to envisage a champagne-popping target, other than back in the garage, and drinking in the garage is not an experience entirely unfamiliar to me. It's not exactly the victorious mountain ascent, or meeting the challenge of the furthest coast, the last navigable road at the end of the continent. Lots of people have made it to my garage; it's really not that tricky. So the challenges of negotiating entrance into visa restricted countries and across borders don't really represent victories; only more borders. Until eventually the circuit has come round to the point where, free, unannounced and unprepared, travel is permitted. That will be followed by unmanned borders and ultimately to a land where the language once again is understood. Having no actual exotic and far flung destination translates as no direction and in turn no drive, little enthusiasm and constant indecision due to infinite choice.

When I arrive at Motocamp the gates are locked and no one is home as they've all gone to Sofia to see Bon Jovi. I call Polly, "I'm back at Motocamp where are you?"

"Oh, we're halfway there, we'll be back in a few hours." Her dad comes and opens the place for me, I re-erect my tent in the prime position and help myself to a beer. That'll do for today.

I spend the night contemplating carburettors in relation to the rich and choking running problems and in the morning I strip the bike of its luggage, tank and seat. Pull off the carb and look at the jets. Yep, there they are, unblocked and in position. I don't know then, it's been suggested to me that I take a strand of electrical wire and run it inside the main jet to reduce the diameter and therefore the flow of petrol and ultimately the mixture. Now, in theory the bike will run leaner and possibly not splutter and cough when the air is thinner on mountain passes. It is at least a logical and feasible alteration. With the float height adjusted to its recommended level, I put it all back together.

In the afternoon I ride with Polly to see a man with a MIG welder. Her bike breaks down twice on the way and I can't go above 50 mph without mine popping and missing; it's not the most pleasurable of rides. The welder is an English expat with a purpose-built workshop. His gas tanks are near empty, he's nearly run out of wire and he can't really see. It's not looking good, however on the plus side my silencer was easier to get off than I thought. The long open seam soon has a strip of glowing weld along its entire length and as it cools and I refit it, I listen to more views of what it is like to live here. It's a realistic and level account and I still like what I'm hearing. From this more elevated location, the mountain views are most impressive too. I'm a little vulnerable now and concerned as to the fee for this much needed work; however it's a perfectly reasonable price; some beer credit to be put on his Motocamp account. Absolutely, consider it done.

I ride down the hill with closed throttle; there is no popping. Then onto the main road and up to 70 mph, the bike is strong and responsive. Problem sorted. So that's all it was, a lack of back pressure due to a split in the exhaust. Mountains will no longer have me coughing to a halt.

My log book has arrived in Sofia but thanks to a change of plan and now the use of a proper address, tomorrow it will be delivered to Polly's insurance broker just 12 kms away. That saves me a four hour journey in the wrong direction. And as a final little bonus a Scot has arrived in Motocamp returning from Turkey, and he speaks very fondly of it. So, bike is running well, enthusiasm is fired up and documents are in the country. The Scotsman even gives me a lonely planet phrase book he no longer needs; it's not much help though. I still find it hard to understand him.

In the night it rains hard and I have a surround-sound of nightingales and frogs, plus a few unknowns, all competing over the sound of soothing rain on a good quality tent. I can't imagine more tranquil nocturnal sounds. If I'm going to be kept awake this is the soundtrack to listen to.

I have a free day. It's the perfect time to try again to find the elusive space ship monument. I ride backroads up into the mountains; I'm still not convinced this is right. However as the altitude increases the bike continues to run fine, in fact I think it's running better at a few thousand feet than at sea level. I recognise a bit of the road and then I'm at the bloody Shipka monument again, but wait. There is a sign to Buzludzha. Oh I see, it's past the Shipka monument. The road gets narrow and goes through woods but continues to gain altitude. I'm totally confident I'm going to find what I'm looking for now. I don't care how long this road is, how far it takes me, I know sooner or later that on a barren hill top I will see a... there it is; a massive concrete spaceship. Like the Taj Mahal, Grand Canyon and the pyramids, you know exactly what you are going to see and there it is. It's as exciting as the expected but previously un-witnessed can be.

As I tentatively ride the path that takes me right up to the door, it becomes clear I'm the only person here. It just feels wrong, that this giant, extravagant, once-decadent symbol of communist might, which was occupied by the powerful and elite, is now, only 30 years after its completion, lying vandalized and abandoned.

A long wide staircase leads up to the doors which are locked and to be doubly sure, steel bars have been placed in front of the already secure entrance. I'm a little disappointed; I thought it was possible to get inside. It is of course, but abandoned buildings don't have entry signs, you have to be a bit sneaky. Around the side (if cylindrical spacecraft replicas have sides) are some glass bricks that have been smashed. I pull myself up and crawl through the hole. There is hardly any light; I can hear the wind whistle and birds inside squawk. I'm on a stairwell, and as I walk on, all light disappears. I have to assume the next step is always going to be underfoot and I'm not sure I want to. Neither do I want to crawl and feel my way. My eyes adjust slightly but there is debris all over the damp floor, if I were to walk into a bit of exposed and twisted rebar it could all turn very nasty, the place clearly doesn't encourage visitors. I've walked about a quarter of the way of the inner circumference of the building and then come to another set of stairs; they lead up and bring me into the inner sanctum; a vast flat area the size of a base ball pitch, with steps around the sides. The walls are lined with signs of soviet occupation and mosaics, portraits of what I suppose were once revered leaders.

The centre of the ceiling has a giant hammer and sickle mosaic but the surrounding roof of glass and steel has long past its weather proofing days, it lets in not just light but birds, snow, rain and wind. Although the anger at the past occupation has been vented on every surface with graffiti or just sheer blatant destruction, the lavishness of the place cannot be completely eliminated. The outer circumference is basically a corridor with views over wind farms and mountain ranges. Apparently this structure was deliberately placed to dwarf and look down upon the Shipka monument. A monument which celebrated Bulgarian victory over a Turkish invasion is belittled by this higher, grander more vulgar display of power. An all-seeing, all-powerful, all-victorious, communist governing headquarters. It's all very symbolic and being the only person here, the little background information I have helps me to understand the war of symbolism.

The nation's inhabitants are now free to symbolically deface a building of such extravagant indulgence. On the one hand I would have loved to have seen it in its glory days but what that would have represented would have been more than some selfish sightseeing. Better to understand why it has been reduced to this state in a country that now has the freedom to destroy in the name of protest. I think that has just become my number one favourite abandoned monument. Well worth the perseverance, I've spent a lot of time here.

When I get back to Motocamp it has the same amount of occupants as Buzludzha did. Everyone has gone to town for supplies and to pick up my log book. I put my bike undercover as a storm is coming; I have a beer and wait to see what will arrive first. Unpredictably, it's four English expats with multiple containers of fresh homemade curry. I'm a little surprised, they are a little miffed.

I call Polly. "Did you order a curry?" She'd forgotten they were coming, so we sit, drink, wait, talk and that thing occurs, that thing that happens whenever there are several Brits abroad together: the beer fridge suddenly becomes empty. Luckily I know where there's more. The only thing better than waiting for a curry to be delivered, is a curry being delivered that you didn't even order. Polly and the others arrive with the yellow and red DHL envelope that means I can leave. There is a heap of food and it's really tasty, made with home-grown ingredients. It's like a typical English Friday night; beer, curry and rain. Although in this case the rain comes in an electricity-cutting violent flood of a storm. I've met so many Brits who have relocated here and they may have kept their British habits of alcoholism and curry but one remarkable transition has occurred in them all. They have all lost the inherent need to moan about everything. That surely makes this quite a remarkable country to relocate to. Over the course of the evening it's mentioned the Virago club are coming here for their annual rally meet, so I think I'll be off.

DAY 20

EDIRNE, TURKEY, 222 MILES

I've got a lovely little hangover to battle with as I dry out my tent in the sun and slowly pack everything onto the bike. Yet another couple of Brits turn up, out on a Saturday morning ride. These ones have been here 8 years and obviously seen lots of changes, therefore they have the most realistic views of all, but still they sing the country's praises. Worryingly though, they are drinking beer at 9AM. Still, I'm sure they know what they are talking about. I also get a golden little tip from one of them: Edirne, the first town I come to in Turkey, was the former capital during the days of the Ottoman Empire. This means many things, not least there is some incredible architecture, including a very impressive mosque—a brilliant piece of last-minute information, just in time.

So here I go. I've actually got some pre-leaving butterflies, which is a good sign I think. I've also got too many clothes on, but I'm sure once I've settled into a steady pace the warm breeze will bring temperate comfort. Before the engine has even warmed up the bike splutters; I've run out of petrol. I've been siphoning it out for cleaning and stove filling, so it's no great surprise. I lean the bike right over in the hope of getting the last dregs from the other side of the tank. It works, and I limp to the petrol station. However, this operation doesn't do much for my already overheating body. Still, I won't let it taint the day.

I'm not thinking anything much, but when I do I realise I am looking forward and not back, which is a relief and a revelation. At bloody last; it's taken nearly three weeks to get to this stage, and it's very welcome. I'm thinking about visas for the 'Stans, and although I don't want this to play heavily on my mind, it shows I have motivation and desire, and this all adds to this morning's feel-good factor. So with a good state of mind, a strong running bike (especially when it has petrol in the tank), and nothing on the road except shadows from the tree-lined verges, all is well. Although I have travelled this road before, it's such a beautiful day I stop to photograph the sites that only turned my head last time. I think of what my first day in Turkey will consist of. I definitely need to get a map; a big, large scale, clear, new map. Then I can consider my route through this, the largest country so far.

There is an abundance of blossom in the meadows I pass; yellows, reds, and purples. It is quite simply a lovely day. This ride really has all the right ingredients. Even when I stop for a Marmite sandwich, the whole time I am parked not a single vehicle comes in either direction. A less relaxed mind would consider the possibilities of some major incident that has caused this absence of traffic. I'm not considering this at all.

The same smiley man is working at the Bulgarian border, but today I too have a smile to match his and Monklet's. Right, back into Greece, this shouldn't take long; it's only about half an hour to the Turkish frontier. I wonder if I can travel through the entire country without putting my feet down—I don't want to get them greecey!

I've got a song in my head, "Istanbul not Constantinople," but that's the only line I remember and it's getting quite annoying. A city appears on the near horizon, and I know I'm running out of Greece, so I'm thinking that must be Edirne. The road takes me through a little village, past a café of bikers who all return my wave, and then I arrive at a little border. A big fat Greek woman takes my documents. She wants to see green card insurance.

"What, for Greece? But I'm leaving Greece now." Her demands continue, but this is the EU, and I'm leaving anyway. I show her my comprehensive European cover. It's not what she wants. She wants Turkish insurance.

"I'll get that when I get to Turkey."

"No you must have now."

"OK; where can I get it from?"

"Turkey."

We're not getting very far are we; last time I tried to cross I had to do a U-turn, now I'm just going round in circles. What she wants I can't give her, and it's amazing how rude people become when protected by glass partitions. Actually, I don't recall any other border patrol officials so far who have been so shielded or so rude. I can feel the sweat running down my legs as I stand in the blazing sun squinting through this window.

"You go," she says.

"Go where? I'm trying to go, but you won't let me. Why can't you tell me where to get insurance?" She points in the opposite direction to Turkey. Well that's a big help. Predictably, a line of traffic has built up; someone is trying to move my bike.

"Oi, leave it," I say in my best *Eastenders* voice. I move it and go to a side door. It's unlocked, so perhaps I can get insurance in here.

It turns out to be the door that goes into fat and stroppy's office, and she is not happy to see me again, even less so as she no longer has the glass to protector her.

"You must go to Bulgaria and cross there." Funny how my last impression of Greece is so different from my first; it is also the one that remains. I am now drenched in sweat, there is a line of cars at the border post, and for the third time I'm heading into Bulgaria.

It's only bloody Turkey, how hard can this be? Apparently quite!

I've been in Greece for one hour and twenty minutes and it's been utter shit.

Back to Mr. Smiley, the Bulgarian border control man. The smile remains, but the forehead says bemused. You and me both, mate. So, third time lucky? Top up with fuel one more time, and here I go again. This time there are miles of stationary trucks. I pass them all, and there in front of me is a huge border control.

There are lots of lanes leading to the canopy of shade where the processing cubicles are. I get in the slowest line and push my bike one car length at a time up to the much appreciated cooler shade.

"Vehicle document."

"Yes, right here." Ha, first hurdle crossed. I'm making progress.

Next cubical

"Passport." I hand it over. "Visa."

"No, not yet, where do I get it?" I walk to another cubical, and for a small price, a sticker is obtained and I have one less blank page in my passport. I need to keep six pages empty to get through the 'Stans and back, so depending on how intimidating the person with the stamp looks, I try to direct them to a space on an already stamped page. It's not essential, and I would rather have a stamp than none at all, but if they use up all my empty pages it could have repercussions later down the road. The last cubical wants to see my green card insurance.

"No, not yet, where do I get it?" I have to leave the bike in their care and go into a big building that is a cross between an airport and a motorway services. There are restaurants, duty-free shops, and a line of insurance sellers. It's all bollocks; I can't imagine the policy will pay anyone anything. No details other than my bike and my name are taken. It's good enough to keep the officials happy, and now I just have an inspection to go through. I wasn't expecting that. A young lad, who must be on work experience, asks me if I have any TVs or DVD players. I must have looked so confident with my answer that a search was not required. And now I'm in Turkey, at last.

First impression: diverse. Cows wander down the road, and tractors with trailers full of female farmhands with covered heads and faces chug past stylish pedestrians in designer fashions, hair flowing and with big sunglasses. There are plush hotels next to housing blocks of satellite dishes and flaking paint. I haven't quite got a grasp on it yet.

"Oh my god, now that's a mosque; it's massive!" This is exciting.

I do the end of day performance that can take anything from fifteen minutes to several hours, but today it is relatively easy: Side street. Sign. Park. Ask. Yes they have a room. I walk up four flights of stairs to a large but dirty bedsit -type room. The bike will have to be left on the street, but the reception is open 24 hours, or as I see more frequently as I head east, "nonstop." It just means "open 24 hours" but sounds more exhausting. The place is run by some young gay youths. Mincing round the reception desk is just fine by me, but I could do without the snide comments and laughter as soon as I'm out of sight but clearly not ear shot. The room's not exactly Turkish delight(ful), but it will do, and man, am I looking forward to a shower. Four flights of stairs three times pushed me well over the limit, a limit I passed two borders ago.

So what happens in Edirne on a Saturday evening?

Phone shopping seems to be quite popular, and in the large pedestrian areas there are plenty of shops catering to the mobile-buying masses. From dinner to washing powder, all my purchases are easy, however, I can't find any kind of map in this cosmopolitan town. The mosque is so big I can't take it all in. I need a roof-top or hill to capture its eight pillars and vast dome.

I have elevation and a view from my room, albeit in the wrong direction, although through the housing blocks I can see a red sunset and the hills of eastern Bulgaria. It may be out of sight, but I am able to hear the mosque; the sound of prayers drift across the evening sky and through my window. Unlike the sound of taunting laughter, which floats up from reception, the recital is more relaxing than the ridicule. Now I feel like I've travelled to a foreign country. I think I'll have an early start tomorrow.

DAY 21

ALASEHIR, TURKEY, 379 MILES

Fuelled by a strong urge to photograph the mosque in morning light, I'm out of my room by 6AM. The streets are not empty by any means, but I can do my purposeful on-a-mission stride without the risk of colliding with dithering pedestrians. There is simply no vantage point to capture the grandness of the mosque, and rather than being impressed by its sheer magnitude, I'm just feeling frustration by my inability to view through my lens what my wide field of vision is seeing. It's more than a place of worship; there appears to be a school and library, baths and a market. Although the walls are low and sporadic, it just feels intrusive to wander round, particularly this early on a Sunday. I know it is not a holy day for Islam, but the actual temple-bit is full of the kneeling faithful. Having walked the perimeter I think I will just appreciate its elegant exterior from a distance. Where's a hot air balloon when you want one?

Apart from this mosque complex, the other noticeable thing in the town is the national flag, flying from every post, window, and building. This is surely beyond some patriotic pride; judging by their cleanliness and quantities something significant is going on. But my curiosity doesn't last long; that pastry shop smells good. I effortlessly make a purchase and soon have a warm, flaky, freshly baked, slightly greasy, pastry-patty type thing in my hand, my mouth, and over my camera.

The camp boys are not around this morning so I can pack up in peace. My exhaust, though not loud, still reverberates around the tall sleepy terraces of this back alley. Its single cylinder tones say that both my bike and I are alive, independent, and in control, a familiar sound in a strange country. Cats cower, the dormant are disturbed, and those who are in a position to, look to see the source of the sound. It's only me, lucky me, out in the warm morning sun, riding out of town, or trying to. I follow a trail of dropped pastry to the main road. I ride past the mosque one more time, mainly because it is east of my room and on a main road, which are two things that will help me exit the town in the direction I want to be heading. The plan works well; at least it does until the main road is closed. There are police blockades and no clear diversion. From what I can see my chosen street is being prepared for a procession or a celebration of some kind. I've got a feeling I'm going to be missing something big, but although this place is not a typically drab desolate border town, I still want to get a little deeper into the country.

Some time ago I decided I didn't want to experience the killer traffic and expensive toll highways of Istanbul. There is an appealing alternative, which involves a ferry crossing. As the hours pass, I'm getting a better grasp of the country. Fuel is, as I expected, outrageously expensive. In fact, Turkey has the most expensive fuel prices in the world. Equal to Norway in cost per litre, however, the difference is Norway is a rich country and everything is expensive, so the wages reflect that. Fuel there is only 7% of weekly expenditure, but here it equates to 35%, because the rest of life's necessities can be significantly less than in Western Europe. Although I'm riding slowly to conserve fuel, eventually the time comes when I need to buy some of this essential liquid. Every pump has an attendant, and the first thing they do is make a note of my registration number, after all, there is a strong incentive to do a runner. I have a daily budget of £50, and after topping up the tank, that wasn't even empty, I only have £13 left, except I need a litre of oil too, and that's another £10. To soften the blow of having £3 left for food and accommodation today, I am given a little freebie map, which shows the whole of the country on an A5 size leaflet. It's a lovely gesture, but I could use a little more detail. Another sweetener to make up for the extortionate price of fuel is free Wi-Fi, so I can get online and re-mortgage my house. I don't have to do many mental calculations to realise that Turkey is going to be a very expensive country to cross.

I somehow expected Turkey to be plains of red dusty soil, but right here it's very green and mostly farmed. Cows, sheep, and crops fill the hillsides. The road is in good condition, and often on this long straight dual carriageway I can't see another car in my mirrors or ahead. To break the monotony, the authorities thoughtfully station a police check in a dusty lay-by, and I'm flagged down. It's quite a noisy check-point, lots of shouting and loud engines. I pull past the makeshift desk standing in the shade of the tree, trying to find my own shade and a place my bike will stand stably on the soft ground. I take off my helmet and get my documents out of the tank box then look up to see who is most interested in inspecting them. It's at that point I see the cause of the shouting; it's directed at me, and the only word I understand is *goodbye*. Oh, so you don't want to see my documents after all? I'll just continue on my way then. Whether it's a case of foreign documents can't be processed or overseas travellers are not to be held I don't know, but I'm happy to continue, not that I had anything to hide or lacked what was required. I realise this as I ride off, and it feels quite comforting. There have been times when modest and discreetly placed contraband has caused a little discomfort, due to an unexpected game of hide and seek when a surprise encounter with authority occurs.

The ferry port is easy to find. The Sea of Marmara is what gives Istanbul its southern coast, but down here it is little more than a wide river. If there is a system or choice of ferries it's not obvious to me, and I'm soon sandwiched between waiting vehicles. When I get off my bike to look around I'm ushered to a kiosk to buy a ticket, which although it is the most reasonably priced thing I have purchased today, now means the budget is in the red, and it's only lunchtime.

I ride onto the boat, right to the front by a vertical unloading ramp. There are no securing straps. As I wait for the other vehicles to load, I look over the side; there are jellyfish swimming in the clear water and among the vessels crossing this busy stretch of water is a sub-marine, but seeing as it's visible I suppose, technically, it's a super-marine. From this starboard railing I can still make a dive for my bike if I see it wobble, whilst getting a bit of a view as we cross. Four hyperactive and giggly teenage girls push past me to get to the disembarking ramp as we come into dock. It's my cue to go back to my bike. However, the movement seems to remove my cloak of invisibility, and I become the object of their unwanted attention. Over-excited and full of bravado in the safety of their little clique, they are over familiar, playing with my earrings, ponytail, the floppy filler hose of my Scott-oiler, and they are much too rough with Monklet's tail. Having exhausted every phallic accessory on my bike, the phones come out for photos. I don't have a choice, but my anonymity remains intact; you can touch but you can't tag. The experience is wholly embarrassing, especially knowing every driver behind me, impatiently waiting for the ramp to come down, is watching. I feel captive and corrupted. I certainly seem to be an object of entertainment to the youth of this country, regardless of gender or sexual preference. When the ramp finally comes down I take the wrong direction on the only road. So then I have to pass the girls again, delaying their need to find something else to giggle at.

My new road is dull, hot, boring, and there is nowhere to stop, no shade and nothing much of anything positive. When I do come to a service station I try to find a more detailed map, but no one stocks them; demand must be low. I have to assume everyone here knows the way already. I never intended to get to the destination of my first Turkish site today; I still don't, but with nowhere to camp, the miles continue.

I leave the main road. There are mountains in the furthest distance, and they appear to have snow on them, which seems strange in this heat at relatively low altitude. The tired and sun-beaten farm workers are leaving their fields, sitting in trailers behind tractors. My day has been hard too, I think to myself. I've been riding for eleven hours now. Shepherds, ditches, and vehicles, every faint possibility of a wild camp has an obstruction. I don't envy the labourers, but at least they know where they are staying tonight. This is not meant to be an endurance test; I just want somewhere to stay, so I can stop riding. A hotel appears out of the evening haze, so it's got to be worth a try. The receptionist speaks English, and the price is way less than I was charged yesterday. No wonder they were camping it up in the hotel reception last night—I was fucked on my first date in Turkey. Speaking of dates, it's explained to me that today, 19th May, is a sort of Turkish Independence Day or at least the celebration of the start of the war of independence nearly 100 years ago. So that explains the flags all over the place. I'm sure I will sleep better knowing this, but anticipated dreams of red silk flags shimmering on a warm breeze in a dusky sky are kept from my tired subconscious mind by a pesky mosquito. It's gone 2AM when I finally manage to wound it enough to prevent any more disturbances.

Day 22

Pamukkale, Turkey, 68 Miles

It's not a welcome or invited audience that witness the packing ritual this morning. The interaction and entertainment is minimal, for me at least, although for a grand finale I pull away without removing the lock. It's much too hot to be crawling around under bike panniers wearing black riding trousers whilst trying to pull a jammed padlock and chain from between the spokes. Embarrassment and heat combined means this is another day where the freshness has left before I have.

Today I'm going to the salt terraces; it's not very far to ride because yesterday was. However, I ignore my sat nav as I am drawn towards some attractive mountain roads, so indirectly I find my way to Pamukkale. From a distance it just looks like dirty snow in early spring on the side of a motorway embankment.

The town is tourist hell, with camels and coaches, campervans and swimming pools with water slides. It's like an inland seaside town, built to entertain the masses who come to see the once natural beauty of the place. Deep joy, if I'd have got here last night I could have left this morning, but now I suppose I better stay and go and look at what I have come to see. I find a campground and give up my passport without resistance, which later annoys me. This visa stamped document is overpaid collateral for a pitch on a patch of grass. I have full view of the salt terraces. Actually it's calcium carbonate, or was before it hardened and became travertine.

I wasn't very good at the sciences in school, but some were compulsory subjects if I wanted to do the engineering class, and I did. I was so bad that my grades didn't meet the school criteria to be automatically entered into the final end of year exam. This was fine by me, I got to spend the lessons at the back of the class with the other non-entries who were mainly girls reading the problem pages in *Jackie*. The fly in the ointment (the chemical components of which I was unsure of) was that my father had paid the fee, so I would still be entered in the exam. The teacher, however, was unaware of this fact until the day of the exam, which was only a week away from when I left school forever. He was not pleased to see me, mainly because my failings would bring his pass average down even further. Had he been a good teacher he would have had nothing to worry about. Luckily for me and also my teacher (I use the word loosely), the exam was multiple choice, and I went down the page circling a,c-d,c. I wasn't about to fail; I was to be saluted. I got a grade 3! Nevertheless, who the hell has heard of travertine? Looks like salt to me, and I'm not about to lick it or cook with it.

It's white and hard, and there are hot springs and the sort of stalactite formations associated with caves. There is a constant procession of tourists who walk from their tour buses against the water overflowing from artificial pools and then up to the source of the springs. It reeks of over-development and under-planning. The fact this place is twinned with Las Vegas says it all really. What the hell am I doing here? I go sit by the pool, but the loungers are uncomfortable, and anyway, I didn't come here to sit by a pool, so I doze in my tent. I have no desire at all to join the hordes and take my place in the line of sightseers.

I take a walk round the town; it's worse than I thought. Loud and bolshie restaurant owners stand outside their premises demanding I come in and eat. Tacky plastic souvenirs are on sale everywhere, and postcard sellers get in my face with their string of perforated pictures. I buy a few food supplies at predictably inflated rates. On my way back I pass a place called "Natural World" that's as natural as triangular cheese. It has fake palms around a bay-shaped swimming pool. Two weeks ago I was in Auschwitz; now that was real. It too was depressing but in an expected way.

I sit in the shade by my tent, and a hungry, poorly, and suffering cat comes scrounging. I give him some of my sausage, and he scoffs it down, then sits nearby digesting as I look over my Central Asia maps. I'm distracted by the distressed chirping of several birds; the cat has just caught a chick that fell from the nest. One of the birds is dive bombing the cat, but it is unperturbed as it crunches into its windfall dinner. It's a little barbaric, but it's the most natural thing I've seen here.

With no other pleasure to be gained by seeing what Turkey does to its natural beauty, my mind races forward to the 'Stans. When I get to Turkmenistan I have just 72 hours to transit to Uzbekistan, and with delayed ferry departures from Azerbaijan this could leave me with only 48 hours. A $1,500 fine is issued if I outstay my visa by as little as an hour. I can get a guided tour for less than that, and I'm thinking it may be worth the cost, as it will relieve more than time pressure. It also means I don't have to think about route, navigation, accommodation, food, language, or even deal with any bureaucracy, from currency to bike importation, for five whole days, and I get to see some sights. The more I think about it the more I think it seems to be one of those situations where spending is actually saving in the long run. It also eliminates a lot of pressure, as Turkmenistan is the strictest of all the 'Stans I will be visiting. All this cyber research also brings the discovery of a recommended route across Turkey. I am now quite keen to get to Ankara and start the next visa application process, but a little diversion via the south coast seems quite appealing.

Whilst I was riding this positive train of thought, the evening arrived and the tour buses left. What looked like a fence across the white terrace was in fact a continuous chain of tourists. Now that there is a break in it I think I may go and have a look for myself. Armed with iPod to drown out the chatter, and my camera to capture the scene, I walk up. It's actually pretty good; I can see the attraction. Best of all, I can see it uncluttered, silent, atmospheric, and enhanced by evening light. Snow topped mountains are reflected in pools of still clear water, although slightly obscured by steam. It's not entirely natural, the flow of water is controlled and the pools are staggered too precisely to have occurred naturally.

It's still unique, and as an added bonus, when I reach the plateau the original Roman city ruins are visible; arches and pillars still stand and the area they cover shows that this place was densely populated long before the dawn of tourism. Bright sodium lights keep the stars away but create some interesting shadows. Tourist attractions attract tourists; that's their objective. It's not mine. I'm the after-hours observer. I like to peek later. I don't follow the crowds; I'm just behind them.

DAY 23

KAS, TURKEY, 210 MILES

Gooooooood morning Pamukkale, would be the inaccurate translation of the amplified wailings from the mosque at 4.50AM. I can see how this could be most annoying if it woke you every morning, especially if you weren't even of the faith that broadcasted it. But I don't have to go to work this morning. It's just getting light and the temperature is ideal, it's not like I want to spend the day under the covers. On top of that, although the sound quality could be better, the chanting is in tune, stirring, and exotic. For me it's not an alarm clock, it's an opportunity clock. This morning I want to be ahead of the crowd.

With yesterday's ticket and a look of intrigue and ignorance, I blatantly walk past the unmanned entrance and back to the deserted mound of hardened calcium carbonate, as it's referred to in certain scientific circles, not that I move in those circles. This morning I'm not moving in circles at all; I'm zigzagging, dodging, and weaving, feeling very conspicuous being the only moving being on this white deserted hillside. I find a place to sit between a terrace of pools that allows me a view of the rising sun, yet keeps me mostly hidden. Mostly, but not entirely. Just as the light was reaching its photogenic crescendo, out the corner of my eye I see the imposing figure of authority approaching. Bollocks. Mustering as much contempt as I can at this interruption of my imperative photographic work, I produce yesterday's entrance ticket. Apparently it would seem it is not valid for today, and I am pointed towards the ticket office. There seems to be little to bargain with, so I reluctantly walk in that direction. He follows at a distance. I know this because every time I check over my shoulder to make sure the feeling of eyes staring in my back is not just paranoia I see his intimidating presence is not far behind. This has become a game now. I've missed the best of the sunrise, and I just need to get out of here without spending another 20 lire. I manage to lose him as I approach the gift shop and double back down a ravine. I climb some rocks and poke my head up; I seem to have found a completely different part of this attraction. Trying not to consider snakes or other possible undergrowth hazards, I ramble on and discover more ruins, a huge but collapsed stone-built arched bridge, no doubt built for the passage of Roman transport.

This is great, an inadvertent diversion from the tourist trail, and although the sites may not be the most spectacular, their inaccessibility and solitude make them all the more authentic. That, in turn, makes me feel like a discoverer. No, that makes me sound like a four wheel drive. Explorer, that's better. It occurs to me that every feeling I'm getting from this experience has a vehicle named after it. Brilliant, I must be doing something desirable. My thoughts *Focus* on how permissible this is, what the penalties might be, and can I a*Ford* it . . .

Thoughts of *Midnight Express* enter my head. I see myself emaciated and suffering from malnutrition in a Turkish prison.

"What was your crime, Englishman?" the heroin-addicted paedophile would ask. "Espionage? Arms deals? Drug smuggling?"

"No," I would weakly reply, "I didn't pay my 20 lira to a bad ticket machine, and for the price of £6.50 I have bought myself this enslavement."

"But Englishman, don't you see, it doesn't matter if it was 20 lire or 20 thousand lire, the Turks love to catch foreigners."

Right, well I've got a couple of good photos now; I think I might head out. I pack up my tent and collect my passport then, although this could be the complacent behaviour that results in my capture, I opt to have some breakfast in view of the travertine of trespass. When I get back to my bike, there is something on the seat, a warrant? No, it's a sticker. I've been given a sticker to remember my holiday in Pamukkale. How lovely.

Back on the road I head through the city of Denizli, which lies at the base of the mountains I'm heading for. I'm sure I read this is a temperate region; it feels bloody hot to me, especially watching the countdown on the traffic lights. It's a long 90 seconds waiting for the green to show so I can leave this radiating heat between my legs behind me.

The cool of the mountains is a long time coming, and the road just about keeps me entertained, with views of opium poppy fields and other flowers I'm more familiar with. My mind goes back to the distressed sounds from the bereaved birds yesterday, as the cat ate an offspring. This morning there is one less mouth in the nest to feed, a few less worms to find. I wonder if birds get depressed and how long the mourning lasts. The fragile life beyond the civilized world; there's not much time for sentiment when food and shelter are the only necessities. Sparrows don't hold court, the cat doesn't need a defence lawyer; there is no justice, just instinct. You are hungry, you kill, you eat. Our society has come so far; we are hungry, we get food, but we also get club card points. Fantastic.

I start to gain altitude, everything gets better, the views, the temperature, the road, and as the air gets thinner, my ears pop. I try not to swallow because I like the engine sounding so quiet; it's more dreamlike as I lean round shallow curves that overlook dry stony river beds in the valleys. There are occasional grey streaks down tree covered mountains, where the land has broken free and taken all the vegetation with it as it slid down the valley floor. Some snow still remains on the very top of the grey rocky tops. It's a good ride. I'm glad I'm doing this. It's not direct at all but it's pleasurable and that, after all, is the point of the journey.

A squadron of Dutch registered campervans comes towards me; I can tell they are part of the same group as they all have big yellow numbers stuck on their windscreens. They have broken their chronological order, but that's where the initiative seems to end. A convoy of campers; I'm so glad I'm going the other way.

The scenery becomes so impressive, I have to stop, and for the first time, I take out the tripod. It's a bit of a palaver but actually doesn't take as long as it seems. Just pull it out from under the bungee, extend the legs, fasten the camera, select self-timer, and go strike a natural pose beside the bike. It's not exactly spontaneous. The thing is it's very easy to discover every scenic photo of the trip has a bike in the foreground, and by using the tripod, I can break this pattern by putting myself in the frame. Although the whole operation takes less than five minutes, it's still a pain in the arse, and it will require some quite spectacular scenery to justify going through this procedure again.

Occasionally I'm graced with a signpost in both Turkish and English; I study the words trying to find some similarities, clues to the translation, but through my dyslexic eyes there are no patterns or logic; it's all Greek to me. Another thing that I don't understand is why other bikes are not waving. I've seen several machines now with the whole aluminium pannier thing going on, but my recognition has produced no response at all. Looking at the photo I just took of myself and the bike, it seems quite obvious I'm of the overland-type breed. Drybags strapped on panniers, what else can it mean?

The mountain road has wound down to the coast, and the heat has returned. Now I head in my preferred easterly direction, glancing down at the turquoise shades of the sea it looks very inviting. In fact, there is no doubt in my indecisive mind that I will almost definitely be staying around here tonight.

I stop to do my point and mime scene at a little shop and get all I require; tomatoes, bread, cheese, and a little human interaction. There is a campsite opposite, but I'm not really ready to call it a day yet. The owner speaks good English, having worked in Wales, and we even exchange some pleasantries in Welsh. I learned a little from a Welsh girl I once dated. I refrained from playing my Welsh trump card, which translates to "I want a kiss." I'll save that one for best.

The road becomes a cliff-clinging ribbon, and below me is the occasional village running down a peninsula, ending in a wooden jetty with a few boats moored to it. There is a general feeling of pleasant, relaxed unobtrusive living. I think I will leave with that impression rather than go down and ruin it.

I ride on and find something already ruined; a scruffy dirty, rundown, rocky campground, too close to the busy road and the wrong side for the sea. But it's cheap and shady and has a shower block. There is a popular little town down the road, and I walk the coastline to it as the sun goes down, past expensive boats and timeshares, which are all part of gated marinas. All very lovely, I'm sure, but I left my wallet at camp, so I won't be indulging in any of the luxuries this complex offers. Sea and swimming pools aplenty, water everywhere; I'm thirsty and I don't have enough money for a bottle of the stuff. I was never meant to belong in such a place anyway.

DAY 24

SEYDISEHIR, TURKEY, 287 MILES

I never went camping until I was old enough to have sex. That wasn't a mandate imposed by my parents, well not directly, but it didn't take long to figure out if you wanted more than a quickie in a Mini, the overnight camp was the ideal opportunity. So I came relatively unprepared to both these experiences simultaneously. One of which, with instinct and enthusiasm, I got the grasp of quite quickly, especially as it didn't require any expensive equipment. The camping on the other hand...tricks, tips, etiquette, equipment, preferable pitching locations have all been learned the hard way, and there is so much to know; what food travels and keeps well, weather conditions and preparation for them. There are a plethora of pitfalls in this pastime; it's as complex as gardening or cooking. So with no instruction, I was thrown into the wild outdoors without even basic foreplay knowledge, such as tent peg insertion technique. I feel adequately prepared these days, but I fear there are some gaping holes in the fundamentals. For example, I never quite know what is expected of the newcomer entering a site. Should I wave? Interact? Introduce? More often than not my arrival is met with hard stares from over the top of tabloid newspapers held on beer bellies squeezed into plastic chairs. Although I have no desire to converse with such people—because I'm much happier to silently judge them—I wonder how my campsite experience would differ if I were to go for a chat.

On this particular site what do I have in common with my fellow camper? We are both foreigners, they Dutch, me English; and we are both transient. Them in a camper, me on a bike; there isn't much else really.

"I see you have ridden from England." "Yes, I see you have driven from Holland." "Indeed."

74

It's no wonder I keep myself to myself. This morning, however, I'm feeling uncharacteristically sociable, so I ask the usual, "How ya doin'? Where ya been? Where ya goin'?" I gain little in the way of useful information, other than learning that yesterday a procession of seventeen Dutch campervans left this site. Apparently they travel that way for safety and also, I would imagine, to avoid having any interaction with anyone outside of their posse. I'm told they were heading for Pamukkale. I bet they'll deplete the campsite's sticker stash.

The morning had started when I took my cup of tea across the road to sit on the beach. Somehow whilst nodding to a dog walker, I strayed into the path of a car. Thankfully, it was the only vehicle on the road, and it managed to swerve and miss me, so I didn't spill my chai. So when I pull out of the campsite I'm doubly sure to check for traffic. I ride to the little town of Kas to shop at the market I saw last night. Then I ride up to the high road and pull over into a grassy parking area. It's perfectly positioned to look down at the town, with its whitewashed walls and terracotta tiles, all neatly situated around a mosque. There are more islands than ocean in the bay, and from my vista point I eat some breakfast and try to work out how one would navigate their way out to sea. I really seem to have slowed my pace, and I'm quite pleased with myself. So with these self-congratulatory thoughts, combined with the simple nautical musings from a panoramic vantage point whilst enjoying my fresh bread, I'm close to contentment. It will take more than a sprinkler spontaneously squirting into life, soaking my sandwich and seat, to dampen my day. It occurs to me I'm feeling better about everything now, or is it just coincidence this feeling has coincided with switching off the sat nav? It was always flashing on and off due to charging issues; there are plenty of better things to look at than a fading screen. The simple appreciation of scenery. I may not quite be in the zone, but I know its round here somewhere.

The coastal road continues, the ocean on my right and snowy mountains on my left. I've decided although the colour makes the ocean holiday brochure inviting, having stood in it up to my knees yesterday, I think I prefer to just look at it than be in it. There are no waves to surf. I don't have a mask and snorkel. Other than shorts I have no equipment for aquatic pastimes, just a camera and an appreciation of a pretty picture.

There is a glossy wet-looking tar strip on the road. It looks slippery, so I avoid the knee scraping leaning that the coast hugging curves tempt me to do. I also become aware that my horn has stopped working when I come across a motorist who desperately needs honking at. Shouting is futile, and anyway, I don't know the Turkish for "Would you drive any better with that phone shoved up your arse?"

The road shoots up to two thousand feet, and today's blossom is yellow hawthorn, accompanied by the smell of pine trees. The problem with Turkey is it's not just where east meets west, it's where the transit meets the trip, and it's such a large and daunting country to traverse. The suggested route I read of yesterday seems quite satisfying so far. The Turkey *Lonely Planet* was a big and expensive guidebook to buy and carry, so I don't have one. This indirect route across the country is a good compromise between a straight line and an all-encompassing tour. I've got a basic route to follow and no real idea what I will see on the way.

The signposts are doing their best to generate excitement by announcing my approach to Olympus; I get caught up in the hype and decide a 12 km detour is worth the effort to see such an historic spot. The road turns to dirt, and it seems strange that this prestigious area should have such limited access. I do my first river crossing; it's not too challenging. I find myself in a traveller's area of wall to wall guesthouses and restaurants. I think there is something here I am not understanding. I stop at a little restaurant, order a kebab, and utilise the Wi-Fi. Turns out this is not Mount Olympus, that's in Greece (I'm sure I knew that), this is Olympus, the Roman ruins. I'm from bloody Colchester; I don't give a shit about Roman ruins. I can't dig up a potato without my spade hitting an ancient Roman artefact. Still, the river crossing was fun.

There is some cloud cover now, and the road is taking me into Antalya, which appears to be a very big city with a coast line of white high rises. I'm not looking forward to negotiating my way through this place. I stop to fix my horn and prepare myself for this city of traffic, lights, delays, and distractions. With great velocity I head into the outskirts on a fast highway. There are car dealers of every make imaginable, exhaust and tyre specialists, but not a single all-purpose shop that might sell maps. Not that I have time to stop. The road flows between the beach and the city. There are no lights, just fast uninterrupted concrete highway. This is going to end; it has to. How the hell do the city dwellers get to the beach? This road is uncrossable; it's built with the sole intention of getting the traffic, nonstop, from one end of town to the other. Its works perfectly. I've never been through such a fast city; I didn't even put my feet down. However, once I'm out the other end it gets horrid, even faster but with traffic lights, the same stinking trucks keep overtaking me and the stop start is tiring. It's a hard ride; sticky, sweaty, humid, and with dirty air. I don't have to endure it for too long. I pull off onto the road that will take me back over the mountains and towards Ankara. I stop for supplies and eat them by a rusty and burnt-out tour bus. There are good camping possibilities, but it's too early to stop; so hard to combine the right location with the right time of day and adequate supplies.

Up into the cold of the mountains where a camping spot would be easy to find but an uncomfortable temperature, I look down at lakes on the warm flat arable plains and see no pitching possibilities. Once the daylight starts going, I decide I will have to pay for a hotel, if I can find one. I can, but I need to be more specific; I want one that has a vacancy. Eventually, in a quaint little town square, I find a room that stinks of mothballs. But I have a balcony that overlooks my bike, a little fountain, and benches in the square. Further, I can see over roofs of tiles and corrugated tin to the pillars of a nearby mosque, framed against craggy mountains where snow still lies in the sunless crevices. It's the low budget version of a view with potential. I keep the door to the balcony open so as not to obscure the view, or be overcome by moth-repelling fumes, and also if anyone tampers with my bike below, I will hear. It's just cool enough so the mosquitoes are kept away and sleep is not.

Day 25

Ankara, Turkey, 256 Miles

No need for dodgy hotel artwork, not with the view from my bed; a clear dark blue dawn makes the snow stand out on its rocky canvas. I feel a part of it, especially as the chill air has filled the room. A gasp of admiration is visible when I exhale. No pannier wardrobe fashion dilemmas today, straight out of bed into all my bike clothes; the stairs circulate the blood and generate some heat as I take my luggage down to the bike. As I load it, I notice the nut is missing from the side stand bolt. It's always something, and if not, it's something else.

Today's audience has polite intrigue, anxious to help but respectful of space and property. They see me off with waves and gentle expressions; it's a very positive start to the day. I've had pistachio nuts for breakfast, left over from last night's dinner. I could look round here for food, but I have an urge for the road.

An industrial area I passed last night offers hope. I find it again this morning, and it meets my expectations. Unit after unit, row after row of vehicle-orientated supplies. I pick one. Yes, he has oil, yes, he has the nut I need, and it's nylock, and yes, he has a cigarette lighter/sat nav charger. However, before we can get into any of my desires, we must have chai. I feel that his delight at my presence is genuine; talk about customer appreciation. I'm just happy to have found proper bike oil to replace the stuff I left home with 4,500 miles ago. I converse with the elderly owner as best I can. His boy looks on attentively. Chai finished, hands shaken, and gratitude shown, I leave for wherever it is I'm going.

It's Thursday, so should I go to Ankara and start the visa process or wait for a new week to start? The alternative is Cappadocia, the other attraction I was aware of in Turkey. No, I need to know the visa situation, then I will have a better idea of a time frame. Good, I've made a decision.

Since I wrote this town by town itinerary the other day, navigation has been quite straightforward. I think I can get through the rest of Turkey now without a detailed map or by relying too much on my flickering sat nav.

I have three one-litre oil bottles hanging off my bike; I need to find an appropriate lay-by to do the dirty deed. I find the perfect spot behind a pile of rubble. There are some empty discarded plastic bottles around, so I pull out my sump plug, which worryingly, is only finger tight. It's a bit messy, but I manage to collect most of the hot black oil in an old bottle. I'm not bothering with changing the filter, not here. I replace the side-stand nut as the oil drains, get out my stove to boil some water for tea, and heat my copper sump plug sealing washer over the flame so it will expand again, ready to be compressed by a correctly tightened bolt. Replace oil, wave hello to farm labours passing on a horse and cart, clean up, pack up, and I'm ready to go. It was a slick little oil change, discreetly hidden by a heap of concrete debris. Nothing too extreme, just a little hardcore. I discard my oil cans in a petrol station skip, and the operation is complete.

This isn't the main road to Ankara, but it's still quite fast and busy. Police cars sit on the hard shoulder facing the oncoming traffic and pointing their speed guns through their windscreens. They seem to be taking quite a risk just to write a ticket. But then it would seem this road is full of risk.

Another town and another efficient bypass around it. However, this one has an enforced slow speed limit. Just as well really; a car comes directly towards me on the wrong side of the dual carriageway. I hoot my now functional horn and flash my lights. As if avoiding a puddle, with no urgency at all, he opts for an arc in his trajectory, and the situation becomes an insignificant moment in history.

I've seen quite a few tortoises lately; another one crosses the road ahead of me. It really is a road of frequent hazards. I'm not sure who would come off worse if we collided, but why does he want to be crossing this wide busy road anyway? To go to the Shell station?

Things often happen in threes if you have the time to count them. Another vehicle comes towards me. This one is reversing down the lane I'm in because he missed his exit. There are no strict road regulations here, just get to where you are going, regardless of the others. Maybe this behaviour has come about as a result of the high fuel prices; maybe it's just Asia. I am officially in Asia now, without ceremony or any clear boundary crossed, I'm east of Istanbul and that's good enough for me. As I leave the town's bypass I slow down for a red light. The lights count down the time until they will change colour, and with 14 seconds to go a truck passes me and steams right through the red light. Where the hell does that leave me? Braking on green? I can't assume anything on this road. Things aren't happening in threes here; they just keep happening.

I turned my back on the mountains this morning, but I've still been riding at altitude, I don't know this because of shortness of breath, thinness of air, coolness of the day, but because now as I round a bend the road drops down to some hazy flat plains. My god, that looks dull. Think I will stop here and stuff my earphones into my helmet. I need some audible stimulation to cross this featureless landscape. Despite all the choices on my iPod, I opt for a classic and happily listen to some sounds even more familiar than the wind in my ears. With the bike now serviced, there really isn't much left on my to-do list, but it doesn't last long. As I pull on a strap to tighten the tank box, a fastening buckle snaps. The list continues.

The road is as dull as I predicted. I recently discovered that the afternoon drowsy feeling has been diagnosed. It's to do with blood sugar levels and can be instantly cured with a can of coke. As I pull up to a little market, my iPod has just reached track three of *Dark Side of the Moon*, and the song of praise from a mosque harmonizes with the synthesized music beautifully. It fits as perfectly as a shadow into the crescent of the moon on the Turkish flag—one of those moments of serendipity.

It's a jolly little shop stop, with the inevitable chai being offered, even the nearby mechanic comes over to cast an inquiring eye over my bike and seems satisfied with what he sees. There are storm clouds ahead, but in this heat, the thought of cloud cover is quite refreshing so does not deter me; I'm keen to ride towards them.

Sullen sky and thoughtful mood take me into Ankara. All I've read and retained, along with half known hearsay about getting visas for the 'Stans is now at the front of my mind. The quicker I get some facts and the process started, the sooner I can relax and think about other things.

I ride straight into Ankara, trying to remember the name of the area where all the embassies are, but it won't come, so I have to find an Internet cafe and refresh my memory. I head up steep hilly streets until I'm in the vicinity. It's a really pretty city, built on several hills, making it easy to get my bearings. I envisage a hotel with secure bike parking and a room overlooking mosques or ancient architecture, sunset hills or a valley sunrise. I'm not that picky, but I will be here for a while and want somewhere inspiring to wait out the bureaucratic process. I ride up and down. There are no hotels at all. I see everything else you would associate with the business district of a capital city, but I can't find accommodation. It's just a matter of time surely. I try going a block off the main streets, still nothing. When I do find a place they want 180 euros.

"No, I only want to stay for a week."

"That's per night sir." Yeah right. I ask where I might find cheaper, and I am told the old town. I don't want to be that far from this area, though, as this is where I will be spending my time.

I try again; a local biker in a hurry can't show me but confirms the only cheap accommodation is in the old centre. It's rush hour now, and I head into the midst of it. I find a place for £6 a night. I'm told it is safe here with hardly any violence; well, I didn't really expect there to be. So there is no risk of a stabbing in this smelly box with no toilet or shower? I think I will try to find better. There is definitely more choice here. I'm glad it's not baking hot as I set a new record; four hours, four bastard hours to find a hotel. My bike is left on the street, and the room looks out over a car-park, but it's clean and there is a leafy courtyard dining area.

Here I am in Ankara where the preparation for the next part of the journey begins. This area is full of activity; there are busy street markets and eateries, and everything appears to be available here. Once again, the bike cover proves to be worth its weight and volume. Parked in an alcove, locked to some railings, and covered with its all-encompassing cloak of discretion; it's hardly noticeable.

I find a place to eat and accidently order a meal for two. As I struggle through this coronary feast, I'm asked by a waiter if I speak English. "Yes," I say, ready for the next question.

"Where are you from?" he continues.

"England." We both find this really funny, but I think you had to be there.

My little triangular room has a pleasant feel, and although it's a bit cramped with my luggage stacked inside, I'm happy with my choice. That is until about midnight, when I'm woken by drunken laughter, banging doors, and moaning whores. It's a bloody brothel. Brilliant, this noise goes on through most of the night, and the only sound that isn't fake is the banging doors.

DAY 26

ANKARA, TURKEY, 44 MILES

Today is V-day, visa day, the much anticipated application for admittance documents into countries whose names all end in 'stan. It starts with a laptop in the shaded open-air dining area as I have my breakfast of bread and coffee. The staff are all male, friendly, and attentive, although none of them speak English. Despite this, much like the girls who work here, I get the feeling they will bend over backwards to accommodate me. The place is quiet this morning; the paying customers and working girls have all left. I have not the faintest idea what either looked like.

I don't know what my man at Stan Tours looks like either, in fact, I don't even know what country he resides in. All I know is in 6 months of communication, regardless of what time zone I was in, I always got an instant response. I don't think he ever sleeps. Between us we tried so hard to get my Iran visa, and we almost succeeded. Now further letters of invitation (LoI) are needed, and today I've been told the price of a guided tour through Turkmenistan. It's not cheap, but the peace of mind it comes with is worth the expense. I'm having quite a productive morning online, but I'm supposed to be on the streets. I read on one thread from a particularly well-organised adventurer he has all seven visas needed to get him from the UK to China. They are already in place in his passport before he leaves. On the face of it that sounds like a wonderfully stress-free way to travel, but what strict deadlines. What if the bike breaks down? What if you find a place you want to stop for a while? There will be daily distances that need to be done and no room for deviation. There is no easy way to traverse this area, but those deadlines would cause me more anguish than this application process. Well that's what I think sitting here with my second cup of coffee. I better get out and discover the reality.

The bike is stripped to near naked, and I'm wearing a lot less too. This week I will be mainly a commuter; I've left the adventuring in my room.

OK, I have addresses in my sat nav. Today is its chance to shine. I have multiple inner-city addresses to locate, and this is the reason I brought the thing. I have cross-referenced this on Google maps and even drawn a little map of my route as back-up. It appears to be a straight line to my destination, seven miles to the embassy area.

This is my plan; I already have my Russian and Kazakh visas, their entry and exit dates overlap so I have some flexibility in my schedule. Kyrgyzstan is the only 'Stan who has dropped their visa requirements. I want a double entry for Tajikistan, as I would like to cross the Wakhan Valley into Afghanistan, depending on the situation when I get there. A visa for Afghanistan can be obtained instantly in Tajikistan. I also need a Gorno-Badakhstan Autonomous Oblast (GBAO) permit to travel the Pamir Highway. I think I can get that where I get my visa. The Uzbekistan visa can take about five days, and if I opt for the tour, all my Turkmenistan documents will be sorted by the agency. I will pick them up in Azerbaijan, the visa for which I will get in 24 hours without a letter of invitation in Georgia, the visa for which I get instantly as I cross from Turkey. Simple, what could possibly go wrong?

Based on all that, I first have to find the Uzbekistan embassy. The straight road goes into a tunnel and forks. Really? A junction in a tunnel? The subterranean choice I make is wrong. Bollocks. A slip road comes down and joins me; now where? When I'm thrust out into daylight, I make several dangerous U-turns across busy roads and get back on track. I come to the area I rode round yesterday; I recognise some of it. The sat nav is saying I'm nearly here. One more junction, no wait, one more junction, another junction? For fuck's sake, the sat-nav's frozen; it's never done this before. The one reason, the one fuckin' reason I brought this bastard piece of shit electronic, moronic, time and petrol wasting bit of useless gadgetry was for today's operation, and it's bloody frozen.

I turn it off; it won't turn back on. The willpower I have had to exercise the restraint I've had to apply to stop myself giving this little box a violent death over the last three weeks has all been achieved by knowing that it will redeem itself in Ankara, and what does it do? Absolutely fucking nothing. Bastard, bastard, bastard.

Luckily I have my laptop with me, I didn't shut it down, and the map page is still displayed. OK, I think I know where I'm going, if only I had a physical paper street map it would just be me, the map, and my glasses, I would be in control. I move on. I find myself on a fast road with nowhere to turn round. It goes on and on. I eventually come to an IKEA where I'm able to turn back. The Uzbekistan embassy website said they close for lunch at midday, and if I don't get there soon, I will be too late. I don't understand the street numbers; there is no logic I can see, so I ask and am drawn a map (I've mislaid the one I drew).

I go a little way; again I'm confused. I ask a taxi driver; he points. I think I'm getting close, no I'm not. I ask another taxi driver. I'm definitely getting close. I come to a building with flags flying, security fences, and lots of people standing around outside, being held back by armed security. I wasn't expecting this. But I park my bike, lock it up, and approach the throng. This isn't the Uzbekistan embassy; I'm told it's the United Nations building. I'm not sure if I'm relieved or not. The Uzbekistan embassy is across the street. It too is surrounded by security fencing, but there is no one around. I press the buzzer, a camera scans me, the gate vibrates and opens; so they aren't at lunch then? I'm inside, phew. I go into a tiny room; a few bits of paper are pined to the walls. Behind the bars is an official. He gives me an address of a website I have to download a form from; can't you just give it to me? No, they are closing for lunch now. Back on the street it looks promising, like there might be an Internet cafe, and there is. I fill out the form online and print it out. I also get multiple copies of my passport while I'm at it. Then I sit in a Burger King having a nasty Whopper and try to work out my entry and exit dates and realise I don't have much time. The Russia and Kazakhstan visas dictate the end of the trip, and the bit between here and there has so many unknowns. I could have given this more thought. Shit, I think I've given it quite a lot already. OK, I'm ready to commit. I fill in some dates. Back to the embassy; everything seems in order, and I can pick up my visa in five days or in Azerbaijan.

"Can I pay an extra fee to fast track it?" I tentatively ask, neither implying nor denying a bribe is in the offing. OK, I'll pick it up at your Azerbaijan embassy, another place I have to try and find. God, I hope I'm doing the right thing here.

So to the Tajikistan embassy; it's this way right? The sat nav is dead. I see a hillside of plush and newly built individual buildings, all with their national flags flying. I just can't get to it; some road workers explain the way. This feels much better. I pass Kazakh and Japanese flags. I see the Mongolian flag. I stop at the Palestinian Embassy, and they point the way, on past the Lebanese and Croatian Embassies, South African and Chinese. What a peaceful little gathering of countries; it's like an Olympic ceremony, all come together for the great game of the visa application. Actually I think they have more important business, but to a scruffy Englishman on a dirty bike, riding round international establishments of limited access, it's pretty obvious why I'm here.

I have heard nothing but positive things about the Tajikistan embassy, how incredibly helpful and friendly they are. The ambassador himself deals with your application whilst you sit, drink tea, and discuss how Japan has the best view from their embassy building. That, however, is not the experience I have, I'm the only one in the little office. I'm given a form to fill in, and when I return it, I'm told to come back Monday. Then why the hell have I filled it in now? No point in arguing. Well that's it then. I'm weekending in Ankara.

Once again it's rush hour, and to fit in, I ride like there is no future through the gridlocked traffic. If I can get through a day of bureaucracy like this, I must surely be immortal. I clearly am, because I'm still alive when I get back to my little ho' away from home. After a shower, much like my fellow guests, I hit the streets. The market has lots of low priced, low quality junk, and I find a USB charger to try one last time to breathe life into the sat nav. I buy my first Turkish beer; its £1.50 for a can. I drink it on my tiny terrace and have a bread sandwich to accompany it. I've had nothing but my own company for a whole week, and this is the first beer too. It's all been pretty good really.

I make a new schedule, draw up a calendar to work out countries, and approximate transit times so I can fill the appropriate dates in the appropriate boxes. I think it will all work out perfectly. I plug the sat nav into my new USB charger, then I put in my earplugs, a pillow over my head, and a loud Turkish voice on the TV in the hope that this constant noise will drown out the intermittent slamming and banging. Let it begin; I think I'm oblivious.

DAY 27

ANKARA, TURKEY, 0 MILES

The pillow just about kept the noise the right side of annoying. In the night I think to myself I'm going to leave, but the mornings are so tranquil. I really like the little courtyard area; it's a pleasant place to begin the day. Well it was yesterday. This morning sitting at another table is one of last night's left overs, playing five second snippets of music on his phone. It's really annoying. I wonder if he's downloading something, as the Internet is also annoyingly slow this morning. I'll blame him anyway. I think I'd better do something else. It's a good opportunity to do some laundry. I get carried away and do all my outer bike clothes and liners; even Monklet gets a scrubbing.

Out on the streets it's so vibrant; there's quite a buzz in the air. I walk up to a castle. It's very close; not surprising really, my hotel is named after it. Mind you the Miami motel on the A12 in Chelmsford has a name that's a little misleading.

There are some good views, so I think I will come back for sunset, but for now my tummy demands some attention.

What do I fancy? Fish, I think, and as if by magic I don't just find fish but a heaving stall besieged by hungry Turks waving money and then scurrying off into some shade to eat their hot freshly cooked fish laid in a half loaf of bread. Bread has been my staple diet for some time now. It started somewhere in Romania, and now I'm in Turkey it comes out at every meal, in a plastic box big enough for several puppies to sleep in. After Islam, I'm sure the second most popular thing here is bread. There's nothing wrong with it; they bake a good loaf. I could just use a little variety in my diet. However, in this instant, I'm going to get myself a fish sandwich. After all, a market full of gobbling Turks can't be wrong.

The details of my guided tour of Turkmenistan have come through, and as with so many of these applications I've done lately, I have to commit and pay. It may not come direct from my wallet, but I always find spending money far less painful, almost pleasurable, if I've had a little drink, so I go and buy a couple of cans. Anyway, I feel a bit sick after that sandwich, so a beer or two ought to sort out the situation.

When the sun starts its colourful descent I go back to the castle, a popular spot in the evening. Several older gentlemen are sitting around a table playing dominoes. One of them sees my camera and wants his photo taken. He grabs his mate, and with a genuine hug and spontaneous smile, they look into my lens, and I capture them beautifully. They like the little image they see on the back of the camera, but it's not until I see it full size on the computer screen that I realize what a lucky shot it is. There is blurred low sunlight seeping through summer foliage in the background and perfect focus on the last wispy hairs on a balding head and fresh ones on a sagging chin. Laughter, age, and wisdom lines frame dark and happy eyes. Damn, I wish I had a way of finding them again.

I sit on a castle wall looking west, and the city's dusty atmosphere glows orange as the sun silhouettes the hills it sets behind. It would seem I have got the view I wanted, I just had a short walk to find it. I think I may get another beer or two to celebrate.

Much as I love my room I feel a little captive, and after a few drinks I decide to hit the streets again; maybe another bite to eat. It's not that late, but it's like I've stepped out into another city altogether. All the shops have closed up; shutters are locked down. The streets are empty. The place is desolate and foreboding. I feel like a street fighter in a city on lock down. I try to project an image of boldness, just in case I'm about to be mugged. I find an empty Burger King and go in for some fries; it's then I realise my fly have been undone since

I left the hotel. The place does not feel safe at all, so I go back down some side streets to the sanctuary of my room. The banging starts at 11PM, but the next sound I'm aware of is morning prayers.

DAY 28

ANKARA, TURKEY, 28 MILES

It's not proper sleep, more like determined denial of disturbance. Sometime after dawn my sat nav sprung back into life, not with a humble and sincere apology and not pleading for forgiveness. It just interrupted the brief silence between morning prayer and barking dogs to announce I was exceeding the speed limit. And what, I wonder, is the maximum velocity of a plastic box being hurled from a third storey window. It is doing nothing to extend its very limited life expectancy.

Breakfast is beginning to get a bit repetitive now; the only difference today is there is no sachet of honey, still, I haven't paid a penny yet to be here, and it's a globally recognized fact—no money, no honey. I look up some "must see" sights in Ankara and draw a little map on how I will walk to them. I quite enjoy a walking tour of a city; it reminds me I have a perfectly adequate sense of direction.

I head out onto the Sunday-silent streets and get lost almost immediately. I do stumble across the museum I read about. I really am very close to everything round here. I walk round city parks and come to a Hilton Hotel, which is always a good source of information and freebies. Sure enough, I'm given a little street map of Ankara and somehow get involved in a conversation about the merits of horses over motorbikes. The map is ideal, or at least it would be if I could see it; thing is I didn't bring my glasses. Luckily I stumble across a market where a lady is selling off-the-shelf, or rather out-of-a-sack reading glasses. She is very helpful, and once we have chosen a pair she thinks suits me, I'm given a small book to read to ensure they have corrected my impaired vision the required amount. I hand the book back to her with disappointment.

"I can't read it," I tell her. "It's in Turkish."

"Idiot," she probably says as she smiles tiredly and takes my money. I wave and wander off with a renewed sense of direction.

If you own a great big camera you either go out with the sole intension of taking photos or you go for a stroll. It's not something you tuck in your pocket on the off chance; a 350mm zoom lens in your pocket just looks like you're bragging and attracts the wrong kind of attention. Today is just a stroll; I have my phone camera to capture the spontaneous and the unexpected. I find myself in a chic shopping street full of designer names, where well-dressed girls strut arm in arm with their fashionable friends, hair flowing and bags swinging. I could be anywhere; I think I'll go somewhere else.

The thing I'm beginning to learn about mosques is they are best viewed from a distance. For me their beauty is when they are part of a landscape or cityscape not when I'm craning my neck to view a solitary minaret. I've been walking for five hours now, and that is all the sightseeing I need to do. I do wander up to the castle for sunset in the hope of seeing the photogenic domino players, but they aren't there, maybe gone for a pizza.

Tonight I put my blow up mattress on my mattress-sized balcony and sleep outside. I hear them knocking but not cumming.

DAY 29

ANKARA, TURKEY, 19 MILES

Well, there is certainly variety at breakfast this morning; there isn't any, not even a chai. Oh well, I'll just make an earlier start on the day than I expected. I almost find my way back to the Tajikistan embassy perfectly. They don't answer the buzzer on the gate, and when I am let in I have to wait twenty minutes in the empty room to be seen. I will not let them wind me up; if they want to play their games they can play them without me.

OK, here I am, like I was on Friday, now what? I have to go to their bank and pay my visa fee into their account. Then come back at 4PM, show the receipt from the bank, and bam, I will have my visa. But I'm told they don't issue GBAO permits here. I could be paranoid, but I think they are deliberately being awkward. My suspicions are confirmed when they won't buzz me back out of the gate. I just stand there, not wanting to antagonize the masterful man who's in control of the button but wondering just how much rudeness and humiliation I will take from one little embassy jerk. He is the first face of his country, and the impression I'm getting is not encouraging. If this is how they get their kicks, their lives must be very shallow. The bank, however, is super helpful, and today's chores are done before 10AM.

Back home I wander the market and get some fresh supplies and make a big fat breakfast in my skinny little room. I haven't cooked for ages. This isn't really cooking, its boiling eggs and cutting cheese and fruit up but pushing my culinary skills to the limit.

Time to get myself educated with some Turkish history. Museums make my back ache. I can stand in pretty much any situation, concert, party, bar, bike show. I'm quite good at standing; I don't wobble, I have relatively good posture, but the second there is art or artefacts in front of me, my back starts aching.

91

Thankfully, the Turkish authorities have found a cure. Six separate buildings, each dedicated to a different part of the country's illustrious past, and only one of them is open to the public. The other five are being simultaneously renovated. It takes me about ten minutes to look at fragments of carved rock before I head to the gift shop, and what do you know? There on a rack are the elusive, larger scale, comprehensive, road maps of Turkey. As a bonus, they are available in every European language there is...except English. I opt, of course, for Spanish, not really understanding quite how a Turkish map can be translated, anyway. Half the places I can't pronounce in Turkish or English, now I've just got one more incomprehensible choice, "¿Donde estoy?" I'm having it anyway, trying to find a map in this country has been harder that any destination I've chosen so far. What a great museum piece, and it comes in a souvenir plastic bag, perfect. I'm at a bit of a loose end as to how to fill the rest of my day though. Spreading the map out on the bed, I see it has roads of scenic distinction highlighted in green. There is one that takes me south out of Ankara. I will take it tomorrow.

If I'd have checked into a hotel this early on any other day I would be unpacking and relaxing, but because I know I'm leaving tomorrow, I'm already in the preparation stages and refilling the panniers. Killing time impatiently.

At 4PM I press the buzzer again, and with an ineffectual smile on my face, take my banking receipt with me as I enter this Tajikistan embassy for the third time. Within ten minutes I have a big colourful visa and one less blank page in my passport. Sorted. Seems like a lot of effort for little reward, but now I'm free to go on to other countries to continue the application process. I'm no longer anchored down in Ankara.

Day 30

Cappadocia, Turkey, 251 Miles

I'm not even going to bother with breakfast; I just want to go now. I uncover my bike and notice that I was so busy securing it yesterday that I left the key in the ignition. If it wasn't for the cover that wouldn't be there now, however, if I hadn't covered it I may not have left the key in the ignition in the first place. Explain that to the insurance company, "Yes I left my bike outside a Turkish brothel all night with the key in it, and in the morning it was gone." Anyway, no harm done. I bump it down the curb in between parked cars then run up and down stairs loading panniers, camping equipment, and dry bags, slowly doubling the weight of my bike. I get my bill; it turns out all the cups of chai I was given every time I came down to get a Wi-Fi connection were complimentary. All the staff wave me off, the strange long-haired Englishman who spent so much time staring at his little pink lap top, stayed in a whorehouse for five nights, and never shagged a single one of them. I leave them with whatever mystery my behaviour created. Over the course of my stay, I did see a few of the girls, but nothing I saw encouraged me to put my hand in my pocket.

I want to find the road that's in green on my map and take it south. I find myself on my first Turkish motorway; there is no traffic on it, and I fear an expensive toll. It appears to be a new ring road; it's not even on my Spanish map, "¿Donde esta aqui?" The city has defined boundaries; it doesn't slowly meander into spacious suburban areas that fade into fields and grassland dotted with the occasional established village. No, the new white high-rise housing blocks just stop as if on a cliff edge, and then there's countryside. Well maybe not countryside, that word conjures up images of streams and meadows, leafy trees and butterflies. This is more like desolate undeveloped grassy wasteland, but it is free of any structure at all, not even a shed. The Turkish are clearly not a nation of allotment lovers.

The sat nav is alive again, but this incarnation is equally infuriating. It wants to send me on some convoluted route and doesn't understand there is a green road round here that will be a wonderful alternative. But even with my map and frequent signposting I still can't find it. I stop at a truck stop and eat some leftovers (my leftovers, I'm frugal but not digging in bins, yet). I try to work out where this attractive but veiled green road is hidden. I'm pretty sure it's behind me; I turn around and find the road with the right number, but it's going west not east. I go back past the truck stop, and soon after I see a signpost for it. The sat nav was trying to send me this way the whole time. OK, so it was right for once, I was wrong, but we don't work in harmony, decisions are not made after reasonable discussion; bitter conflict determines the route to the last resort. And neither one of us has a good track record.

This is undeniably the green road; now the only question is why? What on earth has this road got that elevates it to the prestigious level of green? How did it meet the criteria required to be in the same category as scenic mountain twisties, deep valley gorges, or coastal cliff hangers? I can only assume this road was the way to the house of the cartographer's lover, or maybe he had no lover and filled the void with an unhealthy fetish for petrol stations and trucks, because the road offers little else.

Like a lonely cartographer, I too have needs. On the road there are always needs; it's only the ease of fulfilment that varies. This morning it involves a slight detour into a tiny village. A single dirt road leads me past a shop that only really stocks compromise, and even that has passed its shelf life. I'm pointed to another hovel that has fresh bread, or at least it would have been fresh if I'd have been here last week. I think I'll move on.

My new needs are not met but exceeded; a lay-by with a natural fresh spring, I can wash my hands before I eat and drink. I even have a slab of rock for a table and a bit of a view. It's little unexpected luxuries like this that would go unnoticed and unappreciated by people of means. Now exclusively in my own company I sit and enjoy my one person picnic.

Back on the road, a Dutch registered camper comes the other way. I instinctively put up my hand and wave. Of course, I get nothing back, except the realisation that I have been without company or any real conversation for quite a while now. I'm into my routine, and on reflection, I think whether you live under a cardboard box or out of aluminium ones, there is a weariness that exists, the routine of a daily uncertainty, where and when will you eat and sleep. Of course, I have infinitely more choice than the hopeless homeless, but homeless I am. Living on the road, living for the moment, well I am at the moment. The romance of a nomadic existence is not always the imagined sweet smelling ruggedness, it can often cross into a smelly desperation. That is why lunch by a fresh spring can wash away some road-worn reality and help to feed a fantasy.

According to the map, the road stopped being rated as green hours ago. Now it's just average and acceptable, without hype or expectations. That is why, when I round an insignificant corner and there at the side of the road is a hoodoo, the moment instantly becomes one worthy of capture.

It's not a total surprise; this is what Cappadocia is, an area of distinctive rock pillars of varying height and shapes. But this one seems to have strayed from the pack; its solitude alone makes it worth a photo. My descent into the valley brings me into a forest of hoodoos more than you can point a zoom lens at. This is one of those moments when independent overland mid-size motorcycle travel gives you its big bonus. It's not just the fuel economy or cheaper tyres, the lower purchase and maintenance costs, not to mention less depreciation. It's not the fact it confirms the poverty you plead when haggling for a room or the fear of theft whilst you're in that room. Today it's the ability to just leave the road and ride over to the most appealing hoodoo I can find. It's so good that there isn't even a tripod dilemma, that's how spectacular the scenery is; I just have to be in the picture. These moments are infrequent and short, but they are the moments of utter contentment, when all the choices made result in an outcome that could not be better. So the tripod, I suppose, is my champagne bottle because it only comes out when there is a celebration of scenery, and this is one of those.

With my helmet clipped on the back of the bike, I ride around the landscape, dwarfed by these pillars of erosion and time, without restriction of fences or signs. I ride down little gorges of limestone to hidden wonders so undiscovered even a car hasn't been named after them yet, although the Hoodoo 650 dual sport is probably only a prototype away. I take dirt tracks to a plateau of large cone-shaped twisted spires. If Mr. Whippy built a theme park it would look like this. I love it when the natural looks unnatural; such an oxymoron. The town is predictably touristy, but the expanse of the geological phenomenon means people like me can avoid the quad bike and camel riding convoys. Another area looks like a gathering of Ku Klux Klan members. White-pointed columns, the tops of which resemble hoods, appear to be standing, subservient and manipulated in the shadow of their grand wizard. Obviously, they are not Klan members; hoodoo I think they are. The rock is soft, and many of the larger formations have been hollowed out and inhabited. They have windows and doors and even driveways with cars parked in them.

At one particular vista point, excited to get a photo, I park my bike precariously. When I get back on, before I've found my balance the bike decides it wants a lower centre of gravity and falls over. I'm sure it's the petrol pissing out of the tank that gives me hulk strength, not just the danger of ignition, but the anger at the sheer bloody waste when it costs so much. Vertical again, we are both a little unstable, and I'm standing on the bike's right side. I lean over it to pull the side stand down. I'm shaking with adrenalin caused now by the surplus strength that I managed to muster. I trap my thumb, and a blood blister pops up like an air bubble under a pannier sticker. How quickly a tranquil little scenic stop turns into a sweat and petrol-soaked frenzy, with bloodied and greasy flesh. That's the problem of going off the beaten track, there's no one else around. One of the screen mounts has broken and another buckle on my tank box fastening.

To work off the fury and frustration, I go ride some proper roads, looking for wild camp possibilities. I'm realising that a lot of these formations are inhabited. Some have been carved out so subtly it's hard to tell a home from a hoodoo that isn't hollow. I don't want to trespass or intrude. I really need a good night's sleep after my brothel residency. I find an official campground. What it lacks in view it makes up for in serenity and security. I watch the sunset from a vista point a restaurant owner told me about, then with my helmet strapped on the top box, I ride back through a labyrinth of twilight rocky tapered pixie hats, some with magic mushroom nipples on top, sometimes viewed through jagged eroded arches, some through blurred swaying foliage, and sometimes through watering wind-whipped eyes.

DAY 31

NEAR NARINCE, TURKEY, 345 MILES

I know that noise, but what is it? Sounds like the side door of a panel van being slid shut, but it keeps going. As I slowly become more lucid and more logical, I limit the options and remember where I heard that sound before. At a hot air balloon festival.

I jump out of the tent. The sky is full of them; I count 40 hot air balloons, some so close I can hear the roaring flame from the burner. It does sound a little like a sliding van door, especially when you're waking from a sleep you've been deprived of for nearly a week. This, I find out later, is what you do in Cappadocia; you pay two hundred and fifty euros to get in a basket with twelve others to look down into the valley of hoodoos as the sun rises. It was beyond my knowledge and budget, but as a ground-dwelling early riser, I too get some good views of these silent voyeurs passing overhead. This is clearly a daily occurrence, but the campsite dog is still very excited by it; so excited that he doesn't stop barking even when the last balloon has passed by. Thoughtfully, to drown out the dog, one of the staff starts a stationary tractor and revs the engine to drive a pump to start a flow of water into the stagnant swimming pool. The racket replaces the calmness the balloons left in their wake.

I make chai and do some bike maintenance. Somehow three and a half hours pass between me waking and leaving. Still, no one but me to please, no justification needed, no deadlines, and no destination today. I do have a calendar now with some city names filled in on certain dates, but that's just to remind me of my visa deadlines; it gives my aimless wanderings a little structure.

An old man on a donkey waves. A wave always makes my day, and how often do you get a spontaneous wave from an old Muslim donkey rider? It's certainly not a regular occurrence in Essex. The rock homes continue as I leave the area on a quiet narrow easterly road. It's been the most stimulating of scenery, and all the head-turning slowed the pace, which reminds me that progress is what happens when there is nothing else to do. I'm heading towards a big snowy mountain; it was the backdrop in my sunset photographs yesterday. Inevitably, the hoodoos peter out; the scenery and accommodation changes to arid plains and single story stone houses. Ahead is the promise of mountainous terrain, not that this is dull, in its own expansive way it's quite thrilling. The occasional bird of prey is perched and still on stone walls. Little villages with tractors in the yard and pylons, loads and loads of pylons. How much electricity do you need out here?

There is high cloud today, and I think I may take advantage of this cooler temperature to do some long comfortable miles. I've seen my sights, my two known Turkish delights, and now I'm excited about getting to Iraq. The road is flat and well maintained, but best of all it's empty. Gone are the trucks and impatient motorists; the pace is slower, due in part to donkeys being a popular form of transport. Those who have a need for speed have upgraded to rusty old Fiats and Renaults. When I do find an inhabited area, there is a lot of sitting around. Is it me or do people seem friendlier now I'm further east? Senses slow too, long flat straight empty roads dull the mind. There is a fuel station approaching on my left, but the road is about to divide, so I just ride on the wrong side of the road for a while until I get there. It's the Turkish way of driving, you just do what you want, when you want. Assume nothing, certainly not responsibility.

I only just realise in time that the attendant is about to put diesel in my bike, an expense and delay I could well do without. There is still some concentration needed out here. I have to think for myself, no one will do it for me or even for themselves.

The plains finally meet the mountains, and I gain some elevation, looking down on valleys of flowers and kids on donkeys herding goats. The road rises to 6,000 feet and has turned to dirt. I'm level with snow now across the valley on the other range. At this height I've got big views, and the pylons are bigger to keep their blot on the landscape proportional. There are roadworks and rough uneven surfaces. Of course, the labourers stop to watch me pass, and I fake control, determined not to fall off on this loose stony surface. I fake it so well my ability has no choice but to keep up, and I cross the excavations like I have caterpillar wheels.

The descent brings back warmth and smooth road but also a military checkpoint. I'm getting closer to the Syrian border now, so I suppose this will become more common.

This road is an alternative to the most direct route; it's a perfect compromise. It keeps my forward momentum but avoids the people with tighter deadlines. It's not just the road that's slow; time has gone backwards a bit. An old lady in an apron and head scarf is washing her pots and pans in the river by her wooden shack. Somehow the road has gradually led me towards these traditions, and this conduct seems only natural, perfectly in keeping with the surroundings. The scene is expected; out here a dishwasher delivery would be cause for a photo stop.

When I come to an unsigned fork in the road I let the sat nav decide, instead of stopping to put on my glasses and look at my map. It takes me down a road to the construction of a power station and then refuses to recognise anything else. So I take the initiative and go through a one horse village, a direction which is clearly wrong. When I pop out I'm back on the main road, just further back from where I turned off, the old woman has finished washing her pans in the river and gone inside. I've come around for a second look at this leisurely rural life, their progress still just a little faster than mine.

Another checkpoint. The officer speaks good English, which is rare in Turkey. After Turkish, German is the language they want to use. He tells me where I am on my map and where I am going. Yeah I knew that actually, but I congratulate him on his English all the same.

You can't ride back roads forever, lost somewhere in time and then found again by a world where there is never enough of it. Down a slip road that converges with the fast and furious, the archaic French cars are replaced by fast German ones.

Another petrol stop; two in one day. Shit, this being sensible thing is very expensive. But how annoyed would I be if I stopped for a drink and didn't top up only to run out later? It's that time of the day when I need some coke to keep the mind alert and my eyes open. I never drink the stuff at home, which is why my tolerance is so low. I feel the effect almost instantly, and it lasts longer than my fuel seems to. Having made my purchase, the lady cashier insists I stop for chai and leaves me alone in the kiosk while she boils the kettle. She's gone for ages; I check my oil and get out my map. Then she sets out a chair and table for me in the shade under the canopy. A distinguished older man comes and sits with me, and we look over my map. He points at the Syrian border, only 50 kms to the south, and says, "Bombs." "Yes, I know," but I don't know the appropriate facial expression I should use to accompany this affirmation. Pity? Horror? Anger? Disappointment? It was only two weeks ago that two car bombs killed fifty Turks in the border town of Reyhanli, which is 350 kms from here. Clearly a tragic event, but when your neighbour's war knocks on your door what is your reaction? The residents of Reyhanli had welcomed the Syrian refugees and in return suffered a gruesome act of state terrorism. I don't think his pointing at my map was meant to open such a heavy topic of conversation, so he changed the subject to marital status. *Married* or *bachelor* are the words I catch in a sentence spoken in Turkish. I show him my hands, and the confirmation of his suspicions ring true. Blood blister, oil ingrained, wind cracked and tanned where the fingerless gloves don't cover. An oval tan on the back of my hand where the Velcro fastener doesn't meet is the closest thing to a ring on my hands. I think he knew the answer already. It's a privileged little encounter and takes all the pain out of the purchase. But there is more pain to come. I'm enjoying the easy miles in this perfect riding temperature. It's been a long day, and I should be thinking about an evening meal, but in a heartbeat my attention is taken from my needs. There are blue lights up ahead and cars everywhere, not in a traffic jam, just utter chaos, scattered up embankments and across the road. There are people yelling and running; the panic in the air is too urgent to think about bike security. I put down my side stand and hurry to join the main throng. They are looking down a ravine. People are standing on the concrete bridge that spans it, the railings are intact, but at the bottom of the ravine is a minibus, battered and crushed. Cases and possessions are splayed all around. By the bus are three emergency workers and six bodies, five of which are covered with sheets and tarpaulins. The sixth is surrounded by three paramedics. It's an horrific site. Other people are down there, sitting on their haunches or standing back from the mess, either in horror, respect, or shock. I go back to my bike; there is nothing I can do; it's not my business. I think I can get through this array of abandoned vehicles. As I slowly squeeze past, the medics and many others are lifting the person whom I assume is still alive up the embankment into an ambulance. Everyone cheers and claps when the mission is complete. At the other side of the bridge I can see the carnage more clearly. The bus left the road before the railings began, and it must have overturned immediately as the roof rack is left flattened at the start of the eighty foot drop. It's chilling. Others are leaving the scene now too; there is nothing we can do. Actually there is one thing; oh how carefully everybody drives now.

It turns out the next big town is quite close; I even spot the hospital. There are hotels and possibilities in this place of palm lined streets, but I don't want to stop here. I think I'm a bit traumatized by what I've seen, and I need to keep riding. I never ride this late; it's not totally dark yet but lights are needed. For some unfathomable reason the oncoming trucks have red headlights, well that's not confusing at all is it? Like I haven't got enough to contend with, trying to find accommodation and food, without glancing up to see a truck that appears to be reversing towards me in the other lane. I leave the main road. There are summer crop smells, and bonfire smoke drifts under my visor and hazes the last of the light.

I've got to find somewhere to stop; it's really dark now. I'm hungry. I passed up too many opportunities, and I'm left with a dark empty road, which I think would be quite scenic if I could actually see. There is a hand painted sign; when I shine my headlight on it I see that it says camp 10 kms. I'm looking for any place to wild camp now. I ride into a farming village with a road surface of cow and goat shit, landslides and cobblestones. There's nothing here surely, but my hope is kept alive by half a wooden sign. So I continue down this single-track road past farmyards and darkened wooden shacks. There are lights down in the valley, but I'm not going all the way down there. Shit, I've ruined a good day by stringing it out too long. Where the hell am I now? There is no wild camping potential here at all. That sign must be years old; the paint was faded and the wood rotten, but then there is another one. It points left; I follow its directions and ride down a dirt driveway. It's just a house with a barn and patch of green grass. A security light comes on, a dog barks, and a youth comes out.

"Hello, camping?" "One people?"

"Yes, one people."

"There," he says, pointing at the grass area; oh the relief. I never ride at night; I hate it; it's a waste of scenery. I get out my tent, and he climbs a ladder and fiddles with some electrical wires until a light on the side of the barn comes on.

"Is there any chance of some food?" I ask.

"Yes, what do you want?"

"Anything. Whatever you have, whatever is easiest." When I have got my tent up, I go to the barn, which has a toilet block under it and a dining table inside. He tells me it's traditional Turkish food. It's delicious; hot and tasty, with the obligatory bread and chai. Well I really pushed my luck hard today, but it didn't break.

DAY 32

SOLOPI, TURKEY, 310 MILES

Good sleep, squat toilet, cold water; OK I'm ready for the new day. It's already hotter than yesterday. There is no-one about and no breakfast on offer, but whilst searching for life, I notice some postcards by the counter in the barn. They are pictures of Mount Nemrut, ruins and statues from around two thousand years ago. I saw the signs for the place yesterday. I bet they would look great under a starry sky. However, an exposed hill top in this heat has not the slightest appeal, neither does sticking around here, but will I ever be this way again? It's just ruins, and the thought of traipsing around in bike boots, out of view of an unattended bike, in bleached out bright sunlight, is not encouraging me to go. No, I don't want to go, well I do, but not enough. Iraq, I want to go to Iraq.

Last night, I rode out onto the edge of a valley. There are spectacular views this morning, and as I head back the way I came in, I'm reassured that I didn't miss a single potential wild camp site. Looking down to the south there is a wide dry riverbed, but to the north I can see a canyon of water. I think that somewhere out of my sight there must be a dam; the water level is too high to be natural in this burnt brown climate. I have aeroplane views as I wind down towards this brimming canyon. Well, glider views, as I have switched off my engine. I'm beginning to wonder just how I'm going to cross, as from my higher vantage point I saw no road crossing. My questions are answered with a dead end and a small ferry boat. There are a few people standing around, and there is a little chai shop too.

"In a while," a man who is probably the captain of this twenty-foot vessel seems to indicate. There is no ferry terminal bustle here, just a road reaching a river, and no urgency. I instantly feel the chilled-out atmosphere that is in

103

the air. A little girl from over at the café waves to me. She says hello, so I order chai from her, leaving my bike in pole loading position by the ferry ramp. She and her little sister have a few English words, and together they bring over chai and sugar. Some local onlookers come over to say hello too and ask where I'm from. This brief exchange seems to exhaust their English skills. It doesn't matter though, the following silence isn't awkward; I could sit here all day. And soon sitting around all day will be the only occupation left. Up river, giant concrete A-shape structures have been erected; the supports for the imminent bridge, which will take away several little livelihoods overnight. The brief glance down into the canyon the crossing motorists will have won't ever reveal this social service, specifically here for the time-rich traveller who wishes to reach the other side. That's how it happens. That's how the world speeds up and communities disappear; that's how interaction is replaced with automation. The destination will be reached 45 minutes faster, and the time saved could never be spent as rewardingly as it could be spent here. Time-efficient devices come at such a cost; from supermarkets instead of individual shops, from Internet instead of interaction. It creates a generation of isolation; a person's day can run so efficiently they can get back early to their boxes and stare at screens to relax before it all happens again tomorrow. If only the Western world knew the pleasure gained in waiting for a ferry to cross a river, I'm sure it would be a happier and healthier place.

I'm beckoned onboard and ride in a semicircle so I can lean against the railing and face the loading ramp. There are two other cars and also a herd of sheep. Not the *Sun* reading, special offer, booze cruise, kind of sheep that you get on cross-channel ferries. Real, woolly sheep, herded by a father on his phone and his six year old son. (The phone, I assume has a sheepdog app.) When they are all aboard the loading ramp lifts, and we chug across the reservoir. I'm pretty sure it's a reservoir now, because sticking out of the water, for no apparent reason, is a stop sign. I don't think it is a command for any water going craft; it's just the highest point of what lies beneath. One of the sheep takes the opportunity of this romantic voyage to mount a yew while she is still trying to find her sea legs, so I guess it's not so different from a booze cruise.

This is night and day different from my last ferry journey in Turkey; it's relaxing, it's scenic, it's exciting, and friendly. The deck hand comes to take my money; he says eighty but must mean eight, because I get change from my ten lire note.

The other side of the water is the Turkey I always imagined: a red and dusty land with rocky outcrops, where goats and sheep wander freely on the hilly arid terrain.

When I cycled in Thailand, there was a point when I celebrated my one thousandth kilometre, a significant moment on an insignificant bit of road. It wasn't much of a celebration, just a little yelp of joy and perhaps another application of Canesten. Anyway, a cyclist came towards me; he too was English.

I told him of my elation and recent celebration. He proceeded to tell me he had cycled here from the UK and had done over fourteen thousand kilometres. He also told me that the worst bit was having the shits whilst crossing the plains of Turkey. He said there was nowhere to hide, and he had to just stop and squat. It sounded awful; in fact, cycling Turkey sounds awful, regardless of your tummy's condition. I know there are lots of people who do it and love it but I'm riding slowly, I'm seeing lots and travelling far. A dull hour and a half for me is a dull day for the cyclist. I'm sure they see things I miss, but with my zigzag navigation across this country, I think I too have seen things they have missed. Each to their own. Today and yesterday and all those other good days, and even on the bad days, I didn't ever think it might have been better on a bicycle, or a campervan, or a tour bus, or a 4x4. So I think that I am, once again, doing exactly what I want to be doing.

It's so much hotter today. I think I have enough fuel to get me to Iraq. I stop for supplies and eat in the shade of an abandoned petrol station then take a big drink of water and put the phone on charge. Now I'm ready for some long, hot flat miles. Side stand up, chin guard down, bandana up to my nose, shades down to my bandana and I'm protected from the sun's rays and glare. I look at the quadruplicate images in my broken mirror, select first gear, let out the clutch, glance over my shoulder, and ride into the hot air. This is what I do; this is what I love, and that is why I do it.

As if I have the power to conjure up what I imagine, out of the shimmering heat haze a cyclist appears, flying a Polish flag; I wave as I pass. It's sixty kilometres to the next town, sixty dull featureless kilometres that will probably be where his day ends. I'll be there in less than an hour; I might even be in a hotel in Iraq tonight. I know it's not a race, but I'm winning. I also know I was only just singing the praises of slowing the pace. As the cyclist watches me disappear into the horizon, he could be tutting at my misguided and ever-changing views. In his eyes I might not be winning, I may be losing. It's true, but I ride alone, and I'm free to change my mind, my direction, my schedule, and my speed without any justification. I'm just happy, and that's as much as you can ask from the road.

I see my first army convoy coming towards me; the colour scheme is not dissimilar to my yellow and black combats, so I think they may be staying in the dry bag until I reach more politically stable areas. I don't want to be a case of mistaken identity. I also decide that, although it's less direct, I will avoid the road that hugs the Syrian border. I expect there will be a lot of check-points on that road, and they are rarely the high point of any day. Plus, this alternative route will take me through Batman, which I know nothing about; in fact, I haven't even seen the movie or read the comic books. Still, I need to get a photo by this sign.

As soon as I stop, every car and truck hoots and waves, but back on the road I'm an obstruction they detest, cutting me up and passing too close. But this willingness to wave must mean they don't consider their inconsiderate driving techniques to be anything that would cause offence.

It's a very dry heat, being stopped, fully exposed in the midday sun. Pratting about with my tripod in bike clothes has me overheating, but the sweat cools me as soon as I pull back onto the glistening black highway.

Batman turns out to be a big oil town; high security fencing with watch towers protecting huge ugly holding tanks. It's not a very pretty city, and it's really hot now. The irritability that comes with heat discomfort is blackening my mood; red lights make the heat inescapable. I leave the city from the south and the road follows a river, not just any river but the Tigris. Regardless of its significance, it is wet and accessible. I ride off the road and down onto the stony banks, strip off, and jump in.

A spontaneous skinny dip is a wonderful thing. Once again it's taking advantage of what's around to fulfil your needs. I'm hot, there is a river; I have a vehicle that can get me down to it. What else is there to think about?

Actually there is something on my mind; I wonder if my bike clothes would be better left in the sun to dry the sweat or in the shade to keep them cool, just another one of the road's little dilemmas.

On the other side of the river are high cliffs, and swallows swoop down from their nests to catch the bugs in the air. It doesn't take long to cool my blood. Neck deep I look out at my bike in the blazing sun in admiration and respect. I put my hot dry clothes on my wet cool body and think to myself that I made the right decision.

Hasankeyf; never heard of it, haven't read about it. Vienna means something to me, but this place doesn't. Ruins of another ancient civilization, some of the architecture dates back 4,000 years. The city is perched on cliff tops above the river. There are cave dwellings carved into the cliff face. Protruding from the river are supports from a thousand-year-old bridge, and on the hill is a mosque built around the same time. Unannounced and unvisited, it's an ideal way to get my artefact fix and marvel at a beauty that hasn't been swamped with overdevelopment, like so many other places I've seen. Turkey for me is getting better and better the further east I get.

The road once again is barely used and twists through this canyon created by the Tigris; why isn't this road in green on my map? The surprise of it all just adds to the pleasure. In the space of two miles I have a herd of cattle cross the road in front of me, then horses, then donkeys. I think the cyclist will enjoy this road when he gets here, in a couple of days. He probably won't have the frustration I have at the petrol station, either. Just a few litres are all I need; I don't have enough to get to Iraq, but the attendant pumps away, and I'm distracted by some inquisitive kids.

"Stop, too much!" Damn, I'll be importing the most expensive petrol in the world into a county with one of the biggest oil reserves.

The scenery is rugged and wild now; endless rocky terrain and mountainous horizons, inhospitable and undeveloped. I absolutely love this. This enormity is what I most enjoy; it gives me a feeling I so seldom get. I got it on the barren steppe of Kazakhstan and again in Mongolia. The desolation giving feelings of exhilaration and peace, the knowledge that out here only I am available to take the blame for my actions. This is why I do what I do; right here, the emptiness, the endlessness; it leaves me in utter awe. I'd cycle this bit; I'd definitely cycle this bit. If there was a square meter without a watermelon-size boulder I might even consider camping here.

As I continue I see a solitary two storey building. It sits on the edge of this rock-strewn plateau and overlooks range after range of parched and naked mountains. Outside the building, on a dry barren shadeless clearing, three people are sitting on red plastic chairs and playing cards; it's surreal. A gust of wind would have the pack carried off into distant canyons. I'm not sure they are playing with a full deck.

The quiet river on my right becomes a boundary, as rivers often do, this one between Turkey and Syria. There is always a watchtower in view; they are uprights between the barbed-wire fencing. It doesn't look very crossable; it doesn't look inviting at all. I've rejoined the main road. The trucks are back, and for a while we run alongside the Syrian border. I dithered this afternoon; it's OK, but I see no point in dealing with a border crossing today.

Silopi is a very dusty border town. On the outskirts there are soldiers behind sandbags and in tanks, barbed-wire check-points but only it seems for people coming the other way. They seem quite prepared to let anyone in. The single street has open-fronted shops on both sides; ironmongers, butchers, grocers, all the usual supplies, the necessities for life. The town is immersed in a cloud of dust; it comes up from the road, blows across from the desert plains, then sits in the warm still air before settling on the populace. I ride to the Iraq border just to see what it's like, past miles of stationary trucks at the side of the road. More lie dormant in truck stops and on the loading ramps of bonded warehouses and TIR trailer parks. It's very much a freight orientated crossing. I'll deal with it tomorrow. I saw one hotel as I came in; The Grand Hotel it was called. It is grand too.

I was cycling in Thailand years ago when I got the inevitable runny bum. I knew I had a particularly hilly bit ahead of me as I headed towards the Burmese border, so decided it would be best to get a room until this thing passed and I could regain some strength. Being, as ever, on a tight budget, I found a really awful cell of a room, with unpainted concrete walls and ceilings. The pipe work was exposed, loud, and leaking. There was only a curtain separating the squat toilet from the room, and the bed was a metal-sprung dilapidated thing in the middle of an otherwise empty concrete box. It was an awful place to feel awful.

Whenever I am in such situations I always imagine how it could be worse, "worse troubles at sea" kind of thing. I imagine being in a real cell, wrongfully imprisoned, or with open festering and untreated sores, being forced to get up to work and earn my bread. Believe it or not, these thoughts always make me feel better and more appreciative of my situation.

After 2 nights in this place, I began to feel a little better and decided to see if I had the strength to get up and get out. I walked out into the bright street feeling very weak and overwhelmed, having left my solitary confinement. Not far away was a big plush hotel with guarded gates and well kept gardens. I considered how much better it would have been to feel ill in such a place. The next day, somewhat emaciated but with a happier tummy, I was able to leave and slowly continue my journey. When I reached the next significant town a few days later, I found a bit of a travellers' hangout. I casually mentioned my story of woe to some backpackers I met.

"Which town was this?" they asked.

"It was called Tak," I said. They knew of the town and the posh hotel I was talking about, because they had stayed there; the price was $5 a night. I learned an important lesson that day. Never assume it's beyond your budget. The better the hotel, the better the English of the reception staff, therefore the better your chance of negotiating an affordable price. If you don't ask, you will never know.

Now, for £35 I can have a suite with a mini-bar, air-conditioning, large flatscreen TV, Wi-Fi, and big soft towels. I have hot water and clean bedding; I even get breakfast. I'm having some of this; I'm sure I'm worth it.

DAY 33

DOHUK, IRAQ, 73 MILES

The great thing about grand hotels for me is they are not a very common part of my lifestyle. I'm sure Lady Ga Ga would be most disgusted with the amenities, which is why I didn't invite her along. I, on the other hand, relish the luxuries on offer, not least the view from my window. This morning I realised it wasn't tinted, it's just a layer of dust. There was a constant procession of trucks going past all night; a large proportion of those were car transporters carrying 4x4s that would not look out of place in this hotel's car park. There must be some money in Iraq, because there's a lot of expensive metal heading that way.

I think I've used every complimentary service available to me and should have worn my combats for breakfast to fill my pockets with supplies, but they were a bit scruffy for this "Grand" environment. I eat like a camel these days; nothing, nothing, nothing, LOADS, nothing, nothing, nothing. For a finishing touch as I leave the hotel, I hold my booted foot against the buffing wheel of the shoe shine machine. It's not quite up to the challenge; it was a tall order. The only way I will be able to see my face in them is if I look through the hole whilst in front of the mirror.

Here I go, back down the road to Iraq, past all the trucks and straight to a booth, show my log book, and I'm stamped out of Turkey. I proceed past a holding area, with the obligatory barbed-wire fence and cameras on poles. I follow the arrows painted on the concrete that take me to a group of Iraqi police. There is not the hint of a threat from them. Inquisitive and helpful, they direct me to a large building. They tell me it's OK to ride there, and I have nothing to worry about leaving my bike unattended. Inside the air-conditioned building are hundreds of chairs and not a single person. It's modern, with high ceilings, unobtrusive lighting, and the dampened echoes of a large empty space. There are two booths each with

110

an official behind glass, I give my documents, and they are inspected and returned. I have a stamp in my passport that says, "You have to visit Directorate of Residence within 15 Days." It's issued by the Republic of Iraq, Kurdistan Region.

Is that it; am I in now? A rather effeminate youth is standing by the exit doors. He offers me a bottle of water.

"No, ya alright mate," but he insisted; it's a gift, no strings attached, the seal is unbroken; and there is nothing to be suspicious of. This is unheard of; no one ever gives you anything at a border crossing, except a hard time. I'm already sweating, and the drink is much appreciated. What a pleasant first impression. I show my stamped document to the policeman in the box; he waves me on. Surely that isn't it? It isn't. Now there are more obstacles. I pull up behind a BMW with British plates, owned by an Iraqi who used to work in Manchester. He has to come through the border every forty five days, as his car is only temporarily imported. He is a school teacher in his thirties, and he has to get back to work; but his forty-five days have expired. He has to pay a fine. However, he will help me through the process, which he is well practiced in. He curses the complication of the system as we walk from building to building and back again during the vehicle importation process. The only other two vehicles here are also European-plated but owned by locals. At one booth I need to get my documents photocopied, but I have no currency they accept. A man in the queue next to me insists on paying for me; he hands over some dirty high denomination notes on my behalf. After receiving various documents, I go elsewhere to get them stamped. I even have to leave my vehicle log book in their care; I'm given an official looking receipt and told I can collect my original when I leave the country. It's not the ideal scenario, but did I have a choice? I had intended to exit the country from here, anyway, so it's no hardship.

The process nearly complete, I have to take my fist full of documents to be seen by the main man. He has an office of his own where I have to wait for the guard to let me in. He sits behind a big desk and has an aura of importance but not intimidation, well not to me. He checks all I give him and writes neatly on one of the forms from right to left. My assistant says he has commented on my T-shirt. I look down; it's wet with sweat and sticking to my chest. I don't recognise the design and realise I have it on back to front. I laugh out loud when I realise this and voice that it's the wrong way round. It breaks what little tension there is in the office.

"It's like your handwriting," I say, pushing my luck, but with smiles all round the big man gets up, shakes my hand, and wishes me a pleasant stay in his country. My Mancunian Kurdish assistant gives me his number so I can visit him when I get to Erbil. With that, I am free to leave the compound and ride my little £700 eBay bike into Iraq.

I hand my last receipt to the policeman on the gate. He tells me Iran and Syria are dangerous and not to go there. I don't want to be contradictory, mate, but a few people might say that about your country too.

First impression, when I stop laughing in my helmet at the sincere warning, I can see a billboard that advertises Royal Tea, London; ah that's nice. Other than that it's just a dirty area to begin with, old trucks and dusty streets and lots of satellite dishes. I pass a market place that appears to be closed.

Right, I need fuel and money. The first town is called Zakho; it's not far away. They won't take credit cards at the petrol station, and even though the fuel price is cheap enough, they won't give it away. I'm beginning to wish I'd come last night. It's Friday, the day of rest in the Muslim week, the shops are open and business is good. The streets are crawling with shoppers, but the banks on the corners are in darkness. All the banks are closed, and any ATMs there might be are safely locked inside. There are no money changers, and no one accepts credit cards. Bugger. I'm so hot riding round this heavily trafficked town, up and down every street, so many hotels but no way to pay for one, I'm stopping constantly to try and find a bank or cash machine.

At one junction a man leans out of his car window, "Where you from?"

"England."

"Welcome to Kurdistan," he says and passes me a pack of chewing gum; I might have to live off that if I can't get any money.

"Do you know if a bank might be open?" I ask.

"Not here. It's Friday. Tomorrow they will be, but you could try in Duhok." I was just beginning to think that myself. People are pouring out of a mosque; it's midday and I just want to get some air circulating round my baking engine and body. I leave the town; the signposts are clear and frequent, written in both Sorani, the Kurdish language, and English, my language. The sat nav is packed in the tank box; I don't miss it one little bit.

I'm quite glad that Turkish attendant yesterday put more petrol in my bike than I wanted; it's very useful now as I ride along this smooth but scorched and desolate road. I have US dollars, Turkish lira; I have euros and even Czech crowns. But if I can't get any Iraqi Dinar I won't be having any dinner. More worryingly, I'm out of water now too; this is not a very pleasant situation to be in. I'm a bit irritated and very preoccupied. I'm lacking the basics, and my vulnerability is taking away any enjoyment that might be found in this new country.

The petrol station signs all say they take visa cards, but when I ask they say no. I'm half tempted to fill up first then point out their visa sign when they refuse my card, but I'm not that desperate yet.

Duhok is looking very big, modern, and promising, although not the mountain town I was expecting. I see a sign for a shopping mall; it's closed but out the front is an ATM. I practically run to it. On the screen in illuminated letters it says in English: "out of service—sorry for any inconvenience." This really is quite fucking inconvenient. Exactly how sorry are you?

This overland travel malarkey, it's not hard work like toiling in the fields or unloading trucks by hand, but it's not a bloody holiday. It's not sitting by the beach listening to waves crash, as an immaculately dressed waiter brings chilled cocktails to my sun lounger, whilst I watch bikini-clad women strut along the shoreline. Soaked in sweat, dehydrated, and with no local currency, I stand by a bike that is now running on fumes. In the inadequate shade of a solitary tree, in the empty car park of a closed shopping centre, heat radiating up from the black asphalt, sweltering in a strange city somewhere in the Middle East can bring the question to mind: Why am I doing this again? This situation will not sort itself out; it requires dedication, perseverance, and positive action. That, and only that, will change this uncomfortable predicament. I ride into the city, choose a hotel; and park outside. Yes; they have a room; it's fifty dollars. I can't pay that, but the receptionist calls to her boss in his office.

"Is he a US citizen?" I hear someone say in a Texas drawl. "Naa mate, I'm from Essex innit" would probably be a wasted line. So I'm invited into the office of this American hotel owner. He's quite perceptive, can see I'm soaked in sweat and possibly a little faint. He offers me a small bottle of water; it's like offering the captain of the titanic a tube of stop-leak, but it's the thought that counts. He tells me nowhere will accept a western credit card but changes $50 for me.

I'd like to stay here, but I just can't stretch to that price. The fourth hotel I try will do. I have a street view, shower, and Wi-Fi, but I have to take my bike to an undercover car park and leave it in the protection of a bunch of kids. Then, conspicuously, I walk back through the streets dressed in thick heavy bike clothing.

Back in the hotel reception I take some water from the fridge and look at my new currency to find a small note.

"Relax, pay when you leave," says the lovely young girl at the reception; her English is perfect, and she's so polite. "Where are you from?" she asks. "Ooo England, my favourite."

I bet you say that to all the shrivelled, dehydrated, stinking, desperate bikers who walk through your door. I look forward to talking to her later and finding out more about where I am, but what I'm looking forward to more is a shower.

This is Kurdistan, make no mistake, in a bright Formica-clad café I'm served by a Syrian waiter. He tells sadly of his family still in Syria and shows me his mobile phone with his two daughters as the main picture; he says he can call them on it cheaply. He lives in a tiny hotel room and is interested in the rooms I saw this afternoon and the prices. He works seven days a week, and when he can he sends money home. He is so honest and open, asking for nothing and telling me everything he knows. "Kurdistan is not Iraq; Iraq is very different. There you go to be killed. The Arabs are crazy, but the people here are good and honourable. No one will steal from you." Apparently during the Gulf War the soldiers came here to the Kurdistan region on leave. There are big plans for Kurdistan; development and tourism; prosperity is coming to all, it's just a matter of implementing the plans. It all sounds encouraging. He wishes me well, and the owner, who has been eavesdropping on our conversation with interest, says my dinner is complimentary. This makes me feel a little awkward when I've just heard such a heartfelt story of hardship.

It's Friday night, and I pass a shop that sells beer. I don't need any other reasons.

I utilize my room's view; four hours pass as I stand by my window like I have a mental disorder, just watching the men in their traditional dress, a sort of khaki onesie with a fabric belt and black and white head scarf very similar to the PLO ones we all used to wear round our necks in winter, and actually I still do. There's a variety of women; some have covered heads, some covered faces too, others have flowing hair and exposed beauty. The traffic is loud but gracious, and the shops' commodities spill out onto the pavement; sacks of grain, coils of rope, and bags of flour, the inevitable plastic crap, bottled drinks, and fork 'andles. It's the perfect place to silently watch my new world go by, and acclimatise.

When it's dark outside, there are fireworks on the horizon. I go down to the shop opposite; I just want some more water and some crisps. Again with a smile, my money is not taken. I trip over a bag of flour as I walk out whilst looking back at the shopkeeper, still thanking him. All that grief trying to get some money, and now no one will take it. Back at my window, I see the shop I've just been to has a delivery. Case after case of water is unloaded; he will never get it all inside. It's stacked up on the pavement, and when he shuts up shop that is where it stays. I've never seen trust and generosity like it. What an idyllic society.

DAY 34

DOHUK, IRAQ, 0 MILES

The soothing sound of traffic outside my open window made for undisturbed sleep. This morning there is a big fat mozzie in the room, too bloated to fly. As it sits wheezing on the window ledge, I squash my life blood out of him. It's a vindictive way to start the day, but I don't have much else to do. No one was vindictive or bored enough to kick over or steal the cases of water that are still on the pavement opposite.

I was hoping to see the reception girl again, but she is never around. I wonder if she was reprimanded for being so forward. Maybe she just gets the weekends off. I would really like to find a local who speaks English as well as she did, just for a chat. I've been two weeks now without company.

I walk the streets and get some breakfast. I can't ask for what I want, but with a big smile and the look of hunger, I take a seat and see what is brought to me. This morning it is soup, and as an afterthought, fried egg and tomatoes and, of course, bread. The bread is a bit like a pizza base and as big as a, well, a toilet seat is all I can think of that's a similar diameter.

Once again I'm approached by the staff. One sits with me to chat. He asks my impression of his country. I say I've not been here twenty-four hours yet, although honour and generosity are two constant and notable qualities. He tells me of the days under Saddam Hussein, and again I hear how wealthy and safe Kurdistan is, and that Mosul, a town I'm hoping to transit through on my return journey, is a place of certain death, kidnapping, and car bombs. Is this a case, I wonder, of locals warning of what they have never experienced, or is it a genuine informed view. This is Iraq, after all; I should take some heed, I suppose. More soup is brought, for desert? And copious amounts of chai.

I haven't smoked in 15 years. The urge is mostly dormant, but an urge it remains, and I would really like a fag this morning, but knowing I'm a nicotine junky, I can't have just one. I exercise the willpower that is needed when a distant addiction makes an unexpected plea. A smart but brattish looking boy who I assume was dressed by his mother this morning had been sitting at another table. I saw him as coming from a wealthy family, and he appeared to be rude and condescending to his waiter. But on his way out he comes over to my table and just says, "Welcome," smiles, and leaves. Books and covers, books and covers, will I ever learn?

I'm told where to find a bank and wander off in that general direction. Of course my meal was their pleasure.

The bank is closed. I walk back through a labyrinth of market stalls; a place buzzing with activity, it sells everything I can think of and even stuff I can't. I'm going to spend another day here; there are so many photo opportunities. I see a man with a sewing machine as I walk back, so I go and fetch my jacket. I show him the flapping Velcro on the cuff; he diligently double-stitches it back in place, then goes over the one on the other sleeve, even though it was fine, but still he doesn't give me my jacket back. He looks all over it, inspecting every seam for weakness or a loose thread. And then he actually has the audacity to charge me for the repair. Well I'm most outraged, how dare you expect money for your services; no one else does!?

It's a theme that seems to continue though; damn capitalists they are here. I'm in search of replacement buckles for my tank box. I ask at hardware stalls and keep getting pointed down the alley. I get to a dark and musty shop where a gentleman, the sole proprietor, is kneeling on his prayer mat immersed in the ritual. The shop looks so promising that I silently wait for him to finish. When he has finished, as if his pause button had just been released, he gets up.

As a child I always found musicals on the TV baffling. There would be the cast, making a song and dance about something, half a sixpence being better than half a penny or summer days, drifting away. Then when they finished their performance they carried on with the plot as if nothing had happened. It was so ridiculous to me. I couldn't go skipping down the street, into the sweet shop, and glide to the counter on my knees with my arms outstretched whilst holding the last note of a catchy song then get up and say, "Packet of Golden Wonder, please," and expect the shopkeeper not to look a little unnerved. But that's movies for you, not reality. Anyway, after the active act of prayer, this shopkeeper assumed the role of provider I'm more familiar with.

He looks at the broken buckles I show him. He quietly considers for a moment; it doesn't look good. He shows me some incompatible options, then after some reflection, pulls a hessian sack out from behind the counter. It's full of khaki military plastic buckles still on straps. They are absolutely perfect; I take more than I need, so I have spares. And then he too expects money in exchange for his goods. I'm beginning to come to terms with these conditions of a transaction now, but I preferred the old way.

Back at the hotel I take some photos from the rooftop, until I summon the courage to go down to the street and ask the uniquely dressed natives if I can photograph them. When I make the mental adjustment from tourist to photographer, it's not as difficult as I feared. With my *Overland Magazine* T-shirt on I portray, to myself at least, the air of a professional and look at the scenes around me with a photographer's eye. The photo I most want to get is the groups of old men in their traditional dress drinking chai, smoking, and chatting. I approach one such group. A few look up, and in the most polite and respectful manor I can convey, I interrupt their meeting with, "Good afternoon gentlemen, may I take your photo please?" The response I get is positive; they smile curiously, and in the time it takes me to get the camera to my eye and compose the picture, their expressions have turned to sternness. I snap a couple of shots, and when I take the camera from my face to thank them, they are all smiles and happiness again. Still, I'm proud of my request and appreciative for their cooperation. Later I approach another group and get the same result. I need a gimmick or a second photographer to capture them before and after the pose is struck. I find some steps, and hidden from view, I take some street shots. I'd like to get some photos of the women, but my nerve runs out before I can ask. If I could just see reception girl again, I could ask her what the appropriate etiquette would be. I settle for market traders and their wares.

It's 39 degrees today, and this is an elevated hilly area; how will I cope when I drop down to Erbil? Today is the first day of June; it's only going to get hotter from here. Despite this interaction with the locals, I could use some company that lasts longer than pleasantries. Although it's out of character, I go to the American-run hotel. They have a roof-top bar and restaurant that the owner suggested I should visit for an evening drink. The place is dead; I may as well be in my room. I finish my beer just as a loud group of suited yuppies turn up with their phones on speaker and iPads in hand. I don't care what nationality they are, I'm not that bloody desperate for a chat. I get my bill. $8? Eight bloody dollars for a beer? No way.

"What is this?" I say to the returning waitress. She goes away and makes a call; the next bill is $3. When I exit the lift, the American is in reception.

"Enjoying yourself?" he asks in a snide way.

Everything I've required and consumed today has been provided by locals either free of charge or so reasonably priced there has been not the slightest inkling to haggle; the only person who tried to rip me off was a westerner.

DAY 35

AMEDI, IRAQ, 54 MILES

In a well thought-out operation, I first fetch my bike; I had been a little concerned about its safety in the car park where it was stored. I had reservations about those meddling kids, but I got away with it; they hadn't messed with the bike at all. In fact, they were all so eager the see what was under the cover when I removed it, I don't think they had even peeked.

The roads around the town are mostly two lanes, but there is a central curb, only about six inches high, but it has wheel bending qualities. So I have to go right past my hotel before I can find a place to do a U-turn. Up and down stairs from room to reception then in and out of hotel from reception to bike until everything is loaded. I don't think mistrust and my security conscious practices have any place here, but it's a habit that's hard to break. Paid, loaded, and for the first time riding in jeans, I'm waved off. I never did see reception girl again.

Right, I absolutely have to get fuel, and I know where I want to go to get it, but again this central reservation is sending me in the wrong direction. I'm going to run out of petrol any moment. There is a break in the kerb stones for pedestrians to cross. I use it to do a U-turn. A policeman blows his whistle, and I pretend I don't hear. I don't look in his direction; I just go back the way I came and pull into the petrol station. They need coupons or something; they won't give me fuel. I refasten my now easily removable tank box and go back onto the street.

I'm flagged down by police; the whistle blower had radio'd ahead. Three army officers and two cops surround me, and then a police car pulls up, followed by a second car. Shit, this isn't looking good. Big smile, show my documents; they are taken from me, and I'm beckoned, no, frog-marched to a police box in the centre of a road junction. They surround me like bodyguards, but I don't think my well-being is their priority. I have no choice but to leave my bike unattended; my passport is my main concern. Who has it now? I'm so outnumbered by officials; I do my best to stay calm. I really haven't done that much wrong have I? I'm spinning round trying to keep an eye on my bike, who has what documents, and where they are going with them, all the time trying to be humble and congenial. If I were being spoken to a decibel louder I would say I was being shouted at. I don't understand a word. I wish they would just calm down; it's a volatile situation; and a misunderstood action could have explosive consequences. I'm glad I'm not wearing my combats. A phone is handed to me.

"Hello?"

"You are English?" says a calm but assertive voice.

"Yes."

"Do you know what is happening?"

"There seems to be a problem."

"Yes, you did an illegal manoeuvre on your motorcycle."

"Oh right, I see. The thing is, I really need to get some fuel. I'm about to run out, and if I do my bike will cause an obstruction. It's very heavy; I don't think I can push it. I can see it's a very busy road; I'd hate to be a nuisance." Sometimes I really impress myself under pressure; if only I could be so cool in the company of a beautiful woman.

"Hand me back to the officer please."

I watch the facial expressions as my innocent admittance is translated. The harshness seems to lighten a little. Then, as if I'd just given each and every one of them a crisp $100 bill, suddenly they are all sweetness and light. Smiles and handshakes; my documents are returned, and when I get back on my bike we all pose for photos. Then I ride without my helmet to the enticing petrol station just 100 feet away from where I was detained.

Well that was a bit bloody intense. My tank is filled for a quarter of the Turkish price, and I leave the entire situation behind me. Not surprisingly, I'm sweating already.

As I leave the city, a big black Bentley passes me so close he touches a nerve ending. "Bastard!" I voice to my chin guard. Once past me he drives really slowly, then at a clear junction he just stops, and I only just stop myself from going into the back of him. I hoot as I pass him, seeing my anger reflected back at me in his tinted windows. I check the junction is all clear and pull out. There is a screech of tyres and crunch of metal. I'm upright; I'm not hurt. It's not me. Where did it come from? I turn round to see a taxi has just driven into the back of the Bentley. Ha, instant karma, love it when that happens.

I'm heading into a more mountainous area. In the distance there is snow, but that is on the Turkish side. The heat of the day has brought a haze that takes any potential "wow" out of the scenery. It's not far to where I'm going, so my pace is deliberately slow. I'm enjoying riding and don't want to stop.

The town of Amedi is built on a flat mountain top. The houses are built on cliff edges all the way round. It's a very compact community; I expect it to be a hardcore hamlet, after all, they are living on the edge. It is, I think, another place that is best viewed from a distance. Although I ride the circuit that is the only road on the plateau, I can't get the feel of it from here. So I head back to the area which I think is for the people who are either not eligible to inhabit the flat top or are just acrophobic.

What I want is a place of elevation where I can stand back and take in the view. Like that terrace of cliff-top dwellings up there. I wonder if any of them are guest houses. I take the winding road up to the settlement; the short ride is very scenic. Combined with the anticipation of finding accommodation, it's all quite enjoyable. A solitary armed solider stands by a closed gate, and my hopes drop like a cliff dwelling in an earthquake. He seems very excited to see me.

"Hello, err hotel?" I say, pointing beyond the gate. He shakes his head. He is young, has a defined Dan Dare jaw line, and would be a handsome man if not for his silly red military beret. He invites me for chai. Well I have nothing better to do, and it will console my disappointment at not being able to stay in the place of panoramic vistas. I sit at a white plastic table under a gazebo of scaffold poles and corrugated iron. There is an empty chai glass on the table and some dominoes too. In addition to these he has gone off and left his Kalashnikov behind. It's just there on the table, loaded and available. I could pick it up and go crazy ape bonkers with this thing. Is it trust or stupidity that would make him leave his weapon behind? Has he never seen how John Travolta met his demise in *Pulp Fiction*? He returns with chai for us both, and so begins the conversation in mutually unintelligible languages. I point at his gun. "Kalashnikov?"

"Yes," but he clearly doesn't want to talk about guns. We are joined by a man with the kind of moustache ill-informed people thought looked good during the days of disco; he is wearing more traditional dress and seems to have more authority too. He shakes my hand. I have something specifically for situations like this. I go to my tank box and bring out 15 photos that depict who I am—a bar of beer mats and bitter pumps, a steak and kidney pie with gravy, a thatched cottage, a kitchen I installed, quintessentially British things in my life, and a photo of my American daughter who isn't in my life but is still a part of who I am. This show and tell never fails; I'm shown the soldier's kids on his phone, and then he takes a photo of me by my bike. I take one of him by my bike on his phone, then with my camera, then with his friend/boss then . . . well you get the picture. So I still need somewhere to stay then.

I find a room, well more of an apartment really, one of six that are accessed from a first floor corridor; two bedrooms, kitchen, bathroom, and undercover bike parking, all for $15. I'm the only resident, the price seems reasonable, but the stink, this is not the first time this has happened. They have these translucent perfumed balls they put in the bathroom. They're gag-inducing. I pick them up and throw them down the toilet. This was entirely the wrong action to take; it seems to activate them, and now the stench is so strong I can almost see it. I try to flush them down, but I'm overpowered by the aroma. My eyes are watering. I have to leave the room; I reckon it's the best way to avoid suffocation.

An evening walkabout I think, and at my local convenience store I pick up a few supplies. The boy speaks good English, so I change some money and ask where a good vista point is. He points up the mountain, pretty obvious really. A 4x4 has stopped outside; the boy shouts to the driver, and the back door is opened; the driver and his mate will take me. So, knowing full well I have a pocket full of cash along with my rather excessive camera, I let these two men take me up a rocky track into the mountains. It's certainly a day of interesting circumstance. I sit in the back trying to show gratitude when unease is a far stronger emotion. I'm given a bottle of water, and when we get quite far up they stop, get out, and sit on rocks. "Right, well thanks, then. I'll, umm, just go for a little wander up here, bye," is what I try to convey with my wave.

I don't have to walk up far and I come to an area of military presence. I think beyond this heavily guarded gate there are barracks. They seem to occupy all the best spots, this Kurdistan army. Ain't no chai on offer here; it is made very clear to me I've wandered a step too far. I'll be off then; certainly not here to spy or take photos of your clandestine camp, oh no, not me.

I walk back down past my chauffeur and his mate, "You could have bloody told me," says my shrug as I continue down. I think if I climb over those rocks I will have the view of flat-top-ville that I want. It's an OK view; I'd like to be higher, but that's not a feeling unknown to me.

I think I'll go back home now and see if the perfumed balls have dissolved the porcelain toilet bowl yet. As I go back down the road, I see a couple of youths sitting on a grassy knoll. I wave as I walk past; they run out and catch me up. They are students doing their homework, it's about anatomy, and it's all in English. Then another one comes and another; where were they all hiding? They speak English and are overpoweringly friendly. One loves my camera, and against my better judgement, I let him take it, emphasising the importance of putting the strap over his head. He snaps away whilst I chat with the others. They study here, although they come from all over Kurdistan. They walk back with me and insist that I come back to their place. My god, how many students can you fit into an apartment block? About twelve per room seems to be the average. Mattresses are laid all around the walls like four-foot skirting boards.

Come in, sit down; other than the mattresses the rooms are empty, not in a squalid squat kind of way, just minimalistic, no excess. Much like the chai that is brought for me; no sugar, no spoon, and not even much chai, but what the place lacks in furnishings it makes up for in graciousness.

It's not just conveyed to me, although I'm the spectacle of the moment, but the sense of community is so strong, so sober, and not a girl in sight. They all sit around me and ask their questions. A laptop appears, and they find me on Facebook. It's fun, but intense, an exhausting interaction. Before I leave I'm taken to all the other rooms on that floor, all occupied by multitudes of male students, every one of them is genuinely welcoming and shakes my hand. This is what a celebrity must feel like. No time for any of them but hello to all of them. I'm escorted back to my hotel by the original party I met. It was an honour, an exhausting honour.

DAY 36

ERBIL, IRAQ, 141 MILES

I have my very own kitchen; I use it to make a Marmite sandwich. The oppressive smell from the bathroom keeps me out of the shower. I go down to load my bike. There is a man wandering round, clearly an artefact short of an ancient civilization. He just stares as I load and then wakes the boss from his mattress in the storeroom.

Maybe he got out of bed the wrong side, maybe he's just a conniving sneaky bastard, but this morning the price isn't $15, it's $50.

"Don't give me that; you said $15, that's 18,000 dinar, and that's what I have here in my hand for you." There is not an ounce of credibility in his performance, motivated by greed; he tries to play on the fact that the way he speaks my language the two amounts sound similar. Then he drops his price to forty too quickly; there is little I can do. Other phrases that sound the same are *thank you* and *fuck you*, especially if I say it through a closed visor. Can you guess which one it is?

I ride out with teeth grinding resentment. Great start to the day; I'm out of money again now. I hope he is suffocated by his balls. What these greedy rip-off merchants don't realise, apart from the fact the money they extorted will never bring them what they need (only what they want), is that I have to try very hard not to take their torment with me; it's infectious and destructive to mood and reaction.

Negativity eats like rust into the morning and is fed by the first scene I ride past after the city. On the edge of the road, stretching down the hillside, is all the rubbish from the town. Dumped and incinerated, it sits there festering and smouldering. These aren't misty valleys I'm seeing; this is the smoke from burning plastic hanging in the toxic air. Up and coming? Modern and prosperous? You've got some improvements to make before you can start promoting your avant-garde society. Any other day I would be disappointed; this morning I'm utterly disgusted.

But it's Monday morning; I'm riding my bike through a foreign country on mountain roads. I'm not working on them like the crews of construction workers are. I should try and change my mindset. Five weeks I've been on the road now; spring is a distant memory. In this forty degree heat, scorched trees stand on sun-browned grass, tired and exposed. If there was ever spring greenness here, it's long been burnt out.

The scale of my map seems inconsistent; I can't judge how far I've come and when I should turn. I'm following a fast running but grey river. All rivers flow to the sea, but what sea is this one running into, the Caspian or the Persian Gulf? Because there is a significant difference. I'm heading east to go southwest, and it feels wrong. I stop at a junction and ask the uniformed men inside a shack; I'm not sure what their role is. They can't read the Roman character names on my map, seem to have no awareness of their country's proportions or neighbouring communities, and I can't pronounce the names well enough to be understood. They flag down a car, and between the four of us, a translation is achieved. I should head towards Howleeeer (that is how it's pronounced, regardless of the fact it's spelt Erbil). The name is written for me in Arabic too, should I have to stop and ask again.

Route confirmed, I head off. At the time, those little interactions seem like an inconvenience, but upon reflection, although commonplace within my day, for an Essex boy these are outrageous exploits. Asking the help of armed uniformed men of unknown forces; leaning over a map with a pristine white robed Arab. It's just not yer average "Turn left at the Kings 'ed, mate, then fork right at the co-op." This is another aspect of travel lost by the addition of a sat nav. If it's telling you where to go, you don't have to ask.

I ride on through valleys and over mountain ranges; nothing too extreme, the biggest obstacle is the oppressive and inescapable heat. The sun is at the top of the sky; I can't navigate by it at all. My arms cast shadows on my thighs.

Another signpost and another checkpoint, Kalashnikovs everywhere. I look down at the baked plains I'm heading into. There are plenty of Iranian number plates on the cars but no signs for Erbil. I half expect to see a Las Vegas type oasis, but all I get are dust storms and twisters. I just close my visor in time, but the turbulence blows me across the road. My reactions numbed by delirious heat, I think my non-aggressive response helped to keep me vertical. Who the hell decided to build a city in this hot desert? It better be pretty damned impressive when I get there. I join a really busy road and see a sign that says, "Erbil 10 kms," but there's nothing 10 kms away; I can almost see that far from here.

I don't know what unit of measurement they use, but forty-five minutes later this brown parched land gives way to construction, homes, and hotels with concrete and cranes everywhere. Wide streets with green irrigated grassy central reservations of palms and flowering plants; but this token greenery is ineffectual in the searing city outskirts. It's going to take more than a strip of vegetation to turn this place from furnace to feature garden.

At a red light I notice a skirmish. It's all kicking off; a fist fight, police trying to restrain opposing parties. I think it's some road rage that has spread to the pavement. It's the heat, it's got to be; it drives you mad. What a great introduction to the city. An expensive city it appears to be too. I can't find a room within my budget; the only option after an hour of looking is to just pay the price. It's only just after lunch time; I want to spend my time looking at sights not trying to save a few quid whist sweltering on my bike.

Erbil is one of the oldest permanently inhabited cities in the world. For over 8,000 years people have lived right here. It puts my little accommodation predicament into perspective, too much perspective. I'm just an insignificant traveller through a city that was established over 3,000 years before the pyramids were built.

The citadel is the elevated area where the old city stands; it's not a natural mound like Amedi is built on. This inhabited hill is elevated through 8 millennia of building in the same place. I'm proud of the geographical knowledge I have gained over the years, I can usually name the unmarked coloured shapes which depict countries on a world atlas. Although occasionally this education overlaps into historical facts, there are ocean-sized voids in my mental world chronicles. I think this is mainly due to the fact I find it far easier to travel through distant lands than through distance times, and my own experiences are easier to retain than those I have read of in ancient reports. However, a town that has been established so long it has risen 100 feet above the plains to me seems like an opportunity to walk through time, and it excites me so much I go back out into the heat of the day.

There is a big restoration program in operation, and the residents have been evacuated. My brief Google search from my air-conditioned room says the place is off limits to the public, but what does Google know? I take a narrow spiralling path on the side of the embankment. I walk through a giant brick arched gate and down the centre road; I know it's the centre road because there is a sign in Arabic and English that says, "Citadel Street." It's totally accessible and, although restored, still has a feeling of unfathomable time. I'm nothing but a blip on its guest list of visitors. It requires so much thought to quantify and comprehend that it makes me hungry, and I wander off to find a kebab.

I'm sitting eating my food, and some women walk into the restaurant, heads covered but faces on display. I just realise I haven't seen a woman in any restaurant I've been in. I must have known on some level, because this sight is as unusual as an ashtray in a pub. About six women come in followed by a couple of men, and they are ushered to a table at the back of the restaurant. I'm looking, trying not to stare, because I've just not seen this before. Then the staff put screens around their table; they are taken from mine and everybody else's view. For their modesty or protection? See, I would have loved to have all this explained to me by reception girl. I'm just left dumbfounded and with half a kebab still to eat.

In the evening I go back to the area around the citadel and watch the street life go on outside. It's a busy popular area: old couples, youths, shoppers, and even some musicians. They all come to sit by the fountains in the shadows of the imposing walls, high above the modern city. With evening light and slow shutter speeds, I photograph blurred fountains and streaking taxies.

DAY 37

SIIRT, TURKEY, 293 MILES

A few days ago I mislaid the pen I write my diary with; it's not a massive deal, but I do like the entries to be consistent in their colour and legibility. This morning I found it in my sandal bag. I wasn't inconsolable over the loss, none the less, the day starts with a good omen, and I think you need that when you are about to head into Mosul, the city of certain death.

The lack of water in the bathroom is of no concern due to a full clean up yesterday, and I won't let it taint the day. So I load the bike, and now I'm ready to head the 80 kms into the place of no return. These are not simply the scaremongering words of the world couch traveller, retelling stories of experiences they have never had. These are sincere warnings from every Kurd I have mentioned the subject to. You go there to die; a one way journey, certain death, crazy Arabs, kidnappings, car bombs, shootings, unstable. I have considered all of this, and I think alone, unannounced, that I will pass through the 20 kms of Iraq and back into Kurdistan quicker than you can say "Grab the hippy."

Erbil has good signposts and wide streets. The ancient city's infrastructure seems to have kept up with the increase in the population. I can clearly see the way to Bagdad signposted and go in the other direction. Once I'm on the main northbound road, I empty the majority of the contents of my wallet at a petrol station; there was enough dinar to fill my tank and water bottle. It's hot of course; it's always hot. Every day has been hot regardless of my altitude, the time of day, shade, or cloud cover; it's just hot and that's all there is to it.

The road is hazy as is the horizon. All around is burnt, bleached, brown, over-exposed, dusty, and barely occupied. There is the occasional grey concrete and steel structure, dilapidated trucks and tyres strewn and stacked, discarded and collected. A sudden dust storm throws a barrier of brown across my path with tumbling plastic bottles and whirling paper. I flip down the visor and hold my breath. The wind brings no relief from the heat; it just concentrates it.

I come to a bridge, would this be the river separating Kurdistan from Iraq? There is a police check-point on both sides, but they don't seem that concerned with me. I see a sign to Duhok, an alternative route if I choose to take it, which I don't. I pass old trucks pumping out black clouds of exhaust. Kids rummage through piles of rubbish. Red and white masts break the flat horizon along with a single plume of vertical smoke; I thought it might be a car fire, but it's just burning tyres.

I stop to put on my money-belt for the first time this trip. Annoyingly, along with the back support that I always wear, this pressure is not helping an already grumbling and uncomfortable tummy. I'm not sure if it was that dodgy kebab last night or the angst of today. Either way I really don't want to have to make an emergency stop on the side of this desolate road. I am now 27 kms from Mosul. I must be in pure Iraqi territory now. I must have left safe Kurdistan behind me. Another 27 kms north of Mosul and I will be back in the safety of semi-autonomous Kurdistan. Kurdistan is both south and north of me. Its squiggly boundaries appear to overlap Turkey and Syria. However, for now I think it has left me in a similar terrain but with another name because its borders skirt Mosul like a ring road.

Once again, there is a junction; the majority of traffic slips off to the right and joins a queue to the check-point. I continue straight ahead. The road is empty now. Where are the inevitable trucks that cross every dire road in the world supplying the unfortunate inhabitants? There is always the diesel burning life blood, chugging along the veins of highways across the planet and giving me a sense of hope, camaraderie, and support. I understand everything about their role; the driver's state of mind, the load, the lorry, the engine, the cab, the trailer. It all makes sense to me, and I feel comfortable sharing the road with them. But even these big brave road warriors have diverted, and all that's left on the road is me and a 650cc single cylinder engine sweltering between my legs. It is complaining about the cheap oil that is breaking down in the heat, a heat that keeps the radiator roasting as the boiling fluid is pumped around it. A few cars remain on the road, but it's not exactly reassuring; it's not camaraderie, it's not a distraction from the trouble I'm riding into. And on I ride. 10 kms to go now and another checkpoint. It's army now, and they are more protected than any motorcyclist stupid enough to pass. The soldier looks at me with his big brown eyes under the shade of his helmet.

"Mosul," I say and point. "Yes," his eyes say, "I know it's that way; what the hell are you going there for?" But his authority bows to my stupidly, and he lets me continue to my imminent death. In less than a mile there is another check-point, a big one this time—armoured cars, watchtowers, tanks, sand bags, barriers, and the soldiers; soldiers? They are solid individual killing machines, covered in weaponry and bullet-proofed. My god, they could kill a terminator with that lot; automatic weapons, belts of magazines, hand cuffs, mace, and a big knife at the front. Masks up to their noses and helmet down to their eyes, with some kind of safety goggle perched on top which probably has 3D, X-ray, see in the dark, laser beam projecting and sight-correcting qualities. These men are as secure and bullet-proof as any walking human can be. I thought I was hot in my bike gear. They must be sweltering.

I choose to pull down my bandana, lift up my chin guard, and use my biggest smile; they bring on their highest commander. He is decorated but not defended by armour, just girth, knowledge, authority, medals, and a very slight grasp of the English language. He asks where I'm going. I figure I'm near Mosul now, so I give the destination of Turkey.

"I can go via Mosul?" He plays a low card, but it beats mine. "Where is your visa?"

"Look; it's here."

"No, this is for Kurdistan; you need a proper visa," he says leafing through my passport, "like these ones, but for Iraq."

To be honest, I'm ready to turn round now anyway. I came, I saw, and I realise I have seriously underestimated the situation.

"Here is great danger, bombing, and kidnaps. It is very dangerous. You cannot proceed; you need to go back 10 kms and turn left, continue in that direction."

My appearance here is a break from the fear of every other passing vehicle. It has brought a host of tooled-up military, all smiling, all friendly and with their questions in their pidgin English. They all are shaking their heads at my being here. One of the man-machines indicated I must be hot in my bike jacket. I point at his regalia, "Looked in the mirror this morning, mate?" but it's all in fun. I'm not here to defy or to be obtuse; I just wanted to try to see. This is a war zone, and I'm far too insignificant to be protected but unique enough to be a victim of opportunity. Anyway, I don't even have the right paperwork. But since I've come this far can I have a photo?

The high ranking man offers to take the picture. I stand by my bike with three of the terminator terminators. I feel safe with them; they are so friendly and smiley and have so many weapons on them. When I put my arm round one I can't help but touch a weapon of destruction. After the big man has had enough of my souvenir day, I take the camera and take a few more shots. Luck well and truly pushed, I confirm the new route and say goodbye to these very honourable men. But not before a phone is produced and my photo is also taken.

I wonder what their stories are, how long they have been doing this, and how much longer they will be doing it. I hope if they ever fire those guns in self-defence they shoot with better precision and training than they did with my camera. Still on last night's settings, the photos are as over-exposed as I am to this heat, this city, and all the dangers that I've been warned of.

There is not the faintest hint of disappointment as I leave this checkpoint. It was my mistake. I had to try; had to see for myself. I'm still intrigued as to the street life of the city behind the barricades; it can't be all burnings, bombings, and badness. There has to be the overlaying appearance of normality, shops open, and people passing. It's not going to be a burning pit of hell, but I'm sure it can turn into one pretty damn quick.

I take the road I was told to but there are no signposts now, and I take a guess at a junction. An unshaved man in jeans and a T-shirt, with a Kalashnikov and a radio comes out and stops me. He is the scariest figure I have seen all day. He turns me round, I go back to the junction; more men on radios point me down another road. As I ride down it another armed man walks out from a hedge and stops me.

"Duhok?" I ask.

"Yes. Where are you from?"

"England."

"On this?"

"Yes, yes, all the way."

"Good, good, welcome to Iraq." That friendly little interaction is all recorded. I have it on my voice recorder. I was speaking into it as he approached, and I didn't get a chance to turn it off. It could have been a far more sinister meeting. I was scared; armed men with unknown intentions. Listening to that recording makes me shudder and then smile when I hear the trepidation in my voice and the assertion in his. I think I can say this last hour in Iraq has put the adventure into my biking.

The road is blocked again, by construction this time. I take dirt tracks and squeeze through a gap in a barbed-wire fence. Should I really be riding dirt roads between barbed-wire in such a volatile area?

I get back on track, and the Kurdistan flag appears. It makes me feel safe, and slowly I leave signs for Bagdad and Iraqi flags behind. I pass a field of sunflowers, the most peaceful, pretty, and pleasurable sight today. Then I head north through less intimidating check-points back towards the Turkish border, a place, which ironically, is making the headlines for its riots and political unrest. But somehow it's a little more Eurovision and a bit less fallen dictator. But it's only lunchtime, and this day is not half over.

My little circuit of Kurdistan is complete; I'm back at the same crossing I came in through. I have to be. I really would like my log book back, although the surrogate one they gave me has been readily accepted by all who asked for it, and there were many. I don't see a single person I dealt with when I came in. I pass from building to building. Eventually I exchange a fist full of stamped and signed paper for my log book and a German passport. I have mine in my pocket. It's always handy to have another, but I think in this instance I'd better be honest.

I'm helped through every step of the process by an enthusiastic and pushy man. I don't know what his role is when I'm not around. He seems to work for the love of it; he never gave a hint for recompense. By the urgency of his actions to get me processed I suspect he may be practicing for a record attempt at fastest border crossing ever. The Turkish side is the same shift as when I entered, and I'm processed with ease. I'm back in Turkey. I pull over in the shade of a parked truck to swap maps, currency, and bring out the sat nav, cus I've missed not having anything to argue with.

Silopi is still a dusty and disreputable little town, but now amongst its few attributes are familiarity, and that can give the most uninhabitable dump a sense of harmless security. I pass right through all the same.

I'm not driving a big fat truck on a tight deadline; I'm ahead of schedule on a laden but slim bike. I'm taking the narrow route on my map, and what a good choice. I'm led through valleys and over mountains. I ride by rivers, immersed in the terrain. It is so close and all encompassing, progress is slowed by an insatiable need to photograph and capture this pleasant surprise in surroundings. The colour green is back in the landscape, I've really missed it. The bike is performing faultlessly, but now I'm back in the land of costly fuel I'm frequently freewheeling, silently hurtling down hills. I think it's more for fun than economy, which is why I have to stop at a petrol station. A glass of Coke is brought out to me as my tank is filled, and then food is offered too. The attendant's mime implies there is no culinary alternative between here and darkness. It's a lovely offer and makes for a stronger bond than "Av ya got a club card?'

It's beautiful here. Is it because I've been so deprived of lush fertile countryside? Around every corner there is wild camp potential, herded goats and sheep, rolling hills, clusters of pines, and steep rocky cliffs.

Once again, I have no supplies for a spontaneous pull off and stop. The visual invites become more frequent and welcoming with a wide and fast-flowing river in a deep and steep canyon; I can't not sleep in this place. I will continue to the next town, and there I will grab a bite and a few basic provisions then happily double back to this place of unpopulated beauty. But this little dream is a town's endurance away, and it's not going to plan. There is simply nowhere to eat. Children play and rubbish is stacked; there are no cars parked, no shops, just residents who have no instinct to move out of the way of a passing vehicle. The choices are few, so I opt for a market, buy bread and fruit, and that will have to do me. Oh for an all-encompassing cloak of concealment, but I create a crowd. Twenty youths watch me pour water into my insulated container and then put my crushable fruit into my cool box. "Pretty cool, eh?" I say to break the silent intrigue. They are suitably impressed.

Now all I have to do is get out of town, that's all, just the way I came in. But it doesn't work out at all; fury and frustration, cursing and swearing, circles and dead ends, staring and annoyance. Then to top it off, as the light fades and darkness eats into my deadline, I come across two delicious looking restaurants followed by another fifteen minutes of circling and seething as I try to exit the city.

I ride like a screaming demon when I find the road to the canyon, using both sides to lessen my braking and hasten my pace. Then down to the river, onto the gravel, into the shadows, and out of sight. Serenity now, I crouch on the rocky ground. No, no one can see me here. I make a hasty sandwich and in the darkest dusk erect my tent. I'm wild camping in a canyon by a river with a stomach full of bread and a dark and stealthy tent. My bike is covered too, and I can just lay and let the thoughts of a very long day flow away into the night, a night that will be over before I'm ready to start again.

DAY 38

ADILCEVZA, TURKEY, 131 MILES

It's light at 4.20AM; that's June for you. I lie in the tent and say to myself that what happened last night will never happen again. I am not going to get so low on supplies that I have to ride desperately round a town as it gets dark in search of some basic foods. I'm going to pick up food when the opportunity arises and keep a tummy's supply in my little cool box.

There is a sticky, sweet pungent smell outside my tent. Almost like sewage, but not quite as offensive, it comes and goes. The outer layer of the tent is crawling with ants. I pack up what I can and then unzip and jump out. The sun is late to rise and shine into this canyon. Cows are walking down by the river. Typically, the other side seems to have lusher, greener, grassier banks, but I have no idea how to get across this wide fast-flowing river. I seem to be talking to myself more and more. When I catch myself doing it I say things like, "I see you're talking to yourself again, Flid." The reply is usually "Shut up, I'm trying to live in the moment."

It's about now I should try and find some company before the point when company tries to a find an excuse to avoid me. There's reflection, there's introspection, there's isolation, then there's a journey so deep into yourself that you will be left incapacitated. Unable to communicate in any social situation, in desperation you will sweat and stutter, shake and squirm. Spittle will fly from your dry lips as you blurt inappropriate words. Your knuckles will crack as you wring your hands with anxiety. The only appropriate exercise left for fingers and wrists will be the keyboard, and you are destined to become a naysayer on Internet forums. And we don't need any more of those go nowhere, do nothing, negative, opinionated, contradictory messengers of doom.

135

Not that such pessimism could ever come from this effervescent bedroom that I am rolling up and putting in my top box. But it's important to be aware of the pitfalls that await the lone and the incommunicative.

Last night's unfinished dinner becomes this morning's breakfast, and the thought of boiling water for chai never even occurs to me. I'm not taking a stove next time; the amount of space it takes up is disproportionate to the amount of use its gets.

Out on the road and into the perfect temperature, sunny, fresh, early morning clear. The scenery, too, is ideal; as I lean round corners on a road that follows the flow of the river, there are views of distant snowy mountains. The road indirectly takes me northwards, crosses into a different province, but no real changes are evident.

Judging by the overhead warning signs, I think I'm heading for a very long tunnel. I have a short wait for the oncoming traffic then take the single lane for 5 kms of darkness. I take the opportunity to stab at the glowing sat nav with the supplied touch screen scribe. I get little reward or satisfaction from my efforts.

Finally, the map has decided the road deserves green recognition; I'm losing confidence in their rating system.

After I've climbed to a chilly 6,000 feet, Lake Van comes into view, and the road descends a little to its "mile-high" shore. I've been deliberating what side to pass on, but having made a decision, I make a last minute change of plan and take the western route. I'll never know if it was the right choice. Such can be the tortures to an idle mind; would fulfilment of all desires lie on the easterly route? Probably not, but annoying if it would have, to think after 30 years of searching, I only just missed it by a few miles.

If not meeting every need I've ever had, it's still very lovely on this side, and I ride down to the water's edge. I sit and look across the clear water at green hills on the other side that rise to snow covered mountains. It's a tripod moment, and that's as much as I can ask for. I wash my hands in the water; it's all slippery, oily, and salty. I wasn't expecting that at all. Once again, my progress is slowed by beautiful scenery, natural and man-made. There are modest mosques against the dark blue of the high skies. I ride down a rocky peninsula, simply because I can, then inland to a grove of aspen trees and purple blossoms. There is a lakeside campsite, but it doesn't feel right. By accident, I find a hotel. The owner is delighted to see me and enthusiastically takes me up in the lift and shows me a room of windows and views, then down to a basement of supplies that doubles as secure bike parking, all for the same price as nine litres of fuel.

It's an early stop but a pretty location. It would be all the better if I had company. Locking up the bike this early when you're the only stranger in town can make for a long afternoon, especially after the nonstop stimulation of yesterday's ride. Sometimes getting off the bike is when the best things happen; sometimes the best things happen when you stay on. Today perhaps should have been a staying on day.

Day 39

Dogubayazit, Turkey, 158 Miles

I really don't know what I do between the time I wake up and get on the road, but at least two hours pass, usually more. Still no rush. I'm not even sure where I'm going today, how far, or what route I will take to get there. Just north, that's all, head towards Armenia. I'd happily stop somewhere for a few days if I could find the right place.

I follow the road around the lake, which I know more about this morning. It's the biggest lake in Turkey, it has no exit much like the Dead Sea, and its slippery texture I felt yesterday is due to the salty sediment that comes from the rivers that fill it. All makes sense now, well almost. A lake that is constantly filled but has no drain—surely that makes for some high spring water levels. I bet satisfactory carpet insurance is expensive in such a flood prone area.

I see a signpost for Iran! What a tease, if the trip preparation had gone according to plan I'd be taking that route now. The proximity of Iran brings the feeling of disappointment back.

I have done 6,000 miles since I left home, which is twice the distance of the direct route to Iran. I would have missed so much if I'd taken that 30-day visa in Vienna, which started on the day of issue. It would only ever have caused frustration, but that signpost has triggered a barrage of destination-related thoughts: Are the 'Stans a compromise or an equally exciting alternative? Will I ever make it back this way again to go to Iran, and if so then where, Pakistan or the other 'Stans again? It's a bit premature thinking about future destinations when I don't even know where I'm going today. The moment is not being lived in; it's certainly not being appreciated.

The scenery when I pull myself back to the here and now is actually quite stimulating; there are some wonderful primary colours. The dark blue sky sits on white mountaintops. The melting snow gives way to bright green vegetation and fields of poppies and yellow blossom. The road is empty and so is the land; I'm getting closer and closer to the Iranian border. I can see fences and watchtowers on top of the hills. So many enticing countries Turkey has for neighbours. I come into a town and make myself stop for bread and supplies, the inevitable chai is offered, and when I go back to my bike, parked right next to it is an '89 Austrian-registered BMW.

Wow, company, European bike riding company, I moisten my lips in anticipation of the meeting. A couple come out of a shop with supplies similar to mine. We meet; we greet and then struggle to connect. They are envious of my map. They are going the same way I am. We pack our food simultaneously, commenting on each other's bikes. We are both ready together; it's a little strange as we haven't said we will ride together, but we know now we are going the same direction and that we travel at a similar pace. We leave together. This is weird; are we together now or what? After following them out of the little town, they slow and slow and then just wave me past. Great, is it me? Is it an Austrian thing? Is it a BMW thing? Is it a couple thing? Is it even worth considering? It's a little disappointing, but worryingly, it just makes me laugh out loud. I divert up a hillside towards a border outpost. The remains of last winter's snow is still up here; it's a long way from the baking I was getting in Iraq a few days ago. I find a place to stop at the side of the road to eat the fresh bread. I look at the view and come to terms with my dejection by losing myself in a sandwich then ride back to the main road. Comfort eating is not the answer to any circumstance. That's why I call it breakfast, and if it happens again I'll call it lunch. I'm at 8,000 feet now, and the bike is loving it, running so strong; it's a good sign for the elevation that's to come in the 'Stans.

Round a corner all self-indulgent thoughts are instantly dispelled, as there in front of me is Mount Ararat. It is absolutely "stop-dead-in-your-tracks" stunning. Nearly 17,000 feet of magnificence. I just stare at it dumbstruck. Two consecutive tripod days; Turkey has certainly saved the best till last. Like the supposed bright light at the end of the tunnel, blinkered, I'm drawn towards the mountain.

Luckily, to break this spell I come into the town of Dogubayazit. It's got a seedy border town feeling but sits surrounded by ancient architecture, built in and set against natural beauty. It's a location of certainty; I will not be going any further today. I see a campsite sign, but it stands alone without direction. I ride east through the town towards Iran, but no site appears, then north towards Ararat, but again, no camping is evident. Back into town, right into the centre, I see the Austrian BMW in a hotel car park and carry on up towards the palace. It's built on a rocky plateau beside a mosque on a cliff, so in-keeping with the natural surroundings that it's easily missed, especially if you take a photo with an attractive, desirable, beaten-up overland bike in the foreground.

On route to these sites is the campground—the day seems to be falling into place nicely. It's not ideal. It's a bit tacky. There are some dilapidated fairground rides; rusty monstrosities. It's a stain on this picture perfect scene, but quite typical of the Turkish idea of tourist entertainment. There are a few nailed-together accommodation shacks and a restaurant. The place seems to be run by clueless youths, but it's all that's available, and I've ridden round most of the area now. They start to play some pounding dance music from the restaurant as I erect my tent; surely this is not for my benefit. It's still early, so I use this open but secluded space to remove my panniers and do some bike maintenance. I come across my Turkish phrase book, I forgot I had it, but like gym membership, just owning it does nothing, you have to actually use it.

Some young Turkish tourist girls have arrived, and with blatant rampancy, the youths escort them round the fairground rides. They make the girls scream with delight as they push the archaic machinery to its limits, hoping the swinging and jerking and spinning will make their knickers come off. The music is turned up to distortion, and a half-played 180 beats per minute electronic sample is broken off into amateur silence before being replaced by another. The boys jump around with their hands in the air like they just don't care what twats they look. I go to the shower block to wash my hands and decide I can put up with it for one night. As I walk back to my tent, I decide actually I can't. As calmly as I can, I pack up and get the fuck out of this failed fairground of seduction. I'm finding it increasingly preferable to want company than to actually have it. I ride up to the palace and take in some tranquillity.

I want a view; I demand a view. If I'm going to stay in a shitty town surrounded by beauty, then I want to be able to see that beauty. There are a few hotels in the town that offer nothing except close proximity to the town. Back out on the main road is a tall hotel, suggesting splendour behind smoked glass, but it's a smoke screen. As I walk in, rubbish bags are being taken out through the main entrance. I see a mouse drop out of the bottom of a bag and run to the door. The receptionist sees I see it, and the price is low enough not to have me following the mouse.

I have a balcony; I can see Mount Ararat and the palace and mosque. Perfect. The walk to the beer shop is further than I thought, and I miss the changing sunset sky. Still, it's a great place to just sit and take in the view. It's not camping on any level; it's actually hotelling on the fifth level.

DAY 40

ARDAHAN, TURKEY, 168 MILES

Totally busted at the all-inclusive breakfast!

I am just leaving the roof top restaurant with some extra emergency hard boiled eggs in my hand, and the manager and cook come up to shake hands with me. Oh well, I'm sure they have suffered bigger loses. To add to the egg on my face outside the hotel, two Dutch businessmen approach as I load up. Typically, they ask my destination. Armenia was my general direction, and they tell me all borders are closed. There are some quite significant reasons for this; it doesn't take much of a search to discover why relations are so fraught. The fact the Turkish massacred 1.5 million Armenians around the time of the First World War coined the phrase *genocide*. The grudge is still not entirely put to rest.

Right, Georgia it is then—luckily, I'm quite flexible. I was going to Georgia anyway to pick up my Azerbaijan visa; I just thought I might go via Armenia. Well that's just put a little jigsaw piece in place on my empty table of historical knowledge. Bring on the pub quiz.

It's cold this morning; the sun is deceiving. But again the road is scenic; the fields of poppies stretch off into the horizon, shining bright red like thousands of little Ducati trees.

Again, there are watchtowers on my right, but this time they look over Armenia, possibly the most hostile and protected of all the Turkish borders, and I've seen all but one of them now. The day gets colder as I ride through a town called Kars. So this week I have been from Van to Kars on a bike.

The downside of my chosen transport is about to reveal itself, as ominous stormy skies are ahead of me and lightening shards shock hill tops. I can see the darkness fall like a pastel smear on a canvas. The turbulent sky is full of nastiness; we meet each other on a hillside, and hail hammers down. It turns the road white and whips my fingers raw. I stop to put on my winter gloves, but my hands are too wet and cold to slide them on. Thunder is cracking all around me, and the wind is gusting and shaking the bike. Isolated violence is what it is, and I've stopped right in the middle of it. My fingers still not located in my gloves, I ride on fidgeting and wriggling my hands around. The slate roofs of the farm houses are white from the hail storm, and the landscape has become Dartmoor-like; heather and moss, rocky and barren.

My feet are soaked after that intense little storm. The grey sky is not appealing at all, and then my speedo packs up. The needle has been a bit jumpy lately, and now it's resting in the stationary position and my daily statistics of distance travelled are gone. I see no point in riding this landscape in this weather. I'm cold and wet and ahead of myself. I see no point in enduring this day's riding any longer. I stop in a town, and again, the tent stays in the top box and I stay in a room.

I strip the speedo drive. The seal has disintegrated and worn down the gear drive over thousands of miles; it's beyond repair. The only answer I can see is alcohol.

It's a small town centred around a square of shops, and despite the impossibilities of finding one, I am looking for a KLR parts shop as I go about a more realistic and successful quest to find beer. Next door to the beer shop is a seedy little brothel. I know this because a scantily clad girl walks out of a battered door as I go past, and a fully covered Muslim woman looks at her harder than I do. In my defence, my staring is not purely lust driven; I just didn't expect to see so much exposed flesh under the dismal skies of such a cold and close community. Judging by those hot pants there is a Speedo shop in town.

I decide to get a pizza, but it was dinner and nothing to do with comfort eating at all.

DAY 41

HOPA, TURKEY, 145 MILES

I'm one day away from Georgia, one day away from the sat nav being cast aside forever. But now that I need it to tell me my mileage, this parasitic device has wheedled its way onto the rest of the journey. It's like the crack on my windshield; it can't be given up or removed. Inside the tank box it refuses to pick up a signal so insists on being on display. I loathe the thing; I reconsider the state of the speedo drive.

I have a mate in England, a phenomenal engineer, and I think to myself, what would Andy do? I go back to my bike, and in the fresh light of a new day I wonder if a small washer would increase the height of a drive gear, bringing it once again in contact with the other gear. I select the perfect washer and cut a narrow slice out if it. I push it over the tiny axle the gear spins on. It appears to work, now engaging with the other gear. I put the wheel back on and spin it. The needle on the speedo rises to the occasion, then there is a grinding, crunching noise from the hub, and the needle falls like a syringe from the arm of an overdosed smackhead. Back in my room I order a £20 used drive off eBay to be sent to my mother's house. I figure out how to get the sat nav to record distance; turns out it's been doing it the whole time.

Soon I'm up in the snowy heights again, and my fingers numb in the chill wind, but I can see the descent into sunny valleys, so I endure for a little longer. The road hairpins down, but with gravel corners and potholes there are no leaning opportunities, so I just turn off the engine and freewheel past the pastures. I startle some goats who expect to hear an engine before they see a vehicle. I don't care, it's just the way I roll. Sunshine changes everything; the cones on the pine trees seem to glow and the wild flowers pose with a confidence, no longer the shrinking violets under yesterday's darkened skies.

Practicing my new mantra, I stop for basics, and soon after I'm rewarded with a picnic spot by a river in the shade of a weeping willow. It would have been a great place to stop for the night, but perhaps it wasn't so appealing last night. Birds sing and the shallow river mumbles as it passes; there are no other sounds. I'm not even talking to myself, but it's not an awkward silence.

The road twists as it goes through a skinny little canyon, with no traffic at all. Since I left Iraq I've ridden day after day on spectacular roads. I absolutely love eastern Turkey. Gorgeous though this may be, I take advantage of the surface, bends, and vacant road. The KLR with Mefos can, when required, metamorphose into something quite thrilling. The term *sport bike* might be a slight exaggeration, but I can scrub my tyres and scrape my centre stand as I lean and weave my way through the canyon. Only focused on the road ahead, what I loose in scenery I gain in adrenalin. It's such a wonderfully diverse machine, and it's in its element today.

I take it up a dirt road to a vista point, which just happens to have a 1,000 year old church at the end. It's one of those "and then and then and then" days.

The delicate river I had my lunch by had turned into an expanse of water 300 feet wide. The canyon must have been plugged, as the water level has risen up the sides and everything here is on a grander scale. The scenery gets more impressive round every corner, and there are a lot of corners. The dam I was expecting comes into view, but what I wasn't expecting were the giant statues and cliff-top ruins that overshadow the town of Artvin, a town that clings to the canyon walls above the reduced flow of the dammed river. This is Turkey's grand finale, and it's going out in style.

And on it continues; pristine roads, sweeping bends, a wide deep green river wedged between the steep canyon walls that this road has been carved from. Fast like a racer or slow like a sightseer? Maybe I should do it twice. The scenery becomes a long line of distorted images, blurred by speed and a narrowed field of vision. Then 2,000 feet below me is the Black Sea, signifying the end of this stunning ride, unquestionably the best road of the trip so far. This view will look great as a sunset. I slow the pace looking for somewhere to camp, but the road is dropping quickly and opportunities are few.

I stop dead because a truck has overturned, goods spread across the road. Within minutes, around another corner I come wheel to bumper with a crawling truck that is overtaking in my lane. This too could have been another dead stop, especially the way I've been riding.

I just stare at him. "What the fuck?" I'm not going to push my bike up hill and he can't back down; it's a Turkish standoff. He is so nonchalant, "You have blocked my path, but you could have blocked my future, damn you." I should say nothing; my face says it all. I can't help myself though..."and another thing!" I move onto the verge and squeeze past, then recompose myself; my throat hurts from my spontaneous yelling, I didn't do my Do-Re-Mi vocal warm up first; I hadn't even been talking to myself.

There is nowhere to camp, and the Black Sea is not looking so pretty close-up; the shore is just a rubbish dump, not discarded litter, but dumped refuse. Hopa is just a seaside town and not my scene, especially after the beauty I've just travelled through. I ride north along the coast up to the Georgian border, but other than dusty truck stops, there isn't anywhere to pitch a tent. I do a U-turn and ride along the water's edge hoping there must be somewhere on this strip, but it's inaccessible, rubbish strewn, or rocky. Reluctantly, I resort to the seaside hotel. The sun still sets, but the setting could have been stiller.

DAY 42

BATUMI, GEORGIA, 26 MILES

All I have to do today is cross a border. The first city I get to in Georgia is where I will stop and apply for my Azerbaijan visa. So I string out the morning as long as I can, which isn't nearly long enough. As with my entry into Iraq, this morning's crossing was sized up the day before. The difference is yesterday there weren't trucks parked in the unlit tunnel without lights on. There's always an obstacle waiting for the unobservant rider; with miles travelled will luck run out or will experience be gained and the unexpected less likely to surprise? Either way, I make it to the border where two Ukrainian bikers have just cleared into Turkey. I give them my phrase book, and I'm ashamed to say I've not learnt a single word. Phrase books, like cooking recipes, don't really help me; the words just blur on the pages, and nothing is understood or retained. Anyway, I can probably use my Russian words from now on: Hello, yes, no, beer, and thank you. Just the basics.

With high cliffs on one side and the sea on the other, it's a skinny little border crossing and nowhere really to go wrong. The pedestrians are processed on my right where there is a clear distinction in dress between the Georgians and the Turks; the Georgian ones are shorter. Flaunted eastern European beauty is back; modesty and discretion are left south of the frontier.

In less than an hour I'm free to ride a new country. No insurance needed, and the visa was stamped in automatically and for free. I spy the first and most welcome piece of architecture any overland border crosser wants to see, a concrete block on the side of the pavement which houses a cash machine; I get some Georgian lira and battle the honking traffic; the driving standards have not improved with the human aesthetic, only the distractions. But I like it. It's still got the Black Sea coast seaside town feeling, but the most noticeable difference is flesh, exposed bodies everywhere. I hadn't realised it was missing, but now it's back it's a bit shocking, I almost feel prudish at my reaction to what is blatantly displayed. Almost, but luckily I'm quite adaptable. So apart from that what else, I can't honestly say I noticed anything else; I mean the eye is drawn to beauty and once found why look away. With sex and money being so closely related, I notice that the fuel seems to be half the Turkish price.

The city of Batumi looms, but it's quite a simple city to negotiate, helped by two huge landmarks. There is a building similar in design to the Empire State Building but in a blue and white colour scheme. Unlike the one in New York, this one has, stuck in the side, three quarters of the way up, a London Eye-style big wheel that's outrageous. I think I like it; it's certainly striking. Next to it is a lattice framework 26 storeys high supporting an Epcot Center-like disco ball. God knows what its function is, but it's got attention-seeking intent. Apart from these garish modern structures, there are gold-top churches and Gothic architecture, big town squares and paved pedestrian areas. I find the Azerbaijan embassy easily. Now I just have to find somewhere to live.

I really like the feel of this city; it's Sunday quiet but not in a desolate way. I find a discreet little sign for a guesthouse and walk up several flights of stairs inside a housing block. I'm visualising squalid, but when the door opens I see light and clean, open and communal; this could work. I'm taken up more stairs to an attic room with low ceilings but spacious, fresh, and self-contained; yeah this is lovely. I haven't quite grasped the exchange rate yet, 150 Gel is the price. I say *Gel*, but it stands for *Georgian lira*. As I go back to my bike to get my passport I try to figure out the exchange rate. I make it $93; surely not, she must mean 15 Gel, but $9.30 is too cheap. Back up the stairs I have to clarify; yes it is $93 a night. I mean it's lovely and everything, but sorry, that's way beyond my means. She asks what I want to pay, "Err, $9.30?" I'm shown the door. I get a sinking feeling; what if this is the going rate? I have a guidebook, but it's 13 years old, so prices are not that relevant. I move on and find cheaper but without vacancies.

Like any other city, Batumi has its less glamorous outer edges with railway sidings, street markets, fast traffic, satellite dishes on rusty corrugated tin roofs, dirt alleys, and roaming dogs. It's a place where I belong, or at least where I can afford to belong. I have a little balcony that looks out on all of that, also the unaffordable beauty and extravagance that's still visible at a safe distance. Below I can see my covered bike chained to a lamp post, once again invisible to the constant procession of pedestrians and shoppers.

The place is asking to be explored, and I've viewed enough to know jeans and a T-shirt will have me looking like a local. I've barely got into my stride when I come to a giant beer barrel on wheels under a gazebo. Some chairs are scattered around; the price by the pump is 1 Gel, so I stop, I look, I calculate, I order. This draught pilsner even comes in a proper glass. In Turkey the beer is so expensive six cans equated to the price of a room; here I can get 50 pints for the price of my £18 room! I start with just two, though, then walk on. It's a city of contrast, a city of visual stimulation; it feels friendly. It's got history yet is contemporary; it's got beaches, religion, authority, and protest. It's got pleasant parks and arty structures; it's got clever lighting enhancing traditional designs; it's got Soviet housing blocks and glass and steel extravagance. It's got casinos and restaurants, multinational names and local business. But best of all, this variety is contained within a walkable area; compact and diverse. The afternoon turns to evening as I wander. The clouds come down from the mountains and hide the sunset, and as I walk home I pass an English theme pub. It's called The Quiet Woman. Not based on an Essex pub then?

DAY 43

BATUMI, GEORGIA, 0 MILES

It's visa day again. By all accounts it seems quite a straight-forward process. The condition Georgia imposes on this Azerbaijan consulate means it is the only Azerbaijan office in the world where a letter of invitation is not needed to get a visa, and that's why I'm here. Not that it's difficult to get a letter, but it's another expense, and this place was on my way. It's also issued in 24 hours. The tricky bit seems to be getting the 24 hours to start ticking.

I walk from my ghetto, down dirt streets to the more cultivated business part of the city. I have all my documentation in a carrier bag and present myself to the guard on the gate. He says, "10AM," which gives me half an hour to find some breakfast. When I get back he says, "11AM." This is fun, isn't it? I find an Internet café. It seems in this Russian influenced Caucasus state, along with physical beauty and drinking culture is the shitty rude abrupt attitude. Service is offered with misery and bloody mindedness. All I want to do is print out my Turkmenistan letter of invitation that has been emailed to me, and I need help. I can't make the computer print; they seem to have a different operation system here. I think it's Georgian Windows. The objective is finally achieved, but with maximum fuss and minimum ease. Back at the consulate I'm let in and given three-page forms in duplicate to fill in. This is going to take a while, and it's not going to be processed today. I may as well go and do it in my room.

Batumi has a lot more to offer to the wealthy visitor than it does to the tight git. Being the latter, I walk the streets only able to guess what wonderful luxuries lie behind the posh hotels, casinos, and enticing restaurants. However, it turns out disco ball and big wheel buildings are nothing more than a façade; the new government didn't want to continue to invest in the extravagant. Their exteriors were completed, but they remain empty and unused. If their construction was to encourage foreign investment then it worked; most hotels are financed by oil rich Kazakhs, but the Georgian properties remain vacant.

Having done as much looking as I can, I decide an afternoon snooze is in order, but it's not to be. A young lad and his translator come knocking at my door. The lad wants to buy my bike. He really likes it, and he's only seen the cover. Today there is no price in the world that would make me part with it. We are getting on just fine, and after four wonderful days' riding, the bond is strong. He couldn't have picked a less likely time in the trip to ask. Everything has a price. But what would I be doing if I wasn't doing this? Eating in posh restaurants?

Everything I read, (the *Lonely Planet*) and everything I've heard (my friend in Germany) leads me to believe Georgian wines are very good, so I buy a bottle. Maybe I chose a bad one. With such good inexpensive beer I'm reluctant to experiment much more. It's a rainy night in Batumi, so I stay in. My balcony rocks, well it does tonight with iPod and nasty wine; I sing out loud as I watch life go by, and it never stops.

Day 44

Pasanuri, Georgia, 250 Miles

I don't think it's real sleep when there is so much street noise outside and nasty wine inside. Trains shunt just 50 feet from my window, clearly the cause of my headache. I don't mind watching the trains when I'm awake, but when they pass they are so loud I'm unable to hear the barking dogs, car horns, and stomping on the stairs.

I'm not exactly sure when the consulate opens for visa collection, but I've got time to eat a hot cheesy pastry thing on my balcony and watch the day shift go past. Traders push their barrows of fresh fish and fruit beneath my balcony and are overtaken by ex-military Russian vans carrying what would be classed as scrap in most parts. It might be scrap here, however, I get the feeling renovation and repair offers more profit than recycling. Extreme gardening equipment is wheeled out of shops to be displayed on the pavement; machinery like rotorvators and a sort of two-wheeled rudimentary combine harvester, which looks a bit like Edward Scissorhands in a wheelbarrow race. A rickshaw chugs past a blind and tattooed beggar in a wheelchair—was he blinded after the tattoos I wonder? How much appreciation can a blind man get from a tattoo? Surely scarification or piercing would be better choices of body art. There is a strong presence of Ladas, and watching the horrendous driving makes getting out amongst them quite a daunting prospect. A mother stops on the railway tracks to burrow in her bag; her daughters are demanding something, must be something important. The rotorvator is causing a lot of interest; men are peering and prodding, whilst simultaneously relaying their findings down the phone. So next time I come, I'll bring a spare bike and a rotorvator; the objects of Georgian desire.

I can't eat my other cheesy pastry, so I put it in my cool box as I pack the bike. Now uncovered it's attracting attention but the agricultural machinery still wins the popularity stakes, I don't think I mind. Outside the consulate are several other Europeans: a Spaniard, an Italian and a French couple. We are all paying different amounts for our visas, but collectively we have an extensive knowledge of the current visa and border situation from here to China. It's impressive how informed we all are. Secondary to the visa debate, my bike is a popular topic. I look at it loaded with potential and credibility; it's not glamorous and extravagant like the city's architecture, but it's absolutely functional, and that puts it above the two highest buildings here.

One at a time we are ushered into the consulate. When it's my turn I see the same man I saw yesterday; he seems a bit happier today. I take a seat as he thumbs through my passport,

"Alone?" "Yes."

"Are you worried?" he asks.

"Err no, should I be?" I think he means am I worried about loneliness, not about the dangers of being alone.

"Entry point?"

"Oh, um, I don't know, well I do, I need a map though; I've forgotten the name."

"State?"

"I'm not sure; I need to look at my map."

"S'date, what date will you be entering?"

"Oh right, um, the fourteenth," I blurt out without any real consideration. I wasn't expecting the Azerbaijani inquisition. He sticks a big blue visa in my passport, writes on it, and hands it to me. I give him the money.

"This is too much."

"Do you have change?"

"No."

"Oh just keep the change," I say, and he looks at me like I've just offered a bribe, although I don't know what for. I'm asking for nothing more than I'm entitled to.

"It must be exact amount." I'm very flustered now. I go back out to the street, ask one of my fellow Europeans, get change, and breaking all protocol, I walk right past the guard and back into the office. My passport is handed to me with something that could just pass as a welcome. Only two more visas left to get and a GBAO permit, but now it's time to ride.

First stop is a petrol station, where strangely the attendant manages to get 25 litres into my 24 litre tank, and it's not even empty. Still, the stuff is cheap here, so it's not worth arguing about.

I can't make up my mind about this climate; there are pines and palms, there is coast and mountains, it's wet, it's sunny, it's dry, it's cold. However, these concerns are nothing compared to the worry about the traffic. They are utter bastards on the road. They will not stay behind me, although they can see there is something directly in front of me. My braking space is barged into, but on the way they take any breathing space from the side of me, they pass so close. It's totally unnecessary, infuriating, and antagonizing and takes any pleasure the road could offer, which isn't much under grey skies with intermittent rain. To add to this ride of discontent, my sense of smell is irritated too, by the black clouds of stinking diesel fumes pumped out of the old Russian trucks. Turning diesel into fog at the expense of momentum is a talent Russian trucks excel at. Much like how Harley-Davidson has achieved the turning of petrol into noise without the side effect of horsepower. This road brings back memories of riding to Sochi in Russia, and I realise that too was a Black Sea coastal road; it's just up from here.

I stop to put on more layers; it's raining constantly now. I'm impressed to see my cool box has kept my cheesy pastry thing warm, so I eat it just to get the taste of exhaust out of my mouth.

My map is a very large scale, so quicker than expected, I arrive at the road I want and turn off to a more peaceful pace and pleasurable surroundings. Now I don't have to look out for traffic, I can look around. In overgrown gardens there are frameworks supporting grapevines, hanging over rusty farm equipment. Every roof has a satellite dish. There are many pigs walking down the side of the road, with piglets in tow.

Funny the things you remember; another trademark of Russia was the water pipes. They run along the sides of the road, supported about 10 foot above the ground, bright yellow with right-angle bends to gain height over driveways and junctions. They are here too.

With precision timing, my mother calls just as I've stopped in a dismal town to get a coffee. She is at the DHL drop-off point with my speedo drive; they want £49 to post it to me. It's not a necessity, just a luxury, and depriving myself of such things is what keeps me on the road longer. I can ride without it.

Lots of people are selling their wares at the side of the road today. There are clay pots, then bread, and later hammocks. Communities don't seem to diversify in the products they manufacture; just one craft per village seems to be enough.

I'm rapidly approaching the capital, Tbilisi, but I don't want to go there, not yet, so I decide to ride up the (slightly legendary, depending on the circles you move in) Georgian Military Highway, a road built across the Caucasus Mountains to Russia. It's an easy decision to make, especially with my now extended stay in Georgia, as my Azerbaijan entry date is still four days away. That and my continuing endeavour to actually sleep in my tent.

Tehran is signposted from this highway, so Iran continues to tease me.

The motorway splits south to the capital and north to my road of choice. As I take the slip road, without warning, another road joins mine and has priority; the only indication of this is a dotted white line. I have a little weave to avoid a car, but I've been doing that all day. Instantly there are sirens, and I'm pulled. Bollocks. Of course, we can't communicate; we don't have to; this game is played around the world, and the rules are universally understood.

My documents are taken back to the car, and I'm left sitting on my bike. I watch a big black cloud come towards me, its contents bouncing off the road. Even though I'm stationary, a heavy rain storm comes to meet me. I just sit there, exposed, unable to move to shelter; I'm feeling a bit pissed off, truth be told. The policeman waits until I'm drenched before bringing me my documents back.

He gives me a proper, legitimate ticket, which is refreshing, that and the soaking I just got. It's hard to keep a smile in such circumstances but even harder to imagine why someone would still be smiling, and that is how I get my twisted little victory from the situation. The fact that I didn't give way is, of course, a façade, much like the landmark buildings in Batumi. I'm the slowest and most careful driver on these roads. What's strange, though, is that no bribe was requested; it just seems wrong.

Well that's put a bit of a damper on the camping potential, however, the road ahead is dry, and as the sun reappears, there is a ruined fort by a large lake. Just as I'm reconsidering the whole camping thing the rain comes again. I'm hungry, and the day is getting on. There is something promising ahead, so I pull over. Before I've quite figured out if it's accommodation, building site, or restaurant, a very large strong drunk man pours vodka down my neck. Then to keep it down insists I eat a cold dumpling. Yum. When I get away from his forceful friendship, I'm shown a room and the restaurant. It's only a little wooden shack of a place, but it's got a homely family feel, so I make my reservation in what appears to be the only room.

Is no one else feeling cold? Everyone else is in shorts and T-shirts, yet here I am in a fleece and scarf and still shivering; they're a hard race of vodka drinkers, and I'm nothing but sodden prey for the police. I get some hot soup and dead animal parts. I'm too cold to drink cold beer. I think I've eaten too early, because the place livens up when I'm drifting off to sleep. The laughter of drunk and hysterical Russian women rattles the windows. The image I have of them is not sexy and giggly, more haggard and wrinkly, challenged by gravity and drinking to escape the reality of their years. This makes last night's trains seem preferable. When they have had their fill, and the vodka bottle is dry, the soothing sound of a running river replaces their babblings.

Day 45

Tbilisi, Georgia, 146 Miles

I'm still cold, and I've got no money, as annoyingly I've allowed myself to run out of local currency. Thankfully the US dollar is accepted even in places as remote as this; don't leave home without it. I exchange what I have for what I got, and with the change I buy breakfast, or beef soup, but being the first meal of the day, by definition it is breakfast.

I wonder if I should continue to go up the Georgian Military Highway, what with me being cold and skint 'n all. This is why I am here; I may as well, and if I run out of fuel I can just freewheel back down. I'm given some chocolate as I leave; it's little gestures like that, and the vodka too I suppose, that put a smile on the face of the lone long distance traveller. The smile lasts for 2.5 kms, until I realise my phone's still on charge in my room. I turn around and do it all again but don't get any chocolate the second time.

I've got a lot of clothes on this morning; my optimism stretches further than I can see, and I hope the road will lead me up above this cloud cover. It's possible; aeroplanes do it all the time. As my tongue pries at stringy beef trapped between overlapping teeth, the result of this wet weather is revealed in white waterfalls against lush green hills. The occasional reclusive house sits at the junction where the vertical descent of water joins a free flowing flatter river.

I come to a monument that looks like a one storey colosseum. There is no roof, and it has murals painted on the inside. It was built to signify unity, a gesture of Georgian/Soviet friendship. It's basically a viewing platform, but for me it's a place to park and fiddle with my USB charger that isn't working. It's not the ideal place for solitary electrical repairs, and soon I'm approached by a heavy handed but well-meaning local. A man of weathered skin and good intentions, he stabs my Swiss army knife into the dodgy Turkish charger in an attempt to split it apart.

"Easy, easy, e . . . " the charger catapults open, and the contents fly. If you could just give it back to me now before all hope of repair is lost . . .

Up comes a small but high 4x4 Austrian-registered van. A bearded, older and wiser gentleman gets out. He looks at the situation, and in English we discuss the possibilities, if only we could get the charger back in my possession. It turns out he saw me yesterday whilst I was "getting directions" from the police. Then this morning he passed my bike parked outside my room, so this meeting for him was not entirely unexpected. He too is a lone traveller, and I think, like me, has been travelling more alone than he would prefer. The telltale signs are every time the conversation stops and we say goodbye, neither one of us leave, then another conversation starts up. He too has a Russian visa in his passport, however, his is valid now, so he can actually cross the border; my entry date is weeks away. As we chat, what few sightseers were on the platform of friendship have left, along with the clouds that cramped the view. Having the place to ourselves, we move our vehicles into position for "been there" photographs. Indulging in the luxury of no self-timer or tripod, we hand our cameras to each other and pose proudly by our vehicles. After what I thought was our last goodbye, my new and lonely Austrian friend returns to my bike, this time with a quality little USB charger. "A gift from Austria," he says; "Road karma."

It may be free but it charges, so it's goodbye but with a good connection. I was OK, but now I'm better. I hope the Ukrainian bikers I gave my Turkish phrase book to get as much use out of it as I will from this charger. The road surface deteriorates; it's muddy and rutted. I cross streams and then rivers and pass by waterfalls; despite this my water bottle is empty. The road takes me into a curved and unlit tunnel. It's absolutely black, my eyes won't adjust, and it feels as if my lights are not working. I can't see the light at the end of it; I can't see anything. I have to stop. I put my hand in front of my headlight, and yes, it's still there; I can see my fingers, phew. I creep forward; the road is at least paved in here. Damp and dripping, it's a cavernous vacuum of vision. Without knowing it, I round the corner within and daylight shines on the far wall. That was intense. I like that stuff, though, the unexpected challenges, the assumption that roads are open and passable, that if it's mapped it must be driveable when actually weather conditions and choice of transport dictate the possibilities of passage.

I'm up into the dirty stubborn snow now. As disappointing as a seaside town in winter, midsummer snow has no appeal, but the road does, it's got defiance and rewards for the perseverance. There is the modern, an ATM and petrol station; the old, a fourteenth century church and other ancient architecture; and then there is the natural, spectacular Mount Kezbek and its surrounding national park. All accessible and visible from a road that enhances my experience based on my choice of vehicle. It could be warmer; it could be sunnier. However, on this rare occasion, I think the broken cloud and colourless sky keep the eye drawn to what little colour the landscape offers. There are no little girls in red coats, but the subtle colours of brown cows, terracotta tiles, and the rust of corrugated iron all glow like rainbows in their subdued surroundings. I pass through little farming villages and bigger towns, scraping a living from a yet to boom tourist industry. It's a road of variety in surfaces, services, and scenery. The miles pass slowly but without monotony.

When I stop for supplies I hear Boney M is being played, there are still certain countries around the world where their music never died, man I'd love one of their royalty cheques. The road is paved again and I take it all the way to the Russian border. It was well worth the ride, this is a U-turn I'm happy to do, it was my pleasure, here I come again.

I stop for lunch, looking down a valley at a herder leading his cows through a river. My field of vision takes in the sky and snowy mountains, the grassy hillsides, and here in the foreground, my grey dirt-covered boots. With the sole flapping and torn duct tape somehow they have more beauty than the shiniest shoe in the shop. I wave at the Austrian as he continues his four-wheel-drive journey into Russia. Now I'm ready for Tbilisi.

Back at the junction of entrapment, I stop to look at what other drivers do. In fact, I film the traffic on my phone. I even capture an ambulance that had right of way and lights flashing having to slow for a truck that, like me, didn't give way at the dotted lines. For the sake of a £20 ticket it's not worth the protest; it's just to reassure myself that the only thing I got wrong at that junction was the time I was there.

I take off some clothes to prepare myself for the inner city hotel search. It's a scenic entrance; the road drops down to run alongside a river. I'm wondering if *centre* has a different meaning in Georgia, because although I'm following the signs, the road seems to be taking me around the outside. I take the initiative, cross over the river, go up a steep hill, and see a hotel. It's close enough to what feels like the centre, and since I have stumbled across it so easily with no sweat or contact with the merciless traffic, I think it's worth the extra few quid. I pull my bike up onto the pavement next to the entrance and chain it to the railings, as instructed by the two gorgeous young receptionists, who have nothing to do with my decision to stay here. Once I'm all moved in, I show them the ticket I got from the police yesterday. They point me across the street to the railway station. Inside is a bank and a sort of ATM that does everything from phone top-ups to electric bill payment. There is also an icon to pay your police fine. It would be so much easier if I could just read it. I'm helped every step of the way by a pretty bank employee. It seems I can't pay the fine until three days have passed since its issue. A nearby policeman confirms this. "But I'll be gone by then." I can go to the main police station to pay it, but that's miles away; the whole point of getting this hotel is to avoid riding around the city. On the plus side, the ATM offers US dollars as a choice of currency, so I top up my supplies, as I will need them in Turkmenistan and Uzbekistan.

Because I'm on a hill, I soon find a place where I can look down over the river. Wow, this city is like the Georgian Military Highway; it has a bit of everything. There is the modern in the form of large pedestrian areas with fountains and strange glass structures, play areas and dramatic bridges crossing the river to the older, more established and traditional part of town where there are cobbled narrow alleyways and large streets with decadent buildings. To the west of the city the orange evening sky is silhouetting old churches on the hill tops, but above that the one big thing, the absolutely undeniable beauty, is in the city dwellers themselves. It's like every street is a cat walk; the girls are absolutely beautiful. Their height, their figure, the way they dress, and wear their hair, I'm in awe. I first thought Rio de Janeiro was the city of the most beautiful women in the world, then in Vietnam I had to rethink my ratings, and again in Odessa I'd never seen such consistency in attractiveness. Now, here in Tbilisi, straight in at number one is a city of jaw-dropping beauty. I sit at a pavement café and feast my eyes. The white stilettos and muffin bellies that cuss their way round Essex town centres at night don't touch this refined elegance.

I've been noticing this summer, since Turkey, that red and white seem to be popular colours to wear; these are the colours of both the Turkish and Georgian flags, but I don't know if it's significant or just fashion. Also the Union Jack is popular on T-shirts and jumpers. A legacy of our Olympics last year or just a really cool design? I always see it as a friendly and smiley flag; just to be used for special occasions, much like the phrase *I love you.* The ultimate three words which, particularly in America, seem to be a substitute for goodbye. Pretty soon by over-use their currency is devalued and lack meaning and sincerity. I wander back through the pedestrian area and notice the fountains are not only musical, they also light up. The big one is approaching its grand finale; as water spurts in various directions the classical music reaches its crescendo. Just as I think the peak is reached, the music flawlessly turns into *Land of Hope and Glory.* When I realise which song is playing I laugh out loud, and several people look at me sternly.

"What? It's my song, not yours.'

Swallows swoop to catch the bugs in the last of the light, and I go back to my room. The hot water tank in the bathroom is about to blow; the water comes gushing out the tap under such pressure that rubber seals blow out with it. The room fills with steam. The reception girls, although a little suspicious, come into my room to see what I'm trying to explain, and I give them a demonstration of the danger of such unreleased pressure. Then I show them the debris that was forced through the tap. The power is turned off; they apologise for the inconvenience, the lack of alternative, and then continue to express their sorrow for the whole incident with the police and my ticket. The heat, the pressure, and the cause is cured, I'm left to chill. Good night Tbilisi, "I love you."

DAY 46

LAGODEKHI, GEORGIA, 167 MILES

I can't get to sleep; I just can't sleep. The hours pass; active mind, pointless thoughts, and still no sleep. Dawn appears through my window, and just as I consider going out to photograph the sunrise, I fall asleep, and then it's 7:30.

I notice from my guidebook I've missed an area of glaciers and mountains, but I console myself with the thought that Tajikistan will provide me with all of that and more, and it's getting closer every day.

I go back to the stunning sights of the old city and sit at a street café, nursing a coffee and watching all the pedestrians who clearly got their beauty sleep last night. My reception girls are keen for me to vacate my room, and that helps with the "should I stay or should I go now" dilemma. I try again to pay my police fine, but the machine will not acknowledge my number. I'm about to become a fugitive.

When I uncover my bike I see again that I've left my ignition key in it; where is my concentration? This is ultimate proof I'm not living in the moment; it screams distraction.

I'm pretty sure I know my way out of this city. I head out on narrow easterly roads that take me over tram tracks and through the poorer, working side of town then to a lake and up to a monument; this isn't right. I stop to take in the view and realise that at some point yesterday I lost my bandanna. The one day I am cold enough to need a scarf, and the bandanna, which is permanently round my neck and over my mouth for wasp and dust protection, has been left somewhere. I do that thing when I just can't believe something is not there and repeatedly look in the same places for it.

I just can't find a main road in the direction I want. I try to get some oil, but the only motorcycle oil is fully synthetic and outrageously expensive. My bike isn't used to such refinement and quality; it would be like me eating fresh fruit, my body wouldn't know what hit it.

The frustration and wrong directions continue. It's not that big a city, it can't be, because I keep coming across the same sites, I just can't get out on an easterly road. There are mountains to the north and south of me, and the sun is overhead, I'm losing my sense of direction, and the signs are of no help at all.

I find a bypass that's potholed and full of trucks. It's elevated, and three hours after I left my room, I find the road I want. It's so tiring, especially after a sleepless night. I stop for a snack as it's 3PM already.

That was utter shit. Again I search for my bandanna; its loss along with the loss of sleep and the infuriating inability to exit the city has taken the mojo away again. The mountains too have disappeared from view, and the road winds down very slowly to hotter temperatures. I'm going through the wine region, but not being a connoisseur, to me it's nothing more than fields of vines and less dramatic scenery. I pass through one village after another, none of which are noteworthy; they just make my progress slow and tiring.

Despite the lack of inspiration I have something to say into my voice recorder, but it slips from my hand. I brake and turn my head as it skids to a halt in the middle of the road. I quickly do a U-turn and ride back to it. Hastily I put the bike on its side stand but have to wait for a car to pass. One of the big fat destructive tyres of this black 4x4 makes contact, and it explodes into pieces, four pieces; the two batteries, the cover, and the recorder. I gather it all up, put it back together, and the screen lights up; it's alive. It's got a few new scars, but it still functions. Now I've got something to talk about into it.

Yesterday's thrills have not spilled over into today, and the tiny challenges the day brings are chores with no achievement. I'm sure I reflect the way I feel, because the reaction to my trying to find oil, for example, is not met with helpful suggestions, just indifference at my pickiness.

I vaguely know what to expect in the various 'Stans: camels and plains, mosques and mountains, culture and architecture, man-made disasters and nature at its most spectacular. However, what I'm dwelling on is the visa complications, the unreliable ferry across the Caspian Sea, the thorough customs procedure crossing into Uzbekistan, the heat of the summertime plains, the expense of the transportation documents, and the confirmed unknowns and delays from the ever-changing protocols. I've let the naysayers' negativity get to me, and I don't like where it's leading.

This road is leading me down to the plains; the heat is becoming uncomfortable again. I'm tired of trying to get motorcycle oil, and in the end I just buy car oil. Anything is better than nothing. A German cyclist is having his bike repaired at the village garage where I stop, but he is preoccupied, keeping an eye on the mechanic. I fully understand; I would do the same, especially after yesterday's repair incident. I top up the engine oil and pour the rest into my oil bottle strapped onto the pannier. I take out the little reversible and retractable spout to do this and fail to replace it.

Georgia is not a large country. From the Black Sea coast to the Azerbaijan border it is less than 300 miles. That's the same distance from my home in Essex to West Wales. It's only the slow back roads that make it seem big. At this reasonable pace, even with my constant circling of the city, I seem to have reached the country's eastern limits. There is a camping sign in the border town, but I can't find the site so ask a policeman, who has been eyeing me suspiciously as I've ridden up and down. He misunderstands and points me to a guesthouse. It's friendly, it's welcoming, and is family run. The daughter speaks some English and tells me her mother is called Madonna, a name not easily forgotten. I'm shown to a hot but clean room, and my bike is safely stored undercover behind big gates.

When Madonna summons me down for dinner, I follow her to a table-for-one beside my bike. It has been set with ten different dishes; from cold pizza to coleslaw and all kinds of fruits and cheeses, even a plate of chips and a glass of wine. It's not so much a meal, more like a celebration. Well I am on holiday.

DAY 47

SHEKI, AZERBAIJAN, 94 MILES

The morning's breakfast is eggs accompanied by all the things I didn't eat last night, which, I think, was what didn't get eaten the night before that. Today is Friday; next Thursday my guided tour of Turkmenistan starts. I still need to get my visa from the embassy in Baku, the city on the Caspian Sea, which is also where the ferry leaves from. Baku is 250 miles away; the embassy only opens for visa processing on Mondays and Fridays, if I get there today and there is a problem I still have Monday to sort things out before my ferry leaves, assuming there is even a ferry on Wednesday night or that it will sail. Delays of up to 24 hours are common. I could just ride the 250 miles straight to the embassy, but I will see nothing of the country, which is today's dilemma.

As soon as I leave town there is a sign that says, "Azerbaijan Border Good Luck." Humm, do I need good luck to cross it or once I have? It's an ambiguous little statement. At the Georgian side I hand over my passport and concentrate hard on the reactions of the officer as he scans it. Sure enough, the computers have connected; he is alerted to my unpaid fine but points to a single window in a small building, and there if I want, I can pay it; the choice is mine. Seems like an opportunity worth taking, just to clear my name; maybe I'll be back someday.

The Azerbaijan side is very friendly; at least five officials greet me and welcome me to their country, but processing is slow. It's as if I'm the first foreign motorcycle in the history of Azerbaijan ever to cross this border, but eventually I have a stamp that says, "30 days," next to the visa in my passport, and off I go. I have no money, little fuel, and there are absolutely no signs of life on the road of this, my thirteenth country so far this trip. There is no first impression; there is no impression to have. The road is adequate, there is a slight embankment each side, and nothing else remarkable. No people, no cars, no buildings, no animals, no view, not even a signpost.

Around a dull corner in the bland terrain is a very exciting petrol station. The attendants are thrilled to see me, I'm happy to be here, and when we establish a currency they will accept, they fill my tank, take my euros, and give me change in local currency.

I'm not going to get right across the country today; it's pointless to try, I'll just use the weekend to slowly see what is on my way. I ride through a town and spot a carefully hidden ATM; I buy some bread and, once again, am dependent on nothing and no one. But I can't retain perspective when there is no communication, and I'm lacking motivation again.

This mood is spiralling out of control now. I stop in a bus shelter and tell myself it's for shade, but it could just be to hide. Wearily I get out the guidebook. It says the town I was heading for is a popular place for the city's inhabitants to come at weekends. Brilliant; so I'm both disheartened by my isolation and depressed by the promise of populace. Cars hoot when they see my bike, and I'm not reacting. I make no eye contact, and when I lift my gaze from the guidebook it's only to bury my low self-esteem back inside my helmet. With a now undesirable destination and the bonus time these extended midsummer days gift me, I opt for a slow and meandering back road. The surface is potholed, and the concentration needed conspires to steer my thoughts away from where they were going.

There is a theme of whitewashed walls; they have random black shapes painted on them like a Friesian cow. The effect is meant to look like stonework, but it doesn't work.

The road condition is so bad it has the traffic crossing from one side to another to avoid the potholes. I play chicken with the oncoming cars, as right of way means nothing here. Might and attitude determine who gives way. The hardest bastard wins, and today I really don't give a shit.

When I get to Sheki I wonder what the attraction is. I ride up a dirt road in the hope of a wild camping space, but it ends in a horrendous holiday resort. I try another one alongside a river into a village of cobbled streets. It's almost OK but somehow has a feeling of inbred intrigue and unwanted attention. I go back to the town. The problem with these long summer days is it takes wild camp opportunities away; how can I tuck myself away in a hidden knoll at dusk when dawn is only a few hours away? Back in the town I see a motor parts shop and try again for oil. Instead I get a sticker and am given a key ring. It's the first real contact I've had with an Azerbaijani, and it's really quite pleasant.

Although I was hoping for a spot in the cooler mountains for some peaceful and scenic camping, once again I opt for a hotel; no point in going further, I have more time than I need to get to Baku.

Twisting my throttle, I failed to notice how far uphill I had come, and taking an evening stroll down to the town is a long descent. My tummy is grumbling, and the need for a toilet is becoming quite urgent. I see an open-air restaurant full of locals, and though my usual purposeful stride has changed, there is still haste. With clenched cheeks and knees together it's a walk of prevention, overcoming a debilitating bowel. The toilet block is little more than a hut: it has a single squat toilet, there is no toilet paper, there is no running water, there is no more time, there is no choice.

The euphoric relief is brief; now what? I contemplate a sock and look at my feet. They are uncovered; I'm wearing sandals. I'm in solitary confinement; I have to consider basic instinct over toilet training. To wipe or not to wipe; how much is this smallest denomination note worth? It's worth at least a beer, so a decision is made. I use my hand, walk swiftly to a nice bar, wash rigorously, and order a big cold beer. "Good luck," the sign said this morning. I think I make my own, I'm just not sure how good I am at doing it.

DAY 48

A FOREST NEAR ISMAYILLY, AZERBAIJAN, 94 MILES

There are some picturesque views from here, but like a picture, the scene cannot be experienced because the best of the Caucasus mountains are on the Russian side of the border. Their refreshing snow-capped beauty can only be admired from a distance. Like seeing an ice cream van from a traffic jam, I can only imagine now much cooler that locality would be.

My engine doesn't need ice cream to cool it down, a night undercover on the street is enough, so this morning I check the oil level. When I go to top it up, I realise the little red Touratech funnel must still be in Georgia. I don't use it generally, but it has the O-ring seal that the screw top tightens to. One of the few bits of designer equipment I have now has a bit of plastic bag clamped round the cap. The gardener of this little complex has been watching attentively, enthusiastically, and respectfully. When I pull away he clasps his hands above his head in a "champion" kind of pose, and his smile spreads onto my face.

Last night I noticed an artisan market selling scarves. I need something to replace my bandanna; it would be functional and have souvenir value, as well as supporting the local creative types. There are several people loitering around outside the building, so I deliberately park my bike in their view, hoping they are not a conglomerate of thieves. I go through the double doors into a large ground floor room of silk sheets, sarongs, and sculptures. Ineffective mood lighting does not compensate for the dark walls and obscured windows; it would better suit a night club than a place of creative display. The scarves are the size of table cloths and the table cloths the size of curtains. I don't want plain black, it will be too hot, nor white, as it will show the dirt. There isn't much in the way of patterns. I seem to be trying the patience of the sales girl. So quicker than I'd like, I opt for a white one with a purple border. Leaving empty handed is clearly not an option. As would be expected in such an establishment the goods are wrapped meticulously. I throw the package in my tank box, and I head out of town. On the main road I pass a couple of European looking cyclists, and shortly after I pull over in the shade of a large bus shelter type thing. I unwrap my scarf, and in the clear light of day the edging is not purple at all, its bloody pink.

The cyclists catch up with me. They are a Swedish couple. We chat for an hour. They show me their Kindle; it has all sorts of guidebooks on it and is only wafer thin. The space I could save with one of those, but how useful would it be if it had got soaked like my maps? The Swedes camp constantly, and local interaction is the high point of their journey. I'm quite envious. I know that the company of hospitable strangers is what turns a place name into a memory; I just don't seem to be making the connections. However, this bit of Swedish interaction is a good start, if only I didn't have a pink scarf on.

The day is hot, but the road is shaded by tall trees on both sides. Today there are a lot of smiles and waves of encouragement from the roadside; everybody seems to want to be me. I'm not sure if I do or not. The road takes me through a heavily forested area, which is ideal camping territory, but it's still so early. The forest is too good an opportunity to miss, so when I reach the next town I load up with supplies from a shop that seems to specialise in open boxes of biscuits. I get a two-litre bottle of beer, because biscuits make you thirsty. Back in the forest I ride off-road looking for the ideal spot and remember how much I've missed this. On my third attempt I find the pitching paradise, lean the bike against a tree, and go scout about; actually it's better over there, so I get the bike and bring it over. With a bit of bark under the side stand, I wander off deeper into the forest, just in case there happens to be a stream nearby that would make for an even more perfect spot. The best I can find are deep rutted tracks of puddles and mozzies, so I stick where I am. Its 4PM. I open my beer; there's no point in letting it get warm.

I have a good friend at home who, it could be said, drinks more than he needs to. Many evenings have been spent in his company as he repeatedly pours wine from the bottle into a tiny glass receptacle—his drinking glass. It's not impractical, it's his exercise. I took him daffodils before I left the UK, as I'm not sure I will ever see him again. Drinking alone in a forest in Azerbaijan, pouring beer from a large bottle into my ceramic cup makes me think of him, and I send a text.

Back in about '98, I received my first text message on the LCD screen of my king size phone. My first reaction was, "How rude and impersonal. Don't you want to talk to me?" They hadn't invented smilies back then. However, like everyone else, I came to see the advantage of directness over time-wasting pleasantries and unnecessary conversation. In situations such as wild camping in forests in Azerbaijan, I think it's the ideal form of contact.

I discover in a gonzo style of research what a lone overlander does hidden in a forest once alcohol is consumed, when no one is watching. Alone with his thoughts and needs, his questions and reflections, his experiences and explanations, there is only really one true recreational act: he puts stickers on his panniers.

When my beer is all gone and my biscuits lose their appeal, I recall seeing a sign for a restaurant not so far from here. I've done a lot of stupid things in my life, but I decide to leave all my valuables locked and unattended and walk in a straightish line to the road, in the hope that any landmark trees will stick in my mind and not my eye. What could possibly go wrong?

There is a parked car at the side of the road. It's police with a speed gun, and being confidently intoxicated, I casually walk past putting a finger to my lips in a "sushhhh" manner and keep on walking. I have a big fat smile on my face, but their eyes don't burn deep enough into the back of my head to see it.

Sure enough, there is a restaurant; it has outside dining around a man-made lake that looks as if raw sewage is being pumped in. I eat a meaty kebab as mozzies feast on me. It was worth the effort.

I decide to take an alternative route back to avoid the police car. I do the diagonal, and miraculously find my bike and everything still intact.

For the first time in over a week I get the tent out, and as I put it up cows walk past. I'm not sure they see me. It's a peaceful place; fungi grows as the low sun makes shadows across the forest floor, the sound of traffic lessens, and dogs howl in the distance. A quarter moon casts a shadow, and when it's gone there is nothing but total blackness.

DAY 49

BAKU, AZERBAIJAN, 117 MILES

Man, did those dogs howl last night. The best thing about wild-camping in a place like this, apart from the money saved, is the sense of relief when the dawn arrives. My bike is standing in the sunshine, so I drape my sleeping bag over it and walk to the mozzie infested puddle to get some water to boil my eggs. Obviously, I have to boil the water first; the puddle isn't the result of some underground thermal activity. All packed up, I ride out of the forest, just like Robin Hood would, if he needed to procure his merry Turkmen visa like I do.

One of the more noticeable differences from the road having crossed into Azerbaijan is the lack of litter compared to other countries I've come through. It's not difficult to thoughtfully dispose of your rubbish, but a lot of countries don't have that thought in the first place. It can feel strange packing up your rubbish and taking it with you when all around is broken glass and discarded plastic. I like to take away one extra bottle, therefore leaving the place better than I found it There may be litter all around, but at least I know it's not mine.

The road winds down to a wide dry riverbed of grey stone and then up the other side of the valley. Yesterday the informed Swedish cyclists had mentioned this arduous ascent; they were going to try and avoid it. I avoid it, well, certainly the arduous part. With a few gear changes I'm effortlessly up the other side. Bicycles with engines; it's the way forward.

The road falls to Caspian Sea level. The grass is dry and brown, and the fields are being harvested. The dust clouds from the combines hang in the air; the pink of my scarf is toning down particularly around my mouth. Now I'm out of the forest I can't see a single tree; everything around me is exposed on this flat arid land. From one horizon to another there is no shade from the unrelenting sun. No shade means there is nowhere to stop. I'm thirsty, my bum is aching, and I really need a wee.

Some extravagant wealth is becoming evident in the architecture and vehicles. Large shiny 4x4s are passing me, along with the beaten-up rusty Ladas. Everything passes me; I'm quite used to it. This country has the cheapest fuel of the entire trip, and I'm able to cross it on a tank full. It almost makes me wish the fuel was more expensive or the country bigger. The land starts to become more built up. On one side of the road is a large soviet housing block with a satellite dish on every balcony; opposite is a new black apartment building. They have a better quality of laundry hanging from their verandas. There has been nowhere to stop and relieve myself, and now I'm in the city outskirts; the roads are wide, fast, and busy. I figure if I keep heading east I will come to the coast, and then I can think about finding a room. It's so clean, so affluent, so hot. I find myself in the business area; the shade of the tall buildings is a relief, but this is not a place of accommodation. I head on to the coastal road, slower than I want to. The bike is dragging; it comes to a halt in the mall of the city hall. My back brake has seized on.

Here in this baking city of impatient traffic, bursting for a piss, I have a bike I can't even push. I try to pry the pads apart, and in desperation I spray WD40 onto the disc. It smokes, but I don't care. A taxi driver has been watching me, I ask if there is a cheap hotel somewhere. He says a name that usually I would forget instantly, but I write it down; "Araz Hotel." He says it's $10 a night. It's down this coastal road then left, apparently. It's a little vague but worth a try.

My back wheel is moving, but the traffic isn't. There are no gaps to filter through, and the heat shimmers off the shiny paintwork of the stationary air-conditioned cars. I try to go down the centre, but oncoming cars come at me fast and unforgiving. It seems too dangerous to ride and too hot not to. I go inland and through one-way systems of unsigned junctions. At least with the sea on my right I can keep my sense of direction. I've come a long way south from where I entered the city and still not seen a single hotel. I've come past the dock area where somewhere beyond the gates are the offices I will need to find later. A main road goes inland, and I see my first hotel in the city, and it says, "Araz;" what are the chances? But it's not $10; it's significantly more. It will do for now, this is not the time of day to be looking around. The bike is safe and breakfast is included, that's good enough for me.

Baku doesn't seem to have an arse end; in fact, it has no end at all. This part where I am has a newly constructed Trump Tower. In Vegas it would look quite classy, here it's just ostentatious. All of this is a very long way from anything that might be the old city where the real architectural attractions are. I know all this because it's been Wi-Fi in my room research time; the embassies I need are spread around the city. There are two addresses for the Turkmen embassy, and there are also two possible ferry ticket offices, depending on which part of the docks the ferry to Turkmenistan departs from. If there is a ferry at all, and assuming it even wants to depart, there is no system to determine any of this in advance. I only have tomorrow to get my visa, and it's imperative to the rest of the journey.

I can see the future. I see a . . . a cab ride.

DAY 50

BAKU, AZERBAIJAN, ONLY TAXI MILES

The walk to the all-inclusive breakfast takes me past my bike, where kittens are playing, so I bring them back some of the breakfast that wasn't included. We make friends. Mum sees I'm not a threat and gives her consent to her offspring to take food from this stranger. This is much more appealing than the thought of visa application.

I decline the invitation of the taxi outside the hotel; I have a city map and walk the Monday manic streets. This city was not built for pedestrian traffic, and I have to run across multi-lane roads, but I find the place I'd pin-pointed as the embassy. It has flags, high walls with coiled barbed-wire on top, but no door. I show my map to a uniformed man nearby who stops a taxi. The driver will take me to the other Turkmenistan embassy, the new one, the one that's open. His driving is horrendous; he stops in the middle of the road, checks the map, and lane changes without so much as a glance. He really does drive like he is the only car on the road. All the time music blares from inadequate speakers. He stops at green lights, then reverses to missed junctions. I'm just beginning to contemplate getting out, when as if by complete surprise, he points at the Turkmenistan flag.

"You found it!" He revels in my joy and surprise. "It's ok, don't wait, I may be some time."

This one has a door, so that's promising, but annoyingly, I'm not allowed in it. The guards show me a bench and, after some time, escort me up some steps and into the room of authorized entry document application and acceptance. There are a couple of other people loitering inside. I'm approached by a smartly dressed member of staff. Yes, he speaks English; yes, they have probably received my letter of invitation, and yes, processing will be done on the same day . . . but

174

not this day. It is a government holiday in Baku today, and all the banks are closed, therefore I cannot pay the visa fee into their designated bank. He promises, however, that he personally will deal with my request promptly and efficiently when I come back on Friday.

"No, but . . . "

There is nothing he hasn't heard before; no excuse, no deadline, no pleading, no cash bonus incentive, no sob story, and no inflexible schedule. The way he says it is the way it is and that's all, all that there is to it.

Well that's fucked it. Even if I got my visa and there was a ferry on Friday night I would still arrive two days later than expected. My guide is kept on a retainer, which was made clear; he's obviously wasted too much of his time waiting for unreliable ferries. I will have to change the entry date on the Uzbekistan visa that I'm yet to collect. I will also have to stay in this expensive city for at least another four nights. I have a horrible sinking feeling. I lack desire, incentive, and energy. I don't want to deal with this, any of it. I've had enough. I can't face any more bureaucratic hurdles, not to mention the costs involved in this delayed, altered, and rescheduled itinerary.

I should be freaking out but I'm not, I'm just numb; I can't make any more alternate plans, I'm all planned-out. I walk back to the hotel. I email my man at Stan Tours who has arranged all this for me so far. It's been hard, really hard. The mojo has been tenuous, and now it's just dead. I'm very aware that I sound like a whingeing little motherfucker. The problem is I don't really expect anyone to have the slightest sympathy for my predicament, when I'm out here living their dream.

I have one friend who has first-hand understanding of what it's like to have unused visas in her passport and whose advice I value. I draft a letter to her, but it's so depressing I don't send it.

Hi. Well I've made it to Baku, and so starts the beginning of the end of the visa application process . . . So the question is do I spend the next five days in this very expensive city or not?

My heart is not in the trip. I keep saying, "Give it another week, give it one more week," but it's been seven weeks now, and I don't think it's going to change. I keep reading posts from fellow bikers on their various journeys around the planet, particularly the ones in this area, and they are all so wowed by it. I'm not getting that; the things that have them in awe leave me cold. Somehow the feeling of annoyance and disappointment at not getting my visas this morning are not that big; I just think it's a great excuse to give up and turn round. It's very expensive, this next bit, and I see no point in spending money whilst I'm not getting the feeling. It's not exactly inspiring behaviour, but I'm doing this trip for me, and I don't want to do it any more.

I don't know what lies ahead, but I know myself and there is no point in continuing whilst I feel this way. I'm feeling burnt-out and tired, uninspired and unenthusiastic. I pass through nearby "sites of interest" not even stopping or diverting. So I have to ask myself if I'm not interested then why the fuck am I here at all? So many people would love to be doing what I'm doing. But I'm not living their dream; I'm living mine, and I'm not dreaming of this.

The main reason I write this is to sort it out in my own head. It's not like I have somewhere to go, still homeless till September. I've been homeless and nomadic for five months, and it's exhausting. I haven't slept in the same place for more than a week. I think I just might go back.

It feels like a bit of a relief to decide to stop. I've been struggling with this reluctant progress east for so long, and other than eastern Turkey, which was incredible every day, it's all been one long stream of indecision and lack of appreciation.

This is only a Word document; it's not an email unless I send it. There is nothing like mechanical meditation to clear the head, be it a broken relationship, terrible loss, or aborted mission. I sit myself down by my bike and dismantle the rear brake calliper. My little show attracts an audience, but it's not really a spectator sport, and having my shoulder looked over never increased my ability to do anything. A Swiss woman approaches me and says she and her husband saw me in Sheki.

"Oh right, are you on a tour?" She points at a four wheel drive in the car park I hadn't even noticed. "Aha, a Land Rover."

"No it's a Land Cruiser," she corrects. Some people are so picky about second names: land-rover, -cruiser, -slide, -mine; what's the difference? They all block roads. Anyway, she says her husband might have some tools to help me. Later a bearded older man turns up, who seems friendlier than she was, but then I haven't offended him by not noticing his vehicle or knowing what it is. It's not a Discovery, but I discover that this couple have travelled constantly for 28 years across 178 countries and are the holders of several world records. They are also the holders of a clamp that I can use to push the piston back into the brake calliper. The side of their Land Cruiser has all the countries they have travelled through since 1985; I get the feeling there is nothing they haven't heard, and everything they say they have been saying repeatedly for quarter of a century. Having lent me the tools he leaves me to it, but he had mentioned my Mongolian sticker and would be interested in finding out more from me about my experience there. Really? You've never been to Mongolia? I thought you were well travelled? Perhaps he was just humouring me.

My audience becomes uninvited helpers. One vigorously pumps my brake lever to bleed the system, and I have to forcefully remove the helping hand so I can do it gently, properly, patiently myself. The pads are worn at an angle and have glazed from the heat. Although the piston retracts now, the efficiency of the rear brake is severely reduced. Back in my room I have a shower and return the tools to the Swiss couple's room. The door is barely opened; I hand back the tools with gratitude and ask if they fancy eating together tonight.

Apparently they eat in their room. Do they want to see the old city? It's too far to walk, and there is a fee to take in a vehicle; a taxi is out of the question.

"Maybe we will see you in the car park tomorrow" is my only redemption from utter rejection.

So once again I wander the streets alone, find a restaurant, and sit and eat my meal on my own. The background babble of other diners doesn't distract me from my thoughts, mainly because I don't understand a single word. Actually I do, one word, one new international word, more recognised than Coca-Cola and OK. In a stream of unintelligible chatter the word of the 21st century that stands out is *Facebook*.

Later I sit by my bike in the warmth of the evening; I feed the kittens, spin the back wheel, and press the brake lever. Without the forward momentum of a loaded bike the pads stop the wheel spinning. Back in my room I get out my Central Asia guidebook to try and muster up some enthusiasm for what's to come. I look at Google images of Tajikistan, read blogs from the area, and look at the pictures. Before bed I go out to the not very convenience store, the other side of ten lanes of fast traffic. There is the sanctuary of a central reservation where I wait for a gauntlet-sized gap to run through. As I look down the road at the constant flow of traffic, I notice I'm standing next to a sign that indicates a U-turn is allowed.

DAY 51

BAKU, AZERBAIJAN, MILESTONE

I have to make a decision, and I have to make it today. Either I go and get my Uzbekistan visa or I just turn back. On my way to breakfast I see the Swiss couple who are packing up and heading north. They have not seen the celebrated old city, and they are not going to, which seems like a bit of a waste to me. I have a question for them, and I don't think there is anyone on the planet better qualified to answer it:

"What do you do when you just don't feel like travelling anymore?"

I feel like my reply is on their FAQ list. They say they have no boss, no destination, no one tells them what to do, and that sometimes it would be easier to have a dictated itinerary. When they tire of the road their escape, their alternate activity, is their website. That would explain the half-opened door last night, dongle in hand. There were no answers for me in their explanation and no envy of their chosen lifestyle. 28 years in a Land Cruiser; it's not even a proper campervan. They have 14 jerry cans on the roof from when they crossed the Sahara years ago. The cans still sit there empty, catching the eye and the wind. Why would you continue to carry such bulky and useless equipment? Yes, they look cool all strapped up on the roof rack, but they don't need credibility; they are record holders and don't need to carry excessive amounts of fuel anywhere other than perhaps the Australian outback. Leave them stored, sell them, purchase new ones next time. I too have been travelling for 28 years, not constantly, although perhaps with more diversity. We do what suits us. I don't know if they are doing what suits them or they simply wander aimlessly like the undead. He did say he wasn't going to sit and wait for death to arrive; he wanted to go out and find it. You have to allow for inaccuracies in translation, but it almost sounded like the terminal destination is a place he can't wait to reach.

178

None of this really helps my mood or my decision making, but it does seem strange of all the places on the planet our paths could have crossed, they cross here, while I'm feeling like this. Thoughts of our meeting, their lifestyle and choices continue far longer than any other brief interaction I've had.

When I come out from breakfast their Land Cruiser has left, heading north to Russia and the Black Sea coast, a place he said he's not fond of.

I feed the kittens and go to the Internet. I speak to my friend and tell her I decided not to send the email; she insists I send it. When she calls me back she says it's clear I have already made the decision. I have travel burnout and should turn around.

It just seems so ridiculous, so pathetic, especially after the company I have just been with; that having been without a place or permanency for just seven months, I should be so jaded by the road. I email Stan Tours; the reply I get encourages me to continue, not in a profit-orientated kind of way, but a genuine concern and appreciation of my custom so far. But I think that when playing with kittens has greater appeal than biking through wondrous countries you have to question why that is and bow down to your wishes.

Facing challenges is inevitable; it's a regular hazard for the inquisitive. Only boring people get bored; there is infinite stimulation available to everyone. The smaller the mind the less it takes to fill it, but if satisfaction means inactivity then the future will never change. It's not that I want to stop; I just don't want to keep going. I'm not about to torch the bike and fly home to live in my van; I don't need an excuse. I just don't have the desire to continue to what I thought was my next destination. I don't know why, but I don't have to. I should be happy. I know what it is I do want; so many people don't.

Fuck me, I've just ridden all the way to Azerbaijan via Iraq; it's not exactly a failed mission. I've done quite well. I'm not going to take a direct route back home; I still want to tour, I have been reading about Armenia in my guidebook. That sounds pretty cool, soon as I'm in the area . . . and the mountainous and glacier-encrusted side of Georgia that I missed, I can see that too. And eastern Turkey wowed me, so I can spend more time there.

I can feel my drive returning; the mojo rises again. I've made a decision. I know what I'm going to do. I'm going to do what I want to do; I'm going to turn back. That's my desire. That's where I will find contentment. Today is the last day of the old plan; tomorrow the new journey starts. Tomorrow I will take my time seeing places I've never seen before. Every quest has a turning point, be it achievement or failure, epiphany or dead-end darkness. I've seen the light; I've questioned my answer, and now that I've seen the line between desire and contentment I'm going to ride along it.

DAY 52

NEAR TOUVZ, AZERBAIJAN, 269 MILES

It's not the thought of breakfast that gets me out of bed, nor the journey really; if I have any thoughts at all they are fearful, of the traffic that hurtles past my window constantly. I've walked this city witnessing the merciless, reckless, blinkered driving, and I'm really not keen to be out in it. I just want to get out of this city quickly, intact, and unscathed. At 10AM the bike is loaded; no goodbyes, no kittens, and no back brake. Once again, single-mindedly and fully focused, I start the engine and head for the road. I know exactly where I'm going. It's easy, back to the coastal road, keeping the sea on my left and heading south.

OK, here goes; I have to cross five lanes of traffic in a very short distance just to get to the U-turn slip road. This manoeuvre requires a strong will, no hesitation, or indecision, just confidently follow my intended path and don't, whatever happens, throttle back, lose my nerve, or change my intended trajectory. That's the theory, and I almost manage it. I ride on my horn and flash my lights to catch the ears and eyes of the distracted and oblivious. Vans pass, then pull right in front of me and stop to deliver. I feel like a ball bearing in a pin ball machine. I have to stay with the flow; try to keep the pace, although it's faster than I would comfortably choose to ride. I settle into a pace and a style of riding that, although exhausting, seems to be most beneficial to my self- preservation.

I pass the area of the old city; I never visited it. I could blame it on the heat, the distance, the preoccupation, whatever, I don't know; but missing it has its own significance, a mission statement, a milestone. This is the last time this will happen, and if I ever cross paths with the Swiss couple again, then we can talk about what we never saw while we stayed in Baku.

Although the old city is not pulling me in, the flame buildings are too good to miss, still impressive even in daylight. Although at night the three identical skyscrapers are illuminated, there are LCD screens built into them giving a flame effect glowing up the 600 feet structures that can be seen across the whole city, except from where I was. They were only completed last year in time for the Eurovision song contest that Azerbaijan hosted, so not quite the history of the old city but easier to see, eye-catching, in fact.

The wind is strong and gusty, the sea is choppy, the air is dusty, and the road ahead hazy. The bike is jumpy, but the traffic has thinned a bit. Sitting on the dirt outside a row of shops is a large Harley-Davidson shield. It's lacking a pole, but behind it is a bike shop. I turn round and pull up outside. It's a proper authorized Harley dealer, so I go inside and receive a genuine welcome. They clearly haven't seen my bike yet, so this may be short lived. They have the oil I need, but it's expensive. However, it's time for a change, and I have to treat my bike to what it needs. In this heat the crap that is in it must be breaking down; it deserves better. The guy offers me his staff discount and then asks if I need a place to change my oil.

There is a lot of construction going on outside, which is why the sign is sitting in the dirt and I have to ride my bike between unlaid drainage pipes and then up a narrow wooden ramp over the deep trench that has been dug for the pipe. Once over the bridge I'm in a pristine workshop full of enviable tools, all of which are at my disposal. I have the help of two mechanics, but they let me get on with my oil change. I have my own tools, and they seem impressed at my independence and ability. I work on my bike as it stands proudly on a pneumatic bike stand. It's like my bike is on a pedestal, and it deserves to be. The things I could do with this opportunity and all these tools at my disposal!

Having seen my bike, which validates my limited budget, I'm given some extra oil from a leftover can, enough for another oil change at a later date. I can't imagine this kind of service would happen in many Harley shops around the world. They are renowned for their elitist attitude, so this is very refreshing and really appreciated.

My old oil had drained into a Harley branded oil tray, and then without a thought, while it is still warm it is thrown out the door onto the dirt outside! I could have just drained it there myself. Still, they are very generous and hospitable guys, and I'm so grateful for the service and equipment at my disposal. They say that any traveller is welcome, regardless of the bike they ride; we are all "of the road," and it is their honour to be of assistance. I mentioned that on the road there is always something on your mind that needs to be done. I'm helped on with my jacket as I dress to leave and told, "All you need to think about now is getting home safely."

Across the road I fill up with petrol, and then I go back to being battered by the dry gusting wind off the Caspian Sea, blowing sand across the road and cracking lips.

I stop to sort out my oil. I have so much now, I pour my clean but substandard car oil over my chain and put my new motorcycle oil in my pannier container.

What's left I put in a small plastic coke bottle and stash between the engine and the bash plate. I've been a bit sloppy with this transference, and the strong wind hasn't helped.

Riding on with full fuel tank and clean oil, my mind wanders back to the decision I've made. I'm happy. There is a slight pang of sadness that I won't get to ride the Pamir Highway . . . at least not this trip.

There are working oil rigs just offshore, and what I suppose are huge holding tanks stand on the water's edge. Gas flames shoot into the sky from flare stacks; the smell of sulphur gusts under my visor. I too am getting rid of excess, but I'm not burning it, I'm flinging it. The oil-soaked chain is throwing oil over my tyres, boots, and bash plate. Waterproofing, lubricating, and giving the dust in the air something to stick to.

As I turn west, the landscape is just brown, with the occasional scorched township. It's a bland and hostile environment, with white dried salt lakes, and if there was ever any shade or shelter it's melted. Flat, barren land, featureless panorama; it's not scenery it's anti-scenery, but somehow I'm really enjoying being here. I'm the only feature for miles. Through the heat haze traffic is coming straight at me. Trucks over-taking trucks, I have plenty of time to react and do it with lethargic wallowing manoeuvres. Maybe it's the new oil in my bike, but I'm not so much swerving, more "super gliding." When the threat of head-on collision passes, they come from behind to cut me up. It's as if the vehicles are completely incapacitated: no clutch, brakes, or steering wheel, no space or speed perception and no common sense. Common sense is not common at all when it comes to driving skills out here. All they can do is honk their horns. Whether it means hello, get out of the way, or I'm here they just honk, honk, honk. The vehicles are like heat-seeking missiles, and I'm the hottest thing on the road.

I find myself thinking pleasant thoughts about my return, where I'm going now; it keeps away the regret for what I am missing. My mother has been texting a lot recently, as she is very excited about purchasing a summer house. When there is nothing else to think about, I contemplate the cementing of the base it will stand on. Clouds and hills appear out of the haze, and after this 40°C degree heat, both will be welcome, along with a brief respite from this torpedo traffic. There are storms north and south of me, and I can feel it coming in the air, a bit like Phil Collins. I don't mind if I ride into rain; the bike needs a clean anyway, but I seem to miss it along with restaurants and accommodation. At one roadside food shack as I pull into the dirt forecourt, three barking dogs come bounding out after me. I twist the throttle and speed away, wondering if they get a lot of custom. The next one just has a few vodka-drinking truckers in it, far less ferocious, so I point at my empty tummy, and chai and food is brought to me with a smile. I sit at a table outside the restaurant the way I like to, looking at my bike and smiling inside.

It was a friendly little place. They said hello and waved goodbye. I go through a town called Ganja and get completely lost, I just can't seem to find a road out of the place so resort to asking a taxi driver in the end. I'm sure I'm not the first person who's incapable of leaving Ganja alone.

OK, I have a full tummy and full tank, now I need to find somewhere to fall asleep. With my new sense of wellbeing more options become available to my receptive mind. I pass a derelict Russian truck graveyard next to a fuel station. I ask the attendant if camping is OK. He seems to indicate it's not only OK but I'd be a fool to pass up such an opportunity. I'm inclined to concur. I walk around the back of the decaying trucks with shredded tyres, broken screens, and dripping fluids. There is a little grassy patch out of sight from the road, and it's perfect.

I put up my tent and start to read my guidebook, crouched down by the side of my bike. Something nudges my bum. I turn around startled. It's a demented and sickly kitten, dirty white with diseased eyes. I find a plastic bottle and cut it open to pour some water in then break an egg into the other part. I spread some peanut butter on a plastic bag, and although it eats a token amount, what it really wants is affection. So I reach out and touch it, and for an hour it loves me. Although it has impaired sight, it follows me as I gather some rubbish to make shelter for it beneath an abandoned truck. I think its days are numbered, but if I can make tonight comfortable maybe we will both sleep better. I go to the petrol station to wash my hands, and the attendant follows me back to see the home I have made (for myself not the kitten). It's obvious he's not a cat lover as he kicks away the kitten who mistakes his boot for mine. I have a conflict of loyalty but let the event pass unmentioned.

It's a noisy spot; trucks come and go all night, but I'm out of sight and feel safe enough. In my guidebook I read that jackals are a real and dangerous threat in Azerbaijan, to the point people won't leave their houses at night. That was probably the howling I heard when I camped in the forest. I would have been seriously mauled before I had time to open the three-inch blade of my Swiss army knife. I think I'm safe tonight; the kitten will get it before I do.

DAY 53

KUTAISI, GEORGIA, 290 MILES

Well, it appears it wasn't a derelict Russian truck graveyard. It was simply a truck park. This morning when I look out of the tent most of them have left. The state of the things was horrendous, and now they are out on the road somewhere. Thankfully the tanker I camped directly behind is still there, as is the *In Search of Greener Grass* sticker that I put on it last night; it somehow seemed an appropriate mission for a condemned water tanker to be on. Once the bike is packed up, I go over to the garage to have a wash. (I tried turning the tap on the tanker, but I only got a single rust coloured drip.) There are some men doing concreting by a lone diesel pump; I just wave hello as I purposely walk past. They answer in unison, the Azerbaijani for "What the fuck?" so on my return I elaborate, and in one word I captivate—"Moto," I say and make the arm gesture as if I were riding. They all follow me round the back of the tanker. Other than my bike leaning against the truck, there is no evidence that I stayed there. I make the sleeping gesture.

"On the ground? You slept on the ground?" seems to be the response. "Yeah, well sort of."

All these gestures are making my arms tired; I'm not about to do the tent motion. Let them think I'm hardcore, though not in a way that men of their profession might use hardcore. I don't want to be buried like a mafia boss, especially after I've just had a wash. I think they all think I'm amazing, and this morning they could quite possibly be right. The kitten is nowhere to be seen, so once I'm kitted up, I pull out from behind the tanker; all the concreters wave. I always feel a pang of guilt to be leaving manual workers to continue their labours, mainly because I can relate so well to that kind of work, but today more so because the feel-good feeling is back and is fully deserved too I think.

This morning there is high cloud, distant hills, a pleasant temperature, and a sign for Tbilisi, so there is no need to look at my map. I'm not sure exactly where I am going or stopping today, but it doesn't really matter. I pass a tall concrete edifice; its only purpose is to announce the boundary of a new territory, state, or county, but it's impressive enough for a photo. Two soldiers stop; my immediate reaction is that I've done something wrong. Amongst the things I've read recently there have not been many favourable things said about Azerbaijani authority, but I've had little contact, and what I have had has been congenial. These soldiers are just inquisitive young men who want a photo of me and my bike, as I do of them beside it. This brief exchange has been observed by a farm worker some distance away in a field. He seems exceptionally joyous and animated at what he has witnessed; he is waving very energetically. He's either a bail short of a haystack or I just accidentally stood on his juniper bush.

The miles pass uneventfully, and then along comes Georgia again. Wait, I'm not ready for this yet, I still have some currency to spend. I turn around and top up my tank, then driven mainly by hunger but partly by the need to use up the rest of my Azerbaijani manat, I bravely pull up outside a busy restaurant. I'm invited into the kitchen to point at things, and when I walk back out I'm invited to sit with a well-dressed Russian gentleman. He speaks no English but seems to have authority here. The map is always a good bridge across the language barrier, and it keeps any awkward silence at bay as I eat and drink chai with him. He seems honoured that I chose to sit with him, and there may even be a little gloating at the other diners when I shake his hand and leave. I hope I will never feel so conceited that I would deny someone such a simple request. The pleasure was mutual and possibly more in my favour; it's not always easy to be forced into company you have no common language with, but I've had more than enough of my own lately. I couldn't pick him out in an identity parade now, but I still have the memory. Better than a sandwich in a lay-by.

With a smile still on my face, I return to the border, and the officials have news that instantly removes it: I have out-stayed my welcome.

"You late, you late," a jumped-up little official screams. He was clearly bullied at school, and I'm pretty sure his mother doesn't love him either. He's practically wetting his, no doubt extremely sensible and ironed, underwear at my blatant disregard for the law. The problem it would appear is that although I had 30 days on my visa, on an additional piece of paper that was loosely left between the pages of my passport, it states my vehicle has a transit allowance of just three days.

This has just cleared up a slight niggle that I've not been paying enough attention to. I have continually come across this three day entry allowance on the forums, but I thought it didn't apply to me as I had a pre-approved visa legitimately stuck in my passport. It all makes sense now. When I contacted Stan Tours to tell them of the delay of getting my Turkmenistan visa, I was told to get my bike to the customs pound at the dock as soon as I could. I had no intention to do this, but if I had the three day counter would have stopped like a defused bomb. However, if I had what the hell would I be doing now? Well that's all academic. I've got Mr. Cold-shower-for-kicks on my back. Mr. Self-loathing-and-almost-definitely-sexual-stunted-and-unacceptably-perverse doesn't have a single friend in his life, and even his colleagues hate him. His uniform is worn with waxwork model precision, and his meticulous regulation haircut begs to be ruffled by a scarred and greasy hand. His manicured nails and soft skin say menial tasks, and the lack of blisters means he probably wears gloves when he masturbates. Still, he's just caught a fugitive, and there's processing to be done. Blank forms are pure porn to this purveyor of protocol; fines are to be calculated and imposed.

He's having trouble containing his excitement; I dare not look down to see how this is manifested. He's more excited than the farmer in the field earlier. He's nearly a bully; he's certainly bossy, loves his authority, and after his incomprehensible directions have drawn a blank on my face, he marches me swiftly to see the man who will determine my fate. I'm a little concerned how serious this is. I want to have a price in mind to gauge the actual fine by; I suppose $100 will be acceptable to get out of this mess. If I wasn't calculating this I probably would be giggling at his supercilious manner as he strides towards the high ranking man, proudly handing me over with delight and expectations of congratulations and promotion.

Whilst I stand there waiting for this more authoritative and certainly less interested man to calculate the penalty, Mr. Someone-shoved-my-baton-up-my-arse-but-I-don't-mind-it-that-much-so-I-left-it-there stands staring at me. My earrings are of great fascination to him. How could anyone self-mutilate themselves to that degree; it's beyond his comprehension. With indifference, the older official looks at the evidence of my crime; he thinks for a moment—not long enough to cause suspense—and then says, "20 manat.'

"20 manet? Are you kidding me? That's 15 quid; I piss 15 quid. You know what? Fuck it, I think I might stay a bit longer. Here, ya got change for 50? No worries; if not I'll come back next week." Well that's what I was saying inside. Keep smiling regardless of the situation? Shit, it's all I can do to stop myself laughing.

"Seeee yaaaa. Wouldn't wantta beeee yaaaa." I don't know if he felt deflated, but it certainly took the wind from his sails.

I hurry off to the Georgian immigration, where the pretty girl in uniform welcomes me and says I can stay for 360 days, but my bike for only three months.

"But then what would I do?" The welcome she gave ends short of an invitation. "Hey, I could cook you dinner while you were at work."

I stop to put my scarf and helmet back on; some young lads come over to the bike, spurred on by each other, they start fiddling with switches until I raise my voice: "Look with eyes not with hands," and they obediently withdraw, which wouldn't happen at home.

Much as I loved Tbilisi and dislike my new scarf I'm not going to go back there to try and retrieve my bandanna or stare at the natural beauty. I want to head for the glacier region, so I take the bypass that was so hard to find last time and pass that fateful junction of entrapment. I come to a road that looks promising and seems to correspond with the one on my map, so I head towards the hills.

The road, villages, and minds get smaller, and the staring is uncomfortable. The village doesn't seem to have an exit road, which might explain a lot, so I double back and take a fork. It's going OK, and then there are concrete bunkers and armed soldiers, but they don't react, so I keep going until there are more military and closed gates across the road. It would seem, much like the most direct route to Turkey through Iraq, this one is taking me through the republic of South Ossetia. Except it isn't, because I'm denied access. It's a very volatile area, and less than five years ago, there was full-on war between Russia and Georgia over this area. The war was centered around the town of Tskhinvali, the place directly between where I am now and where I want to be.

The Roman alphabet having only 26 characters means I'm rapidly running out of letters to name my altered plans after. I turn back to the motorway and pass three United Nations 4x4s. There seems to be no expense spared in preparing the vehicles for their overland objectives. Shortly after, I pass a walking procession; a funeral march, and an open coffin is held aloft, so I slow my pace in what I hope is seen as respect. Then I pass another one; the coffin is much smaller, and roses are being thrown on the road ahead of the march. What the hell is going on round here?

You know you are in an area of danger when a motorway of Georgian traffic seems like a safer option. I pull into a service area to get some money out and find a new route. When I get back from the ATM, a man is studying my bike thoroughly and taking pictures. He is from Brazil, here on holiday, and speaks good English. It turns out he too was on Copacabana beach on the night of the millennium. "I thought you looked familiar," but he says he doesn't remember me.

The day is passing by, so I divert into the town of Gori, the birth place of Stalin and one of the few places where a statue of him can still be seen, or could be: my guidebook is old and political tolerances change. I see a statue that could be him; the figure does have a moustache, but I was expecting it to be bigger—the statue, not the moustache. This place too had suffered badly in the war, and it is not a place I want to stay.

The problem is I'm not sure where the Republic of South Ossetia borders are. So I try another north-bound road, and again it ends, this time in a deliberately destroyed road. I'm getting rained on, and it's been a long day in the saddle, plus going west I gain time, not that I need it this close to the solstice. I go through a warm tunnel, warmed from exhaust fumes and no ventilation. Then the altitude drops, and the warmth become more natural. The environment doesn't, though, and reluctantly I opt for a hotel, just so I can rest and eat. Kebab and chips, and I buy a bar of chocolate to eat in my room. I can't get the TV to show *BBC World* as the laminated channel advisor says I can, neither can I get the air conditioner/ heater to work or Internet access. So I lie on my bed and listen to doors slam instead.

DAY 54

ONI, GEORGIA, 104 MILES

Doors slam all night, and whilst sitting in the bathroom I discover the door of the vanity unit bangs shut very loudly on its sprung return hinges. Desperate to join in with local customs, I open it and let it slam several times. Whilst packing up to leave I go back to check I've left nothing in the vanity unit, and the door crashes back again. This is very small-minded, and if it didn't achieve a spiteful satisfaction I wouldn't bother to do it at all, but it does, so I do it a bit more before I leave. It's hugely satisfying behaviour. My bike has taken its vengeance on the place too and leaked oil from the sump-plug, which is a quarter turn loose. Whilst we made our audible and visual mark on the accommodation of displeasure, the morning's blue skies have turned to low cloud. Karma?

Now I am on a road that really will take me north, however, I seem to be on the wrong side of the river. The valley is wide and there is nowhere to cross. The skies either side of me are blue, but the cloud is trapped between the hills and hangs over me. I've got a good song in my head, my tank is full, I've left the traffic behind, and it's going to take more than a little rain to ruin my mood. Perhaps I accidently transmit that thought to the rain gods because a little rain turns into a torrential downpour. There is a bus shelter at the side of the road, so I turn round, look at the double concrete curb and decide I can probably ride up it into the shelter, but soon realise I can't. Bollocks.

It's not too difficult to pick the bike up, so I get back on and go round for another try. The cows must find it much easier to enter than I do, as the ground is covered with shit. I use my top box as a table top and have some breakfast whilst watching my spilt fuel make rainbows in the puddles outside. There is something quite satisfying about utilizing a bus shelter as the rain bounces off the road. Rain this hard rarely lasts long, and before I have run out of things to occupy myself, the road is steaming and the sun has broken through.

It can't shine bright enough to take the gloom out of the next town, though. Tall, oppressive soviet housing blocks each side of the road create a valley of their own, and I ride in their depressing shadow. They really are structures of condensed misery. I see a holy man, an orthodox priest, traditionally dressed in black robes with beard and long hair; a large golden cross hangs from his neck, just like a biker dressed for an Ozzy Osborne fancy dress party. I find the look a bit intimidating; maybe I'm just paranoid. Their grey beards make these guys look older than their years, but perhaps it's because they never say dye.

I'm quite happy to pass on through the town without giving anyone the chance to change my impressions of it. The road climbs steeply away, and I pass two European cyclists, a young girl in a purple anorak and an older man wearing a Johnny Cash T-shirt; they are both wearing flip-flops. When I find a place to pull over I stop, and as they pass by I say, "You don't have to stop if you don't want to break your momentum."

They say they have no momentum and lay their bikes on the ground and both light up cigarettes. They are German and justify their smoking by saying they don't want to get too healthy. They have flown in for a month of cycling in Georgia and got soaked yesterday; their cycling shoes are drying on the bikes. Unlike their flip flops on their pedals, we just seem to click. We stand talking and laughing, swapping the information we have. They smoke continuously as pigs forage around us looking for more than cigarette ash. Neither of them has any water, but they don't seem that bothered. They are everything the organised and informed Swiss were not: Ill-prepared, with little more than a vague plan and some determination, a travel style I can wholly relate to.

Now I've reached the hills the distances between destinations are short. There is also more evidence of a tourist industry, with money changers, hotels, and signs written in English. T-junction decision time, I opt for east on instinct, even though I'm supposedly heading back. The town of Oni has guesthouse potential, but I'm not ready to stop riding. So I continue, and the road turns to dirt. I know it will come to an end eventually, as Russia looms over this north-eastern part of Georgia, and there are no through roads. However, the roads that exist are remote and rugged. The cloud is sporadic, but I can see snow on the mountains I pass between. I follow a river and go under a concrete aqueduct that water falls onto from the cliffs above. I shelter under it whilst another cloud of rain comes across; I've been quite lucky finding shelter today. On I go past meadows of daisies and cross the kind of river that may, with a storm in the mountains, quadruple in size. The high water mark indicates what it's capable of, and it's far greater than my river crossing abilities. Then I have the luxury of a low wooden bridge where the river has nearly dammed itself with pine trees it has swept away and then jammed under the supports.

The track is getting narrower and finally takes me into a village, the village at the end of the road. It's a bit scary, quite exhilarating. Old women dressed in black sit on wooden benches worn shiny from the bums of time. The houses are made of stone and tradition. Electric cables have been strung from anything of height, and my exhaust is much too loud for such a remote and unvisited place. The other side of this settlement the track takes me down to a dry rocky river-bed, used to retrieve more building materials brought down from the mountains when the waters are high and powerful. I can see a glacier but no way to get closer to it. The Russian border must be very close to here, if it is defined at all. I turn round and manage to get lost in the tiny village. The landmark benches of wrinkled women are many; the faces all look the same. In a Hansel and Gretel style I look in the mud for my tyre tracks, but I've already done a lap and they are misleading me again. Eventually, having attracted the unwanted attention of just about every inhabitant, a hard-faced youth assists in my exit strategy, and I'm back on a single line of my friendly Mefo tracks, the ones I left on entry. Once more, the KLR does what it does best, taking me to the isolated and inaccessible, and best of all taking me back again.

It's much too early to camp and not really a place I can hide. I've been seen and continue to be seen by lumberjacks, herders, and the kind of people who, for whatever reason, swing pickaxes at cliff faces to bring rocks tumbling onto the dirt track, before leaving them there. I ride past with my rain face on.

Back in Oni, I find a family run guesthouse where they speak German; it adds variety to the daily custom of incomprehension. I'm lead up the end of the driveway. There are ducklings and chickens running round, and I'm taken up the stairs to the terrace of a wooden building and into a dark musty room, where the single window has nets up keeping light out. Where the dusty bookshelves stop, the walls are adorned with paintings conceived by a disturbed mind. The veranda faces north to the mountains and has a threadbare couch to sit on. There is memorabilia everywhere, from farm and torture implements to crockery and vases of dried flowers. It may not have abandoned trucks, but it does have a Lada decomposing in the garden, and I would be a fool to pass up a night in such unique, rustic, and bucolic accommodation. And tonight is not any night, but the shortest one of the year.

Food is prepared for me in the family kitchen: the soup is good, the rest is iffy, and I'm yet to taste a Georgian wine that doesn't seem corked. Conversation is frequent and friendly, but futile, and when they can't find anything else to bring to the table, I excuse myself and walk into the town on a quest for beer.

There is magic in the air on solstice evening. I feel it. I love it. Sitting on the veranda watching the rain fall, I can smell the smoke from burning wood drifting past on damp air. I clear all the cushions and blankets off the couch and get in my sleeping bag, listening to the rain patter on the wooden roof and trickle off my bike cover. It's so peaceful, tranquil. There are cloud-obscured views from my antique balcony; the mountains come and go, and the rain calms the evening to a trance. There are smells of old enchanting times gone by; I'm surrounded by a lifetime's accumulation of treasures. There are spirits here. Sometimes I feel so glad to be this free. I could be on a ferry to Turkmenistan now, but instead I'm drifting through the thoughts of past solstices, immersed in the elements, but just sheltered enough as the unseen sun finishes it longest performance of the year. There is nowhere else I would rather be tonight than here on my own surrounded by a wondrous world on the apex of summertime.

DAY 55

ZACHENDERIL, GEORGIA, 97 MILES

I always feel a slight twinge of disappointment when the summer solstice has past; now over the hump we are all heading into darkness from here. Every season has its appeal, but there is nothing as enchanting as the extending days of late spring, the reward for enduring a winter. I doze on the veranda with my hat on; the bird song is the only sound. It really is the perfect spot between camping and a hotel; I think I will choose to be a dweller of the balcony from now on. Downstairs in the little bathroom is a water heater cum log burner. I was shown how to use it last night, so continuing in my primitive rituals I split some wood with an axe and light a fire in the small box beneath the water cylinder. Fire and water, what a traditional way to start the day. It's so much more satisfying than pop-up toasties and a power-shower.

When I go down to the house to pay, a breakfast has been prepared for me, and it appears I misunderstood the room rate last night. It is significantly less, £7.50 for two meals and that glorious accommodation; I'd stay another night, but they have city slickers coming for the weekend, and another night here would never be as perfect as last night was.

"Where are you going now? Where will you stop? What will you see?" I don't have a single answer but indicate to the family that staying here gave me a great big smile.

In nineteen slow kilometres, I see just one other vehicle. I expect to see the German cyclists again, actually I hope to; in fact it's occupying the majority of my thoughts. It's becoming obsessive; it's getting annoying. I need a diversion and I get one. At a junction the road quality deteriorates and the scenery excels itself. The dirt road squeezes through a tight gorge and fights for dominance

194

over the river; it doesn't always win. This is more like it; this is what I want. Docking in Turkmenistan? No way, I'm rocking in the ravine.

I go through a tunnel of cow shit, mud, and darkness; this seems to be a trait in Georgia, these unlit obstacle-strewn tunnels. I usually poo poo the over-lit adventure bike, saying the day has gone seriously wrong if you are still on the road at night. It's a pointless mission, missing what you came to see at the expense of progress. But for short periods in this country a piercing beam of light would be quite useful. I do have spot lights on my bike, as they were on it when I got it. They don't really do much except set off the buzzer, which tells me the battery is getting insufficient charge; the buzzer ironically taking yet more juice from the battery. When I come out the other end of the tunnel there is a lake beside me and it ends predictably in a dam. I get a pristine strip of sealed road, and before I can get into fifth gear, it abruptly turns back to shaking potholes. At midday I meet the German couple; we will try and meet tonight in a village beginning with "Z"; the problem is the faster I go the longer I will have to wait.

I pull into the last town of any significance on this route to Europe's highest permanently inhabited settlement. I fill my little cool box with my usual staple foods. Nothing quite takes the urgency out of the day more than knowing you have to wait for some cyclists. Am I really that desperate for company? Yes, actually I am, especially company that I know has chemistry, and I'm in no hurry to be anywhere. I ride down to a river to have my lunch; everything I do today is done at a slower than usual pace, I have time on my side, and it makes for greater appreciation of the simple things. Like the side stand sinking into the soft ground, and the bloody bike falling over while I'm eating a sandwich.

Although the road is rough it attracts traffic, mainly foreigners, Ukrainian cyclists and a German campervan. It's not surprising; the scenery is the best I've seen so far, and I've seen some quite magnificent stuff already. What if the Ukrainian cyclists meet the German couple, and they decide to camp together? It must be a good day if that's all I can find to worry about.

I get to the village which is to be our meeting point; there is nothing here at all, a single dirt track between some wooden shacks. I ride right through to a little vista point on the other side and stop to look for camping opportunities. A 4x4 Lada is parked up, a local driver chauffeuring a Polish couple; they have food spread out on the bonnet and offer me a shot of whiskey. We chat a little and I'm given another shot before they pack up and leave. I head back through the village to see if I can find something that resembles a shop, and on a particular muddy bit of the track, I manage to fall off. Whiskey-numbed reactions mean I'm not hurt at all, but I have bent a pannier and a hand guard. The bike is filthy now, and I'm quite muddy too, so I find a quiet spot and completely unpack my pannier, then with a rock I bang it back into shape. The panniers have lost a lot of their strength now. They were first smashed when my bike flipped in Mexico. They were beaten back into shape and have been mounted on several different racks, so the backs now look like Swiss cheese. Unpacking them also reveals they have leaked again, but none of the contents have suffered too much. This operation is being watched from a distance by a farmer, and I get the feeling he won't stop watching until he sees me leave, so I do just that so he can get on with his not so busy day.

Due to the amount of time I have and the lack of shops here, I decide to go back to the last village where I know there was a little store. I buy a big plastic bottle of beer and wait for the Germans. A few vehicles stop to see what I'm doing, and I'm told they are not far behind. I'm sure this beer would be much easier to carry if I drank a bit of it now. When they arrive we decide to buy two more bottles and then an extra one just in case. I now have eight litres of beer on my bike, and most of it is still in the bottles. We find a really good camping spot at the side of the river and away from the road. I put the beers in the river to cool down and gather up some wood. The sky clears; snow lit by the last of the sunlight on the tops of rugged cliffs stays illuminated by a full moon; our faces glow as we sit round the fire. These are the moments that produce photos of deception. Yesterday the cyclists got soaked and their clothes are still wet; I've been agonizing over routes and destinations. However, right here by a wild river, warmed by a fire, under the light of the moon which shines on distant snowy peaks, is a slice of the journey that everyone wants to taste. These tempting morsels come at a cost, and it's a price that most aren't willing to pay. Sometimes the planets align, and everything falls into place. It's exceptional, but all the more rewarding due to its rarity. A day that starts and ends in fire will be branded into my memory for many more moons to come.

DAY 56

USHGULI, GEORGIA, 23 BRILLIANT MILES

The morning is a little subdued, and as we sit around last night's ashes, the only warmth is in the sun. The scenery soars up from the river, which is flowing far easier than the conversation. Last night we did what has been done since the invention of fire: warmed ourselves, told stories and jokes, sang, and laughed. It is the oldest of human habits, along with reproduction and eating, but I was too busy drinking and laughing to indulge in anything else; I was single tasking.

My tummy grumbles from the liquid diet. The only remedy, other than responsible drinking, is to ride. Packed up and cleared away, I now have four empty beer bottles strapped to my bike. I say my goodbyes and head back to the track. I'm really glad I made the effort to have company last night, and having got my fix, I'm equally glad to be moving on without it. Motorcycles only ride with bicycles when they are filming the Tour de France.

In less than a kilometre I come to the other part of the village, the part that has a shop. I know this because there is a sign that says "shop" in English. I'll know next time. I'm not sure if it's because it's a sunny day or a Sunday, but lots of local folk are out on benches watching me go by. I wave and they wave back, because I'm a happy person today, this morning, at the moment, well, this second in time at least.

Another day with no real destination. I just want to ride. The track is getting very muddy in places. I suppose it will only get worse; I don't expect to see tarmac today. A river crosses my path; I stop, look, assess, go forward, and fall off. I pick up the bike and continue. My hand guards are getting pretty bent out of shape now. At the next river crossing I use some of the skill and experience that I have picked up over the miles I have travelled, as opposed to all the picking up I have done over the miles. With more concentration on my riding and less on my hangover, I cross the river like a bridge. It's a beautiful performance. The bike is getting washed by rivers then covered by mud again on a road that deteriorates with elevation. Both the bike and I are getting a bit beaten up now. Apart from the cracked windshield and bent handguard, the aluminium tool roll is very dented, the chain guard is rubbing on the tyre, and the back brake is still ineffectual. I stink of fire smoke, have a flapping sole on my boot, and my bike trousers are frayed and soaked. There is no one out here now but me, unless the hills have eyes. Best not think about that.

Do I like this? Yes, I think so. Alone into the unknown, I'm not even at the pass yet; the road is going to get worse than this. Ahead of me a mountain appears. It's so close, so big; a glacier creeps down towards the base, and against the blue sky it towers so steeply I can't lift my head far enough to take it all in before my helmet digs into the back of my neck. It's absolutely stunning. I can't look around as I ride, but when I stop I see waterfalls and natural beauty all around me. The mud is replaced with rocks and boulders, and I feel like I'm gaining more control over my bike as I weave between the spoke snapping obstacles. It's the perfect time of year to be here. There are meadows of buttercups and daisies, and everything is green and alive. The road increases in elevation, and the scenery becomes even more breathtaking. I have no breath left.

Ahead of me are some very rutted and muddy tracks. Alternate routes have been tried across churned up grass, though none seem inviting. I surge on ahead, and the bike gets bogged down and comes to a halt. There is no way it will continue, and I can't pull it back either. I lean it over and drag it into another rut. The rear tyre feels flat, but it's so caked in mud that I can't even tell. With all my force I pull the bike back a foot at a time, then opt for another track, but again the bike just gets stuck.

I will burn out the clutch trying to force it through this. It's exhausting. Eventually I do what I probably should have done initially; get off and walk to find the path of least resistance. There is only one option left now anyway; it's tall grass but firm under foot, and the bike effortlessly crosses the marsh on this, the third try.

There is the occasional house sprouting out the side of a hill. Most are abandoned, dilapidated, a formation of crumbling stone and rusty iron. The buildings that are occupied seem to scrape an existence from the surrounding land, a hard life rather than a good one.

I'm wet with sweat now; it's a road of constant challenges, no time to rejoice in achievement. I come to washed-out bridges and white-water rapids I have to cross. It's so steep and rocky now, there is nowhere to stop, so I have to maintain momentum. Standing on the pegs, I have to keep my visor up because the sweat is making it mist up, but the air is thick with mozzies. They are sticking to my wet cheeks, sucked into my mouth as I gasp for breath. I have to grit my teeth, then a fat one flies into my eye, and I screw it shut. I lose perception, and a twig from a tree pokes my face, so I'm glad I had my eye shut.

Still I can't stop; I'm just riding into more abuse. A boulder-strewn and submerged track, I'm basically riding up a river bed against fast running water and clouds of mozzies. This track continues steeply, zig-zagging up a hillside, and finally the river and road separate, and I can stop and put my feet down. Man, that was some demanding and relentless riding. It's the best kind of exhaustion there is with your clothes on. A massive glacier appears ahead of me—this road is spectacular. I round hairpin bends which climb up mountainsides, but I can't stand it any longer. I need to stop and take a breath; I need to get the tripod out. I may have missed Tajikistan, but this is more than making up for it.

I'm at 7,000 feet now so stop for a sandwich and finish the last of my water. I sun-dry my sweaty body, but when the sun goes behind a cloud the temperature drops like a clumsy mountain goat. Putting my arms back into the wet sleeves of my jacket does nothing to warm me up.

The road continues to wind up and then into a valley of vivid green hillsides. I'm above the timber line; there are sporadic pockets of snow, which look like white sand bunkers on a vertical golf course. The contrast in colours is so defined; dark blue altitude sky, bright green grassy hills, and a layer of resilient snow between the two. A basic photography technique is to divide a landscape photo into thirds; it's done automatically here. It's all so untouched, unchanged, no human contact, nothing but nature and seasons.

When I get up to 8,000 feet I fill my bottle from a waterfall. A hunter once told me never to drink from a stream, as you don't know what is up river; an animal could have drowned and be decomposing in the water above. I've always born that in mind, but here I can see the source. I can see up to the frozen snow on the ridge and the stream flowing down from it until it cascades into my water bottle; it's clean and pure as the driven snow. It's also very refreshing, as is the wind on my wet and cooling body.

The descent starts, and like the post-solstice dawn, I feel a little sad the best is over. It was the highlight of the journey so far. A village comes into view, and I chug down into it. There are tall stone towers all around, the road is still dirt, some Russian trucks are parked up, and there is a small restaurant. A few plastic tables placed in the yard outside are the most unnatural thing I've seen all day. I stop and sit down; a Swedish couple are sitting at the other table. The motherly owner comes out and tells me in English she has soup, which sounds ideal, so I order a Coke while I wait. I instantly feel myself relax; there is a good vibe here. The Swedes tell me of the guesthouse they are staying in. It sounds good. I think I want to stay here too.

I cancel my Coke and order a beer. This place has staying power. More people come and sit down, Polish, Argentine, German, everyone is happy, everyone is laughing, everyone only just met. Again the planets align, if they ever fell from sequence. There is instant interesting banter, no small talk; this medieval village is in a time of its own, and it's a good time. The restaurant too has a room to rent, I have a look but want to see what else is on offer; everyone sings the praises of their own places. Because of the village's isolation, meals seem to be included in room price. There is no Internet or phone signal up here, but there was no accommodation here for travellers at all when my guidebook was printed.

As well as us tourists, there are some military men who have been at their own table; they come and go in trucks. They had watched me drink beer, and now in full view, I clip my helmet onto the back of my top box and ride off down a path into the midst of the village in search of a room. It was only when I stopped at the end of my one minute ride that I realised the back tyre had thrown up cow shit all over my helmet. Don't look so cool now, do I?

I look at two more guesthouses before I make a choice, but I find one with a view of the entire valley, even though the walls are thin, the floors creak, and in the common bathroom water trickles from the shower. The owners help me drag my bike up from the dirt alley and lean it against a wooden fence. After my trickle shower, I sit with my fleece on, order a beer, and look out at these strange foreboding stone towers standing against the most incredible backdrop of glacier encrusted mountains. If I hadn't stopped for a Coke I might have missed all this. No, I'm sure I couldn't have passed through this timeless place without giving it a little of my own.

Day 57

Ushguli, Georgia, 0 Miles

It's just so relaxing here, chilly but chilled. Down at breakfast I chat to the Swedes across the room, as I seem to have been seated on the naughty table in the corner. I've decided I will stay another day. If they had asked I would have hiked to the glacier with them but they didn't, so I make my own itinerary. They have quite an unruly child, so after their departure I bask in the tranquillity of being the only resident in the guesthouse. Then, as my bike isn't going anywhere today, I think it will be a good idea to let the chain soak in some oil, and whilst I've got the spray can out, I do the hinges on all the doors in the corridor. The squeaking echoes down the hallway at night, but this good deed may also mean I get a better table at dinner time. It's only a little village, but I still haven't taken it all in yet. I take a walk up the hill to an old church. A big grey hairy wolf-like dog joins me; he seems to just want someone to walk with. I know how he feels, sometimes at home when I wander out to the fields to watch the sunset I feel a bit self-conscious. I sense I'm being eyed suspiciously by the dog walkers who have a justifiable purpose for being outside. Big Dog, as I have called him, seems to know there will be a point when I will just stop and sit down; he therefore finds the best place and stops there. He sits with his back to me, looking at the mountains as I gaze down at the towers in the village of stone. I'm sort of absent-mindedly half stroking and half play fighting with Big Dog and then realise I have my forearm in his large jaws; he clamps down with a respectful force. Bah, he doesn't seem to be a threat, although it's rather forward behaviour, bordering on stupidity. There are no services up here. I can't see my travel insurance paying for me and my severed limb to be airlifted out when they discover I put my arm in the mouth of a half-wolf I'd just met.

There must be 40 stone towers in view from up here; some are over 1,000 years old, built to protect the families from nomadic mountain invaders as well as from village infighting. Some are still inhabited, but they look like very cold places to be besieged in. They are striking in appearance and unique to this area, in fact, the whole village seems to be lost somewhere in time. I don't know if the *Lonely Planet* was being discreet or indifferent, but they certainly play down this remarkable place. I wander round the narrow dirt alleys; I've just walked into the Middle Ages, not a Disney theme but a genuine working way of life.

I walk along a well-trodden path between stone walls and irrigation streams diverted from the river. There are small half-wild pigs that have coarse hairy Mohicans along their backs, horses too wander free along with cows, goats, and chickens, so there is a real need to look where I am treading while viewing the scenery around me.

It occurs to me that if an animal has four legs its name changes when it appears on a menu; pork, beef, venison, but if it only has two legs it stays the same; chicken, pheasant, turkey. It may not be relevant, but it's something to chew over.

I end up back at the restaurant, mainly because it seems to be the meeting place of the small travel community. Before I have finished my soup of the day, which was not unlike soup of yesterday, I'm joined by a German couple. An hour of tale telling distracts us from the passing rain.

Back on the viewing platform of my guesthouse I have time to read more about this area; Georgia as a whole and Armenia too. I think I may be here a while; this in turn makes me realise my Russian visa will become valid before my intended leaving date and I start to look at new routes utilizing the visas I do have. But I never really liked Russia that much, it was only ever going to be a place of transit; seems pointless to go just because I have a visa.

I've enjoyed this journey all the more since I aborted that plan. I'm just happy to be happy; seems little reason to change anything.

My landlord is on the doorstep below me. He plays a three-stringed rudimentary guitar, characteristic to this area. Apparently its sound changes depending on warmth and humidity, which seems logical, however, they say they can forecast the weather from the sound it makes. "And now the weather forecast: There will be a smoky mist on the water, being burned off later by a fire in the sky." To accompany his strumming he sings in a three-part harmony. I'm pretty sure it's just him but don't want to lean over the balcony to look in case he stops.

At dinner my good deeds have allowed me to sit with the observant Swedes, who recognise that the film poster on the wall is of our landlord. With a little persuasion he proudly tells us of how he was chosen to star in a movie based around the people and traditions of the area. He appears to be a very talented but modest man. The Swedes are moving on to the next village tomorrow; we swap emails so we can meet up. Strangely the more I relax the more tired I get, so I have an early night, opting for my blow-up mattress rather than sleeping on the squidgy bed, due to an aching back from yesterday's strenuous ride

I'm woken by fireworks at midnight. The skies have cleared, so I set my camera on the balcony, and with a prolonged shutter speed, I capture a medieval tower lit by the moon, a sky pierced by stars above a snow covered mountain with wisps of cloud blowing, blurred over the summit—one of the best photos I've taken this trip. I really want to wake someone and show them.

DAY 58

MESTIA, GEORGIA, 29 MILES

Noisily the Swedes next door (the only door I didn't oil) pack up and leave, but I stay on the floor in my room. I've never really got the feeling the couple who run this guesthouse like me much. Today I don't even get an egg on my breakfast table, the honey has a fly in it, and there are no tea bags. I woke up cold; the shower was cold and the breakfast is too. Even multiple trips up and down the stairs to load the bike have failed to warm me up. I say goodbye, sad to be leaving this place of living history, and ride the cow shit and boulder-strewn muddy paths to the road. The challenge is instant, and before I'm out of the village I have a sweat on. I force my lazy arse off the seat and put some control into my riding.

Once I've left what little civilization there is, I follow the track along the side of a river under a canopy of trees. There was a military presence in Ushguli, not large but constant, usually sitting around the restaurant. It may not be the volatile area it once was, but it's only five miles from the Russian border, and there are warnings of illegal activities. Mugging and robberies of lone tourists are not unheard of.

A soldier standing at the side of the road flags me down; it's the perfect place for an ambush. He doesn't look threatening, but then the best decoys don't. He wants some wire to fix his broken bicycle and shows me the problem. He is only a young lad and clearly not in the engineering division. Somehow he has twisted the derailleur on his five-speed bicycle so the spring pushes; making the chain slacker, as opposed to providing the tension it is designed to. I fetch some tools. It's puzzling; how the hell did he manage to do this? The chain has no joining link, so I resort to removing the pulleys to relocate its position. It works, but the chain is so dry I fetch my chain oiling, hinge quietening spray can. He's happy to be mobile again, and indicates he will get chai for me. I wave him off; it will take me a while to get all packed up again.

I see his skinny tyre marks as I continue along the track, the sweat is cold on me now, and as it starts to rain, I manage to come off the bike again on a muddy patch. I really am a crap rider, but I'm very good at picking up a loaded bike. Further on there is a gate across the road. I don't see how I could have gone wrong; there is only one road, and I turn back to a minor track I saw, but it just dead-ends. I return to the gate. In this unstable area I'm not sure what to do, so tentatively I open it and close it behind me. It appears to be there just to keep the livestock from wandering off.

On a corner by a bridge is a tiny chai shack, Mr. Military is waiting there for me with his bicycle and a cup of thick black coffee. He shows me photos of his children on his phone, which seems almost standard practise now. I don't know how much this coffee cost, but he doesn't have a drink for himself. He leaves me to it, waving his thanks and taking a steep track up into the hills. I ride to another gate and leave this captive little experience behind.

I'm back in road mode now and start my ascent to the pass. It's a busy stretch of road; I've seen six vehicles in the last hour. A minivan stops ahead of me; a tourist jumps out with his camera in time to take a photo of me as I pass. Because I'm so cool, wild, and free? At least compared to his companions in the confines of the minivan I am. Yeah, I like being me today.

As I come down the pass the sun shines, and yet more glacier encrusted mountains come into view, along with more stone villages with their towers of protection protruding from the green landscape. It's beautiful, but I want to ride on; the ride's too good to stop. It's not over yet, though, I still have a river to cross and a tripod moment to indulge in.

Mestia is a modern town; banks and petrol stations, a big newly-built town square, wide streets, and tarmac, so third and fourth gear can be selected; it's been a while. Despite the modernization, the tourist count is low, and I spot the Swedes walking down the street. They have found a guesthouse with the German couple, and as I follow them along the steep dirt track leading there, they enthuse about the view from the balcony and the high standard of the rooms. There is even a resident puppy to play with. It feels so good to pull into a foreign town and see familiar faces that lead me to a place to stay. It's so easy, so enjoyable. I lean my bike against a fence outside, take off my boots; I go up the steps to the ornate deck that surrounds the first floor. The owner is out, but her daughter is in reception. Without a hint of compassion she tells me they are full, and my euphoric feeling falls from the landing into the mud. Dejectedly I follow it. How bloody miserable, from company and accommodation to solitary homelessness. Bollocks.

I can't turn round on this narrow steep track, so I continue up round a corner. Still there is nowhere flat to put my feet down. The road ends by two open wooden gates; it's another guesthouse, and in the yard is a motorbike.

It has a big yellow number plate the same as mine; it's a British bike. Wait a minute, I know this bike, this rider. He left on his journey to the 'Stans from the Ace Cafe in London; I watched him leave. What are the chances? I didn't even know he was in Georgia. This is going to be funny; wait till I see him. But he isn't in. Three drunks are sitting on some chairs in a lean-to. They avoid my enquiries as to the possibility of a room.

"Drink beer," one says, "It helps you to sleep." "But I don't want to sleep. It's only 1 PM."

"Drink beer," seems to be the only option; what's a guy to do? I drink beer.

"Drink vodka," says another one and pours me a shot. "Oh, go on then," I can see where this is leading. I better pace myself.

"You know this man?" one says, pointing at the bike.

"Yes, Mark, I know him. But I didn't know he was here." They all find this hard to believe; so do I. I'm given more to drink. Then bread, cheese, and tomatoes come out and more vodka to wash it down. I don't even know if I can stay here yet. Wait till I see Mark; he will be so surprised.

"Who are you people, anyway, if you don't work here and you are not guests?" One is a guide and has certainly led me astray; the other is an incoherent drunk; the third seems to be a mute. What stimulating company.

"Drink vodka," comes the demand again. I seem not to be able to assert myself so succumb to the invitation. A lady comes to the table. She seems to know who I am; yes, she has a room.

"I'm really sorry. I'm not usually this drunk. You see, these men here are responsible." Actually they aren't responsible at all and neither am I.

"What is your name?" "Rosa."

"Oh, like the name of this guest house; well that's easy to remember. I'm Graham." She frowns and smiles simultaneously; I'm clearly not the first victim of this misguided guide. I'm not sure I'd be so welcoming to someone as dirty and drunk as I am. I think I will change my trousers. In the middle of the yard I strip to my underwear and slip into something more comfortable, something less offensive, less offensive at least than a tattooed half-naked hippy in the front yard.

"I think I'm ready for another drink now." My room is not prepared yet, so Rosa suggests I stay where I am for the time being. I don't try hard enough to find another option. In-between the somehow quite entertaining yet limited conversation, I anticipate the surprise I am going to give Mark when he arrives.

"Hello Graham," he says like he expected me to be here. My drunkenness, loudness, and my bike in full view took away the element of surprise, but it's still good to see him. We continue as we were, and the guide wanders off and comes back with another bottle of vodka. Oh no.

I haven't even unpacked my bike. I really should eat something. The afternoon turns to evening, and drinking turns to really drunk. Before I go to bed a large lady gives me a hat.

DAY 59

MESTIA, GEORGIA, 1.5 MILES

Where did that hat come from?

My room exits into a large library-cum-parlour, where one of the walls has a bookcase full of Georgian-script books. The spines look intriguing, but I can only judge the books by their covers.

The room has low benches and high tables, which make them terrible for anything but posture. I go down for a breakfast of rice pudding and bread. Rosa only asks your name once; she addresses everyone by their first name. It makes for a Walton family feeling around the breakfast table with some of the residents I'm yet to meet, unless I did last night.

There is a communal dongle, and for the first time in five days I am able to get online. Amongst the usual rubbish is an email from Ted Simon; he has finished my book and said he "found it entertaining." It may still be early, but I defy the day to get any better! The next email informs me I now owe nothing on my visa card; it just did. And another tells me Stan Tours are not charging a cancellation fee. I may be in a place of spectacular natural beauty, but I'm getting quite a lot of satisfaction from the virtual world this morning.

There is a washing machine in the kitchen, which is at the guests' disposal, so Mark and I make a load of clothes that have only been washed by hand for the last two months. The morning passes talking bikes, people, anecdotes, visas, and all that stuff. It turns out that 16 years ago Mark's path crossed with the Swiss couple in the Land Cruiser. He made some observations, thoughts I had considered but was unable to articulate. The fact remains I do not envy their 28 years of constant travel; it sounds tortuous. Mark goes off to look for some friends of his who have also, by complete coincidence, arrived here at the same time.

I go for a wander; this place has had a lot of money invested in it. It's everything Ushguli isn't: it lacks authenticity and originality. A multi-storey police station has been built, the place is over-policed, and bored patrols drive up and down the main street constantly. A bored policeman is usually a dangerous thing, however, I've recently become informed that the new government sacked 97% of the former police force, the corrupt ones. Now they are all above board and honest, which would explain my fine last week. I do wonder what the fired 97% will do for a living when the bribe money runs out. A rather swish-looking pedestrian area has been constructed, but the glass-fronted shops show nothing but vacancies. There are a few pavement restaurants, but the pristine concrete slab of a runway with its smoked glass terminal building is yet to bring in the anticipated trade.

The day is warm and sunny, so I give my bike clothes a wash too and start to clean the bike, but it is beyond a manual clean. I go for a little ride out and find a man with a power washer. I can't prise the spray gun from his hands, so I point at the bits that need squirting and try to keep the jet from cleaning the grease from my bearings. It's better than it was; I don't want mega-shiny any more than I want mud-encrusted. The bike is significantly lighter now, so I fill it with fuel to make up for the weight loss.

The guides of persuasion are nowhere to be seen today, and I spend the evening in the lean-to chatting to a Slovenian girl.

When I'm not looking into the eyes of a beautiful girl or at the bottom of a shot glass, I realise that from here I can see a pyramid mountain top, and the snow turns from orange to purple as the last of the sun shines on its peak.

She says they have some strange dress habits here. She is a fashion designer and notices such things, and here I am in yellow combats and a holey Bulgarian T-shirt. Where's that hat gone?

DAY 60

MESTIA, GEORGIA, WALKING FOR MILES

I need to go hiking. All everyone talks about is hiking; it's even more popular than the visa conversation. Hiking is what you do here, so I think I will have a go. Mark is still trying to track down his friends, so I leave him my laptop and prepare for the transformation from biker to hiker. I'm not going for days into the wild, I just need to take some water. I'm a little concerned about my knee; just over two years ago it gave out on a trek in Nepal. I always land on the same one whether I'm falling from a ladder or a bike. This could be seen as a good thing; it means the other knee is perfect. I've not tried anything strenuous since the doctor said the MRI scan was "just fine," stop whinging.

I've managed to leave so late the day has warmed up past a comfortable point. I'm going to the cross on top of the hill, a destination recommended by Rosa and several others. The path starts steeply; I'm not sure I brought enough water. I'm sweating and gasping already, which is the down side of choosing throttle over pedals. I may get exercise picking the thing up, but I don't get the cardiovascular like the cyclists do. A couple of fat German ladies are panting in the shade of a tree; we all agree it's harder than we expected, but inside I'm determined not to be beaten by the mountain or by them. I continue; it's not personal but I don't want to see them again.

When I trekked in Nepal the first time it was on a well-travelled route; the guidebook practically told you step-by-step what to expect, where to eat, drink, sleep, and what to see on the way. What it didn't give you were hints for small-talk when you repeatedly encounter the same people. You can't ignore them—you get the same bus to the starting point and stay in the same villages at night, but by the third time you've passed each other it's becoming difficult to have an original comment, as it's not even lunch time yet: "Hard work, eh?" "Nice view?"

211

"Steep isn't it?" "Did you see the yeti?" There's only so much you can remark on. I'm not going to suffer that agony this time.

Every time I stop in the shade I'm surrounded by flies like Pigpen in Charlie Brown. After the initial ascent the path evens out, the flies stay beneath me, my head and heart don't pound so hard. The track takes me past wooden fences that appear to keep nothing in or out, then up into flowery pastures, and slowly rises to a full panoramic mountain view. The sky is clear, and the diversity of the peaks is incredible. There is last night's pyramid, a dome like a giant mosque with a roof of snow and grey jagged pinnacles that barely have a flat spot for the snow to cling to. Then there are the absolute big boys that pierce the sky and create their own weather systems. Occasionally I get glimpses of their magnitude between the clouds where I thought there was only sky. There are glaciers everywhere, 300 of them in this area. All this visual stimulation takes my mind from my knee. I take a photo for a couple who don't have a tripod. After I give them back their camera, one of them fills their bottle from a stream, I don't say anything, and when the path switches back, the stream crosses the path and flows through cow shit. They'll learn.

After a few hours the cross comes into view. I can look down at Mestia and the road I came in on. Not only is the view beyond my expectations, but the real joy is that my knee is fine; I'm not too old and crippled for such activities. There are a few people sitting around, some with the foresight to bring sandwiches. I didn't even bring an emergency protein bar from my panniers. I nod acknowledgement to some other hikers and go find a peaceful spot to sit and take it all in. Beyond the cross the path heads north to a lake, but I'm not going to push my luck. Rosa said it's possible to ride a bike all the way up here. When I head back down I meet the fat German ladies still trudging up.

"You were quick," one says. "Yeah, it's closed" would be a pretty mean thing to say.

The track splits, and I take the more rideable one, just for research. I meet trains of horses, and although it would be an easier path to ride than those I have already done, it seems a bit invasive, disrespectful of the environment. Nevertheless I'm contemplating the thrill of riding up to the ultimate campground and sleeping in such infinite solitude. It's very tempting, and the thoughts alone are so exhilarating it makes me shudder. It's not from cold; this alternative route back is taking me way out of town, and when I reach the river I have to go several more miles through dusty road excavations to get back. The last bit really drags on and exhausts me. The vodka drinkers are back, but I need water; they cannot tempt me at all.

Mark has had no success in meeting his friends; he is preparing to leave tomorrow and gives me his brick of a Turkish guidebook. I think I'm grateful; he certainly is for not having to carry it anymore, and he won't even accept my Central Asia one in return. We go out for an early dinner. As we walk back we bump into his friends—a couple I'd seen at the top of the mountain today–

so we all go to a pavement restaurant for a drink. This place is the Koh San Road of Georgia; everyone is connected to everyone else. The cow shit-water drinkers are here, and back from their mountain hike are the large ladies of German descent. We soon have quite an international table. The inevitable visa conversation dominates, but I'm in the company of some experienced travellers. This isn't the gap year crowd; we've all been drunk in a far greater variety of places.

Again I spend the evening in the company of the Slovenian girl. We are both leaving tomorrow, but only she has a destination.

DAY 61

UREKI, GEORGIA, 138 MILES

Alone again. I'm not going to stick around for the next influx of transients. I borrow the communal dongle once more. I have an email from my tenant. The subject heading is "Urgent," which only says one thing to me: he wants out before the end of the contract. Any house maintenance issues would be dealt with in other ways, and yes, he wants to arrange a Skype conversation. Well, I can't do that here, and I certainly can't do that at the top of a mountain. How much would I enjoy the solitude of that mountain wondering about the tenancy? I need to find out what the news is. As I take my tank box down to the bike, the cleaner looks intrigued by it,

"TV?" she asks. Really? Do you really think I have a TV with me? Any way, they aren't even made this fat anymore. After goodbyes, gratitudes, and compliments on guesthouse hospitality, I head out. I never came across the Swedes and Germans again.

One of the benefits of cheaper accommodation is the unavoidable integration. "Community" is built into the function of the place, and the anonymity of a hotel room seems very cold by comparison. As I pull out on the bike, some backpackers arrive, and my short but memorable residency is over; the circle continues.

I need a post office. There are still two postcard people in my life; they don't do any other form of communication. Even the police I ask don't know if or where a post office might be, so they won't be getting a Mestia postmark then.

It's so good to be on the bike: blue skies and snowy views, jacket open and flapping. I ride the smooth concrete at a steady 40 mph, well probably; I've been estimating my speed for weeks now. It's a little sad to be leaving such a good social scene and scenery, but that's the road for you; it's what happens. I just had to get through a disproportionately long spell of no contact.

Melted snow streams down the mountains to join the river, which winds down the valley next to me. The mountains change in profile as I pass around them. They are such good value; not only do they change depending on your view point but through the course of the day as well, with shadows and low light. If that isn't enough, the seasons too give them a variety of appearances. You just don't get that diversity with the sea. I'm meant to live around mountains, not in bloody Essex.

As the land becomes less hostile, farming communities start to appear, the river gets greyer, wider, and more aggressive. It takes away anything in its path as it rushes down to a lake of contrasting turquoise. If you have to leave mountains behind, this is about as scenic and dramatic an exit as you can hope for. There are multiple tunnels of utter blackness that drop big drips of cold water into my wide scanning eyes. Inevitably, the corner comes that leads the road down to the plains ahead. Yuk, they look hot.

I sigh deeply; I want my mountains back, now only a cloud covered haze in my mirrors. However, I know that in a few days I will have a different range on my horizon. For now, though, I have towns and traffic lights, trucks and choices. I stop at an unsigned junction. Taxi drivers whistle and point; how do they even know where I want to go? The road runs alongside palms and grape vines; the aroma of summer flowers is held in the hot air. As transitions into civilization go this one is quite gentle. The traffic gets faster, the humidity greater, and eventually the Black Sea coast comes into sight. I ride down to what was described in my guidebook as a quiet beach camp, but things have progressed, and it is now a resort of solid ugly hotels, shops of garish plastic beach toys and Manchester United towels. It's shocking, horrendous. I ride to the end of the beach road in hope of something better, but there is nothing. I turn round in a place of fishing boats in various states of disrepair; there may be some kind of accommodation here too. I'm allowed to put my tent up in the grounds; it will do for tonight. It's not exactly mountainous seclusion, but the upside is it's easy to find a restaurant with Wi-Fi.

My fears are confirmed, my rental income is going to end prematurely. I'm really glad I'm not in a distant 'Stan now.

Day 62

Vardzia, Georgia, 138 Miles

I can hear the waves break on the beach, but my tent stands in the shade of some fir trees, the ever contrasting vegetation of Georgia's landscape. There is a shower head above the squat toilet. It's a tricky operation, but I seem to come out cleaner. I loosely roll up my dewy tent and bungee the lid down on an overflowing top box. I'm not sure if they just don't want payment or whether it's for me to decide the rate. I've asked twice and leave without paying anyone. It's not like I sneaked out, I have said good morning to half a dozen people and waved as I left, but if they expected payment they really should have said. I can't read the situation; anyway, other than a few gallons of sun heated water, I've taken nothing and left only a small area of compressed grass.

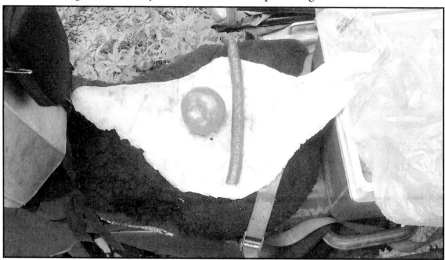

The stalls along this coastal resort road are just opening, so I get fresh diamond-shaped Georgian bread and other supplies. I suppose I got the best out of this place. I have no desire to stay a moment longer. I came up this way a few weeks ago, but then it was grey and gloomy. Annoyingly there are far better camping opportunities just down the road, but oh well. Just more seaside towns, but somehow they seem OK; the sun helps of course. Back past the sellers of bamboo ladders at the side of the road, and before long I see the extravagant skyline of Batumi again. The road runs down by the beach, and although it's still early, the flesh of bathers is exposed and distracting.

The temperature is a long way from its peak, and I would like to get into the hills before things heat up. I do; they are just the wrong hills. It should be pretty straight forward; I've come from the north, to the south is Turkey, to the west is the Black Sea. All I need to do is head east, but there are many choices. I just can't find the road that keeps on going. I ask some police, just because they have a uniform on doesn't mean they have ever left town or even seen a map. Perhaps all the literate cops were fired, and it's just the dumb honest ones left. A taxi driver tries to lead me, but the way he goes can't be right. I persevere in my beliefs and ride with instinct. I pass a big gas works; the smell of gas is so strong I think I could ignite it from here. Eventually I find the easterly road I want.

Back in the hills the road is good, despite the dangerous traffic, wandering cows, falling rock, and gravel corners. I'm probably riding faster than I should, but the road encourages speed even if the obstacles don't.

It's all perfectly agreeable although not that dramatic; how could any road compare with what I've just come down from? The road forks in the outskirts of a town, and assumption keeps me on the paved option, which takes me on a needless detour, winding up through the hillside town, and although I would like it to be the right direction, I have to concede that I should have gone for the dirty option.

It's not fun like the tracks up by the Russian border. It wants to be a fast road, but it isn't; it's bumpy, dusty, rutted washboard with delusions of sealed superiority. I have little respect for any kind of wannabe, and this road generates contempt. It slows progress and offers nothing in return, and return was my original plan, but as it painfully drags out its inadequate existence, I decide I will avoid coming back this way. In a futile attempt to impress, it gains altitude to a ski area that's still under construction. The surface becomes loose and the rocks bigger, blasted straight from the cliff face. The traffic is backed up on both sides whilst diggers distribute the latest controlled landslide. The only good thing about roads like this is the renewed appreciation for the tarmac when it starts again.

It's as if pleasure was put on pause, as now there are castles, mosques, and churches, ruins on hilltops; probably worth more than a passing glance but I'm not stopping here. Riding on I meet another river that flows through woodland with inviting grassy areas of camping potential, but I have a destination in mind.

It's a rare occurrence, and I will not be side-tracked regardless how enticing the track is.

Vardzia is signposted, and one tour bus after another is coming towards me, I'm beginning to fear that another place has developed significantly since my guidebook was printed.

Vardzia is a city of caves hollowed into a cliff face; it was developed around the same time as the towers in Ushguli were built. It once housed, or caved, 50,000 people, and now monks and nuns live there, although in separate caves, I think. Being early evening the hordes have left, and I ride up the valley past the abandoned hot springs, looking for the ideal river bank camping spot. There is a little open restaurant, so I stop there for a plate of meat, potatoes, and grease. They say I can camp on their grounds: perfect.

There is a warm breeze to dry this morning's dew off my tent. Further up river is a large house in need of repair. I'm not sure if it's occupied or not, so not to intrude, I pitch by the river between the house and the restaurant. It is occupied, and the owner, a biker type, walks over to the restaurant. Long hair in pony tail and with a bushy beard, I nod hello at him, but he doesn't seem very receptive. It's hard to read his facial expressions; could be a bit of a nasty bastard.

Across the river from me, the last of the light shines onto the caves. It's Saturday night, and the lawn mower man comes to visit for some evening grass harvesting. Up and down he goes with his smoking two-stroke engine revving at full throttle. This is obviously a time of day for all kinds of constructive pursuits.

A generator is started to pump water from the river into a large concrete circular structure; I'm not sure if it is a water garden feature or an overgrown swimming pool. A vanload of workmen arrives to string power lines across the river, yelling and hauling pulleys and cables across poles. It's like camping in the middle of a bleeding industrial zone. This is all going on around me like I'm not there; I wish I wasn't. When it's too dark to run cables across rivers and cut grass, when the generator runs out of fuel, still I can't hear the flowing river. I hear the intermittent pounding bass from an over-amplified and under-talented fuckwit DJ, providing what some might call entertainment to the revellers on the other side of the river. I hate this place already. At 3AM I get a text; my friend who drinks his wine from a tiny glass has fallen into a coma. My complaints are suddenly very insignificant.

Day 63

Gyumri, Armenia, 101 Miles

Better go and look at these caves then; already two big tourist buses have arrived. However, once I've walked across the bridge to the car park, I'm told they don't open for another hour. How can a cave be closed? I bet cavemen didn't have this problem. As I walk back I mention this fact to an approaching couple; they are English, and we decide to go to the hot springs. There is a pipe sticking out of the ground at a right angle; water spurts from it. I saw it last night but didn't think much of it. Colin tells me it's a discharge of thermal water, and it sounds like a jet engine. The sulphur-smelling steam is projected 100 feet along the river bank. I'm not sure why I wasn't more curious yesterday. Colin has a very enquiring mind and the ability to retain all the facts he stumbles across. He remembers the names of various towns we have both visited across the globe, and he pronounces them correctly too.

On our way back to the caves, he produces a very thorough printed-out guide. He has a hat and head torch; I have a headache. A torch, though, might have been a useful addition for this tour. He goes into every piss-stinking toilet of a cave; he knows what the Frescos depict and all about Queen Tamar who lived here in the 1100s with a modest 350 cave rooms to herself, supposedly for hiding, possibly for seeking too. Colin points out the wear on the walls where horses were tethered. This is all excruciatingly interesting, but I want to get up to the cool shit before the masses arrive. We are already being passed by the shuffling multitude. Having popped into every cavern on route, even Colin seems to tire of this meticulous tour. We head up to a gateway carved out of rock and into the three storey cave, which is the Church of the Assumption.

I can't think of a more aptly named monument to religious belief. But my cynicism is soon restrained; the church is predictably cavernous and, being

219

Sunday morning, is in full service. Three priests stand at the altar; the place is full of women, heads covered, slowly taking communion in turn. We stand at the back respectfully. I look on in awe; it's a very spiritual moment. I'm not taking the piss, it really is a privilege to see this ritual in such a unique place. There are heavenly voices chanting as the communion takes place. I look around to see where it's coming from; the place is lit by candles, and I don't expect to see celestial speakers hanging from the ceiling resonating a pre-recorded sound, especially after last night's incomplete attempts to string power cables across the river. In the corner are four nuns. The sound coming from them is reverberating around this sonic cathedral. I get out my phone and record the harmonic mantra. It's a very calming and divine experience.

I was told that behind this church, further into the cave, is a labyrinth of passages that rise up the inside of the cliff face, so I lead the way. It's lit by intermittent light bulbs that barely glow. This too would be an atmospheric experience in an Indiana Jones kind of way, if not for Colin. He saw me record the nuns singing and starts telling me about his success in electronic sampling; it really detracts from the moment. It's quite claustrophobic, hunched back, stumbling into darkness down very narrow passageways. Having ascended three storeys, the passage ends at a hole in the cliff face that looks out across the valley. These caves rock.

Back down at the church the congregation has dispersed, and it's easier to see the murals on the walls. One of the priests is still hanging around chatting to the parishioners, and what do ya know, it's the biker dude from the house next to my tent. He's not a biker at all; these orthodox priests really do bear an uncanny resemblance, though. I think I've seen enough; the pathways are crawling with tourists now. I lost Colin and his wife, or perhaps they have lost me. I can't imagine a more traditional way to start a Sunday.

Having packed up the bike, I ride back to the thermal jet and have a bit of a wash in it. I've come down from the heights of heavenly choirs to wash in the steaming fury from the pits of hell. Cooled and cleansed, I ride towards Armenia.

The road is empty and twists through modest valleys. There is blossom on the hillsides, and the river flows beside me, but I'm not seeing any of this, I'm thinking of the text I got last night. My mate, Doug, is in a coma now. I hope he is at home; I don't like to picture him in a hospital environment. Strange how I should find myself in church only hours after I heard the news, not that I associate him with such places; a smoky bike shed is where his absence will be most felt.

A town comes into view and pulls me back to what I'm doing. There is a signpost for Turkey. That's convenient; I can go back this way and don't have to do that awful dirt road again. The now obligatory ruins sit on top of a hill overlooking the town, and by object of elimination, I find the onward route I need.

Once again, I am surrounded by high altitude meadows, where the flowers look like they have only just accepted it's warm enough to blossom, and they have done it in unison. For a country smaller than Ireland, it has so much diversity in elevation and, therefore, in scenery, temperature, and landscape too. It's rapidly becoming my new favourite country. Having said that, I'm about to leave Georgia again. The corrugated apex of the shelter over the customs border is visible from a distance, and I consider what, if anything, I should do in preparation for my entry into Armenia. I've heard if you have an Azerbaijan visa in your passport you won't be allowed in. I also have a sticker on my pannier, and I consider hiding it, but I can't do anything about the passport. As it turns out, they don't care at all; one of the easiest transitions of the trip. I'm the only vehicle at the crossing. Judging by the amount of shacks that sell insurance I'm assuming it's compulsory, so I buy some; it's only $12. I get a little sticker that must be displayed on my windshield. The agent watches as I wipe the dirt from an area so it will stick, and then he obtusely sticks it above the clean area.

First impressions of Armenia? Poor and grumpy: much poorer and no smiles anywhere. I go through little villages of rusted farm machinery and cow pats, formed into pancakes and stacked to dry so they can be burnt at a later date. Every yard has a pyramid of cow shit; geese and ducks wander around the yards of scrap iron. Some properties have bee hives, and they all have their washing blowing on the line, but it is Sunday and a good drying day too. A signpost for Yerevan, the capital, is worth a photo. I know I'm in Armenia, but signs excite me more than a passport stamp, probably because they are indisputable proof of how far from home I am.

What I need now more than anything else is not an ice-cream, but when I stop in the first town to use an ATM, a young boy comes up to me and says in an accent he surely got from too many American movies "Cool bike." He has a little ice-cream stall outside a shop, and seeing as trade is good, I figure it hasn't been festering inside the machine for ages so bravely buy one. It's my first purchase in Armenia, unless you count boring insurance. As I stand chatting to him and watching the pedestrians and traffic go around the town square, I decide I would like to spend my first night here. It takes a few tries to find a hotel; I opt for a grander one than I would usually choose. The rate is high, but the reception staff are friendly, so we haggle, because I really don't care if I stay or not; it's not late, I'm not desperate, and it's not one of those baking hot or pissing rain days that you don't want to go back out into.

We have just agreed on an acceptable rate when in walks an American rider; he has all the expensive BMW riding gear. I say hello, and he asks how much a room is. Suddenly the rate goes up for a single room, or if we want, the manager says we can share.

"Look, I really don't want to share, I don't know him. I've known you longer than I've known him," but there seems no chance of getting back to the price that was on offer before his arrival. So we both leave.

Turns out he is German but with an American accent and American sayings too. He has a sat nav that has hotels on it, so I ride with him. We get one rejection after another; we can't even agree on a price at a restaurant cum brothel we stumble across. An hour has passed, and I'm just about to split company from this guy when we find something suitable on the edge of town.

Now the obligations of the day are complete, my thoughts return to Doug. There is going to be a surplus of alcohol on the planet now he is in a coma. I feel an immediate need to do my bit to rectify the situation, and I have no want to explain my actions to anyone.

DAY 64

LAKE SEVAN, ARMENIA, 180 MILES

The restaurant doesn't open until 11AM, which is just fine; I haven't had unlimited Internet for a while and all my complimentary soap has run out too. In this place I can stock up on both whilst my underwear dries, hanging from my mirrors outside. Modesty and discretion have long departed, as has the BMW that was parked next to my bike. Along with soap and Wi-Fi comes the feeling of safety, so I don't bother to bang the hell out of my boots before I put them on to evacuate any nasties that may have made them their home for the night. A morning of planning, organization, and structure is novel, and like any positive new experience, I'm finding it quite appealing.

As I head out of town a truck heading in honks. Was that at me or the girl walking down the road? She's worth a honk; is she accepting the honk? I want the honk; we're both worth it!

The road condition is adequate, and the traffic is scarce, I plod on happily for a few hours. I read some reviews on the Glastonbury Festival on the Internet this morning, where the Rolling Stones headlined, two things that used to be better in my resentful opinion, mainly because I'm a little sad I missed them. Michael Eavis said it was the best Glastonbury ever, but he says that every bloody year.

I come into an industrial town of railway sidings and a power station, where the landscape undulates with endless heaps of coal. It looks like a plague of steroid-strong moles have inhabited the heart of a Midlothian coalfield. The power station distributes its product via a web of rusty pylons that head off in all directions. Then come the drab steel and concrete tower blocks, which house the workers; living monuments to the failed dreams of the inhabitants, multiple stories of unreached potential. Beyond their shadows the city becomes more upmarket with wide shopping streets, trams, and trees but no signposts.

The road I'm on looks less and less likely to exit the city, and it dead-ends in a graveyard.

I try again, a little harder. The road looks promising then it too appears to lose the will to leave. I'm not sure if the broken surface is due to over-use or no use. I get to see things I wouldn't have, but it's a little frustrating, especially when it takes so long for the road to be wrong. Back into the city and at a set of major traffic lights I take the only option left, and it works. It's hard to express the feelings generated by the wrong turns. It's not too hot, and I'm in no particular hurry. I'm riding into areas of housing blocks surrounded by an expanse of concrete for parking, playing, and pissing on. I ride to a well-kept graveyard with extravagantly decorated memorials, then on another route past the captive playgrounds, where children wave from behind rusted yellow railings. The roads turns to dirt at the city outskirts where gardens are used as farmyards; pigs lying in the mud whilst a skinny horse stands by a stone wall waiting for work.

They are the sights of the city, the life I would have missed if I hadn't made a mistake. But when I take the time to recall what I witnessed on my unintended tour, there is not a hint of regret. I think that is another benefit of the hundred day journey; it would have to be a quite significant detour to make a memory if the trip was a year or more long. Destinations and targets may change, but I'm happy that the one thing I consistently get right is the time I take to do my trips. It fits my budget, my endurance, and the life expectancy of my attention and appreciation. The mojo unfortunately has a will of its own, but it seems to be content with the experiences I've been feeding it for the last few weeks.

Now I'm on the right road I satisfy my need for other things. I double-back to a fruit and veg stall, and it takes longer than I'd like to find a surface that won't swallow my side stand. When I do look up I see my sales assistants are a couple of very wrinkled women with polka dot aprons, knitted cardigans, and gummy smiles. I point at a few tomatoes; there is nothing else I need. They are wrapped in paper, tied with string, and then gifted to me. I've been feeling like Captain Wealth as I ride round the deprivation of the outer city, and here I am being given the fruits of their labours. I ask if I can take a photo. They agree willingly, but you wouldn't think it to see the stern faces I have captured. The winkles rise upwards into grins and giggles when I show them the back of the camera. If only I could have captured that too.

Back up into the coolness, over a mile above sea level and another explosion of colour on the hillsides. I choose a field of purple to stop for lunch. I slice my tomatoes on my chest-high top box table and thoroughly enjoy my vertical picnic. The road descends in gusty switchbacks to Lake Sevan, a lake that either failed to fulfil its potential, or lost its appeal, judging by the derelict hotels that line the shore. There are dark clouds overhead, but the water is clear, and I slowly ride around looking for a place to camp, although it's only 4PM. I go off-road down to a place hidden by pine trees. It's got possibilities, but the flies and midges are off-putting. There is a little bank down to the water's edge, water so clear I can see schools of fish, and just as I'm contemplating a paddle, I see a water snake swiftly move across the surface. Bugger that.

Back on the road I keep my eye out for another camping spot. There are lots of possibilities, but on closer inspection they are marshy. If I turn off the engine or stall it there is a buzz in the air but not from excitement; from my boots to my visor the air is thick with swarming insects.

At a little shop I stop for some chocolate. Some military lads have pulled up outside; they're a boisterous lot, and, although I don't generally permit anyone but pretty girls or wide-eyed kids to sit on my bike, I seem to have little choice as they take it in turns to be phone photo'd in the rider's position. Thankfully they seem to have perfected the overlander's high kick in basic training, so nothing is dislodged, and they take their turns with presumption but respect. I think I'll go and eat my Kit Kat down the road a bit; I haven't got a spare finger for them.

The lake is filled from mountain streams, and the source is beginning to have more appeal than the mozzie-infested lake. I make several efforts to find a route into the hills, but the dirt tracks all end in villages of stares and hopelessness. The pine forests are OK but deprive me of the lake views and the hazy mountains on the far shore. When I find the elevation I need, it doesn't come with the concealment I want. I find a rutted track and drop the bike. I'm getting so good at picking it up now; it's a pity I'm not getting better at riding it. I find a spot that meets my out-of-sight sunset needs, and just as I'm dismounting I realise a field of farm workers are all watching me.

It's getting late now; perhaps I'm getting too picky. I'm running out of options and take a track down to the shore again. It ends at a muddy bog, but it will have to do; there is a patch of grass big enough to pitch my tent on. Beside it is a shallow swamp of croaking frogs and the inevitable mozzies, still I have a stunning sunset view as I cook the canned meat I've been carrying for a week. It's barely edible, looks and smells like dog food, probably tastes like it too. The sun shoots beams over the mountain it has set behind– it's a signal for feeding time, and I am besieged by mozzies. They swarm with blood-thirsty intent. I would literally be eaten alive if not for the sanctuary of my tent. I kneel inside looking out through a fly screen that is absolutely covered with them; the hum is so loud. I squash the ones that got in the tent with me. I think I'm safe now. It's a warm night, and there is no breeze, I have a door at either end. I open the cover of the rear one so any breeze there is will pass through. I'm getting bitten and realise with horror that I accidently unzipped the fly screen and they are swarming in. There is a blood bath as I frantically squash all the invaders. And then I just watch. I'm going to need a wee at some point, I can't possibly leave the tent; I've never seen such a fearsome and persistent swarm of mozzies. Thankfully, the feeding frenzy only lasts for a limited time during the last light, then they go back to whatever larvae-layered swamp they came from. It's a noisy night, apart from the frogs there's a lot of other loud pond life. This is going to be one of those experiences it will be hard to keep quiet about when at an English barbeque someone with a couple of bites on their ankle proclaims they are being eaten alive.

"Let me tell you about the time I camped on the swampy shore of Lake Sevan in Armenia . . ."

Day 65

A Hillside near Kapan, Armenia 178 Miles

Something very loud is very close, and it sounds very large. From some nearby trees it screeches an announcement of the arrival of dawn; I think it was saying it had survived the night. This was followed by a neighbour's reply; its mate confirmed that it had too. I have as well, as did the mozzie inside my tent, too full of my blood to fly away, so it doesn't survive the dawn. I wipe two sticky fingers on my sleeping bag; the blood of a midnight feast and a dawn killing. My morning gesture of vengeance keeps any other opportunists at bay, and I pack up without paying any more blood money.

10,000 Armenian drams fills my tank, and I'm out of town before the majority have woken. I have a mountain pass to cross, so I gain the altitude I wanted last night and see the river I'd hoped for too, but from up here the lake is lost in a haze, probably clouds of mozzies. Two cyclists come racing downhill towards me, too chilled or cool to return a wave. The dodgy canned meat has taken its toll, and the need for a hidden spot becomes my top priority. I wash in a river so cold it numbs my feet, while a frog chorus serenades me. Unlike Georgia, the varying elevation does not bring a variety of scenery. I continue to a village higher than Ushguli, which is peculiar, as Ushguli is celebrated as being Europe's highest village. Maybe Armenia is even less European than Georgia; who knows what the criteria is? I'm only judging this by the altimeter on my watch. Anyway it is high. The snowy mountains are a long way off, and they can't compete with the Caucasus wow.

I stop near Sisian. Outside of the town is the Armenian Stonehenge; the details surrounding its existence are sketchy, but it's certainly more accessible than the English 'henge. There is an element of confusion, though, as a new circle of old stones have been erected on the other side of the road. They still bear the ancient carvings, but I'm not convinced of their authenticity. I'm not quite sure how their credibility stays intact when they are not where they originally stood and what they stood for. It seems the understanding of their origin is as unknown as the reason for their repositioning. The site across the road is more permanent and equally unvisited.

With heavy-handed unnecessary haste, I manage to break my tripod, but I have some super glue and generously soak the broken part. If there is one thing that is not needed around ancient stones it's impatience. I somehow manage to transfer some glue to my eyelid, blink frantically, and move my eye ball around as if I'm stuck talking to a boring person and looking for rescue. When I feel the glue solidify in the corner of my eye like sleep, I think I'm safe to look through the viewfinder without sticking.

There is a portakabin selling souvenirs. Inside is a black and orange T-shirt with pictures of the stones (the permanent ones not the rolling ones). This KTM livery is most desirable but has a tour T-shirt price tag, so I leave it.

The wind has got up, and the day has cooled down. I ride on looking at picturesque towns sitting in lush valleys. I'm heading south to tease myself one last time as I approach the Iranian border. A lot of the trucks have Iranian number plates; the inhalation of diesel fumes is the only taste of Iran I get. The road continues up and down over mountain passes, which are just not really doing it for me; the views are hazy, I'm overly critical. Any other time I would be gushing like a waterfall over this landscape, but I peaked too soon up in the glacier covered Svaneti region of Georgia. I know at some point I simply have to turn around, and I'm wondering how much longer I will ride before the inevitable U-turn. The town of Kapan provides the incentive I need. Its tower blocks and greyness, slow traffic and smoking trucks are enough to turn me round.

I buy some supplies and head back looking for a camping spot; the first is too close to the road, the next is too accessible to other traffic, the third has deep troughs of muddy water on a narrow cliff edge. I'd seen a sign earlier that warned of landmines—quite a price to pay for an off the beaten track camping spot. It takes multiple back and forth movements to turn round. I reconsider an area that's almost level; it's on a hillside and looks down over the plains. It will do, like the rest of the day, it's not spectacular, but it's OK. I pitch my tent and eat my food. It's an early stop, but for the last five nights my sleep has been disturbed.

I get a text from No. 6 in Holland; he will be going to Albania in a few weeks and do I want to meet him? I look at my guidebook and map of Turkey; it's a possibility, I suppose, but there is still a lot to see between here and there. He would never expect a simple yes; he of all people knows the fear of commitment. However, it's something to think about, option No. 6.

Thunder starts to rumble; low storm clouds creep over the hills behind me and take the last of the light away. Then the rain starts. I think it might be a good thing that I'm camped on a slope. The lightning cracks and rips the darkness apart; simultaneously the thunder crashes into the void. Much as I love my bike I'm reassured it's going to attract the lightning before my aluminium tent poles do. The storm seems trapped in the valley, and with increasing intensity it displays the anger of entrapment. The rain hammers onto my tent with deafening violence as if it's being hurled from the clouds; gravity alone can't produce such force. The tent stands the abuse, and through an inch of unzipped door I look out across the valley when the lightning illuminates it. The storm is relentless, and I start to consider my survival—food supplies are low, flood and famine are possibilities. There is no sleeping until it rains itself out and rumbles off over the plains.

I love the exhilaration of extreme weather. We don't get any in England; it's never excessively hot or cold, snowy or windy. We did have a hurricane on my 22nd birthday, but other than that, we rarely push the boundaries of bland. We don't even have any animals that will kill you. You can't go into the wild in England, only into the country.

DAY 66

KHOR VIRAP, ARMENIA, 204 MILES

The thing about severe weather is it opens a path to my most surreal thoughts, and I dream further into any weirdness than I can ever conceive with a conscious mind. Maybe camping on a cliff edge enhances such things. I wake at 9AM disorientated and on edge. I never sleep that late.

There seem to be no casualties from the storm; the bike was covered and my helmet was strapped to the bars. The morning is misty and humid, the bike is a bit moist under the cover, and in my helmet there's a puddle of water. Bugger. I think packing-up may take a while. An old man comes up the track; he is wearing wellies and waterproof trousers and is carrying a plastic bag. I say hello, and he stops to remove his waterproof clothing, taking some smart shoes out of his bag. He then stashes the clothing he has removed behind my tent; his appearance is very smart now. Without any question of mistrust, he leaves his wet weather protection and continues onwards to the road. I wonder if he's going to a funeral; I just get the feeling that this is not a regular thing he does.

After his departure, a hot July sun comes out, and things start to dry. Two hours after waking, the bike is loaded, and there is nothing left to do except put my soggy helmet on my head. The post-storm morning has left me sticky and damp, but the air is fresh and chilly at 40 mph.

I misinterpret my guidebook; thinking it implies that Goris is a place worth visiting, I make a small detour into the town. I'm sure in future editions they will elaborate by saying " . . . unless you have a wet helmet on your head." I do find a post office, and although they are not sent from the country of purchase, my postcards are finally on their way, so that just about makes it worth the visit. I ride up the street, round the church, and back to the main road.

While storms have passed overhead, and still now inside my soggy lid, I'm continuing to give a great deal of thought to the benefits of being the owner of an overpriced black and orange Sisian Stone T-shirt. It's occupying so much of my time I have to stamp out the thought with simple logic: a £10 note would disappear in a London pub in the time it takes to pour a couple of pints. Even if it was my favourite beer with the best of company, the experience wouldn't last more than half an hour. The T-shirt will last significantly longer. So on the way back I'll just stop and buy the bloody thing. Now I can think about something else.

Tatev Monastery is going to be that something else. It sits on a high cliff edge; I'm on the other side so I have to ride down into the gorge. There is a new and totally out of character cable car across the valley that would drop me right outside the monastery. I'm sure it has quite the view, but I have my own transport and I'm going to use it. At the bottom of the gorge is Devil's Bridge, one of the more pleasantly located rubbish dumps I've seen. Water rushes underneath some fallen rock. To stumble across it may be satisfying; to purposefully ride to it leads only to disappointment. The ascent from river to monastery is not paved; I'm beginning to see the benefit of the Wings of Tatev world record-holding cable car.

Best viewed from a distance is probably the way to appreciate the monastery. It's OK, but its perch on the cliff-top for me is the high point of the structure. When a cable car arrives it's announced by an amplified chime, much like one heard before an announcement in an airport. It booms across the valley and reverberates inside the monastery walls. I can't wait to go back to the distance and view the monastery a bit more.

Back on the main road I ride faster than I've ridden in months; the road is good, the air is cool, and there is nothing to miss that I didn't see on the way down. It's really good fun, and the engine seems to love it too. I go back into Sisian. There is something I'm not getting here; it's not a large town, and the map in my guidebook is simple enough. There should be two sites. The one with carved ram stones are meant to be in the park; the park doesn't even seem to exist, let alone the stones. The other is the Shaki Waterfall, which isn't "turned on." They use the water flow to generate electricity, and if you want it diverted to the waterfall you have to pay for the loss of electricity. I go back to the main stones; I'm still confused as to why there are two separate groups of them. Anyway, I just want a T-shirt. The black and orange one is out of stock, and the display one is sun faded; the other black one has white writing on it and doesn't have a design I like. So I end up with a blue and white one. I don't even know why I bothered; I hate it instantly. It doesn't matter, the price I paid wasn't for a T-shirt, it was for peace of mind. I'd rather have had an over-priced London beer.

I get a text from my tenant; he will be out in a month, so the clock is ticking, better move on. It's the perfect excuse to ride fast again. I love my KLR (and my

Mefos), it just transforms from dirt bike to race bike at will. I'm leaning hard round the bends, and as I drop 4,000 feet it doesn't miss a beat, its capabilities far exceed mine. The horizon has black skies on my right and sunshine on my left; conveniently the road takes me to the left to continue my drying out process. I'm heading up towards the capital now, but I'm not going there tonight.

The temperature is perfect, and the road takes me through shallow canyons. This seems to be wine country; there are plenty of roadside vendors selling plastic bottles of various coloured wines. I consider strapping one under a bungee, but I've got my treat for the day; gotta have a bit of discipline, I've got a mortgage to start paying soon. The road continues to thrill with winding climbs and sweeping descents and the occasional snowy mountain on the edge of the horizon.

With stunning presence Mount Ararat comes into view. This time I'm looking at the east side, however, its namesake town where I had hoped to stay doesn't quite measure up to the beauty of the mountain. It has a major cement works that, along with other industry, sprawls across the valley floor, making it a good place to keep riding past. It's getting late, and now the traffic is sweeping me up in its rush into the capital, but I'm not ready to go there yet. I divert to Khor Virap.

You'd think I'd had enough of churches and monasteries, but this one I know won't fail to satisfy. It's definitely about being viewed from a distance; it is located in des-res surroundings, although it got its name from a 200 foot pit within the walls. For 13 years the dry well was a place of imprisonment for a man later to be sainted. How annoying to be so close to such a stunning view but imprisoned in a pit. There is a remarkable story surrounding this incarceration and its significance to Armenia's history and faith. I would only be retelling a story that has nothing to do with motorbikes, roads, and scenery if I went into it now, so I think I will let the history books have the honour—it is really interesting though.

I park away from the monastery to take in the whole view. The sun is shooting beams across the sky, and I notice in my bike mirror that my hair looks fabulous. It's a laborious procedure, but wearing a wet helmet for 8 hours, riding at speed, and suffering sleep deprivation during periods of high humidity have resulted in a wild mane flowing over my shoulders.

Having wandered round the grounds, predictably, I end up appreciating the overall view of the place, but it's the near view that really interests me. I want somewhere to wild camp, and round the back of the church looks like an ideal spot. Trying to attract as little attention as possible, I ride out of the car park and then round a barrier away from the road. There are small bleak hills, and I'm very close to the Turkish border. Watchtowers are visible along the dividing river, but I don't think they are interested in me, so I ride around until I find the perfect spot. I have a stunning view of Mount Ararat out of my tent, so I sit and watch a glorious sunset. Once again the mozzies come out in force, and happily

I retreat to my sanctuary. I hear the mozzies' high pitched drone as the evening prayer from the mosques drift over the border.

In the night there is another storm. The lightening shoots down to the mountains over Turkey, and at 3AM I'm outside in underwear with tripod taking photos of a silent storm in another country; this one is undoubtedly best viewed from a distance.

DAY 67

YERAVAN, ARMENIA, 27 MILES

Thunder wakes me; it's light. I poke my head out of the tent; there is a storm rumbling down the valley behind me. Three consecutive days of wild camping brings out a primitive instinct in me, and I really like it. There is homelessness, there is touring, and then there is this: independence, opportunism, calculated, respectful, but devious; " . . . underhand, overland, wandering free . . . " Like a selfish womble I pack up my rubbish and leave with speed and efficiency; I don't want to get caught by either rain or authority.

The wind from the storm has kept the mozzies away. I ride to the vista point for a sunrise photo. The cloud is high, but Mount Ararat is higher and cut off in its prime. I'm deprived of the classic postcard picture; ironically the best views are behind me as the sun streaks through scattered storm clouds. I have nowhere I need to be, so at the side of my bike at the side of the road, I brush my teeth and hair, make a Marmite sandwich and a cup of chai, and wait with optimism for the clouds to clear. For the last four days I've bathed in rivers and sweated in humidity, I've been dampened and blow dried, I've managed a level of hygiene with what nature has provided. I'm not too offensive, in an up-wind kind of way; I'm just a scruffy vagrant with a nice camera. Hot water is my only hope of social acceptance for now.

These clouds are set-in; even if they do clear the low light will be gone. It's time for capital city captivity. The storm has passed, but the road surface has aquaplane potential. It's not slowing the rush-hour traffic. Potholes and puddles all have the same surface, and I'm given no room to avoid them. I'm looking for one specific hotel; I have eyes everywhere: road surface, traffic, junctions, signposts, pedestrians, police, traffic lights, street names. When I'm at a significant junction in the centre, I stop and look at my map, get my bearings, spin round, do a left, and there is the Hotel Shirak, right where it's supposed to be, right where I wanted it to be. It's only just after 9AM, but I'm able to check in; a room with a view of Ararat and my bike undercover. I have a wonderful shower and rush to get the inclusive breakfast. The left-overs are a let-down, but the real problem is back in my room: the maid has been in. I only checked in half an hour ago; I'm not a rock star, I can't trash a room that quick. The bed has been cleared of clothes and all the money I left on it too.

I'm going to have to approach this thief in a very diplomatic manner. At reception I tell them I'm not sure where the maid has put it, so could they ask her. A smart thief would return it whilst I was out of my room and the receptionist was on the phone to the housekeeper on my floor. There are accusations that I'm the dishonest one; I start to get a bit more defensive. Eventually I'm told the maid thought it was a tip, why would I tip for a service I didn't want, need, or expect? Strange how the attitude changes when a confession confirms my version of events.

Back in my room the hotel has a power cut, so I go and walk the streets. The day passes in pavement cafés and searching for sights; it's a tricky transition back into a cosmopolitan city existence after a period of wild life. I stop in a supermarket for beer and crisps to take back to my room for the sunset. In the check-out queue, ahead of me is a trolley full of needs, surrounded by the family it is meant to feed. The father lets me in front of them. "Enjoy your beer," he says in English, and I think, in envy too.

"Enjoy your family," I felt like replying, with a genuine emphasis on the luck he doesn't seem to realise he has.

Mount Ararat is now clearly visible from my room, but there is absolutely no point in photographing it, not from here, but as I drink my beer the temptation becomes irresistible and I do anyway.

Day 68

Akhaltsikhe, Georgia, 233 Miles

I've been here 24 hours but only one night, and that is all I want to pay for. The receptionist says, "You pay today?" "Yes, I pay today."

"OK, 50,000."

"No, I pay today for one day, not two days."

"OK, 25,000." Phew. Now I just have to pay the bell-boy who guarded my bike all night. The bike is surrounded by "parking reserved" signs and has been treated better than I have. It's so quiet out here on the streets at 8.45AM. There is no traffic; I'm not complaining.

One more church to see: the thing is they all tie in with one another, and the more I read the more interested I become (strange how that happens). Clearly I have no religious beliefs, nor am I an expert on architecture, but I can appreciate the age of the structures and historical facts. Paganism overlaps a lot of Armenia's Christian beliefs; this church dates back to 300AD and sits on an old pagan shrine. By complete coincidence, I visit it on the morning when a lone man with a bloody-big hammer seems to have an unstoppable need to uncover that shrine. He is smashing the hell out of the floor in the church. I go in to see the sun send its beams through the windows of the dome tower. The altar is lit by candles, and the place is very tranquil, except for this bloke with a hammer, kneeling on the marble floor and shattering it. The noise is echoing with stained-glass window-shattering intensity.

When he stops hammering there is the sound of him gathering up rubble, and then he swings his hammer again, banging in the morning, in the evening, all over the floor. It's not a subtle way of uncovering the pagan shrine, but blatant force can be an approach that works.

Hammering notwithstanding, it's a peaceful day everywhere; even parked in a lay-by for a Marmite snack the passing cars don't seem to be disturbing me. I must

236

just be at peace from visiting all these churches. I'm exiting Armenia on what appears to be the dullest road in the country; Mount Ararat is over my left shoulder, and I can't see it easily. I intend to cross two international borders today back into Turkey and to see the ghost-town of Ani, the former capital of Armenia, which due to wars, invasions, and moving frontiers is no longer in Armenia. I daydream my way into a town I'm not sure I'm supposed to be in. The road is fast, and the country is all the smaller for it, but I'm making good progress. Of the three, Azerbaijan I could have lived without. Armenia was definitely worth the effort, and Georgia is up there with Mongolia and Alaska, in my opinion. If I'd fallen in love in Yerevan or seen the flaming towers of Baku by night my opinion may be different, but on a lifelong quest for gratification through natural beauty, Georgia scores high. Armenia ends on a low of ugly abandoned factories, depressing to work in and equally drab now they are derelict. The road becomes potholes, the pace slows, and the country gets bigger because of it.

I'm running alongside the Turkish border; watchtowers stand staring. I see a sign for Ani. I can't ignore it. I know Ani is on the Turkish side, and it's a long diversion to get there, so I follow this dirt road to see where it leads. I pass through a tiny farming village and onto a narrow dirt track that ends in a coiled fence of barbed-wire in view of two watchtowers. Across the plains is the city, but viewing from a distance will not satisfy me this time; I actually want to get up close to this place.

I run along a lakeside, which again divides the countries. Usually a body of water is divided down the middle, but not this one, Turkey has claimed it all, and the Armenian villagers can't even fish in it. Lines on a map decided by wars and politics. There is a point where the lake comes up to the road. The barbed-wire border has a bridge built for it, and the water flows under without restraint into the Armenia side. Men sit on the banks fishing in the shallows. It seems so ridiculous; fish can swim under the fences and birds can fly over them, but the humans who make the divide have to obey the restrictions imposed, and that supposedly makes us the superior species. Seeing segregation so close-up is quite shocking. It seems to me these rigid bloody-minded rules are only upheld for proof of power and superiority, when in actual fact it just shows how pathetic the power-crazed can be. Share the lake for fuck's sake; there's nothing else out here.

I leave Armenia with a wee dram coin worth less than a pound, a few mozzie bites, and a little less ignorance than I arrived with. There is one other thing I leave with, and I only notice by accident whilst I'm showing my passport to enter Georgia. I touch my nose and realise I have a blob of Marmite on it; that's embarrassing, it's been there for hours.

I haven't been in Georgia long when I see a sign for Turkey. I follow back roads through more cow pat pyramid villages with horse and cart transport but with the modern twist of the reins in one hand and a phone in the other. The sat nav is acknowledging my proximity to Turkey. It's not a busy road, so I stop for a pre-border wee just in time. Around the corner the road has a barrier across it. From a building a long way off, a heavily kitted soldier comes running up; he's not even out of breath. He has news for me. This border is not for crossing; it's closed. Several other less fit colleagues arrive. They are affable enough, at least until I ask for a photo. Glad I asked before I shot; a good practice to adopt when dealing with the armed I think. I have no choice but to do another U-turn and go to the next crossing, which involves a 60 mile diversion. It's 3.45PM, so I'm not sure I will make it to Turkey tonight.

I thought I'd remember this winding canyon road. It was less than a week ago I came this way, but my thoughts were full of my mate then. I really can't have been paying attention at all, because this all seems new to me, and now I'm thinking about him again. The clouds are dark, and I'm about to ride into a storm. I just miss it; brutal it was too. It brought leaves and branches off trees and spread hail across the road. But as the road esses its way on down the canyon, I catch up with its tail end. There is a convenient bus shelter. I ride into and sit out the downpour. I've been in there a few minutes when I hear a little squeak; under the bench are three tiny kittens; dirty, cold, scared, and huddled together. They must have been egging each other on to draw my attention to them. They are all backed into a corner petrified. Luckily for them, I have some sausage in my cool box, and I end up giving them the lot. They get braver as they satisfy their hunger, mum is nowhere to be seen, and they are much too young to fend for themselves. They are too cold and too hungry to play like kittens should. I wash my greasy hands in a warm puddle and then at the kerb I wave goodbye.

Sun shines off the wet road, and along comes more rain and another shelter. I'm timing it just right, but I'm not getting very far. I don't need to; if I did I'd face the weather, and I'd rather not. Just as I've got going again, a vivid shallow rainbow appears and calls for a photo; it's a tripod moment but I just can't be arsed. So instead I position myself so I can take a photo that looks like the rainbow ends in my tank box. When I've finished playing with rainbows, I ride on to the next town and get a room. A rainy night in Georgia is no hardship at all, it's just a bonus to the day.

With a little bit of Wi-Fi, I learn my mate passed away last night. Ancient churches, barbed-wire divides, starving kittens, perfect rainbows, and the death of a friend. So much contrast, so randomly connected by a tenuous thread. The views, interactions, experiences, and emotions that happen to a man in one day on a bike. Good night, Doug.

DAY 69

HARASAN, TURKEY, 246 MILES

I'm first down for breakfast, and I'm still too late. When were these eggs fried? I mean roughly, just tell me the day. Cold fried egg, it's like eating an oyster with a yoke. A brief checkout chat reveals that I've seen so much more of this country than the receptionist. I enthuse about what I have seen; she hasn't even heard of Ushguli. She asks if I will stay another night, but I have more things to see.

I fill the tank to brimming and slowly head to the border of Turkey and the world's most expensive fuel. It feels like a Saturday morning, which is perfect really, as that's what it is. I'm not sure if my Turkish visa and insurance are still valid, but I hand them over with confidence and they are accepted, then for the third time I leave Georgia and enter Turkey. The scenes remain the same; farming is farming, cow shit pattie pyramids look the same in Armenia, Georgia, and Turkey, the only distinguishing difference here is a single minaret standing tall above the turf-roofed huts of the hillside villages.

Unexpectedly, I ride up to 8,000 feet. This area of the planet is so diverse in scenery and altitude. Regardless of the country-defining borders, the varying beliefs of the inhabitants, and their architecture, the undulating land itself has a far greater variety of viewpoints.

It's been a 500 km circuit to get to Ani, the ghost city I could see across the barbed-wire fence in Armenia yesterday. What I didn't see from my distant view was the hotels, the tour buses, the mini vans, the car parks, and the touts. This doesn't quite meet my definition of a ghost city; I had visions of camping under the stars in the moonlit shadows of crumbling city walls that have stood for 1,500 years. That was not going to be happening; the place has sold out and fallen down.

I lock every pannier as a group of kids stand around the bike. I don't like this at all, leaving my bike in a car park specifically for the tourist trade who walk away from their wealth and go through the city gates. I make a very obvious display of securing what I can but don't put the bike cover on.

Inside is nothing but disappointment. Ongoing disputes between Turkey and Armenia have left Ani a neglected, disrespected mess. If a ghost city crumbles to the ground does anyone hear it? Yes, if the reasons are vandalism, quarrying, and military target practice. The brick shouldn't roll far from the wall, but here the ground is nothing but a rock-strewn landscape bearing no resemblance to the structures that once housed 100,000 people.

I stroll around hastily. I follow a herder with his goats and try to focus on the timelessness of his profession; it's more authentic than the brightly coloured tour parties being rounded up by their umbrella waving shepherd.

Inside one grand church, a lady with a big fat book full of bookmarked pages stands staring at things I don't see. Transfixed and in awe, she takes a single step, flicks through some pages, and again studies a sight that is beyond me. She is clearly getting a lot more out of this than I am. I'm a little envious, but that's education for you; the more informed you are, the more you appreciate. If you only watch Jeremy Kyle you'll never get more than sunny delight.

My need to get back to my bike is greater than my will to wander. This place is no Angkor; it's exposed, levelled, and it would take a lot of research and understanding to appreciate something that, to the untrained eye, looks little more than a bomb site. The city walls are most impressive; I saw them yesterday from the barbed-wire fence and again, today, from the car park. I'm keen to go back through the city gates and leave this disappointing diversion to the tour bus crowds. "Lose yourself in Ani," said the *Lonely Planet*; I could no more lose myself here than on a cricket pitch.

The bike appears to be intact; the kids have gone. As I leave the bustling ghost town complex, I reach for my voice recorder to express my disgust and realise it's not there. Bollocks. This isn't just the recorder; this is two months of comments, thoughts, observations, and feelings. OK, most of it was bollocks, but there were a few inspired remarks. A lot of it is backed up on my laptop, but still, what angers me is the violation; it's like stealing a diary, it is of no use to anyone. I turn around immediately. My mind is racing, and I know what little fucker took it. There is a motorcycle parked outside a shop; without even considering the rider's nationality I tell him to be careful, there are thieves here. He is Turkish, and his English is minimal. The thieving little bastard is loitering, with a butter-wouldn't-melt look on his very punchable face. I yell at him. He knows he has it. I know he has it, but short of jumping on his scrawny little arse and going through his pockets, there isn't much I can do.

"OK," I say, "Polis, Jandarma!"

I go back to the parking area. There are a lot of soldiers hanging around. I ask them for help, but they appear to be here on holiday.

They take me to the ticket office, where no one speaks English, but they are understanding and helpful. I'm handed a mobile phone, and the gentleman on the other end speaks English. I tell him the whole story, maybe too much; I should have just stuck to the facts.

"I'm a writer; my livelihood has been taken from me." He relays my distress to the ticket men, and I follow them outside, where the Turkish biker is coming in accompanied by some soldiers. He has my voice recorder.

I'm elated, "How did you get it back?"

"I told him to give it to me, and he did."

I'm gushing with gratitude, "You have no idea what this means, thank you so much."

Well, what an experience Ani turned out to be. As I leave the complex a second time, I see the same thieving little scumbag walking up the street ahead of me. He doesn't hear my bike.

Remorselessly, I ride straight at him; at the last second he spins around to see me heading for him, and he jumps to the side. I stop, yelling a few tips on how to stop becoming what he is destined to be. He will never understand, regardless of the language I say it in. Then I leave him to rot in his pathetic little existence.

Within minutes, people at the side of the road are waving happily, innocently unaware of what has just happened. I want to tar the whole of Turkey with the same brush, but there isn't enough tar. I should concentrate it; just tar and feather one little bastard.

Once more I reach for my voice recorder to relay the dismal experience into it. It starts up quicker than usual; well at least something positive came out of it.

I've been getting complacent, leaving more and more stuff on the bike; I would never have left the bike unattended like that in England. I should thank the thieving little git for teaching me a lesson.

I'm heading west, and I think mostly will be from now on; better put some sun block on my nose.

My mood lightens. I'm here in Kars again, a Gary Numan song comes into my head, breaks down, and stays there, turning-over for the rest of the day. My progress is steady, the road is dull, my speed is petrol-saving slow. Regardless of where I end up tonight, I will plan a more scenic route for tomorrow. I'm not going to cross Turkey in a bland straight line when my map has some green but indirect routes available, although I'm not convinced just how pleasing the green is.

The monotony of my pace is soon forgotten when the road gets narrower and winds through hills with pine trees and distant, snow-capped volcanoes appear to the south. I ride through little craggy canyons. It would be great if I could find a river to camp by tonight.

A supply stop creates a great deal of interest, a little semi-circle of shops which seems to have its own micro community. Kids follow me from aisle to aisle, and the old men invite me for chai at the table outside. I've got everything

I need except bread, so the kids lead me to another shop. There seems to have been some miscommunication, as this is a plumbing supply shop. Luckily, outside is a van with a picture of a loaf of bread on the side, and coincidently, it's parked outside a bakers.

I've been preoccupied; my bike has been out of my sight, but it's just a fact of travelling, and at this stop, like every other apart from Ani, the only thing taken is photos. Faith restored and supplies replenished, I move on to find a place to camp.

I'm running alongside a river, which is looking promising. The search begins for the ideal spot; off-road, down tracks I find a few potentials, but I've got time and high expectations so I continue. On my fourth attempt at leaving the road, I ride through some tall grass and get out of sight, then away from the road to get my peace, down to the river for my washing needs, and follow it to a bend with sandy banks and a sheer cliff view. It's absolutely perfect. I've got my own personal beach and a soft and shady surface to camp on. The sausage I bought is smoky and not that nice, so I think I will treat myself to one of my emergency meals. I don't anticipate many more emergencies this trip. I discover once again my pannier has leaked and the water has again got through the plastic bags into my maps, so I completely unpack it. Oh look, the top has come off the mozzie-repellent too, and the deet with its acid burning qualities has melted my mattress, tent, and pillow repair kit.

I'm in the ideal place to spread everything out to dry. Off to the river to fill my pan to boil my Lancashire hotpot in its bag—my stove won't light. This idyllic little setting might as well be a hotel room for all I'm getting out of it. Instead of waiting for night to fall, I'm racing against the last of the light to get things cooked, cleaned-up, and cleared-up. So much for an evening of route research. I crawl into my tent beyond the mess of drying pannier contents, and I peer up the side of a wild jagged canyon into a starry sky. The river ripples past, there are no mozzies, the ground is flat, soft and dry, the air is fresh. Tonight for the first time it feels like I'm heading back.

DAY 70

ESPIYE, TURKEY, 308 MILES

"The thieving magpie," until this morning it was just a phrase, a live double album, but now I am a victim.

The majority of my wild camping experiences seem to result with me being woken by an unfamiliar sound. This morning it sounds like something is pecking my plastic soap dish. Maybe I saw the evidence before I guessed the sound. Two magpies have taken all my hotel freebie soap and are attempting to take the container too.

With something between a bounce and a swagger, they arrogantly lurk out of reach, showing no sign of repentance. It's only soap; I make some chai and sit in the sun to write my diary. I press play on my voice recorder and listen to yesterday's babblings. There is the sound of Turkish boys speaking in excited tones, lots of short snippets as they press random buttons, unaware the stolen device is capturing their red handedness on its internal memory. But where are my recordings? They are on the four gigabyte memory card, the one that should be in that slot. FUCK.

I throw down my diary and stomp to the river. The little bastard got the last laugh. No wonder the recorder started up so quickly, it wasn't accessing the memory card, it was just recording onto its own limited storage. I have a strong urge to ride back, drag the little fucker behind the bike till that resilient grin is ground off his face. I walk around the sandy river bank to see if I can find my stolen soap. Slowly I regain my composure and perspective, and realise all I can do about the situation is learn and prevent it happening again. It's not the cost of replacing the memory card, nor the loss of what was recorded on it, neither is it the violation by the thief. The irritation is that the smug little brat got one over on me. Sometimes I can't wait for karma; I need vengeance and I need it now, but I just don't need it enough to ride for three hours to implement it.

Despite the morning's trauma I'm still out on the road early. It doesn't take long to realise I got the absolute prime camp spot, as the land soon turns arable and the road moves away from the river. I need to get at least one good site or experience out of this slab of a guidebook I'm carrying. Ani certainly didn't live up to my expectations; "lose yourself" indeed. Lose your possessions more like.

As soon as I come to a town, I find a bin to responsibly throw last night's rubbish in. That little ritual always make me feel good; can't beat a good dump on a Sunday morning. The streets are lined with pavement cafés, endless tables of mostly older gentlemen drinking chai whilst indulging in their weekly catch up. I see a phone shop; I bet I can get a new memory card there. I pull up and weave my way through the maze of tables on the pavement. I can't quite explain what I need, so I go back to my bike to get an example, albeit four times the size.

An elderly Muslim gentlemen calls out to me: "Monsieur, we would be honoured if you would drink chai with us."

"Ang on, I'm in the middle on a transaction here. One moment, sir, I'll be right back." I continue with my quest; he looks at my memory card, understands exactly what I need, and confirms he hasn't got anything like that at all. I go and sit with the chai drinkers.

The person who invited me is a bear of a man, old but strong and fit, with grey trimmed Action Man beard. Regardless of what he has witnessed behind his bright eyes, they still smile at me. He speaks French but not, unfortunately, Spanish or English. I think he once worked in France. I seem to be the connection, the mind-jog to his fond European memories of when he was a younger man, perhaps the man he sees in me. Next to him is a more fragile man who seems to have been swallowed by his suit.

He sits with a cheeky smile. Attentive but happily stepping back from the conversation, he takes sugar lumps from the bowl in the centre of the table and dunks them into his chai before sucking at the softened cube. I instinctively want to say this behaviour will rot his teeth, but he has to be 80 and his smile is white and intact. I can't imagine he has only recently picked up this habit. Other people gather round our table; the feeling is comfortable and relaxed with an underlying sense of frustration at our inability to communicate in a common language. However, that is overridden with a huge feeling of pride, which I first sense and then reciprocate. I can't remember who initiates it, but photos are requested and taken. I hand the man seated opposite me my phone, and my French-speaking friend puts his arm around me with such strength it feels like he has just been reunited with a long lost friend. That little Sunday morning moment is captured forever. It says so much; it's a bridge over an abyss of religious ignorance and intolerance. Our smiles, our body language don't show the anger at the irresponsible media reports spreading religious hatred like napalm. We sum each other up as individuals, and we like what we see. No guidebook can over-hype this; no tabloid can denounce it. It's just a cup of chai. It's a tiny gesture, and it's so significant. That photo for me says so much, not least because the moment would never have occurred if I hadn't had my memory card stolen yesterday. Everything happens for a reason.

When I go to leave he stands, gives me a firm hand shake, and then puts his hand on his heart. It's emotional. I go back to my bike to find whilst he had distracted me, his friends have pinched my camera . . . only joking.

I left that town with my back straight, my shoulders broad, my arms strong, and my head held a little higher. A meeting like that can have a profound effect upon the day; what a privilege, what an honour, what a wholly positive experience. On my way out of town I stop at some lights, a van pulls up on my left. When they turn green he turns right, straight across my path; the feeling of well-being is short lived.

I head out onto wide plains under big skies, but the road isn't wide enough to accommodate me and the two trucks rapidly approaching from behind. They are running side-by-side in a three mile overtake manoeuvre. I pull over and then slipstream the slower one because it's just cost me £37 for 18 litres of fuel.

A successful shopping stop; I have replenished my food, soap, and got a new memory card. Outside the town I find a peaceful picnic stop. Under the shade of a tree in a grassy meadow, I sit down and have my lunch. I wonder to myself why I don't do this pleasurable picnic thing every day, and then I remember it's because every day is different. I eat my cheese and tomato in fresh bread, and if it wasn't for the flies, I would lie down and have a little doze. I contemplate putting my helmet on, but that would just be weird.

Slowly I'm dropping down to the south coast of the Black Sea. It's getting much hotter; I'd better get used to it, I've got mid-Europe in mid-summer ahead of me. It's that time of the day; I've started yawning, except it's not that time of the day, it's just I got up early and I need some sugar. Not dunked in tea, I think I'll opt for a Coke.

The road continues to take me through some typically Turkish sites, a town built on the walls of a canyon. It's a bit like the thatched cottages and warped walls of timber and time in a quintessential English village, seen but not noticed. These are Turkey's unmentioned marvels, nearly normal and barely noteworthy.

The road continues to wind down, through flooded canyons and eventually to the Black Sea. The road is smooth and fast and so is my bike with this thick sea level air. The wide hard-shoulder is solid with parked cars; everyone is at the beach. I wish they would go home; it's work tomorrow. Don't they have *Antiques Roadshow* here? I see a few camping signs, but it really means wooden terraced shacks, beach huts with beds; it's not very appealing. I don't want to ride any further. I'm tired, the light is going, but the beaches are not emptying. I stop for some food. Looking down over the sea, slowly the bathers pack up their plastic toys and leave their piles of rubbish behind them. I find a campsite and pitch next to semi-permanent tents and caravans. The sun goes down. I walk over to the beach. Tomorrow must be dustbin day, that's why everyone left their rubbish out.

DAY 71

SINOP, TURKEY, 205 MILES

Excited by the dawn, I run down to the beach to get a photo of a red sunrise over the Black Sea. No sandals, no thought, no focus; I cut my foot and don't notice the camera is on last night's settings, so the whole operation is a total disaster. An unnecessarily manic way to start my Monday. There are no showers in the stinking toilet block, and the outside tap has run out of water. No one is around; they know better than to spend the night here and are equally aware it's not a place worth getting up early for. Consequently, I leave without finding anyone to pay; it was almost worth the price.

I'm going to spend my camping money on a lovely breakfast. I come into a town of smartly dressed commuters waiting for buses. Glamorous roadside restaurants cater to the affluent, who are too busy to pour cereal into a bowl or boil a kettle. They prefer to distribute their wealth to the service industry. I sit outside under a shady awning, but the waiter takes me inside to point at the choices; soup seems to be the speciality today. I point at one and go back to my table to drink my chai. In true Turkish tradition, a bucket of bread is brought, shortly, followed by the soup—grey and with the odour of a U-bend, but it's steaming hot and seems to be a popular choice amongst the other patrons in the restaurant. I take a sip. It's atrocious; it's like liquid animal fat, and the bits I dredge up from the bottom of the bowl are simply insoluble body parts. It lines my mouth like I've been chewing on lard. I try just dipping my bread in, but it's a vile, oily, greasy, fatty liquid—boiled lifeless leftovers from the slaughterhouse floor. When the waiter comes over, I shake my head apologetically. My face says all he needs to know, and he takes the bowl away before it coagulates into the form of Freddie Krueger's face.

A month ago, a morning like this would have had me skulking into a hotel, bitterly considering my choices. However, with the big decision made, with the realisation of the ongoing problem recognised and rectified, if still not entirely understood, contentment is in residence, and all I desire is that it stays for a while. U-turn if I want to, and everything is better for it.

Some custard cream type biscuits are brought out for me, and I dunk them in my chai. This is not the breakfast I had in mind, and I'm pretty sure it's my karma for running from the campsite, but I'm wrong because a compassionate waitress has just come on duty and brings me a plate of tomatoes, cheese, jam, another chai, and freshens up my bucket of bread. With grease-lined throat, it all slides down effortlessly. I'm very grateful but a little miffed; will I now have to pay for two breakfasts? When I get up to ask for the bill, I'm patted on the back and waved away. It is gratis, on the house, a gift for the road, their pleasure. Turkey: you just can't judge it by one thieving little git. What wealth of diversity, if it's not one thing it's another.

The day is warm, bright, and sunny. I'm riding slowly, my jacket is open, and I'm looking down at a calm clear sea from a hilly coastline with the occasional gathering of houses on the shore. I've got a full tummy, possibly a little too full; I'm doing animal-fat belches through my open visor. I wonder if the soup I couldn't stomach was just poured back into the cauldron it had been dredged out of. I've ridden every day for the last twelve, mainly because I'm really enjoying the journey. A single gesture can influence the entire day, be it thief, friend, or offering. It's "road mode" at its best; excited to see what is around the next corner, where the road and the day will take me. The mojo is up and running, functioning faultlessly. Having said that, I am perhaps beginning to feel a little weary, and if I can find the right spot, I'll gladly take a break.

I go through a long tunnel whilst having a Charley Boorman daydream; I'm not sure which is darker. I'm daydreaming a lot today, can't seem to focus my thoughts on what is around me. My bike is running a bit lumpy. This morning's fill-up was the cheapest fuel I've found in Turkey; I'm paying the price now.

It's a common occurrence to have no daily destination, but today this is combined with a contented dithering. I have an abundance of time, and I'm spending it frivolously. I stop for a coffee; I need a strong taste to overpower the lingering sediment of the soup. The little cup contains thick, black, high-density tar. The sugar is more devoured than dissolved into the black hole contained within the cup. The bottom half of the cup is a solid mass. It's scary; it can't be drunk, and I don't think it should be chewed. Well, that's focused my thoughts. I need a toilet, and I need one now.

I'm back to an area where storks have their sticky nests on top of lamp posts. Only now on my return, their children have hatched and grown. It all looks quite cramped up there. I'm sure the parents are looking forward to their offspring flying the nest. Still, it's only a six month wait, not eighteen years.

I come into the city of Samsun, a fast and modern place of glass and steel high-rise buildings without character or imagination. The traffic beneath is too busy to notice them. There are signs for Ankara and Istanbul; I read them only for lane and direction assurance. Those names seemed so exotic before, now the announcement means nothing more than the promise of a quieter road, as the majority of the traffic takes the faster routes to more popular destinations.

I have a destination now, a town on a cape. According to the guidebook, it's an ancient walled city and now a quaint fishing port, which sounds like a peaceful place with long-stay potential and fresh fish possibilities.

I see a pizza delivery man in my mirrors riding erratically, not from a conscientious need to deliver piping hot and with punctuality, but so he can catch up and pass me. He hoots and waves; it makes me smile, not just the two wheeled camaraderie but the effort he made to participate in it. I have nothing but admiration for his mission as he weaves through the traffic with his insulated top box.

With the last exit to Istanbul the traffic thins, and again my thoughts wander. I pass a town called 19th May. That was the date I entered Turkey and saw the annual celebration of the beginning of the war of independence.

Briefly, the road takes a more direct hilly route east through pleasant countryside. I can see minarets, like windmills in Holland. At any one time there are six or seven of them spanning the landscape. There can't be a place where you fail to hear the prayer; no peace for the wicked.

My sat nav says I'm riding in the Black Sea; I will forgive it on this occasion as I am. The road is an example of extravagant engineering; the cliffs have been quarried, crushed, and flattened. I'm on a fast, smooth dual carriageway which winds round the water's edge. The only thing between the road and the sea is an endless breakwater of perfectly laid stones. For mile after mile this goes on, through tunnels that are lit with alternating orange and green light projected in streaks down the tunnel walls. It's like riding through the opening sequence of *Dr. Who*. I've travelled through time; several seconds have passed since I was last out in the sunlight. When there isn't a tunnel, there are bridges, and then the carriageway is tiered, split-level, like the M5 in the Gordano valley.

This is a spectacular piece of engineering, and I'm really impressed by it. I'm embarrassed to say I even took photos of it—I think I'd rather be caught with porn. It ends in an anticlimax on the outskirts of Sinop. It has cruise-ship port tackiness; hi-density tourism crammed into every crevice of this over-populated peninsula. I don't even have to stop the bike; I ride round the clock tower and back out on the road I came in on. Another place the *Lonely Planet* suggested I could lose myself. Where were these writers from, Bangladesh? I'm becoming quite despondent with their over rated descriptions. Turkey doesn't need over-hyping; it just requires some responsible reporting. What if I'd have caught a bus here? I'd be committed then, but thankfully, with my independent transport I can just leave, and no commitment has ever really caught-up with me on my bike.

I follow the signposts for a campsite; it's only six miles out of town and has space, peace, shade, and Wi-Fi. Once my tent is pitched, I walk down to an empty beach and into the sea up to my waist. I can see myself stopping here . . . I may go deeper tomorrow.

Day 72

Sinop, Turkey, 12 Miles

My stupid stove won't light. The one I took on my last trip was crap, and this one is being equally temperamental. I don't think I'm going to take a stove next time; the space it takes-up, combined with my general inability to cook or even boil water without burning it, makes it as useful an accessory as an air freshener.

I go over to meet the neighbours, a young English couple on bicycles. They have lived and worked in Turkey for a while now and are cycling around as they await their new positions in China. We sit chatting; I keep saying I'm going to leave, but I don't seem to be. They percolate some coffee in their Italian coffee maker, an extravagant luxury in both weight and volume. I seem to be lacking motivation to do anything much, so I go with the apathy and decide to stay another night.

I suggest we go into town to get some supplies. Jimi speaks some Turkish, and shopping with the ability to communicate will be a treat. He has never been on a motorbike before so, lidless, in sandals and with no pillion pegs, I am honoured to be the rider who introduces him to the world of responsible and experienced motorcycle riding. Of the three shops we try there is little choice, and pointing would have worked just fine, but he does at least exchange pleasantries, and I nod with acknowledgement. Portraying the silent-type; aware, knowledgeable, respectful, and quiet, that's the impression I'm trying to give, anyway, although it's probably interpreted as another Englishman who didn't even bother to learn how to say "hello."

With our limited supplies Rose, Jimi's other half, makes an omelette, and morning drifts into afternoon as subtly as a sidestand sinks into sandy soil. Thankfully, the countries of the compulsory visa conversation are behind me. Speaking to people of semi-permanent residence, I learn a lot more than the guidebook told me about this country. For example, a real delicacy here is the soup I couldn't stomach yesterday. It is not only associated with breakfast but is a popular end of evening snack, much like the kebab is in England. It is regarded as a sure hangover cure; they swear by it and it's called . . . tripe. That explains everything; just the sound of the word makes me dry heave. There are some tastes in life I never need to acquire. In addition to the stomach ingredient, a popular little extra is meat from a sheep's head, specifically the cheek. Yum.

I decide to do a bit of bike maintenance, and again, I remove the speedo drive. It only works when the wheel is turning backwards, which would explain why the mileage is slowly going down; it's all the little pushes out of dead ends that I do. If I could just do a small amount of commitment I could probably get my speedo drive sent to somewhere I will be going through, but I don't want that £20 accessory dictating my journey.

My tyres look like they might make the round trip, depending on the extent of the diversions, and the back brake pads have bedded in and regained some friction, which is reassuring.

Having got myself a bit greasy, I go for a swim and make the Black Sea a little blacker. All day I've been trying to find a good reason not to drink; on this beach there is no reason to be found. I speak to Rose and Jimi, hoping they will help me come up with one, but annoyingly they just encourage me. I get no discouragement from the lady in the little local shop either, even though I have no money or at least a note so big she can't change it. She happily puts anything I want on a tab and smiles rather provocatively.

Two Norwegians turn up in an ambulance; they are doing a charity drive to Tajikistan where they will leave their vehicle and all its supplies for the locals. Well not quite all the supplies. The potato vodka has to be drunk before their entrance into Turkmenistan. Feeling a visa conversation brewing, I do my best to help with the consumption of the incriminating spirit; we all do. They are so impressed and grateful at our ability to make it disappear, they go and get another bottle out of the ambulance. It has completely lost its symbolism of rescue, resuscitation, and remedy and is now just a vehicle with the ability to fast track you into oblivion.

DAY 73

SINOP, TURKEY, 0 MILES

Escape from the heat of the morning sun when you're inside a tent is impossible. I turn round so my head is up the other end. Futile.

I go and have a shower; I can improve the appearance of the exterior, although the interior remains inferior. The Norwegians have brought their breakfast stuff to the table we sat at last night. The empty cans and bottles still stand as a monument to the hangover. I take my meagre offerings over too; it's always amusing to watch a non-Brit gag on Marmite. Rose and I re-have the conversation we had last night, unaware that it's a repeat performance. Once again, I'm captivated; the others remember it, but we are both enjoying it for the first time.

So are they leaving today as planned? Am I? It's OK, we don't need answers. This is exactly the kind of pleasurable behaviour exclusive to the deadline-free wanderer. I go over to the flirty girl in the local shop. She has eggs; she's very proud of them. Is this a Turkish euphemism for fertility or am I reading too much into it? I just want to make an omelette. I'm not sure I can handle a non-verbal exchange with euphemisms. Do I look like I can fertilize eggs this morning; I can't even keep up a conversation. We're not going anywhere today; the place is too peaceful and relaxed to rush. Another morning passes as the coffee slowly filters away the hangover. I let the Norwegians use my laptop as I dismantle my stove. I now have a full understanding of it, and it's quite simple really; still doesn't bloody work, but I see the principle.

Later we are all given a tour of the ambulance, a Mercedes, which is totally kitted-out; not for camping or as a motor home but for picking-up people off the road and patching them up. The cab has a walnut dashboard, cruise-control, leather seats; they're not exactly roughing it. They leave with sirens blaring and

254

lights flashing. I had tried to persuade them to give us a demonstration last night, but luckily, they maintained an air of responsibility, although they seem to enjoy performing their audio and visual display as much as I enjoy watching it—it's an impressive exit.

I decide to go down to the beach to wash my dirty stove-cleaning hands then have a doze to dehydrate and burn for a few hours. It's not the best decision I have made today. I have a strong desire to make a cup of chai with my overhauled stove. It still won't bloody work, so I take it apart again and find the jet is blocked again, clean it again, and fire it up. Then I go and buy a beer from Miss Flirty-pants.

Rose is making a veggie lentil dahl curry tonight; it all seems very healthy and an ideal last supper. They are very good company; I feel super chilled. Just what I needed, and now I'm looking forward to the road ahead even more. I needed a break, although I couldn't have found anywhere less Turkish than this isolated campground. I can't hear a single mosque, no traffic passes; there isn't even a barking dog, just the sound of a gentle ocean with waves that barely break the silence. Rose tells me of her wrongful arrest, mistaken as a protester against the president's decision to build a mosque on a popular park in Istanbul. This action, or more what it represented, has caused a lot of protests across Turkey and headlines around the world over the last six weeks. The arrest was a big deal, and the British embassy was even involved. The whole incident was filmed by a TV crew, and there's a clip on YouTube. It's quite entertaining to watch the Turkish secret police struggle with the resilience of a red-headed northern lass; a handful at any time, but particularly when dealing with false accusations, wrongful arrest, and being forcibly escorted into a police car.

Our hangovers are now a distant memory, and Rose suggests we have another beer, and in the same breath she insists she is not an alcoholic. I say she doth protest too much, she reaffirms she's not a protester either.

DAY 74

AMASRA, TURKEY, 191 MILES

Dawn arrives much too soon, but I get up and start packing anyway; the tent pegs are growing roots, and that's not a foundation I want to be a part of.

I pay Miss Flirty-Pants, who doesn't seem to be gushing with such ovulating invitation this morning, which is unfortunate, as today I feel I could definitely keep up my end of the bargain, vasectomy notwithstanding. I say goodbye to Rose and Jimi. It's one of those meetings that is unlikely to ever reoccur, but with the benefit of Facebook, we will know if our paths are ever crossing the same continent at the same time. It's a testament to their personalities when, after such a short encounter, there is a shooting pang of sadness as I go up through the gears.

I am trying to keep my expectations realistic, despite the *Lonely Planet* describing the next bit of road as Turkey's Pacific Coast Highway. I'm lucky enough to have ridden Highway 101 in California and wonder if the writers of this sensationally misguided book ever have.

The road is deserted, and that's a good start. I come across a deer standing in the road; a beautiful brown red rust colour, his big brown eyes meet mine and for a second neither of us reacts, then he bounces off into the undergrowth. Later I see a fox and then a large bird of prey who takes-off from the road towards me, his imposing shadow making me cower behind my screen. With the absence of traffic, I've seen the best wildlife of the trip. Despite this, I'm still yawning uncontrollably; I need a snooze and find a grassy patch to lie down on. I don't usually do this, but I don't usually feel so tired so early in the day. I only lie down for ten minutes, but I dream, so it must have been real sleep. The only thing wrong with this road is its comparison with the PCH; it twists and bends, rises and falls as it hugs the rugged coastline. It's narrow, smooth and unpopulated, the sky and sea are bright blue, the landscape is lush rainforest green, with dramatic cliffs falling into heaving white waves. There are islets covered with a layer of sea birds, secluded bays of plastic-free sand and camping enticement. Monklet's smile has nearly met around the back of his neck, and the experience is without fault, but it's not the Pacific Coast Highway. Not for many reasons. It's an entirely inaccurate comparison. A Turk from this area going to California would be equally disappointed if he was expecting this. I think I preferred Turkey when I came through from west to east without a guidebook and was wowed without preconceptions.

I once saw a band that was labelled as the "next Pink Floyd." That was a kiss of death to a band that, without such sensationalist marketing, had the capacity to entertain in their own unique way.

I'm still learning; what a pointless exercise travel would be if you didn't learn from it. I have come to realise that the things that thrill me the most are natural beauty; I don't like the tourist crowds, even if what drew them was spectacular. My wanderlust has purpose when I see the vast, the natural, but most of all the unexpected. Eastern Turkey and northern Georgia have been highlights. The guidebook is a double-edged sword. I have travelled to parts of the same country with and without one, and without was the winner. Inevitably, I will miss out, but celebrating the surprises, for me, makes up for missing the celebrated. Once I stop believing the hype, I can just use the book to find a place to stay.

Having said all that, the road is getting better and better. I feel the contrast of the coolness in the shadow of the cliffs to the heat of the exposed road. I realise as I go onto reserve that I had no idea, nor had I considered, how much petrol I had. I know now, and I have a ridiculously short range on my reserve. A small town has no petrol station, and when I see a young lad, I stop and ask him how far I will have to go. He speaks good English; he says "40" then "44" then "4." I thank him and wonder which one it really is. I only have the range to do one of those three distances. Luckily, it's the shortest of the three; £47 to fill my tank, ouch. I need a kebab to numb the pain; I can fill my tummy so much cheaper than I can my tank.

The road has stopped being wonderful now; either the surface has melted or it's just been sprayed with tar. Gravel appears to have been randomly spread; it almost looks like a deliberate attempt to bring the rider off his bike. As I tentatively round the corners, I catch-up a tipper truck, where three men are standing on the back shovelling grit across the road. Ah, so it is deliberate. After that the road becomes dry and dusty; a tanker comes towards me spraying water. I was looking forward to it cooling me off, but he respectfully turns off the spray as I approach. The road becomes really slippery, but the smell of water on hot roads remains, a smell that usually signifies relief, at least it does when it's due to rain drops from heavy clouds that cover an unrelenting sun.

I arrive at my destination and decide to give my sat nav free rein. It takes me through cobbled streets into a very old part of this, my second consecutive city on the peninsula. I'm really riding through time now, backwards. Terraced stone houses are stuck like limpets to an outcrop of rock. I wind up into the centre, which is also the end, as the only way out is back the way I came in . . . or over the edge. I have no alternative but to leave my bike unattended. It looks like a safe enough place, but I'm more cautious now, and I take Monklet off the bark basher. I know of someone who earlier this year got their teddy mascot taken from their bike in Spain. I can't risk that, so I take the trip down well-worn steps to my little guesthouse several times to avoid the frustration of another theft.

Coincidentally, when I have settled in with some Wi-Fi, the same guy who was a victim of teddy bear theft is looking for someone to go and see Iron Maiden with in London next month. I don't have to think about it long and decide to commit. I have a date to be back now.

Down in the town I sort of get another date. As I wandered round the port and the maze of restaurants and souvenir shops, I had noticed a barefoot, dreadlocked, bearded hippy dude wandering the streets, wearing the proverbial baggy clothes. His sun-weathered skin and black matted hair suggests he is local, although he hardly looks like a typical Turk. The other thing that suggests he is a familiar sight on these streets is the body language of everyone around him—there is an obvious display of avoidance from anyone in his vicinity. I've never been able to locate or disable that part of me that acts like a weirdo magnet. Despite trying to copy the locals' body language whilst I'm sitting having a chai by a pavement snackbar, he sneaks up on me and catches me defenceless. And so begins the bombardment.

He speaks at me in English 600 words a minute but delivers them in the manner of John Hurt's character in *Midnight Express*. It's like he is making up for all the Turks I haven't been able to talk to.

He says he is an artist, and being a writer, we are arch enemies. His reasoning being that his work gives an audience free-will to decide what they see, but the writer dictates and controls, telling the reader what image they should see, wanting to be supreme over the artist. It's not exactly a passive introduction; I'm wondering who's dictating now.

When I get a chance to retort, he writes my words down in a notebook with a sweeping calligraphy scroll. Interesting he is writing now and not drawing a picture of my words; he is left handed like me. I haven't had a conversation like this for . . . for a long time; its fun.

"So what kind of art do you do?" I ask him

"It is Dali to the power of a thousand; it is so extreme no one understands it. They can't, the people are too small-minded, so after I create my work I destroy it; I am the creator and the destroyer." He muses over this and then makes a note.

"So you don't have a portfolio?"

"I don't need one; one picture is all I need. I am sending it to the Minister for the Arts, so I can get a grant. My signature alone has infinite connotations."

I want to see the sunset on the other side of this peculiar peninsular. There will be a new moon right behind it. So he walks with me; he has Magnus Pike animation, and as we walk the pedestrian alleys, everyone is looking at us. He swoops and gyrates; he could have someone's eye out if he's not careful. He'd stand a better chance of getting a grant from the ministry of silly walks than the arts council. I have looked hard into his eyes; his pupils aren't dilated, he's not speeding, this is how he is, under the influence of nothing but the torture of a mind that became unhinged. He is clearly a very intelligent man, but somewhere along the line something snapped. He's incapable of functioning in a manner that will sustain his survival. We sit on a low wall, looking out west over the sea into the low sun.

"Do you believe in God?" he asks me. I'm not going to be diplomatic; he is forceful to the point of offensive with his opinions.

"I don't need a messenger of God to tell me what I should and shouldn't do. I know the difference between right and wrong, good and bad, and basically I'm a good person. I don't need a religion dictating to me."

"So if you are saying you know the difference between right and wrong, you are saying you are God," he says with checkmate emphasis.

"I am not saying I am a god; I just know what is an acceptable and considerate way to live my life."

"So you think killing is bad?"

"Yes, you don't just go round killing what you don't like."

"Then you are a hypocrite, because you think it's OK to kill animals so you can eat them, and to take life is theft; if you take it you must need it more than the person who has it."

Theft is a pretty hot topic for me at the moment, but he's smart, quick as lightening, and sometimes just a little irrelevant. We need a subject change.

"So show me your signature." His words, ideals, and imagery all lose credibility when put on the spot. He says his signature is never the same twice and draws a squiring insignia. There is a clear swastika in the scrawled design. I don't point it out, but he does.

"That bit looks like a swastika," he says. He already mentioned Hitler earlier on. What an intense meeting this is. He could be a recruiter for a cult religion. He could be a lot of things. I think I'll just say goodnight.

He reads my T-shirt.

"Overland? You overstand, you don't understand." I walk out to some rocks and watch the skinny Shiva moon set. What a philosophical man; his concepts were almost plausible but tinged with the impossible and with paranoia, spoken with a lack of social acceptance and in an offensive manner. It was a very stimulating conversation. I wonder what he's doing now.

DAY 75

IZMIT, TURKEY, 273 MILES

Last night's conversations replayed in my head and wouldn't let my mind rest. I'm not sure how the hippy guy manages to sleep with such tormented and conflicting thoughts. I'm up before the bread has been delivered. I watch the sunrise with a cup of chai from the little guesthouse garden on top of the cliffs.

I've been back in Turkey a week, and this has been the first night I didn't camp, so returning to my bike to pack and reload is all the more exciting. Plus, dawn exits have a thrill of their own. Fresh and quiet streets, an old man sits on a bench watching my preparation, the tired youth drags his lethargic body towards the port for another day's hard labour. There are cats everywhere; in trees, on walls, catching the first rays of the sun as they stake out their territory. The day rewards the early riser, particularly in a place where the sun will soon bake away the morning's motivation.

I wind down the tiny street, a stream of cobble stones in a valley of terraced houses steeped in history. I have to assume these stones have been re-laid over trenches containing sewage pipes and that chamber pots are no longer going to be emptied out of bedroom windows. My exhaust pops under engine braking as I descend to the market area, where the vendors recreate their displays of fresh produce for the day.

I see my arch enemy the artist. I pull up next to him to say, "Hi." He is wearing different clothes, the same style of course, but he has changed. So he at least has a wardrobe, even if it's contained within a bin liner. He has been writing again. In his hand he has a scroll of paper; he says he has been working on it all night.

"With this," he says, "I can disprove all modern assumptions and beliefs. Society will crumble when they see this truth." I can't help but wonder if this is just another day in his life or if he has achieved his life's purpose. He clearly didn't get much sleep last night either. "So this is your motorcycle?" he observes to lighten the conversation a little.

"Well spotted," is all I can say.

"With which you pollute the air that I breathe."

"Which runs on the highest taxed fuel on the planet. A tax that might even filter through to the cultural department, so they can give grants to artists like you." I thought of that about ten minutes later when I was riding into the hills; my mind is not as quick or sharp as his, but it keeps me on the acceptable side of sanity.

I just say, "You really need to be less offensive."

"You need to be less on . . . lesson . . . listen," he says and laughs condescendingly.

"Be lucky," I say as I leave him to his quest, which if he succeeds, will change everything any of us know about anything. I should have got a picture of him. I wish I had recorded his babblings; he was eloquent, if not fully comprehensible. I met the man who adamantly believes he has the knowledge to change the world we know, if not the ability, but I can't prove it.

I turn my back to the Black Sea, but the road has not finished its performance. It takes me up to where I can take in the view of the port and coastline.

Predictably, my guidebook has a major section dedicated to Istanbul; it's overwhelming. I have decided to give it a miss.

I'm sure it's an incredible city, too good to waste, but it will be much better appreciated as a pedestrian on a city-break in shorts and sandals. I think I won't be getting the best out of this wondrous, historical, romantic city after I've dealt with the stress of negotiating the killer traffic, securing the bike, and then figuring out public transport. Like Paris in the spring, I think the city should be witnessed in company and in love, but Monklet and motorcycle are not the congenial company I have in mind.

So that only leaves one more recommendation on route: Safranbolu. My experience does it an injustice; I'm just burnt-out on historic towns. I wander the narrow alleyways under a canopy of grape vines. I climb a hill to look over the mosques, baths, and tombs. I buy a bracelet then make like the Red Sea and split. Motorcycle boots in summer heat don't enhance the sightseeing experience. Despite the contrast in architecture, it reminds me of a place in Mexico called Campeche, also a World Heritage Site. I stayed there for two days, bouncing around like a slack chain on a worn sprocket. So it's not you, Safranbolu, it's me. I just need some space. It's all been a bit too full-on recently. I just need to go for a ride. I'll call ya.

Back on the road there is nothing remarkable as far as sights and scenery are concerned until I see a Scania 141. Wow, how nostalgic. I think back wistfully to school days in science class looking out the window at the busy road, the constant flow of trucks heading to and from the ports of Harwich and Felixstowe. I remember how I wanted to be a truck driver as soon as I got out of school. The reality didn't quite live up to the daydreams, but the days' dreams continued and still do.

I'm driving myself crazy looking at fuel prices. They've gone up; deal with it. It's not even relevant anymore; one more top-up will see me out of Turkey. I contemplate my strategy for crossing Istanbul and think I will stop this side of it and get up super-early to cross the Bosphorus back into Europe at dawn. I can consider all these things now the road has dulled down. It runs parallel to a toll road, and all the trucks seem have opted for that. I don't need a fast road. It's pointless on a slow bike, and this road is all the better for its lack of traffic. The day has sped past again, and I'm riding into the afternoon sun. It's an "iPod and distance" day, but the earphones get uncomfortable inside my helmet after an hour or so. When I can't stand it any longer, I pull over, jump off the bike, remove my helmet, take them out, and put them in the tank box. I get out the sun block and coat my nose, helmet back on, and I'm ready to go with pit-stop efficiency. When I look up I see a van driver has watched the entire operation. I smile a wide smile; it's got much larger lately, it must be the muscles I keep using. I feel it beam broad across my face. I can tell it's an impressive smile because it gets such a good reaction. A smile is the most important thing on the packing list, but only time, practice, and knowing what pleases you gives it radiation qualities. It won't last forever, nothing ever does, so it's best to share it, no point in saving it.

When I stop to get water, I impulsively buy an ice cream too. An old man comes up and brings me a chai; he shows me on my map where he grew up in the east. A family have stopped in their VW to let the kids run off some energy. We all seem connected; there is a feeling of community in this petrol station forecourt. On the speaker system a poppy song is playing, "I knew you were trouble when you walked in." I can feel it; there seems to be a Friday afternoon feeling in the air, an end-of-the-working-week buzz, willing the weekend to start. Probably be a good time to be in Istanbul, party all night; that's where everyone is heading. Sounds a bit tiring. If I see Istanbul's dawn it will be after sleep, not before it. I'm still 100 kms away, so I head on. The driving becomes more erratic—it's dangerous. 50 mph is not getting me out of people's way; this is not a road for saving petrol, it's a road for saving myself. I go faster, accelerate out of situations. They are all destination-driven, end-of-week crazy. I pass a container terminal. Trucks are queuing up on the road to get into the port. Yuk, Friday night at the container terminal; how many frustrated hours of my life have I spent doing that?

I stop for a half-tank of fuel, so I can get out of Turkey without stopping tomorrow morning, another chai, and I'm pointed down the coast to a place I can camp, this time on the south coast of Turkey's egg-timer waist. It looks OK; pine trees and picnic tables. This could work. There are a few people around, and it's too early to put up a tent, so I occupy myself pratting around with my luggage. The guidebook is about to be buried into the depth of the pannier where the European atlas has been residing.

There is a family of four at a picnic table by the sea. They beckon me over. I would prefer to remain alone but that is not an option, Turkish hospitality will not allow it. So I go and sit with them. As has been the case most of the trip, we have no common language.

I'm invited to eat with them, but there isn't much happening in the form of food preparation. I'm with a father and his big fat daughter in her early 20s and her slightly older and slimmer friend, who is with her boyfriend.

Eventually some coals are poured into one of the free-standing grates, and I'm left with Father as the other three drive off in the car. It's all a bit strange. I get some fuel from my tank to help start the fire; there isn't much else I can offer. When the others return, they have brought a feast of additional food; bread, salad, chicken, peppers, potatoes, and Pepsi. I wonder if they were going to do that anyway. They are meticulous about hygiene, and the offer of my chopping board, which is stained black from rubbing on the inside of an aluminium pannier, is politely declined in favour of a foil covered table top.

Slowly the food is prepared. There seems a lot of attention paid to time. Phones are repeatedly looked at; are we waiting for someone? It is getting dark. With everything cooked, chopped, and laid out on the table, we just sit; seems like a good photo opportunity, so I capture my hosts against the dusk sky. Their father picks at a piece of bread sheepishly and is chastised by his daughter.

And then it all makes sense. The song of prayer drifts over from a mosque, then they also say a prayer of thanks. It's spoken a sentence at a time for me to repeat, but other than *Mohammed*, I don't understand a single word I'm saying until the "amen." The daily fasting of Ramadan is over, and we all tuck in. A classic example of how the benefits of watch-and-copy stopped me from embarrassing myself by snacking before the bell tolled. I'm not one for praying. Sometimes I wish, often I hope, but usually I just get on with making my dreams come true. Reciting an Islamic prayer could be seen as hypocritical; I see it more as respectful. What else can I do? I don't understand what I'm saying. I don't have their faith. Even if I could communicate, my views are irrelevant here. I'm not about to convert to Islam, but my hosts deserve respect; they are about to feed me, sustain life, and that's all I need to know about Islamic beliefs tonight, and I can live with myself on a chicken wing and prayer.

An extra plate of food is prepared and taken over to another family who have lit a fire to make chai; in return, chai is brought over to us. To have is to share seems to be the principle. I'm told it is dangerous to camp here and I am to follow them to a better place, but that isn't going to happen anytime soon. Music is played on a phone, and father and daughter dance with each other. I decide to brew some chai of my own with my English Twining's tea bags; it's accepted but not appreciated for the taste, only the principle of the offering. Slowly things are packed up and put into plastic bags that are then thrown into the sea. The horror! Such a polite, friendly, generous, hospitable family, and then with an absolute disregard for the environment, all rubbish is thoughtlessly discarded. They no more consider it wrong than I do to eat before dusk.

I was under the impression we were going 10 kms to the safe place to camp. It's night time now, and I'm following them as best I can. We head back the way I came in, past the docks; all the trucks are gone now. Against the dark sky the minarets of the mosques are lit in greens and blues, seen all the better as the street lights have been turned off. We divert off the main road, through a town of housing blocks. At 10.30PM we come to a park. It's really busy; I'm not camping here. I shake all their hands, express as much gratitude as I can, and then ride off. I find an area of shadowy pines next to a railway track. It's flat and concealed and will have to do. The night is hot, so I don't unpack much, and I won't be here long. I lie in my underwear on top of my sleeping bag and consider the day, the evening, the outcome. There are voices close by, and at some point I hear drums. It disturbs my sleep, and I have demon dreams, but nothing lasts forever.

DAY 76

MOTOCAMP, BULGARIA, 506 MILES

At 3.38AM the mosque chants into life. Blue and red flashing lights are projecting through the tent; the cops are the other side of the railway tracks, but it's too close. I quietly pack up, making sure tent poles don't clink. I wish a train would pass. I don't know if what I'm doing is wrong, but a bored cop on night shift could easily kill time at my expense. I'm already sweating by the time the bike is packed up, and although I've been silent up until now, there comes a point when I have to start the engine and ride out of the trees onto the road as casually as Mr. Wood, the tree inspector, at the end of a long shift. I ride past two police cars outside the park I was told to camp in. They all seem preoccupied, and I plod past as inconspicuously as I can. The fact it's still dark helps. Round the corner, between the housing blocks, and out onto the dual carriageway where I hope I will blend in. I'm going in the wrong direction until I find a place to do a U-turn by a green fluorescent Christmas tree. Cops outnumber the traffic at this time of day. I've got 50 lire in my pocket, half a tank of fuel, its 60 kms to Istanbul, just getting light, and I'm not wearing sunglasses, but I am wearing fingerless gloves. My hands are greasy with the humidity, my face is covered in a sticky shroud of sleep deprivation, but for now I feel good, alive, and alert. With little effort, I flow down the road into the city. There is nothing to stop me; all I'm looking for is the other side. High-rises come into view, and planes come in to land over my head. That's how I'll arrive next time. Fast tourist buses pass me, but there is little else on the palm-lined road. Building sites are the only spaces within the high-density cityscape. The sun starts to shine on the tallest buildings, which are becoming more extravagant, with spiralling twists and slanting gold mirrored walls.

I was under the impression it was impossible to cross the Bosphorus for free, or at least you are not supposed to. The toll for this and all other roads has to be bought in advance in the form of a chip, which you have to stick on your number plate, but there is a minimum payment and it is five times the cost of a toll bridge crossing. I haven't got a plan of action, other than to stop and take a photo of the bridge, my bike in the foreground of course, as I cross back officially into Europe. The sun is still low, the water is calm, and I have eyes everywhere as I cross between continents. There appear to be no toll booths, no alarms go off, and without incident I've left Asia behind me. The road takes me over more bridges, but they aren't as thrilling. High-rises are replaced by houses, and then suburbia is replaced with sunflower fields. With calmer surroundings I consider the rest of the day.

Right, now what? Most days don't have plans. I ought to be used to it. Just go to Bulgaria, but before that I need to eat. I stop at a big truck-stop for breakfast; I'm getting so brave to be eating in such big public places. I get the obligatory bread along with a token egg to indicate the time of day. Not that time is having much influence on my actions lately. I want another snooze. I find an abandoned factory and ride round the back but can't sleep, the excitement of scavenging and the creaking steel structure echoes the sound of heavy tyres on the road with spooky acoustics, and the flies on my face mean closed-eyes is as close as I come.

Back on the bike I keep my mind awake with some calculations. I have crossed Turkey in exactly a week, and I've done it with only two and half fills of my tank, three nights' wild camping, three in a campground, and one in a room. I've spent £140 coming back across, so despite its size and the price of fuel, it doesn't require a great deal of endurance or money.

Back at the border town where I first entered, I still have a few Turkish lire left, so when I see a Carrefour I make one last stop to buy some luxuries like peanut butter, mozzie coils, and wet wipes.

And with ease I'm back in Bulgaria, and my phone provider is now charging me 24p/minute to make a call as opposed to £3/minute. Which means I can now use my phone for more than just telling the time and currency conversions. Two months ago Bulgarian driving seemed brutal, but now after the deadly Georgian demolition derby antics this seems gracious and relaxed.

I feel dirty, so when I find a little rest area I boil some water, have a shave, and discover that you get what you pay for when it comes to wet wipes. These supermarket own-brand ones are like wet toilet paper.

The transition back into Europe calls for clean underwear; little treats like this can give the day a new lease of life. I'm going to the seaside I decide, but it's Saturday and so is everyone else. At a service area of cars, kids, and general chaos I realise this is only going to become more concentrated as I head for the Black Sea's west coast I opt for the mountains instead. Still, nothing appeals that brings me to a stop. I'm absolutely directionless now, and just because fuel is cheap it doesn't mean wandering aimlessly is fun, rewarding, or advantageous.

After a few half-hearted attempts to find somewhere to camp, I let my bike take me where it wanted to go in the first place.

16 hours of riding gets me to the gates of Motocamp, where I'm hoping it's not too crowded. Careful what you wish for; the gates are locked and no one is home. I ride up to the house of the expats I know, and everyone is there; it's like coming home. Everyone knows my name.

I left here saying I was heading to the 'Stans. I was concerned at how my failure would be received. I needn't have worried, there is no judgement here.

Ivo says to me, "Body OK?" "Yes."

"Bike OK?" "Yes."

"Then there is no problem, is there?"

A barbeque is in progress, a beer is put in my hand, and without a moment to make the transition from road warrior to home-comer, I'm shown the latest progress on the restoration: the new deck, plumbing, and hardwood floors. I can't handle this. Last night I was waiting for dusk and thanking Mohammed for my food. This morning I woke in a pine forest to the call of a mosque, ate breakfast with barefoot truck drivers, dozed in derelict buildings, washed in a secluded lay-by, and now I'm inspecting the shims that level a deck. It's been a ridiculously high-mileage day, and now being thrown into the familiar I'm shocked and unprepared. Bulgaria feels like home, and I'm not ready for that yet. This transition has the immediacy of air travel, not the gradual progress of overland transport. This isn't me being back, and I didn't even know I was coming here. I should see it as a friendly terminal while I wait for my connection, because with a ferocious clarity, I'm hit with the realisation that I'm not ready to go home yet.

DAY 77

MOTOCAMP, BULGARIA, 38 MILES

I've got a bastard of a headache. I think I'm just run-down; I'm certainly dehydrated. There's no better place to recoup. I've got a room this time; they are all named after bikes. I'm in "Harley" room, which seems appropriate, as yesterday I couldn't stop and today I can't get going and I certainly can't handle going for a ride.

After a lot of effort I do go for a slow ride into town, I need to get supplies for me and the restaurant. My underwear situation has reached critical levels; washing powder is imperative. On my return I do my laundry and spend the rest of the day discreetly commando. An American turns up wanting to store his bike; he's just spent two years in Africa but has some unexpected business to take care of and needs to go home. Probably a bit more serious than lack of clean underwear I would imagine.

After a couple of beers he opens up a little, and we start to really hit it off, so we ride out to a restaurant for some dinner. There aren't many things better than a summer evening ride with a little beer buzz (I'm talking about the one in my head, not the American). It accentuates the feeling of warmth, the sunlight, the summer smells, freedom, speed, confidence, and probably gives a false sense of security too, but what a wonderful way to go.

At an outside table by the road I ask the American why he travels. Same answers, different accent. Broken marriage, worked with cancer patients and sees how precious and brief life can be, too many friends are dying, life is too short for shopping on Saturday, drinks on a Sunday, work on Monday. Life was not wholesome enough; all his friends have family commitments. Africa has never appealed to me, and I ask him, like I ask everyone who has been there, to sell it to me. He does the best job anyone has but says if I like my privacy forget it, there you will always have an audience.

268

Two bikes turn up, a Sportster and a British-registered Speed Triple. It's Polly who runs Motocamp with the expat who is responsible for my introduction to plum wine; they have been on a two day ride-out, and their enthusiasm about it is infectious. They join us, and the vibe is upbeat, friendly, and exhausting. So here I am sitting at a roadside café, in good conversation with a new acquaintance when two friends from a few months ago ride up. This really does feel like it could be my home. I don't have a social life this good in England.

Back in the room I feel myself relaxing. I can see why people just come and stay, apparently riding directly here from Istanbul is not uncommon, if not intended. If I'd have known, I could have taken a far more direct route.

DAY 78

MOTOCAMP, BULGARIA, 26 MILES

I wake at 8AM. There is bird song, cow bells, it's a cool sunny morning, and in the distance is the sound of a chain saw. A horse and cart trots past my window; that's it, that is Monday morning rush hour. I go out to the veranda and have chai looking over the open restaurant, gardens, and bike patio that is Motocamp. I notice that "BMW" room is located round the corner, close to the bathroom, nice and easy to find at night (they are renowned for losing their bearings). There is nothing hectic about the day. I wander to the clubhouse for some breakfast.

No. 6 has been dragging his feet too. When he left work he sat around for two days staring at his panniers, unable to find the energy to pack them, on top of which he broke his thumb, and although he is still going to ride, he's unsure of his levels of endurance. Therefore, he can't say for sure if he will make it to Albania to meet up.

Plum wine rides up on his Street Triple, T-shirted and lidless. I remind him little acts like this have to be appreciated, particularly on a Monday morning. I work out I have done 3,800 miles since Baku, and it's time for an oil change. I'm told where to find what I need and ride off into town, but there's too much choice and not what I really want. I end up with "photosynthetic." What the fuck is that? Not mineral, not 50/50, not fully synthetic, oh no, let's make another obscure blend and fail to explain its composition on the can. Choosing the oil is the most difficult aspect of the change. Back at base I just pull the sump plug, let the black stuff flow out whilst I anneal my copper sealing washer over my stove, and then give the engine a transfusion of the photosynthetic. It certainly looks attractive with its golden appearance through the level-glass.

270

I now have the rest of the day free; the power has gone off, so with no Internet it's even more relaxed. I get out the map and look at a route through Macedonia to Albania. I might be able to catch Roger Waters playing in Croatia if I time it right. I should be thinking about leaving, but the elusive Doug, whose name is on the gate of this haven, has broken down on the Greek border, and I would really like to meet him, so I'll stick around a little longer.

Polly's dad, the former mayor, brings over chicken soup and baked potatoes for us all to eat. We sit in the clubhouse upstairs and watch a movie. I watch half the movie and then go back to lie on my bed in "Harley" room. My batteries are now fully charged, but I don't have the energy to turn over. I'm ready to see if there is any more adventure in this trip.

DAY 79

MOTOCAMP, BULGARIA, 0 MILES

A new level of relaxation has been reached now, almost to the point of boredom, and that's a dangerous thing when I have access to a workshop full of possibilities. I take my rear brake apart and look at the sad, worn pads. I file the glazed surface away in the hope of gaining a little more friction, but there is very little pad left to play with. Then I take the speedo drive apart again, but I can't drill-out the pin to remove the drive gear in the hope of raising it on the shaft. So, after those failures, my chores are all done.

Skype time: my mum is glad I'm safely back in Europe after my exploits in Iraq and a prolonged stay in Turkey, which has been grabbing all the headlines with national protesting. My friend of "U-turn" advice is off to Tajikistan tomorrow with her KTM bicycle, flying out to ride the Pamir highway for . . . well, as long as it takes. No return flight is booked. This is her second attempt to see the country, so her success is something we both expect.

A Bulgarian biker arrives on a Transalp; he speaks perfect English and is super friendly. He says he has a pair of tyres he took off his bike that will fit mine; they are at his place in the capital, Sofia. I can have them if I want them but I have to collect them tomorrow, because after that he will be back at work. Am I going to stare at the mouth of a gift horse? That's a very attractive offer. It would be satisfying to complete my circuit on the same set of tyres, but peace of mind is more practical than the pressures of worn, puncture-prone rubber. Obviously, I can't commit immediately, but I take his number and give the offer a great deal of consideration. Thunder rumbles; he is anxious to get back home. I'll almost definitely see him tomorrow.

The storm arrives at the same time as a couple of Danes. We shelter in the restaurant as they delight in their good timing, while the rain hammers down on their exposed bikes. I assume they are a couple, but as soon as the lady leaves to claim a room and unpack, her riding partner confides in me that it was a match made via a website, not a dating one; "tag-along.com" or something, and all he is seeing is the rose tinted benefits of "going-alone.com." Lately, the riding partnerships I've seen are seldom as they appear; he's clearly not even getting a shag out of the deal. Greener grass, everyone's convinced it's out there, but they won't find it. Greener grass is like a rainbow; you see it, you appreciate it, and when you try to get near it you find it's best viewed from a distance. Rainbows need rain to appear, so does green grass. I've come to the conclusion they are best viewed in your mirrors.

Day 80

Sofia, Bulgaria, 177 Miles

Its fleece-chilly but sunny. The indirect return is about to continue. I'm excited about the possibilities of new countries, new roads, and I've got three weeks left; that's a usual amount of time for a holiday.

The owner, Doug, never did turn up. I'm sure I'll be back this way again sometime. I've got a new second-hand pair of fingerless gloves; they have a circular pattern, which will leave some interesting tan lines, like symmetrical liver spots. Waving a gel-padded leather-gloved hand like a black, pus-filled palm-blister, I leave Motocamp again.

I've texted my man with two tyres to say I'm on my way and take the recommended middle road to Sofia, probably the least direct but apparently the most scenic. I pass that Buzludzha flying-saucer monument again—can't miss the bloody thing now. As I wind round the mountain roads my Mefos behave endearingly, as if they don't want to be dumped, and with pannier-scraping traction on tight twisties I question the wisdom of replacement. The hours are passing quicker than the miles, as plodding is my new cruising speed, perfected in Turkey and continuing on through Eastern Europe. My thoughts are turning over as slow as the engine; nothing much is stirring, looking forward to a possible meet with No. 6. Then I'll finish up with a hard endurance, tunnel-vision ride back home; getting through expensive central Europe as quickly as possible, unless something else happens.

Sunflowers and pine trees, Bulgaria doesn't feel foreign to me at all, it just feels friendly and familiar. Maybe in a previous life I was Bulgarian, obviously a mute and illiterate one, judging by my inability to grasp any of the language or alphabet. I could see myself living here; there are laws, but freedom to interpret them as you please. The country appears to be going through a period of

274

modernization; there is a pleasant mix of traditional and contemporary. Horses and carts are still common, but McDonalds have descended on the country. I'm yet to see a "trot thru."

I approach a transit van. The back doors are held open; from floor to roof are smiling gypsy faces all peering out and waving; gold teeth glint in the sunshine. Is this human traffic? My smile is one of bewilderment as I wave and pass by the happy transients.

As I approach the outer ring-road of Sofia the mountains remain to the south, and it turns out you can get a ski lift up to them from right here in the city. This country has everything, from flying-saucers to Toys 'R' Us, and it's half the size of the UK. I find the arranged meeting spot and wait for my tyre man, Vasil, to arrive then follow him to his workshop. VWs are his first love, and in this workshop are some examples of true labours of love—the sort of restoration projects that only a real enthusiast could ever get excited about. He gives me a couple of perfectly useable Heidenaus. I strap them on the top box and now look even more "outback overland" in this cosmopolitan capital city. There is nothing low profile about my appearance as I follow Vasil right into the centre of town. There are some beautiful buildings, but I'm more concerned at the no-entry signs we are going through and the one-way streets we are riding down the wrong way. I'm a bit wider than he is; this is not my element.

After the gifted tyres comes more generosity, and I'm taken to a restaurant, followed by an invitation to stay at his place, then entertainment. Tonight we are going to do what residents of Sofia have been doing every day for over a month now; we are going on a protest march. Vasil has spent a lot of time on his phone this afternoon; my arrival has thrown his schedule off, but I still seem to be top priority. At his place I'm shown my room. A chair lift goes right past my window, so I can wave at the passing ascendees. I could lean out and practically shake hands.

We await the arrival of his lady friend, a very pretty girl with a sophisticated and intellectual beauty. I think she has her own business; she definitely has a spectacular bum but the most unfortunate Pat Butcher earrings. Apparently she speaks English, but I'm not hearing it much, although she can definitely listen in English.

I'm not sure what to expect here; should I take a camera? Or should I be streamlined for a swift response in case things get riotous? She drives us into the city; I haven't been in a four-wheeled vehicle for ages, travelling and not looking where I'm going—what a treat. I've only been on one protest before and that was a poll-tax demonstration back in the early 1990s. It was a success because, along with 88% of the country, our opposition to the unfair taxation system brought about the downfall of Margaret Thatcher before the year was out. The great British apathy was disabled, and something actually happened. I don't think the country has been so united or passionate about anything since, perhaps with the exception of the death of Princess Diana, but that was shock and grief, not oppression-driven persistence. That was long before the advent of instant communication. Somehow pressing "like" or "share" doesn't have quite as much impact.

So with a 100% success rate, I better try and find out what I'm going to be protesting about. It would seem that some old communists are being reinstated within the elected government. One in particular is also the head of a major TV network, and therefore, news coverage of the government's strategies, policies, and electees is somewhat biased, if reported at all—at least that's the way I understand it. What I witness, though, leaves me in no doubt as to the passion of the people. The red, white, and green of the Bulgarian flag is everywhere; the noise of whistles and horns are deafeningly defiant. But other than that, it's more peaceful than a parade of Buddhist monks. There are families with young children, old couples walking their dogs; a clear cross-section of society.

We all slowly march down a main street, then stop outside the parliament building, and the sound escalates. Chanting, whistling, horn blowing—it's all turned up to eleven. I see someone scurry through the crowd; has he just planted an incendiary device, thrown a brick? No, he's putting his empty water bottle in the rubbish bin. Protesters have climbed statues and mounted monuments, but it's done with a respect; the only objective is to be seen and heard. The TV crews are out, along with various freelance reporters with mics and cameras capturing the crowds. The police presence is low and discrete. It's a lovely place for a demonstration; the city's finest buildings and a warm summer evening. As the crowd slowly disperses, people wander on to the park or sit by fountains in the square. The road is opened to traffic again, and there is not a trace of litter anywhere. No alcohol-fuelled behaviour that the papers love to focus on; it was just a loud and peaceful display of a country's very strong feelings, respectful, passionate, and non-threatening. What a great way to see a city; a walking tour with 7,000 other people.

With the calm, I get to chat to Desi. She is lovely, and her English is fine; she just couldn't find her voice in the crowds. We head to a park, past a four-storey building covered by a Roger Waters tour poster. He is busy building his *Wall* all over Europe this summer. It makes me smile. Always the ego in the band, he's not quite got over himself yet. This giant banner is bigger than the Bulgarian parliament building we just marched past.

Nice one Rog, did you really want to appear bigger than the political discrepancies of a European country? These are the pros and cons of concert promotion.

DAY 81

KOPAONIK N.P., SERBIA, 214 MILES

I thought I was given the spare bedroom, but I was given the bedroom. Through the other door is just a cupboard. I feel a bit embarrassed to see the couch had to be turned into a bed.

We study maps, discuss routes, cross check on Google maps, look at photos taken on said routes, consider distances, and decide on daily destinations. Looks like I'm going to Serbia then, although in my head I keep calling it suburbia, another name that is associated with unrest (Serbia that is; I only associate Buda with suburbia). Anyway, that is in the past, and when a country finds peace it's time for the outsider to find the country beyond the news reports. I still think it's ironic that after all the countries I've been through recently with volatile reputations: Georgia, Armenia, Iraq, Turkey, and even now heading into former Yugoslavian states, it's the peaceful and unobtrusive Bulgaria where I find myself involved in matters that are not getting the coverage they need to.

Before I left Motocamp, I managed to get rid of a few unnecessary items to lighten my load, and now I'm carrying two bloody great tyres. I have an absolute inability to travel light. Before I leave Sofia, I'm also given the scarf in Bulgarian colours that Vasil was waving last night. I may have casually said something just in passing along the lines of "I wish I had something more patriotic to wear." Now I do; actually it's a great little souvenir, a reason to look forward to winter: "Why are you wearing an Italian scarf?"

"Actually, it's Bulgarian. It's from the time I was involved in a protest in Sofia against the government"

I'm like a subtle little Che Guevara, and this is my motorcycle diary. And with these delusions of grandeur, I press the button and the engine starts its revolutions. Once again conveying a gratitude that seems inadequate, I head back to the open road.

Open it may be but only just; road-works, congestion, and confusion, this outer ring road is revealing just how big Sofia really is. It seemed like such a compact little capital, but now I'm stuck in its suburban sprawl that spreads out in the direction of the Serbian border.

Once I'm on the right road I pass a biker café; it's tempting, but ridiculously I worry it could be over hospitable, and I don't want to offend. I just want to be anonymous for a little while and pass through a few places without obligation. Anyway, I've got no more room for gifts.

In fact, when I do stop for supplies my efficient little packing routine has lost all its grace due to the cumbersome tyres. I get the feeling of a dealer entering a festival. Too valuable to throw away, they will be useful later, but right now they are a pain in the arse.

A flash of the passport and I'm in Serbia. First impressions? Well, the churches have domed roofs, the houses look well-maintained, bright terracotta-tiled roofs, and the place seems clean and spacious as hills roll into the distance. The farming seems labour-intensive, but there are some rusty tractors in the fields and some rusty Skodas on the road. There are still the sunflower fields; in Turkey they were withered, in Bulgaria they were in their prime, here they are yet to flower. Local transport is outnumbered by a procession of Dutch number plates; it is prime holiday time now. I have no more guidebook references, so from this point on I will only see what I stumble across, which hopefully won't be holiday destinations. The road signs are in yellow, which makes them look like diversion signs, but at least there are signposts. I'm still trying to figure out which alphabet they use here.

For the last two days my sat nav has disagreed with my decisions, but I really don't give a shit about what it thinks and says; just record the mileage and shut up. I come to a junction that has no signs, diversion or otherwise. I make the wrong choice. The road is severely potholed, and if the open-mouthed staring is anything to go by, I'm heading to a place where fiddling might be a popular pastime. I stop for some lunch; there is a small spot where I can stand next to the bike in the shade of a tree. I pull out a water-injected, tasteless, tomato, which is far more satisfying to throw at a tree trunk than it is to eat. Its dripping diluted contents attract the attention of the flies, and the oak tree has a branch that keeps scratching me and pulling at my hair. I hate having my hair pulled; it's like my instant piss-me-off button. Perhaps the tree hates having a tomato sliding down its bark. The pollen is making me rub my eyes; it's not the kind of picnic that I want to prolong or remember. In fact, the camera has not been out of the tank box for a few days. So I head back to the junction, take the right road, which is slightly less atrocious, in the hope of finding a sight for sore eyes.

Serbia feels like a football game that's yet to get going; a lot of casual passing, no defence or attack. Or a bike race that's biding its time without passing or competitive riding. Serbia is just being reserved; nothing significant is occurring, like a sunflower that's yet to blossom. Then again, if it showed its best at the border the rest would be dull. "Don't shoot your magazine too early" is a phrase a German friend of mine likes to use.

I need to get on a motorway to head north a bit. I'm seeing toll-booths on the exit slip-roads, but I didn't go through one to get onto this road, and I don't have a ticket. I'm wondering how they are going to be able to determine the charge. When I get to my desired exit, I've already prepared myself for what is to be my first Serbian interaction. It's not as complicated as I feared. I point at my map to show the man in the booth where I joined the motorway, which seems to be all the confirmation he needs. He counts the junctions between there and here, then charges me a modest amount based solely on where my finger rests. When I stop at a supermarket I'm less impressed by the reception I get. The language sounds almost Russian and is spoken with the same aggressive harshness. Regardless of the words, the actions and demeanour are unfriendly. After a break of peanut butter and Pepsi, I liven-up a bit and so does the scenery as I reach my intended destination, the national park.

I'd like to camp by a river and change my tyres, but the only spot I see is already occupied, so I ride up to alpine meadows a mile above sea level and pass some military activity, which does not encourage me to wild camp. Then I come to a ski area; there is a big hotel complex. It looks to be a Russian/Serbian partnership, mainly under construction or refurbishment but still open to the public. It has no appeal at all. As I descend, I pass a snake in the road, but I'm still determined to find a camping spot here. Anyway, I don't have any local money. My third off-road exploration ends with a secluded spot, out of sight and overlooking endless layers of mountains. It looks like a Joy Division album cover. It's not an easy spot to stand the bike on or pitch a tent, but it's worth the effort; clearly a lot of people don't know the pleasure of camping here.

I have a really hard look at my tyres, the ones on the wheels and the ones on the top box, and I manage to convincingly talk myself out of changing them over. The difference in the amount of tread is not worth the effort. I compromise and tighten my chain; it's been banging on the swing arm. When I stop fettling and deliberating over tyres, I sit and take in the view. Nothing like a ticking clock to make you appreciate the time you have. I'm sitting on a hillside of long grass and purple and yellow flowers, hidden by pine trees and facing the low summer sun over misty mountains. Just me, my bike, and my tent plus all the unknowns that are present and all that came before me. Looking down at the little villages, I wonder what this area was like during the war years of 1991-'99. Were these hills a place of ambush or refuge? I wonder what I would have done. A whole-hearted believer fighting for the cause? Not having any facts to hand, I can only really see me running to the hills. It's what I do best.

DAY 82

GUSINJE, MONTENEGRO, 179 MILES

No dew, so packing up is easy as the sun rises over the mountains to shine on me. Last night my stove worked fine. This morning, nothing. I'm never going away with it again; it can go in the power-cut box with the candles and matches.

I didn't realise how close I was to civilization; before the engine is warm I come to a village of chopped wood and stacked hay, sagging grapevines and old women in head scarfs. The bike was running rough yesterday, and it's no better this morning, but I want to put some petrol in it before I start to pull the carb apart looking for a blocked jet.

As I wind down out of the park I get hit square on the cheek by a bee with hard rock velocity. I can feel it bruise as my eyes water (my cheek, not the bee, I'm not sure what injuries it suffered).

I take a left instead of a right and accidently come to the Kosovo border. I consider turning round, but I think it looks incredibly suspicious to do a U-turn in front of a border crossing, and anyway, why not go through Kosovo? If they'll let me in. An official says I should buy insurance to enter the country, then confides in me that if I'm only here for a few hours there isn't really much point. They're the kind of laws I like, the ones that don't count if you're lucky enough not to get caught. Well, I'm left in no doubt as to what the Kosovo flag looks like; it's hung from every telegraph pole and lamp post.

Unsure of No. 6's progress, I'm going to Albania anyway; the cyclists in Turkey spoke highly of it. I've never been to a country beginning with "A" that was awful, and I liked Alaska too; it's not a great reason to go, but it's no reason not to either. Anyway, I've got an "M" country before that.

I ride alongside a disused railway line; there is something romantically mysterious about it. A destination no longer serviced, it's unmaintained, reclaimed by nature, the hard labour of laying a track wasted. Why is the route no longer desired? Expense, attractive alternatives, or perhaps blocked by moving borders? The track leading into Auschwitz was also abandoned, but its demise was rotten brutality; this one has a dreamy decay of chocolate commercial wantonness.

The countryside is pretty and delicate. When I see a brown sign that indicates a place of interest, like a zombie sensing living flesh, I instinctively follow the arrow. It's only a renovated monastery, obscured by power lines and looking about as authentic as a Disneyland castle, but at least I made the effort, even if it didn't take my breath away like a zombie bite. I think I can stay on this road and take a back country shortcut via a mountain pass.

None of the cars have number plates. I'm the only vehicle displaying one, and I feel like I'm wearing Speedos on a nudist beach, conspicuous and over-dressed, uncomfortable with my nonconformity. My sense of direction tells me I'm going the wrong way; the sun tells me different. My sat nav has lost the plot entirely, and my phone says welcome to Slovenia. I trust the sun, which is something I'd never do in England. I think I must be heading west, therefore in the right direction, but I could be wrong.

The land is funnelled by coiled barbed-wire, which narrows to a military check-point. There are armed guards, uninterested and out of uniform. The Kosovo flags still fly, and there are big roadside billboards saying, "Obey the peace resolution," and, "This is Serbia." I'm totally bloody confused now. Still, it's a lovely road and below me is a turquoise reservoir. I only see it intermittently; there are a lot of dark bendy tunnels. Inside I slow the pace waiting for the curvature to meet the exit straight and shed the light onto the road. There is more barbed-wire, this time stretched right across the road. A single armed soldier stops me; he has a handheld radio with an unfeasibly large aerial you could catch fish with. The other side of the roadblock is a passenger helicopter. The blades are spinning, and when a couple of dignitaries have jumped in, with a display of hollow, echoing, chest pounding power, it levitates in front of me in an attention-seeking performance. When I'm allowed to proceed, I pass a line of armoured cars and another security checkpoint, another border. I would love to ask where I am, but it seems a bit rude, I should at least know what country I'm heading into, as I think I might be back in Serbia.

I enjoyed my little diversion. I ride through hillside villages; garish houses painted green and pink and orange surrounding a single mosque. I'm confused again and then another frontier; now I'm entering Montenegro, a bloody big sign tells me so. What a thoughtful country, it's like wearing a nametag at a conference of ex-Yugoslavian states; I know exactly who I'm dealing with now. I mean shit, I'm not hiding my identity or nationality, why the secrecy? This would never happen in America; you always know where you are there, boy.

I definitely need insurance here. My documents are taken, and I follow them up some stairs and wait outside a door. It is confirmed I categorically need insurance to travel through this country and then assured there is absolutely no one available to sell me any. After some hectic and assertive activity from some quite high-ranking officials, my documents are returned, and I'm told to go. I'm free to enter the country . . . without any insurance.

On first impression it seems Swiss-like; pretty villages, neat and tidy towns, smooth twisty roads, steep cliffs, deep canyons, tunnels, and gorges. Montenegro may have shot its magazine too soon.

The driving standards have gone downhill, so has the rubbish; dumped over the edge of the road down the canyon, it tumbles into the light blue water that breaks white as it flows onto boulders and takes piles of decaying debris with it downstream. At the first sizable town I head for the centre, park by a pedestrian area, and stride forth in search of an ATM. They use the Euro here. I'd like to eat but feel far too scruffy to stop and dine in this smart and affluent area. I know my place, and it's at the side of a river but not by the rubbish dump. I unwrap my supplies: the sausage is full of fat, the tomatoes full of water, my cheese has gone hard, and the yoghurt I bought turns out to be cream. Nice scenery though.

The distances are much shorter than the map suggests, and soon I realise I've gone much further than I should have. It starts to rain, so I stop to put on some more appropriate clothing. No. 6 has texted his location; he is in Albania. Cool . . . I'm closer than I thought I was; I can get there tonight. This map Vasil gave me is quite detailed once I cross to the Albania section.

People are driving really slowly, the speed limits are slow, and I have to obey; I have no insurance. I don't know much about Montenegro, but the name makes me think of mafia and corruption—not sure where I got that from but best to stay in line for now I think.

I apologise for suggesting it shot its magazine too early. This is stunning; dark grey, formidable, imposing snow-covered, rocky mountains. They may possibly be on the Albania side, but combined with crystal waterfalls and wooden bridges over sparkling rivers, it's a wild paradise of dramatic scenery. In this little town is the end of the road. I see a sign that says bikers welcome, but I'm not stopping. I've got another country to get to today.

My map is misleading, and I seem to be on the wrong side of the river heading west. On the cliffs the other side a flat line has been carved out. It could be a road, but I stay on the track I've chosen.

Branches woven together with sticks make fences that enclose livestock and keep phallic haystacks out of reach. The track deteriorates to dry riverbed and then into marshy grassland. The road splits, and every option ends in barbed-wire boundaries and dead-end disappointment. I have no option but to return along the unnecessary and over-optimistic miles of quite challenging terrain. I head back to the carved out cliff; its pristine smooth tarmac, newer than my map, and after a few sweeping bends I arrive at the Albania border. This is rugged and remote; two men, one shed, and a barrier. They are friendly and process me out of Montenegro with smiles and handshakes. The Albanian side is just as friendly, but again, insurance is needed though unavailable here. I'm shown on the map where to buy it at a busier and better equipped border post called Hotit, but they still let me in.

Within a mile the road ends. I go over a wooden bridge, round a corner, and am thrown out into a rocky expanse. Other than some compressed stony tyre-tracks, there is no evidence of road, direction, or boundaries.

I love this. It's scary, undeveloped, untamed; it's just me versus the elements. Well, not quite, now and again a painted football-sized rock indicates, to me at least, that this is some kind of route. I come to a line of concrete dome-shaped bombproof lookout fortifications. Here I am surrounded by nature's unhindered majesty, and the only evidence of humans in this pristine landscape is what's been spoilt by war. What a mess. We fight for it, we pollute it, we concrete it, we divide it, and guard it; and when we declare ownership of it, we rob it of its minerals, beauty, and sustainability. It's all going to end it tears.

I come to a tiny settlement of dilapidated houses built of riverbed stone and with wooden shingle roofs. They're wrecked and isolated but beautiful, set against the rough and rocky cliffs. I ride though wide shallow rivers so clear I can see the bed for any potential obstacles. The river is the only sign of movement and direction. It's as wild as Mongolia but so much closer and convenient.

On this rough terrain, something is thumping under my bike. I thought it was the chain yesterday, but I've tensioned it. Now I see that the rubber buffer on the centre stand has come off, and it's banging on the shock mount. I spot a discarded old work glove on the ground and cable-tie it round the cross section of the stand, and the problem is cured. However, the problem of navigation remains. My map says the road goes down the west side of this, the most northern part of Albania, but I can't find anything. The occasional painted rock gives me hope but leads me to boulder encrusted river beds, absolutely unrideable, or grass inclines that end in fallen trees or boggy marsh.

The bike is getting stuck. I'm losing balance, dropping it, and dragging it. It's exhausting. I'm wet with sweat, panting from exertion. The only indication this could be the right track is I'm in the valley, but there is no evidence that any kind of vehicle ever comes this way. It's taken me half an hour to do five kilometres.

Out of options, I ride into meadows under canopies of trees along the grass in the middle of two tyre track trenches that end against sheer granite cliffs in black dense forest. I have to turn back. If this is the right direction, it's beyond me; if it's wrong, the map is too. Back to the abandoned village and find another track on the east side of the river. Exhausted, I drop the bike a third time. It's a bad one; I tuck and roll, but the bike goes down hard and is on an incline. It's laying flat on a pannier, wheels in the air above the engine, the screen is broken, the bark basher has bent, and the front brake lever has snapped off. But no time to assess damage; petrol is leaking, and there is no way to lift this dead weight at this angle. I have to just drag it along the ground, the agony of scraping stickers. I couldn't be any wetter if I fell in a river.

Adrenalin fuelled, I summon all the strength I have left, pull the wheels over a rut, and get under the bike arching my back. Straining my muscles, pushing it up past the point where it will pivot on my body, and I can push it up onto its wheels. I'm laughing, convulsing, gasping, sweating, shaking, hysterical, in defiance. It's vertical, and I'm spent, fall to the ground, parched and panting. An exercise of necessity, a predicament with only one option. A situation that required an immediate reaction.

I catch my breath. How quick happy travelling turns to serious incident in this environment. Where the fuck is health and safety now? Eh? How would you deal with this, ya limp wristed, conforming, regulating cowards, fearful of spontaneity? Interfering and intrusive, eliminating instinct and improvisation. I'd happily meet my demise out here doing this, and if I don't, I'll taunt you some more you country-crippling controllers.

I'd hold back my head, wide-eyed at the sky, and do a primal scream if only I had the energy. I roll over, crawl to the broken plastic, and stand up. It's not good. It could be worse, but I have no front brake lever, and my back brake has been inadequate since Azerbaijan.

Well that's it; I can't go on. I couldn't find a navigable route when the bike and I were able, but now we are both knackered. I have to head back, through the rivers, along the compressed stony track. My stub of a brake lever has no leverage at all, so I have no stopping power front or rear. Ego, bike, and body are all battered. I couldn't find a road that was passable.

Back at the border three hours and 15 kms later, I show the guards my broken bike; "Your country has just beaten the hell out of me." If they can't understand a word, they can see the evidence in my expression, in my exhaustion, everything about me, and the bike screams brutal extreme exhilaration. In front of me is a well-dressed man in a 4x4. He looks a bit mafia; when he opens his mouth he removes all doubt. In a Brooklyn/Sicilian accent he says, "It's a gonna be OK, they a gonna sort ya out, don't a ya worry." I don't have to reply; there is something about this level of fatigue that speaks all it needs in any language. If he were a vulture, I'd be worth his wait.

I head back to the biker welcome sign, where a large man sits at a table outside the restaurant; this is clearly his domain. He has a deep reverberating voice and a Schwarzenegger accent, also with a hint of Mafiosi.

"We're gonna get it fixed for ya," he says and speaks into his mobile. I have a shower and hang my sodden clothes on the communal undercover line. I go down for food and beer. The main man wanders round; he speaks to everyone, the old locals, the waiters, the newcomers, the passersby, but no help materializes. He comes and sits with me. Conversation is forced. It's busy beyond the gates; a lot of pedestrians all dressed up for a Friday night in this little party town in the shadows of rain clouds and dark mountains.

I mention the prettiness of the passing girls. Wrong thing to say; he calls over a peroxide Amazonian Serbian hooker. He says she is a waitress, but she's just waiting with sexual prowess. She sits with us, smiling at me expectantly. Well this is awkward, and then he bloody leaves us together. She speaks no English, and I don't even know what language Serbian whores speak.

It starts to rain, so we go into the restaurant. She orders a drink; apparently it's my pleasure. Then she plaits my hair, while I'm thinking about how to splice together a snapped brake lever, what size holes to drill to avoid weakening it, what tools I need, and how I can improvise. What I'm not thinking is what it must be like between your thunderous thighs. Now make yaself useful, leave me hair alone and go find me a drill.

I go to my room, put a photo of my fallen bike on Facebook, and mention the damage. I get more gratification than I would with a damaged and fallen woman. I will not let this stop me; it's easy to let such problems have end of trip connotations, but I'm keeping perspective. I'm not going to be waiting for DHL; there has to be a way to splice it together. I have no choice but to contemplate this until 3AM; pounding bass, live bands, karaoke, loud fairground. What's going on here? The streets are still full of people; it feels like such a lawless party place. If I'd had a different day, maybe I'd be part of it, but I wouldn't swap today for an oversized tart and a line of Charlie. Ask me again tomorrow.

Day 83

Barbullush, Albania, 138 Miles

Well, Schwarzenegger landlord doesn't need much sleep; I can feel his voice pulsate through the floor boards. It's only when I open the window that I hear it too. Down in the restaurant as I sip an espresso, I'm beginning to think he's all mouth; this place caters to bikers no more than anyone else. He makes more promises of fabrication and repair, but he can't pimp my bike like he can his so-called waitress. A Facebook friend suggests, "If you have a pair of mole grips you can use them as a temporary lever."

With caffeine induced speed, I get them out and clamp them on my stub. It's like putting your last coin in a slot machine and three bars come up; brilliant, solid, ergonomically perfect, 100% functional. I put a cable tie around the narrowest part to stop them pinging off, and baby I'm ready to go. This euphoric feeling is something I doubt Miss Serbia could ever have generated. I wonder if I would ever have considered that fix myself. I'm so grateful for the tip and glad I kept my pessimistic panic under control. Yesterday's clothes are still damp and festering on the line; I stuff them in a bag and pack up. I pay my board to Mrs. Schwarzenegger; the landlord has disappeared off somewhere, and contrary to his reputation, he won't be back.

I get out of this town that seems to have far more going on than I'm aware of, but I have my suspicions. I really need to get fuel. At the next little town I see a petrol station. It's a happy place; the attendants just can't grasp what I'm doing. "Alone? Azerbaijan? All this way? Where are your friends? Who do you talk to?" I show my voice recorder, but I'm thinking, it's you, people like you are who I talk to, and this exchange, like this tank of fuel, will last me all day. They are enthralled by my mole grip brake lever and the bike in general. When I go in to pay they even have a Montenegro sticker. This is turning out to be a brilliant day.

The bike is running great now. Treat it mean, keep it keen, and all that, or perhaps it's just petrol which isn't watered down like my tomatoes were. Maybe all the abuse just banged the blockage out of the jets.

I'm going to take the road over the top of the Albanian border and approach it from the west side. I love my brake lever; apart from anything else it just looks so cool. With 98 octane fuel and smooth roads the KLR has once again transformed into superglide mode. I love my bike too, in fact, this morning I'm just full of loving appreciation. The bike puts up with such abuse; bad petrol, bad roads, bad riding. Regardless of the circumstance it rises to the challenge.

What the hell was I doing when I rode this road yesterday? How did I not notice this scenery on the way in? Low clouds, preoccupied? Blue skies enhance everything, particularly clear rivers and mountainous horizons. If Albania were my through route I would have failed, but this is more than adequate compensation.

When I rode through Kazakhstan, on my third day I came across roads so bad I couldn't ride them; not just the state of them, but the way they just ended. Out in barren steppe wilderness, unable to find anything that resembled a road, I couldn't navigate or negotiate the tracks I did find. I thought the country had beaten me; in hindsight it seems a bit over-dramatic, but that feeling came back yesterday. There are just no roads, no navigable roads. Thankfully I had this alternative that I'm riding today, but if I hadn't, when the terrain becomes too severe, the way unmarked, the exhaustion and battering so relentless beyond ability and endurance levels there is no option but to turn back. It's a guaranteed way to discover your limitations; the realisation you are unable to cross the line you desire.

I turn off yesterday's road onto a narrow and twisty one, dwarfed by granite cliffs. I try to resist taking photos. I've been doing it for 30 years and rarely capture the feelings of awe such scenery stirs in me when I see them in the flesh. But this range of grey and snow streaked rock is so vast it might be the ultimate picture. Oh OK, just a few photos, just to make sure my camera still works after yesterday's pounding.

That tank box is as strong and resilient as the bike is. I can see how the tank box might look a bit cumbersome and precarious, but it's functioning perfectly. From the moment I strapped it on the bike I was ecstatically happy and so proud of it that I posted the construction video on a forum. I should have known better. I just wanted to promote the skills of Zen Overland. It was a big mistake.

The go nowhere forum naysayers who, although I have utter contempt for, still manage to cause a niggle of doubt with their negative ramblings that they peck out in the safety of their comfort zone. "I wouldn't ride a bike like that," they say. Well what exactly would you ride and where to? Anyway, I didn't make it for you. Their gleaming bikes may be adorned with all they can purchase, every accessory in the Touratech catalogue. However, thumb through the plethora of motorcycle trimmings page by page, from index to Internet, and you will discover that Touratech don't sell balls. You won't find the ability to challenge your limitations for sale in an accessory catalogue. That comes from within, from strength of spirit not strength of panniers, and you don't gain that quality slagging off what everybody else says and does. These are the people who put down others to make themselves feel better about their underachieving lifestyle. You can never get the last word with that type; they will always be in front of the computer, because they don't do anything else.

I'm clearly very proud of my tank box and possibly a bit overprotective of it. I see this negativity as being equal to me looking into a pram at a new born baby and saying, "That'll end up costing ya; it's gonna be a headache when it reaches its teens." Babies are generally what parents want, and this tank box is what I want. I will continue to defend it passionately. Ultimately, I will be taking it on my next trip, and that is as big an accolade as I can give any accessory.

A wasp flies under my shirt and stings me twice on my tummy. As I strip off frantically at the side of the road, he falls from my waistband, and I stomp him into his next incarnation.

I see a sign; a corner-cutting track to a point I want to get to, but looking at the state of the surface and after yesterday's experience, I think I will stay on this road. I'm enjoying slowly winding round the mountains; I don't have any want for a shorter alternative route. My only deliberation today is do I go into Albania again? The road is too narrow to go fast, and I'm coming across the occasional logging truck. I don't want to meet one when I'm at a 45° angle on a blind corner with no Armco and a sheer drop.

I round a corner that is anything but blind; it reveals a 180° panoramic view looking south over Albania. The country tempts from a distance but then taunts upon arrival. This road is so continually spectacular I decide to take some video footage on my phone. It doesn't really work, but with Monklet's tail flapping round the clutch lever, my fingerless gloved hand on the throttle with two fingers curled over a cable-tied mole grip, it does capture the vibe of the ride if not the magnitude of the landscape. At certain points I see a track that spans a canyon over a suspension bridge and then disappears into a black hole on a cliff face. When I realise it's railway and not road, for a moment I envy the engine driver; he's certainly had an extravagant route cut out for him.

I've strung out this back road ride as long as I can, and with an increase in temperature, the sound of crickets, and the return of discomfort inside my jacket, the descent is evident. I have a lunch stop at a diner on the junction where I join a proper road. I get tomatoes and chewy ham, which disagrees with me before I've got my helmet back on. All too soon I'm on the outskirts of the capital. I don't want this at all; it's only 3PM. So with masochistic intensions, I head directly to the Albanian border to give the country another chance to beat the hell out of me.

I'm really pleased with myself for not heading straight home, not that I have anywhere to live, but since I made the U-turn decision, I have zig-zagged my way in a very indirect westerly direction.

I'm no further north than I was a month ago. I'm being wowed by the unknown and am happily anticipating the time to come.

I don't spend much time now dwelling on what ifs in respect to the 'Stans. I'm still not sure what I was doing wrong. When the only symptom is unhappiness and the diagnosis is to continue the journey but change the direction, it's a rather ambiguous cure, but it totally bloody worked. If this book was *The Wizard of Oz*, after "Day 51" the text would have turned to colour.

In front of me at the border in Hotit is a British-registered, beaten-up Toyota, and cramped inside are four guys doing the Mongolian rally. They have just bought their Albanian insurance for 38 euros. This is where I was told yesterday to purchase my green card.

"Where are you going?" asks the immigration officer.

"Oh, just round the lake and back again," seems to be the right answer to avoid having to buy insurance.

"Would you like a stamp?" he says holding my passport. I'd prefer a sticker.

The road is bowling-alley smooth, the best surface I've ridden in days; this is very different to yesterday's path findings up in the wild north. My tummy is grumbling; bloody rancid ham sandwich. I ride at the side of a big lake, which splits Montenegro and Albania. The map indicates it is divided down the middle.

That's the way it should be, not like that one Turkey had claimed from Armenia with barbed-wire. I head into Shkodra; it's all bars, cafés, hotels, but with a big ruined castle on a hill—that's the surprise of no guidebook. I find a petrol station with an ATM and toilet just in time; I have a very explosive bottom.

I head south and pass a signpost for a place called Puke. Today I have the shits, tomorrow I'm going to Puke, but for now I'm heading to a Dutch-run campsite that No. 6 stayed at last night.

It's soulless but the toilet block is clean, and I visit it frequently through the night.

DAY 84

DARDHE, ALBANIA, 137 MILES

Fasting is usually my last resort, but I'm going to start now because I don't want a runny bum, especially when I'm about to have a riding buddy. So breakfast starts and ends with black chai. There were strange goings-on in the toilet block last night. When I arrived, there was literally shit-loads of toilet rolls, but they were disappearing with every visit and there are only a few other campers. Supplies got so low I took a roll myself. That's how shortages start; quite often self-fulfilling prophecies. Announce loudly in the supermarket there will be a bread shortage, and everyone panic buys; low and behold, there isn't enough to go round. Same when an irresponsible media reports limited quantities of petrol or any other headline grabbing commodity. In this case I bought into the panic of depleting stocks for justifiable reasons.

Google Maps tells me Split is 400 kms away. That is where Roger Waters is going to be playing in two days' time. Including today, that gives me three days of riding to get there. Having seen the improvement in road quality, I think that's quite doable, and it's the closest thing I have to an obligation in the next two weeks. With that on my mind, I head down to the meeting point.

The mountains look two dimensional and out of reach in this heat haze. The road is horrendous, fast, and busy with impatient and reckless overtaking. I can't pay much attention to the scenery anyway; there are a lot of police speeding up and down, but it doesn't deter the hooting processions of wedding cars. They are driven like the drinking started hours ago, with swaying passengers holding video cameras out of the sun-roofs. I'm glad to get off the road and into the parking area of a restaurant. I stop in the shade where I can be seen from the road, take off my boots and socks, and sit on the ground with my head resting against a pannier. Before long, despite the noise of the constant traffic, I'm dozing with

293

an ear tuned for the 990 V-twin of a KTM. After about an hour I hear it, jump up, wave him down, and before he has taken off his helmet I'm chattering away. This isn't a conversation; I'm just talking at him. I didn't realise I was so starved of company, but after about ten minutes I take a breath. We formulate a plan; it's not difficult; we are heading to the mountains.

There is one thing I really want to do and that's to learn how to pronounce No. 6's name. It is not pronounced how it is spelt. His English is perfect to the point where he wants to learn Essex slang, like "innit." The least I can do is learn how to call him by name. I write it down phonetically and put it in my tank bag.

No. 6 has a sat nav, but yesterday's lesson not learned, we use my map to get into the mountains and find they have drawn another route that isn't there. We end up in a town of hot stagnant traffic, and in an attempt to get some breeze around our baking engines, I lead us to the main road and we complete a big hot frustrating one hour circuit back to the meeting place. This isn't going very well.

I think No. 6's bike is even more beaten up than mine is. After 18 months in Africa and Asia, as well as plenty of Dutch off-road riding, his bike has a scrapyard pick and mix appearance against my KLR's inventive mutation. No. 6 finds us a road into the mountains, although it follows a wide river alongside a main highway so we aren't gaining any altitude. The riverbed is mostly dry and is being excavated. There is heavy plant equipment down there and mountains of stones that could be to complete the uncharacteristic highway, a multilane modern fast-track to Macedonia. I could use some fuel and water, and I need a wee, but I can't catch up to convey this to No. 6 any better than I can say his name out loud. Just as inside my helmet I can sing like Axl Rose, so too I can pronounce his name perfectly, but to attract his attention I get tongue tied, lose my confidence and slur, stutter, or muffle my attempts.

"Yer . . . Ewe . . . Dude, I need to stop for a piss."

The chirping of the cicadas is so loud I keep thinking it's coming from my bike, and the KTM's exhaust tones add to the unfamiliar sounds. When we find a village we stop for supplies. I usually scurry off as soon as I've made my purchases, but we stand outside the shop and chat. Across the road is a housing block; an old woman calls out to me from a balcony. I'm not sure what she wants; waving and smiling doesn't seem to be enough. So, like the prince looking hopefully up to Rapunzel, I stand beneath the balcony. She has a plastic bottle of water she wants to give me; I think she's a little deranged. OK then, I hold out my hands. It's frozen bloody solid; it nearly snaps my wrist. It bends a finger right back. I'm a bit pissed off at this meteorite projectile. You could fracture a skull with that.

We head out, possibly ten minutes later than we should have.

The frozen water slides from under my bungee, hits the road, and shatters, I wasn't going to drink it anyway. The road winds up the side of the valley, and we stop to look down at the black line of highway, relieved we have left it behind. It's little things like this I've missed; a spontaneous stop and chat about whatever has been on our minds or on the road since our last stop.

The road hugs the cliffs and twists round the profile of the mountains. It's like no other road I've ridden this trip; I'm so glad I've given Albania a second chance. When we head back down into the valley, there are kids jumping off rocks twenty foot into the river; I want to do that. I'd really like to plunge into some instantly cooling and cleaning water, but I'm deterred by the thought of the laborious undressing and redressing. There are so many different types of mountains: orange rusty ones in front of the grey jagged granite ones, against the deep blue clear sky.

The heat haze of the morning's view has been left on the plains; we've ridden above and beyond it. We go through a little tunnel carved out of the side of a rocky foothill that meets the river; it's so narrow. We stop the other side at a little snack area and comment that in a campervan you wouldn't get through and would have to turn back all that way to the highway. What a bummer that would be.

"We've still got a long way to go," says No. 6." "Where to?"

"I don't know."

I just have a Coke. There is no food available, and fasting is keeping my tummy happy. We make a little plan. My map is simply wrong; it's shit. We pass near Puke, and I stop to get a photo of me by the signpost. No need for a tripod, I have a sixpod.

He notices there is no memory card in my camera. I took it out last night to download photos onto my laptop and forgot to put it back in, so all this morning's photos don't exist.

The road has higher speed qualities; smooth, with views along the mountainside that confirm the radius of the bends and lack of traffic. Other than a few landslides, the corners are gravel free. I lean low left and right, safe in the knowledge of having seen what lies ahead. The Mefos continue to say, "Trust us," as they cling to the corners with confidence. This road is the perfect match for my bike's power, handling, load, and my abilities. I push the limits of all, and nothing comes up short or wanting; its harmonious motion. Albania, you little bugger, in 24 hours you have made it onto my elite "want to return" list of countries. I'm so into this exhilarating road that nothing else matters. I wait at a spectacular corner to photograph No. 6 coming round. He's not going very fast, in fact he's stopping. He tells me I've ridden 10 kms past the turn we wanted.

"Oops, sorry;" shaking off my selfish lone rider habits is harder than I thought. "Must think of others not just the road and having fun." Back at the junction we meet an old-school Austrian biker in a leather jacket, backpack bungeed on the pillion seat. He has a brilliant map. It clearly shows where I was yesterday and there is no road there. My map is wrong. If I'd have gone south on the east side of Albania it would have been fine. Well, at least it wasn't my fault; I just put too much trust in the cartographer's ability.

We discuss the similarities of our intended routes, and I expect to see him again.

We continue along more cliff edge. I couldn't dream a ride this good; I'm just loving every corner. Another horseshoe bend, another waterfall, another stretch of left and right shallow sweeping curves. At 5.30PM we stop and have some biscuits, the first food I've had in 20 hours; everything seems to be OK now. No. 6 comments on what a hard day it's been. "Really? Not by my standards; you should have seen what I put myself through yesterday." I don't say that of course.

Apart from my riding ability on this type of road, I also become even more aware of the efficiency of the tank box. I can get out my camera and take the shot as effortlessly as the design intended. No. 6 is faffing around in his tank bag to retrieve his DSLR between packs of biscuits and sun glasses; I don't miss all the miles I rode like that. Anyway, regardless of the efficiency of photo taking, it's all academic, as the beauty is being here, experiencing it, immersed in it; that's where the real thrill is, in the here and now, not in the future looking back.

No. 6's guidebook indicates a guesthouse is around here, and we descend a steep, rocky dirt track that ends at a ravine of dark blue water. This is where the roles are reversed. I'm hesitant and heavy; No. 6 with all his African off-road experience rides with control and confidence. The benefit of this is he gets to the dead-ends first and has to ask directions. The descent is so steep and narrow, even though we are going the wrong route down deeper into the chasm, we can't turn round and have the infuriation of riding into a situation we are not sure we have the traction to get out of. It's a cruel pounding at the end of the day, and there is no guesthouse to be seen. On the way up I stop to pick up what has fallen off No. 6's bike. Back on the road I pass him his orange juice, and we have an overland meeting. Onward into the unknown or back the way we came to the twee, expensive-looking Swiss cottage hotel that stood alone? Its 7PM already.

The problem is this road will end and we have to get a ferry boat down the river to get to the next village. No. 6's guidebook says it leaves at 6AM, and we are still 70 kms away. We opt to go on, see nothing, stop, turn round, and go back to the twee hotel.

We have a beer and consider our options. On the other table is a hydro-electrical engineer who speaks perfect English and says there is no ferry any more. That means after a long day's ride I'm further away from the Roger Waters concert than I was this morning. Oh well, I can't change that. The engineer speaks to the waiters and negotiates rooms for us both, and with nothing else we can do about the situation, we order another beer and enthuse about the day and what is to come. Albania has surpassed itself. It is thrilling beyond all my expectations. Although I'm tired, the surprises continue; I didn't expect to see a scorpion in my shower tray. I consider knocking on No. 6's door to show him; but not sure what message that would give out; he's probably seen a scorpion before anyway. I pull all the covers off my bed, shake them, and then decide to go down to the bike and get my sleeping bag, I feel a bit more protected in there. I pull the drawstring tight so the bedbugs won't bite.

DAY 85

KOMAN, ALBANIA, 43 MILES

No signs of scorpions in the night, but there is a zoo outside. I'm up early to do some bike maintenance; first I walk over to a cage in which two brown bears live. They appear to be very much in love; when they stop kissing, licking, and preening each other, a big paw is put through the bars to shake my hand. The claws look very sharp. I hold out my hand, free to make contact if I'm stupid enough, and I nearly am, but sense overrides impulse. I'm sure they are much more skilled at dragging idiots in than I am at pulling away. I have no way of knowing what sadistic or instinctive practices they indulge in to get their kicks. So I just wave and go back to the bike.

The Scottoiler has stopped working, and when I take off the tank, I notice a few other problems. The fixes are straightforward, but it's always awkward to get the fasteners to line up when remounting the tank. When it's all getting a bit frustrating, I remind myself it's Monday morning, I'm warm and surrounded by mountains, I'm not confined by bars, and I am about to go for a ride; the annoyances just float away.

When No. 6 emerges he says he's tired, needs some adrenalin. I say be careful what you wish for and tell him about the bears, saying it's sad to see them caged. He says, "Well they could be dead." I'm sure that's a great relief to them.

Before our engines and tyres have fully warmed up, a bee flies down my boot and stings the back of my calf. He should have got No. 6; I didn't need the buzz.

As we ride I consider the options. I thought I might want to go to the show, but I'm running out of time. There is a national park that looks good; the towering peaks of which I saw from Montenegro where I waited for the promised mafia lever fabrication but only got a hooker waitress. What if we have to come back this way, maybe we can charter a boat. I can't make a decision; we'll deal with the situation when we get there.

A sweet little girl is standing in the road selling blackcurrants in plastic beakers. She is about six years old, blond, and super cute. We both stop. I don't like blackcurrants, but she just deserves the business based purely on her shy innocence and cute smile. I take a photo of her dwarfed by the KTM. She can't be here alone, and over in the undergrowth I spot mum, or at least her owner; a haggard and dark-skinned woman dressed in black from shoes to head scarf. Is this little blond blackcurrant seller really the fruit of her loins? I don't have much local money; still, she seems ecstatically pleased with a euro coin and poses hesitantly with Monklet for a photo. What the hell am I going to do with these? There isn't even a top on the beaker, so I jam the container in the tank box and hope it doesn't topple over. She totally read us; using her sweetness she makes her sales. We've been played; we don't really care. Around the next corner are some older lads aggressively selling the same thing. They are demanding money, pulling at the bikes. We have to force our way past them. They cling on as we pull away. They could take a lesson in sales technique from the girl down the road.

When I put my fuel tank back on I trapped the throttle cable, and now it doesn't snap back. There are a lot of people out on the side of the road today; they all want to do high fives. Due to this accidental cruise control, my right hand is free to make clapping contact.

This morning I found out a friend at home had a baby girl. In a year that has consisted of some significant losses it's so good to be have a birth to think about, and I can't wait to meet baby Charlotte when I get back; one of my favourite girl's names.

We pull over on a particularly picturesque bit of twisty cliff-hugging road. Three heavily accessorized GSs come towards us. The leader throttles down, but as he gets a closer look at us, he thinks better of it and we hear the revs increase. The other two follow him obediently—Touratech triplets.

There is a trickle of a glacier edging down a crease in the shadows of another horizon-hogging mountain; it is a backdrop to a landscape of forested hills that fall into a deep midnight-blue river. From here the road esses down to the water's edge in countless switchbacks, a sheer drop on one side and sheer cliff face on the other. There is the odd token white concrete bollard that won't stop anything falling off the edge. As we descend we have a view of the lake-creating dam and the power generating town beyond it. We can see a T-junction where rivers meet, and the different coloured waters merge like . . . well, like watercolours really; why make a complicated analogy to describe a watercolour image? Over to the west is a small jetty, where two ferry boats are moored, and that is where we are heading. We want to get the facts about the feasibility of getting our bikes downstream. The road to the ferry boats is new, smooth black asphalt; I wonder if perhaps this is a through road, recently constructed, that follows the river to the next town. It isn't. There are two large rusting car-transporting boats. They are nothing more than floating salvage, far too big to even consider chartering. They look like they have been unemployed for a while. If they do go down river, it's bit by rusty bit as they slowly decay. There are a few men drinking in a wooden hut. All they say is "6AM." So there is a boat, or is that when you started drinking? We go back into town and find a restaurant for our now daily overland meeting.

I have a look at the guidebook; I knew nothing of this boat journey before No. 6 told me about it. My first thought was I don't wanna go on a boat, I wanna ride. What I'm reading is written with flowery over-rated enthusiasm.

"The journey along Lake Komani deserves to be one of the world's classic boat trips, up there with the Hurtigut up the Norwegian coast or the ferry from Puerto Montt to Puerto Natales in Chile . . . the boat at times appears to be heading for an unbroken cliff face . . . "

Even taking into account the possibility the writer had only ever been on a Dutch canal, it still sounds like a journey I want to experience. So I've gone from oblivious to not caring for it to wanting it to being deprived of it. I think there is a name for that pattern of behaviour; for now I will just call it familiar.

The Roger Waters show in Croatia is tomorrow evening, it's nearly 500 kms away. I would have to start heading that way now. I can't do that distance in a day. Am I going to sacrifice *The Wall* for a road and a river? It's a hard decision; this gig was the consolation I promised myself for returning early, but I don't really need consoling now. I'm really happy with my decision, particularly with the way things are at the moment. I'm going to be seeing him closer to home later in the year anyway. The roads are phenomenal, the company is really good, too good to be rushed. Yeah, bollocks, I'm not going. Maybe I'll see you around, Rog.

God, how long does it take to make some chips? I'm being patient, though; there is no rush. We decide we will ride to the national park then come back and sleep on the dockside for tomorrow's 6AM departure. It sounds good; I've accepted I'm not going to the gig, now I've just got to stop looking for possibilities.

As we leave the restaurant a young pretty girl is coming in. Confidently, in good English, as if our dilemma is displayed in a neon light above our heads, she says, "Do you want a ferry to Koman."

"Er . . . "

"We can take you;" she points at some older boys behind her.

"25 euros."

"And our bikes?"

"Yes, of course. You want to load them now?" I think I just fell in love. This calls for an immediate overland meeting. National parks of untold beauty and sleeping on docksides are wiped from the itinerary. I look at No. 6: "Whaddya think?"

"Yeah, why not innit?"

"No, innit doesn't work in that context; I'll explain later." I don't have any money, and I need fuel too. She says there is an ATM in the next town; they are going to have some lunch and will wait for us. We haven't haggled, we haven't negotiated in the slightest, we certainly haven't considered they do this every day, and we could get tomorrow's ferry. Much like with the blackcurrant seller, we have been wide-eyed sitting ducks, and we have just been sold a trip down the river.

"Are you going to wait here, or are you coming?" "I'll wait here. No wait, I'll come," decides No. 6.

We ride like demons down windy roads, no time for photos now, alongside a cyan blue river, leaning hard, up and down the gears we race into town. It's temptingly close to the national park, but we have other temptations. However, the mountains are immense; their size and presence beyond description. They are now postcard fantasy surreal with cloud perched on top, leaving the summit to the imagination. Two youths are crossing the road; I ask where an ATM might be. They respond as proudly, helpfully, and enthusiastically as I would if I saw Roger Waters hitchhiking.

I grab some money. It's such an easy operation when there are two of you; no need to lock the bike, I just run off leaving it in the safety of Group 6 Security.

We rush back. This feels so good, so much fun; exploring possibilities, making plans, then changing them. This isn't U-turn deliberation, this is a spontaneous reaction to an opportunity. Keen to get back we don't take the opportunity of getting fuel. There was a petrol station by the restaurant, and anyway, I don't want much. I don't want to make the bike even heavier for loading it onto the boat. We seem to have worked ourselves into a bit of a frenzy.

Mariana, her brother, the captain, and his mate are nonchalantly rounding up backpackers and tourists. They must know exactly where to look; the place seemed void of any foreign presence an hour ago. The petrol station is out of petrol, which was rather short-sighted of us. We just passed-up numerous opportunities, and now we have no choice. You'd think we'd never done anything like this before, but between us we have a wealth of experience; we just haven't learnt much. However, our new guide offers something between a five star service and a money making opportunity. Mariana says fuel can be arranged for collection when we dock this evening.

The backpackers are herded down the road to the boat, and Mariana, barefoot and in a T-shirt, climbs on the back of my bike and perches herself on my top box between the tyres. She gives directions in a way that makes my sat nav and Monklet jealous.

We have to strip our bikes of luggage; I manage to cut my finger in my haste. I would rather we load the bikes backwards, thereby having engine assistance when it's time to disembark. The three strong dockhands have clearly done this a lot, and whilst I'm flapping and fussing like a mother hen, checking ramps, and pointing out a mole grip brake lever, they have manhandled the bike onto the boat carefully and effortlessly. As Mariana is the only one who speaks English, they were unable to tell me to just get out the bloody way, and I did need telling. It's nothing more than a thirty-foot boat with benches down each side and a bamboo canopy held up by scaffold poles. With ten passengers and two bikes we are comfortably full. These are not the first bikes that have been on the boat, nor, despite how special we are made to feel, are we the first bikers. Mariana's first objective in life is to make money; she is much younger than her brother and clearly the boss. In winter she continues her education, and all summer long they cruise the river in this hired boat, providing a service down the canyon, making the most of a gap in the market and the road.

Once we set sail I chat with her. She is much younger than I thought, full of life, smart, funny, and shrewd. I think she has a great future ahead of her. She has No. 6 and I wrapped round her finger, both captivated by this effervescent vision of positivity, zest, and enthusiasm. She has an imagination of infinite possibilities and is entertaining us with her insights. It is exhausting trying to keep up with her. When we get round to introductions, No. 6 tells her his name, pronounced Yer-ren; she repeats it back to him perfectly. My inability to pronounce it makes me the butt of all the jokes. "That's what I've been saying: Yer-ren," I protest.

"No, you are saying it wrong," says No. 6, and he tells Mariana it is pronounced Jeroen in French.

"Well that's what I say to myself when I read your emails; you never bloody told me it could be pronounced that way."

"That's because I'm not French, so you have to pronounce it Yer-ren innit."

"I have been, and that's better."

"No, you've been getting it completely wrong and thank you."

Mariana says later we will stop to go swimming, "Do you want to swim?'

"Yeah, I'll go swimming." She high fives me; the gesture didn't seem worthy of a high five, but that's cool. Cool? It's bloody freezing. No one else is stupid enough to go in, but I've made a promise and sealed it with a high five. I'm pathetic putty in her hands; there is only one way to deal with this; I dive off the side of the boat.

Fuck me, that's cold. If the water wasn't flowing there'd be ice on it. It takes my breath away like the scenery I haven't noticed should have. I think my head is going to implode; I can't feel my legs. Oh, look at me, I'm so cool; the paddling passengers are nearly convinced. One gullible lady takes the bait and jumps in, instantly realising how stupid I am. Mariana seems oblivious to it and swims around like a hard-core mermaid. She makes my efforts seem petty by comparison; she's going to be such a heartbreaker. I've done my duty, honoured my high five vow, now I'm going to defrost in the sun.

Back on the cruise, everything seems more subdued. The dip has chilled everyone out; Mariana seems to have left her smile in the water. Jeroen and I pay a bit more attention to this world class Chilean and Norwegian-competing, fjord-traversing, cliff-piercing voyage. When I get out my camera, I notice the blackcurrants have gone everywhere, so I sit picking them out and throwing them overboard. Finally I give my attention to the view; it is lovely, the colours are striking, the canyon modest but agreeable. There's nothing wrong with it; it's fine. Are we nearly there yet?

When the gorge recedes, the so-called port comes into view, comprising a wooden café and a ticket shed on a tiny peninsula. There is a black arch in the cliff, which is the tunnel, the only way on and off this platform of rock. The bikes are removed with the ease they were loaded, petrol is siphoned from a waiting minibus, and containers are passed along a chain of hands and poured into our tanks. Before I can make any mental calculations, Mariana is relieving us of the contents of our wallets. We wave off our fellow passengers on the minibus, and all too quickly it's just me and No. 6 again. I say to him the next time we see that girl it will be on the cover of *Forbes* magazine.

With cold engines we thud into the black archway. The tunnel is unlit, with a rough surface and bends like Rotherhithe; it's long too. When the light finally illuminates the tunnel walls, it's a soft evening glow; we are faced with a cliff of orange sunlight. It sweeps us round a horseshoe bend. Goats scurry off the track. There is no tarmac to be seen.

A campsite comes into view at the side of a wide river. For me this image encapsulates the overland travel thing that we do. The day, the feeling, the scene of the campsite ahead, a day that wasn't pushed, we simply went with the flow, and flow it did. We didn't rush or stress about the slow frying of chips at lunch, and everything just happened; we let it happen. Roger will be on stage in 24 hours; do I care? A little but not enough. What are we going to do now? I think we have to come to terms with the death of the old plan before we can conceive a new one. Have a drink I think; better put the tents up first. Well just one beer then.

There are kittens, ducklings, and chicks wandering round our feet as we sit at this table under a tree beside our bikes. A full moon rises behind us and sparkles on the river, a river that has come from the other side of the dam. A French couple arrive on a Yamaha and then three Poles: a girl with her boyfriend and his mate, all on individual bikes. They all wave at us as they enter the campground.

"How come they think we are the ones with the bikes?" says Jeroen. "Well you have a big orange KTM logo on your T-shirt, and we are both sitting by our bikes at a table full of beer bottles. I'd think we were the bikers too."

The other tables around this farmyard campsite are occupied by cyclists, campervan tourers, overland car drivers, and backpackers, all sitting quietly, writing diaries or reading kindles, books, or maps. I catch them glancing over enviously at us, the laughing happy chatty table. Soon we become a table of seven, four nationalities with six bikes between us. I'd suspected the Poles would produce some toxic homemade alcohol, and true to their generous reputation, they do. Thankfully, I still remember what happened when the Norwegian ambulance drivers gave me their potato wine. Well, I don't actually remember, but I recall how I felt the next morning, so I just stick with my beer.

The girl says she travels with 12 skirts; when she gets to Istanbul she is flying back to Poland for a wedding.

"So you still have one skirt at home then?"

"No, I will buy an outfit in Turkey."

This gratifying day is going on all night. It's late; the moon is shining over our heads reflecting off the cliffs surrounding us. As I erect my tent, I tell the Polish guy the story of how I came to own such a good quality tent and what a bargain it was.

He says, "Poor people can't afford to buy cheap stuff; it breaks and needs replacing." What a good philosophy that is, a true wisdom.

Jeroen complains, "The mountains are too tall; I can't capture them all in my lens; it's too hot, and there is nowhere grassy to pitch a tent."

"I'll get you a complaint form in the morning; you're not pitching it here, are you, with your snoring and all?"

"No, diva, calm down. I'm going to take it over there."

The crickets and cicadas quieten down. I lie in my tent for the first time without its flysheet; a warm breeze blows over my exhausted happy body. This was the best of days; this was harmony with serendipity.

DAY 86

THETH, ALBANIA, 79 MILES

I learned my lesson; I actually learned my lesson. I didn't drink the Polish poison, and this morning I'm feeling just fine. I have breakfast with the French and later chai with the Poles.

"We don't have a plan for today," I say to the quieter of the Polish guys.

"Well that is a plan too," he says. If I had crossed paths with someone like this back in Baku I wonder how different my trip might have been. It was nothing but my own thoughts and solitary experiences that led to the U-turn decision. If the Swiss travellers in the Land Cruiser had been this philosophical, who knows how my judgement may have been swayed. The more I think about it, now I'm enjoying the journey so much, the more burnt-out those 28-year travellers seem to me.

I am undergoing the acceptance of missing Roger Waters. Looking at a map in retrospect, I now consider how we could have stayed in the national park and taken the ferry today. However, a trip taken in hindsight is always perfectly executed, and just because it's efficient doesn't mean it's fun.

The Poles are catching the ferry this morning; they know it's only the other side of the tunnel, so they aren't wearing their bike gear. The girl is riding a DR650. She must have run out of skirts, because other than her helmet, she is wearing her bike boots with hot pants and a boob-tube. I want one like that. Not the boob-tube, the girl.

"Hey boy," the campsite owner says to me.

"Hey boy?" I repeat laughing, "who taught you to say that?"

He just wants paying: £12 for camping, two meals, and all that beer. For that price you can "hey boy" me all you want.

We need a more immediate plan. No. 6 has been studying the map too. We have decided. No. 6 has decided we will ride to Theth via the bad road, 50 kms

305

of unpaved mountain track so rough that even the goats complain about it. OK, I can go along with that; it's too late to go to Split now. Although it's not mentioned, it seems like we will be riding together for few more days. I'm more than happy with that. We'll just take it a day at a time; neither one of us are forthcoming where commitment is involved. The trip has been so full-on lately, I'm feeling the anguish of an incomplete diary.

Occasionally it happens, when it's nonstop from the second you open your eyes in the morning until you crash at night. It's such a long time coming, and I wouldn't change a thing. However, it's times like these that most need to be recorded, to recall during the inevitable down times, those sad and lonely periods when there is nothing but time to write a depressing monologue. I'll just have to resort to memory, because it's moments like this that have to be lived.

Back on a mountain road, on the edge of another canyon, a beautiful river beneath us full of dark deep waters, another gorgeous day, mountains against a blue sky, just like yesterday. Sometimes samey is just what you want; I hadn't had enough of this scenery. I sit on my bike, taking it all as it comes, watching what's occurring with wonder as I plod through another perfect morning.

As we ride my mind goes over the conversations from last night, the interactions, stories told, knowledge gained, connections made.

More canyons meet the river, which expands into a lake across the valley, the depth of which remains a mystery. I wonder what lies beneath. We leave the classic mountain scene in a haze to be replaced by brown scrub, withered ferns, on a delicate landscape of rock-strewn undergrowth. Then on to pine covered hills and a mosque in the distance—there is something for everyone on this road.

Ultimately, we descend to the flat wetlands of reeds and heat, biting insects that collide with pus-splattering satisfaction on a closed visor.

We ride back into Schroder, hot and uncomfortable in the cross-town traffic. The shock always occurs when I go back into civilization; I can deal with the transition into wilderness so much easier. I don't have to think too hard about it to know which environment I'm meant to belong in.

We ride into the city centre sweltering, and I leave the bike with Group 6 Security and fetch what we need. Teamwork in a place like this means we can get out all the quicker, not that the scenery here is so bad. I don't think No. 6 was really paying that much attention to my unattended bike in this throng of scantily-clad shoppers. I see a ZXR with British plates, not looking much like a tourer. I just bet someone at home is missing that bike and possibly still has the papers for it.

We head out of town to the north on the skinniest of roads; it's newly laid jet black asphalt and encourages a faster speed than its width allows. The terrain is different again, and there is farming in the valley. Then without warning, by a stone church with a three tier spire, the black smooth luxury ends, replaced with a rocky, fastener loosening, tyre shredding track. Some people like this, No. 6 clearly does; I don't. It's hard, really hard. If I were alone I'd probably turn back. I'm sort of obligated; I led the KTM around the paved twisties in a riding style that was unfamiliar to No. 6, now it's my turn to follow the leader's wishes. 50 kms of this is going to take me five hours. The bike, the camera, the computer are all taking a pounding. I'm pretty much riding alone here, which is fine as I don't want to be eating dust. I catch up with a truck; he's going even slower than I am, obviously, or I wouldn't have caught it up. It sways from side to side as each wheel goes over a boulder. It's impassable, taking the entire width of the track. There is a loud bang; did it just rock into the side of that cliff? No, the cloud of dust from the right hand side says a tyre just burst. He keeps driving. It's understandable; there is nowhere else to go. Eventually he wobbles to the side of the road, and I'm able to pass. He waves happily, unfazed by his blowout. There is a broken moped at the side of the road, snapped in half. That's how bad this road is.

I think No. 6 knows I don't like this; he has stopped in the shade, "I'm thinking picnic," he says.

I'm drenched; we've only done 15 kms. My bread is stale, but the shade and the rest are welcome. Forget looking at the scenery, it's all about the road. I really should have expected this. When No. 6 first emailed me to say he was going to Albania his words were, "Obviously, I didn't choose Albania for its culture . . . although its culture might be rich; I still regard culture as a money-absorbing leftist hobby :-). Apparently there's a lot of off-roading, so that's my aim . . . but then again: whatever."

As I sit panting and wringing out my T-shirt, I consider the joys of taking up a comfortable leftist hobby instead of this money-absorbing damage the impact is having on my capitalist possessions. As we eat, the punctured truck passes us, waving enthusiastically. Great, more dust to inhale.

Like coaxing a kitten to go through a cat flap, No. 6 entices me onwards. I hate what this is doing to my bike. I hug the cliff side of the road, regardless of what side that is; I would favour a head-on collision to being pushed off a cliff edge. With a head-on accident at least I can put up my hands and say, "Sorry, I was in the wrong," as opposed to the oncoming vehicle pointing down the valley and saying, "He was in the right."

I pass a young lad squatting at the side of the road. He indicates he wants a cigarette, I'm in no mood to deal with beggars; I'm exhausted and struggle with every revolution of the wheels. Just after I pass him, I lose traction and drop the bike. He runs over to help me lift it. Once I go round the corner I stop; a tankbox fastener has broken and the spare tyres have come loose. I've got a spare fastener and slowly put the damage right. No. 6 is way ahead; when I get going again he is on his way back. My tyres have come loose again, memories of Mongolia, my temper is fraying, and my fastening strap has broken. No. 6 gives me a ratchet strap, and I clamp them down hard, maintaining control. When I do look up I see what glorious scenery we have ridden into. The mountains are snowy, but annoyingly, I have already used up my best descriptions. Anyway, there is no time for that now.

I'm drenched in sweat. We pass a wooden shack selling drinks to the truckers. We should have stopped, but in an effort to get this over with, I shook my head when No. 6 indicated if we should pull over. He shouldn't have listened to me; I don't know what I'm doing, anyone can see that.

There is a brief respite as we enter an abandoned village, I take photos of a barely suspended wooden bridge and a crumbling church. There are power lines here, but no one seems to live in this isolated but stunning location. I bet it's harsh in winter.

I ride beyond my limits to catch up and fall off again; my back protests and aches as I lift my bike up. The scenery is getting better all the time. We are surrounded by mountains. I just hope when we do stop we will still have such spectacular views.

A Roger Waters song comes into my head, *Each Small Candle*; it's so appropriate for this area. I'm happily reciting the lyrics in my helmet when I come to No. 6 waiting on the other side of a river. It's not wide or deep; it just has a steep bank either side of it. I stop, look, assess, and then go for it. My front wheel falls violently into the river and is then slammed into the opposite bank. With no grace whatsoever, I bump up the other side. Vertical, but without balance, my pannier knocks No. 6's, and we both fall over.

"That was completely unnecessary," he shouts.

"Sorry," is all I can say. Next time I catch up with him, we both think we have flat tyres. We don't; it's just the surface is so soft we are weaving like we were riding on our rims.

"Eight kilometres to go," encourages No. 6. I really am struggling; the road is getting even worse. No one ever taught me how to ride this terrain. I enjoy being out in the open wilderness and off the beaten track, but the track has to be beaten flat at least. I've come away for three months and left with cold weather clothes. No. 6 came away for three weeks, his engine is 340cc bigger than mine, includes an extra cylinder and far more power. I'm not excusing my inabilities, just pointing out some differences. With all my luggage I weigh so much, not to mention the additional 25 lbs. of spare tyres. I can't twist my throttle and lift my wheel out the way of obstacles, I just wallow round, bump over and sometimes into them. I haven't got the most effective braking either.

Five more kilometres to go. There have been a few forks in the track, so we are not entirely sure we are on the right route. There have been very few vehicles. Three kilometres to go, and for no reason, my bike spins round 180° and throws me off. It's laying in a bastard of a position, halfway up a bank. No. 6 is way ahead, probably having a shower now. I've broken the new tank box fastener. I'm so completely knackered now, I drag the bike unlovingly down the bank and get it up on its wheels again. It's facing downhill, and I can't use the side stand, so lean it against the bank I just tried to ride up. As I attempt to refasten the tank box, the bike moves forward and falls over again.

"BASTARD!" This time the GPS mount snaps off. The bike has bits hanging off everywhere, and it's still facing the wrong way. Where the hell is No. 6?

There can't be much more strength left in me. With the last of my reserves, I right the bike again. The sat nav screen is scratched, but I don't care about that and put it in the tank box. As I try to climb on I lose my balance, and it falls over a third time.

"MOTHERFUCKER!" I've had a total sense of humour failure now. I'm really angry, I haven't got the energy for a tantrum, but I'm going to have one as soon as I've rested. Somehow, I lift it up again; pure fucking anger is the only energy I have now. I strap the tank box onto the back of the bike, turn around, and ride towards the village of Theth. No. 6 is coming the other way. When he sees the state of the bike and the look on my face, he doesn't have to ask.

At a ridge that looks down to the village, some hikers have stopped; they take a photo of us, not surprisingly, they don't get a smile out of me. I wonder how I appeared in that photo. I follow No. 6 down to the campsite, strip off my sodden clothing, and stagger to a bench. A Coke arrives. I sit in the shade, catch my breath, and calm down. I look at my damaged bike leaning against the fence; poor thing. I didn't even want to come this way.

I calm down remarkably quickly; I hadn't spat out my dummy, so I'm not embarrassed. I don't need to have that tantrum now. In a surprisingly peaceful manner, I go to my bike and calmly start fixing all that broke. Once again, the bike performed better than I did. Therefore, it deserves the attention.

After a hot shower and clean clothes everything is better. The scenery almost makes it worth the hardships to get here. I'm too tired to do anything much, but after some food, I chat to a German couple in a compact 4x4 campervan and enthuse at their mode of transport. All they can do is envy our bikes and speak of the days they rode to Alaska and Africa, the days before they had the child that is sleeping in a hammock above their bed. They seem to get little consolation from the fact they now have possession of a solar powered fridge full of chocolate, but I find it most gratifying.

When the moon comes up I drag my camera and tripod over to the dry stony riverbed, and only now, really become aware of just what we've ridden into. I can't capture this on a camera. I'm surrounded by an arena of looming snow-streaked mountains, under the cavernous blue moonlit sky, a canopy pierced by a few resilient stars like tiny candles that light the corners . . . of the dark.

DAY 87

PRCANJ, MONTENEGRO, 174 MILES

When I was in Turkey I was concerned with campsite etiquette and how, as the new arrival, I should behave. I now realise that it had nothing to do with the appropriate etiquette; the reason I was unsure of how to fit in was because I didn't, couldn't, and had no desire to. Those places are the extensions of the block-paved driveways outside safe suburban semis, where, surrounded by neatly trimmed hedges, stand perfectly polished cars next to wheel-clamped caravans. Of course I didn't know what to say or do in such company. But the people who make it up here are of an altogether different calibre. It's a hard journey; it's an exclusive reward. There is the physically fit cyclist, the courageous climber, the extreme hiker, the alternative independent backpacker, the 4x4 nomadic family, and then there is the well-rested motorcyclist who rode beyond his limits to arrive in a rather bad mood.

This morning, though, I mix like a DJ, the bike giving me far more credibility than I deserve. This is the first day we have a clear plan and we are not executing it.

We sit around socializing and gazing at the scenery. When I turn my seat round I realise there is a whole new view to take in. This place does not encourage rapid movement, and we certainly seem to be under the spell cast by this tranquillity. I'm so glad I didn't arrive ranting and raving from my disastrous journey; it would have been entirely the wrong vibe to bring here. Exhausted is acceptable, expected even, but the place isn't open to Mr. Fuming flaunting his fury.

Five hours after getting out of my tent we leave. I have one objective today; not to fall off. We are taking the easy route, the alternative route, the one the vehicles that service this isolated location use. It's still all rocks and loose surface

310

and not quite as easy as I was led to believe. Then again, the suggestion of anything daunting would have probably kept me staying in the village another day. The only way is up when you are in an area surrounded by mountains, and as we wind our way to even more spectacular views we meet a lot of people coming the other way. A couple on motorbikes; he is too cool to wear his helmet or a jacket. He must be one of those really clever people who knows when he is going to fall and stops to put his protective clothing on first. His Bulgarian girlfriend is struggling with her bike on this road; I try not to be too discouraging about what she has ahead of her.

At a vista point that commands everyone stop, a car pulls up next to us. Two of the passengers are on holiday, coming home. Native Albanians, they were born and raised in the village we stayed at last night. They now both live in East London and have for some time innit? We get a little history lesson: the road was built in 1938, and since then there has only ever been two fatalities. I find that a bit difficult to believe, but they seem well-informed. The place can be cut off for weeks in the winter, and I would imagine in such a small village rumours and exaggeration run rife. So if two road deaths are the retold tally, who am I to argue?

The road is being paved and will be completed by next year. I predict caravan club penetration into these parts. Nothing stays the same, but it's so good to see somewhere before the "used to be better" status applies. They say it really hasn't changed that much from when they were kids.

After they leave, the ground shudders. The sound reverberates around the mountains; a shadow of eclipse proportions creeps over our bikes. We stand in reverence as the most outrageously excessive six-wheel drive, multi-terrain, mountain flattening monster lumbers up the track. It's the most extravagant overland vehicle I have ever seen. When you see an Artic on the motorway it looks perfectly proportioned, compared to seeing it negotiating its way round the chicanes of a 17th century village with parked cars on each side. In this instance, placed in precisely the expansive terrain this model was probably photographed in for the sales brochure, it still looks significantly out of proportion.

Inside this Dutch-registered penthouse on wheels is a family of four, one more than the transit sized German 4x4 with the fridge no longer quite as full of chocolate. Its build is excessive to the point of becoming impractical. Most of the conversation is in Dutch. No. 6 cranes his neck up to the driver's window, and I stand with an empty but congenial smile on my face that says little. I'm trying to calculate how many years I could stay on the road for the purchase price of this thing and how many lavish hotels I could book for the cost of a tank of fuel. Over the course of the brief chat the multi-cylindered engine ticks over thunderously, drinking diesel quicker that I can beer. When he pulls away it takes three shunts to get round the hairpin bend. What's he going to do when he meets another vehicle? How will he get under the overhanging cliffs; what will he do when he reaches a tunnel? I'm impressed by its overall structure but unmoved at its impracticalities. On his third shunt he straightens up and crawls to the next obstacle. I look at No. 6 expectantly, waiting for a translation of the conversation. With a dead pan expression, as if it was blindingly obvious, he just says, "Small dick."

Before we have got our helmets on, another 4x4 arrives; this is a great place for conversations. I could set up a stall here and sell books to the passing trade of like-minded individuals. We head back down into the heat, past major new road construction, until eventually the tarmac starts again. No. 6 has been very patient and always waits for me. I've seriously slowed his progress. Being back on easy road my mind instantly wanders; it's like a shakedown after a long workout. I realise as I accelerate up to a visor slamming 45 mph that I better start keeping an eye out for police again; I never did buy any insurance.

We are heading back towards Shkodra. We have only explored the most northern quarter of this country, and by all accounts, the rest is equally beautiful. Soon we are back down in the flat hazy heat again; up ahead is an old man trying to push start his antiquated Mercedes. His hunched and fragile wife stands at the roadside, only helping by removing her frail body from the payload. We become her knights in body armour; dismount and indicate to the gentleman to get in the driver's seat. We push hard, get some good momentum, but he screws up his end of the operation. We are approaching a junction, but we push again down this slight incline; this time it fires up. Not appearing quite as fit as we thought we were, we walk back past the grateful granny, wearing a slight glow of perspiration.

Our bikes, too, have warmed up nicely, having been left running with no cooling air around the engines. But man, do they look sexy; these two visions of beauty, standing side by side on their side stands, geared up, lights blazing, and ticking over with eagerness. Our tired saunter turns into a purposeful stride. With skilful actions, confident intent, and firm hands we sweep them off their side stands and take control of their wanton desires. There's nothing else around I would rather throw my leg over.

Road karma delivered, we head to the main road for a full tank and a cold drink. The attendant speaks English as well as I do Spanish, but conveys to me in three words and one action news from my home country. He says, "Buckingham Palace," and moves his hand in an arch from his chest to the bottom of his stomach and then says, "Man." Oh right, Will and Kate have had a baby boy. No matter where I am in the world, I always get my royal news from the locals. They have infinitely more interest and are better informed of the goings on in the house of Windsor than I.

A table is brought out for us so we can sit under the canopy by the pumps and have our Coke. I have devised a way to remount my sat nav after the incident up in the mountains. So with my Swiss army knife I make a couple of holes in my windscreen and cable tie the punctured suction cup into position. That's what I was doing, putting a preconceived plan of basic ingenuity into action. What I was not doing was wandering off to have a little cry at the news of a royal birth, but that was the accusation I was met with when I had finished working on my bike.

Now we are going round the lake into the south of Montenegro. As we cross a bridge a large overhead sign states the distances to noteworthy places. Berlin 1,900 kms, Vienna 1,200 kms, Istanbul 1,100 kms are just a few that I caught. At the end of the bridge the road splits. That unnecessary notice must have exhausted the sign budget, and the junction remains unmarked. We go the wrong way, but as we are now by the lakeside amenities, we have a pizza and look across at how remarkably unimpressive the mountains seem from here. All we have done today is come down a hill, and it's already 4PM, but we are fed and can now ride into cooler comfortable temperatures until the light fades.

This is my first border crossing with company; I prefer to do it alone because, as a group, one person's failings can affect the whole unit. This is not the case though. First we take the initiative and ride past the sizable queue of cars. I feel my neck sink into my shoulders, half expecting someone to shout a reprimand. Having reached the front, we are ushered through the pedestrian processing lane. We can just squeeze through with our panniers, and without a mention of insurance, we are in Montenegro.

No. 6 didn't see it, but just before the border was a compound of tarpaulin tents and piles of rubbish; a few lost souls sat in the dust with vacant eyes. I think it was a refugee camp. It looked so hopeless. It's just a refugee camp; it's just an image we have seen countless times on TV, to the point of being desensitized to it.

However, although it was just a passing glimpse, I saw real people in a real life situation, and the situation looked dire. I think to myself that next trip somehow I want to try and make a difference to a desperate life. Because a sight like that makes my journey feel extremely selfish. My whingeing about falling off my bike seems such an affluent problem to endure next to someone who has nothing, least of all a country to live in.

Not surprisingly, the roads become uneventful, or at least less stimulating. It's still a good ride from lakeside to Adriatic coast; we cross over minor mountain ranges. We are sticking to the scenic "green" roads. One in particular is perhaps designated green because of the grass growing through the cracks in the surface.

It's not used much anymore. My tyres slip out from under me on a lefthander and then again on a right hand corner. I think it's safe to say the Mefos have passed their useful life. I have got over 13,000 miles out of them.

I've got the thrilling Croatian Adriatic coastal highway ahead of me from Dubrovnik to Split. It was, when I rode it in 2006 on a 955 Triumph Sprint, the best road I'd ever ridden. The road is so forgiving it really gave me the impression that I was a brilliant rider, and for several hundred kilometres I was. I will change my tyres before I relive that ride in a few days.

We make good progress across the map, then as the road zigzags up a mountain we appear to be stationary, as only the elevation changes. We are both tired, and after my dodgy descent, we stop at a pretty little town on the far eastern edge of Lake Scutri. It has tourist appeal but maintains its quaint charm. It would be easy to stay here, but No. 6 has to be in Slovenia in two days, and time is slipping by. We sit in a restaurant and watch the people pass. Man bags seem to be a popular accessory here. I'm sure they must be very useful, despite how they look. I have one myself; it's at the bottom of the pannier. I use it to keep spare engine parts in. It's more a clutch bag.

The sugar break has the desired effect, and with renewed vigour we enjoy the low light and summer evening warmth as the road continues to wind us through some beautiful countryside. It is narrow, and the sun is in our eyes now but the drivers are very courteous and pull over for us. I take the lead; it's not fair that No. 6 should take the impact risk round every corner. The midges are out now too, and staring wide eyed seems to entice them into the moisture of wind whipped eyes.

The moment arrives when we find ourselves looking down to the bay where the town of Kotor sits; tonight's destination. Although it is so beautiful from up here, I'm considering camping possibilities. One of the major plusses of company is to just pull up at the side of the road and look to the picturesque bay 1,500 feet below and say, "Wow, look at that Jeroen."

"You finally got it right, man, innit?"

Now we are looking down to sea level as opposed to up into thin air. The sun is just setting behind the hills, shining on the water, and the view is gorgeous. I don't think there can be a better time of day to ride this road. Sitting up here from now to dawn would be my first choice, however, I can't find anywhere to wild camp, so I don't even bother to mention it. Half way through the descent, when the only thing left to think about is the ride into town, the road climaxes: twenty-six hairpin bends curl down to sea level. I know this because each one is numbered. It snakes us down in a north-south direction, and as we wind on down the road our shadows follow then they lead, until the last of the light takes their definition away, and all we have to do is find the campsite. That's all.

The town is buzzing under the street lights; it's crawling with evening shoppers, tourists, touts, stall-holders, artists, street performers. There is an imposing castle perched on a ledge above our heads and dramatically lit. The place is full of energy, but it's not sharing its vibrant spirit. I'm seeing it, but I can't feed off it. We continue on past hotels, guesthouses, all manner of accommodation, but no campsites. We have followed the coast road right out of town, riding slowly looking hard, reading every sign; the progress has been slow. Eventually I ask an attendant at a bus park; he says it's all the way back the other side of town.

No. 6 is tired. I can feel his angst. I'm happy to take control; I feel fine. So we turn back through the throngs and round the bay. I ask again in a little shop. The shop keeper knows, but the young mother translates wrongly; another three kilometres, still nothing.

"Another five," says a street trader. I hear No. 6 moan at this news; I think his dummy just got spat out. I'm keeping positive and lead us on down the dark narrow road through authentic fishing villages.

I see a sign for a campsite called Monika. I'm not sure if that's the name of the owner or the site itself, but either way it epitomises narrow-minded, unimaginative, ignorance in reception and design; past its sell-by date, used up, and void of any attraction it may have once possessed. A place, in theory, where people of the road congregate, and it is generally accepted that travel makes you a better person. It opens the mind, expanding social awareness and understanding, becoming knowledgeable and sympathetic to the needs of other travellers, offering help when the opportunity arises. This, however, appears to be one sick person's obsessive and malicious attempt to radiate misery to the travelling community. As if driven by pure spite, there is not a single redeeming quality in this field of loathing. A fleeting glimpse of this septic infection makes the rest of the world so much more inviting. In the knowledge that some suffering should be left to the sufferer who created it, they deserve each other. We don't let it stop us.

I feel like I'm physically pulling No. 6 behind me. It's OK; this evening I have enough energy and optimism for both of us. I have to say this town looked better from a distance. We have come into prime tourist area at peak holiday period; it's no wonder we are experiencing such overcrowding.

At every opportunity I stop to ask the same question. Inside one bright fluorescent-lit shop, the lady at the counter points behind her. Sure enough, there is a campground, but they only have room at the top terrace cut into the hillside. It's perfect. We have this elevated tier to ourselves, and with our bikes we can ride straight up to where the caravans can't. I lead us up to the flat grassy area and turn round on the last switchback to see No. 6 has dropped his bike. I can't let this pass unmentioned. I run over to help.

"Ha, how does it feel?"

"Like that," he says, pointing at my bike; the side stand has sunk into the ground, and the bike is on its side again.

Bollocks. Another perfect day.

DAY 88

SLANO, CROATIA, 88 MILES

The first sight for my morning eyes is a camera-grabbing scene. Without having to leave my sleeping bag, I can see bright pink flowers and palm trees that lead my eyes down to a stone-built seawall that creates a peninsula. Small boats are moored to the wall that protects the church and shore-hugging fishing houses, all constructed from the same natural materials. The far side of the calm bay is in the shadow of thousand foot cliffs. The sun shoots rays over the top to announce its arrival. Gliding towards the town with pirate stealth is a bloody great cruise ship. That would explain the crowds we rode through last night; the artists, performers and traders were all there to create and sell the tradition and authenticity of Montenegro. No wonder we couldn't feed off the buzz, it was created solely for the souvenir hunters who take their photos and make their purchases before heading back to their cabins. From this side of the bay, though, as the sun peeks over the mountains, I'm seeing postcard perfection. It's so peaceful that as the ship drifts out of view, I can hear the shallow bow waves break on the shore.

My camera requires some attention, and I really want to change my tyres, check my email, and have some breakfast by the shore; maybe even a closer look at the castle we saw yesterday, before the throngs and the heat take away the appeal. I've been riding for nine consecutive days, every one of them spectacular, but I'm feeling the need to stop and process before I move on. I can feel No. 6's urgency to get to Slovenia, and now that the roads have improved I will slow him down even more with my plodding progress.

The shower consists of a curtain suspended from a square framework under a tree; a hose pipe is hung over the top of the curtain that doesn't quite pull closed, so there are views both in and out. I think mine is the best though.

317

One of the houses in the fishing village has diversified to cater to the likes of us; we have a tablecloth breakfast with a designer coffee price tag. Having two bikes creates a disproportionate increase in interest. I don't know if it's the two different exhaust notes or the fact that the first bike triggers the awareness and the second receives the attention. We seem to be the envy of everyone; I envy us.

One of those unfathomably expensive boats goes past, the type you'd expect to see moored by a Monte Carlo casino. His momentum has leisurely rubberneck sluggishness about it. The only conclusion we can draw from his pace is that he too is staring at our bikes with lusting envy. Sorry, mate, you can't afford them; you could never afford the price I paid to have this moment. Since I did the U-turn I've been richly rewarded; the dark days of indecision are a distant memory. This is the contentment I came away to find. It comes at a very high price, but No. 6 is paying for the coffee.

We ride back through more fishing villages. The narrow road is ocean drive without the pretence; there are bright colours and strong smell, and always in view the other side of the bay are the striking vertical mountains. I can't think of a better way of seeing this than from the seat of my bike.

As we curl round to the happening side of the bay, we catch up with the cruise ship waiting for a vacancy at the dock, already occupied by two other cruise ships. Private helicopters pulsate across the bay like parasitic insects; there is an obscene amount of money here. Bikini-clad girls ride around on mopeds, displaying their perfect pre-crash and skin graft bodies. The well-dressed trophy wives drive their 4x4s down from their desirable cliff dwellings. Everywhere is transitory wealth and beauty, and none of it looks very natural.

Further on, we pass islands with mosques and churches built on them. When we gain a little elevation, the water gives a still reflection of all we have passed; only broken by the white Vs of surf in the wake of the cross bay commuter crafts.

I have some niggles on my mind. I need to stop; the mental list of chores is getting long. I feel a split coming on. Are we even in Croatia yet? There is such a variety of number plates I'm not sure. The continuous caterpillar of cars means overtaking makes no progress at all. It causes pointless fatigue; may as well just stay in line, there is no front to get ahead of. If I was trying to get to Split now for the concert I would be realising I wasn't going to make it; it's still over 200 kms away. I definitely made the right decision. I'm still teased as I ride past by a poster for the gig though.

The traffic becomes stationary. We pass it all until we reach the border control. I'm sure queuing in this heat has frayed some tempers, so without making any eye contact, we cut in the front, get processed, and get out the other side as quick as possible.

The traffic is horrendous; it's holiday route hell. We pull over at a lay-by overlooking Dubrovnik. I text my friend who I rode here with seven years ago. I'm going to have to stop; this is a waste of good road. It's the first road of the trip I've done before, and I was really looking forward to it. It's so disappointing; overtaking just accelerates me to the next procession of caravans and roof racks.

We pull off to a seaside town. At an open restaurant we have our last supper, a burger made with apathy; the youths who attempt to run the place fail in their roles of cook or waiters. They are the closest thing to chavs I've seen since I left home. It's an ugly sight and disgusting food in a nasty environment. We ended our holiday on a low life.

And that was it; what a brilliant excursion within a journey. I went to places I would never have gone to on my own and had twice as much fun by being two.

I find the kind of campground I now know I will never integrate into. I take the higher ground and spread myself out, do my laundry and strip off panniers to change my tyres. It's a hot, dirty sweaty operation, but I'm pleased at my ability to do it. After the tricky 17 inch rear tyre, I move to the delayed gratification of the more flexible 21 inch front. However, I've lost one of my tyre levers. I sort of heard it ping off as the last of the bead snapped into place over the rear rim, but I can't find it anywhere. It's ridiculous; it just can't disappear. I don't want to believe it, I can't believe it, but I'm out of possibilities. I take the rear wheel back off, let out all the air I painstakingly put in with a bicycle pump, and lever the tyre off again.

Sure enough, in an exercise of inexplicable incompetence, I somehow managed to trap a 12 inch lever inside the tyre. Other than that hiccup and noticing there is nothing left on my rear brake pads, the operation and afternoon pass perfectly as my clothes dry in the sun. I go for a swim to wash my tyre-blackened body.

Responsibly, I watch the sunset, drinking water and rehydrating, then go to my tent for an early night. I press shuffle on my iPod. Eight thousand songs, and the first track that comes is *All Alone* by Mad Season.

DAY 89

VIROVITICA, CROATIA, 366 MILES

It's cool and quiet; my tyres are still inflated. Happy that I didn't nip a tube, I freewheel out of the campsite before 6AM. The bike feels like it's riding on knobblies. I pumped my little bicycle pump all I could yesterday, but I couldn't make the tyre bead pop into position. I'm wondering if centrifugal force will help them locate themselves, but the shaking of the bike doesn't encourage speed. At least I don't have a bloody great tyre lever stuffed inside the rear tyre. As the sun comes up, I pull into a petrol station. They have free compressed air. It takes a lot of deflating, lube, and inflating to get the tyres to sit right, and even then it's not done with a satisfying pop, but a creeping reluctance forced by 80 psi of pressure. I could never have achieved that with a bicycle pump. I pump my own fuel for the first time in two months, spend the last of my Croatian money, and I'm ready for the day.

There are two things between me and the amount of time I spend on the road; one is time, the other money. There are also only two things that are between me and the road, and they are my tyres, which is why this tyre change is so significant to me. I want "hit the road" to remain an expression and not become an experience. The bike is now riding smooth, and as the tyres warm up I take them closer to their edges. I wind round this coastal road, hoping the rubber won't lose traction taking me closer to the edge. After half an hour of reassurance, I pull over at a roadside wheelie bin, and with a short ceremony, a few photos, and as much respect as the action allows, I throw the Mefos away.

There is a four mile stretch of this coastal road where the Bosnian border meets the Adriatic Sea, specifically so the status of landlocked doesn't apply. The road is not living up to my memories. I've avoided the traffic with my early start, but despite my bike's diversity, it's not a transformer. This road is too fast

320

for it. I'm up and down the gears, squeezing the throttle, and pushing it over on the corners. Riding much faster than usual, the bike takes it in its stride, but it's no Sprint. Cars overtake me; that didn't happen last time. Then a sports bike blasts past. That's the moment I have to concede that the thrill of this road is dependent on the vehicle used. Expectations cause disappointment, and because of that, for the first time in 60,000 KLR miles, the bike fails to satisfy my demands. In its defence, I don't think many bikes that could get the best out of this road would have got to all the other places the KLR has taken me. I overtake a car; the bike revs and rattles. I get stuck behind the next one, and there is nothing else for it, I will just have to appreciate the view. The palms, the clear blue sea, the pretty villages, the tree blossom, all witnessed without the blur of speed and kick of adrenalin. Anyway, I don't recall as many villages and solid white lines. This road I rated as the best I'd ever ridden. I've ridden a lot of roads since then, but the rating remained the same. Revisited, it just dropped right out of the chart. I stop to look at the map just at the right moment. From here I can head directly north and take my recently conceived but unannounced return route.

My sat nav has jammed; it's completely froze. I have no way of knowing the distance I am covering now. I leave the Adriatic highway behind me and wind up a cliff of hairpin bends. The bike instantly redeems itself, and the new tyres are performing well too. I stop for breakfast and manage to reset the sat nav; it has now lost three months of data, but I don't care. Half an hour after leaving the restaurant, I realise I have left my back support belt behind. I'm not going to turn back. I don't intend to do any more off-road riding this trip, but it had been with me for a very long time. I'm quite surprised how quickly I can decide it's not worth returning for. I look over my shoulder and see it flapping from the pannier, the Velcro desperately clinging to a bungee cord. I'm glad I haven't lost it, but if it had feelings it would be miffed that it was so dispensable, the Velcro bond so easily broken.

Pretty soon I'm at the proper Bosnia border requiring insurance; I don't have any, and they don't sell it. I have to go to the other crossing a stone's throw away, but I'm not on a stone. I try to cut through north Croatian villages. They all dead-end; I'm getting annoyed at my doubling back and wasted miles. However, I have no time pressure, it's warm and sunny, and the villages are pretty.

I'm hearing metal to metal; I have no pads left on my rear brake. I'm down to just my mole grip-operated front now. When I came to Croatia last time it seemed like I'd ridden to a different world. I would never have thought about limping back from such a far flung destination. Now it just feels like the home straight. I can't imagine I will need a back brake between here and my garage, 1,500 miles away.

At the border I am shown where to buy my insurance, but I have no euros. I have Iraqi dinar and Turkish lira; I have Albanian, Bulgarian, and Czech currency; I have a credit card and large denomination US dollars, but I don't have any euros. There are about seven portacabins selling insurance; most of them are locked, and those that are open can't help. In a café the waitress speaks English; her only customers are the insurance agents from the locked offices. We negotiate an inflated insurance rate and a weak exchange rate with change in euros for a $100 bill. It was all unnecessarily difficult, but the immigration man is happy now, and I'm legally in Bosnia.

What a very neat race they seem to be. The house exteriors and gardens are immaculate, with flowering window boxes, manicured lawns, topiaried bushes; there's a real pride in their properties. There are churches on hills and mosques in valleys, standing harmoniously within the landscape, if not in theology. I wonder if neighbouring countries make fun of the anally tidy Bosnians. Matching socks hang side by side on the line to dry; logs are stacked so neatly I could ride my bike up them. Even the building sites have a clean and organized structure about them; equally, the farming is precise, with onions growing in uniform rows.

I'm yawning. It's only midday, but I've been riding 6 hours already. I am not going to have another Istanbul day. I don't have a destination. I know where I'm going; I just don't know where I'm stopping.

I stop for a Coke in a village shop. They accept my euro coin, and the owner chats away to me in his mother tongue as the two women in shop uniform behind the counter look on attentively. It seems rather over staffed for a village shop. Perhaps he was telling me the difficulties of supporting two wives from the profit margin on the sale of a single can of Coke. His language sounded Russian; he spoke, I think, of the heat from the sun, always a popular topic. It was my first Bosnian encounter, and to sum up an entire race by a country shop keeper may be wrong, but I think Bosnians seem very nice.

Inevitably, after a long spell of stimulating scenery and company there has to come a point when it all levels out. It could be seen as a dip; I don't mind, I realise it can't be spectacular every day. The thing is when this happens the reaction is to just ride, and that will never let anything in to replace what is missing. I could be home in three days, but I don't want that. I've lost my special status now; cars don't hoot any more, people don't stop and wave. There are plenty of laden bikes coming towards me, out on their European tours.

I go into a valley following a river. There are lots of camping opportunities, but it's only 2PM. I'm not opposed to stopping, but I have nothing to occupy my time if I do. Sitting looking at a river with a busy road of Friday afternoon holiday traffic behind me and nothing to eat is no incentive to apply my worn brake. The canyon gets deeper, and flies and bugs come over the top of the screen, hover momentarily in the vortex before picking up a current of air that can take them up my sleeve, down my neck, under my visor, or just out and away to find another windshield to head butt.

Tunnels start to appear as the river takes over the canyon; it's a fast river too— kayak world class, according to the signs. There are slalom markers suspended above the white water and even temporary scaffold grandstand seating for one's viewing delight.

At 5PM and showing no signs of stopping, I cross back into Croatia. All that performance with the insurance this morning, and I'm out the other end keeping my no claims bonus intact. I stab at the screen of the sat nav, but it's in its own little world and not displaying the one I'm in.

I put on my iPod. I'd been saving it for this road, but the battery has gone flat, and I only get half a song out of it. There is village after village, no space in-between to wild camp and no campsites either. I go to the front of a level crossing queue; it would be so easy to weave between the barriers. The evening sun is still hot and I'm exposed to it; there is no sign of a train, and I can see down both tracks. Even if I dropped or stalled the bike, only a bullet train would hit me before I got my bike off the track, and I think I could even dodge one of those too. I daren't go through; Croatia joined the European Union three weeks ago. I bet there are new laws about running level crossings, but god, this is tedious and hot and uncomfortable and tiring but probably better than being hit by a train or chastised by rail police.

I don't get a second wind, but I do get a pretty wave, and that keeps me going on. It's now been a twelve hour day. The area isn't inhabited enough to have a hotel and is too populated to camp. I've really picked the wrong route here.

I come to an area of forest and lakes; it looks promising. As I ride the dirt track, fishermen all glare at me; they look like they are set in for the night. Parked cars, hampers, and night lights. I continue on and catch the attention of a ranger. Bollocks. I ride off into some trees. The route's heavily rutted, muddy, and swarming with mozzies. I drop my bike. Double bollocks.

I ride on to a clearing, but it doesn't say camping to me; it's just not right. I turn around and, now in the last of the light, pass the fishermen who clearly don't take kindly to my sort round these parts.

Back to the main road, above a high fence on a pedestal is a motorbike. I stop and turn round; it looks like a club house. It's dark now. I do what I would never do at home and ride through the gates, down the driveway to the small throng of patch club members gathered round a fire. Time to man-the-fuck-up, Flid.

The men are older than I am. They come over to meet me. I take off my helmet as quick as I can, show my smile, and shake hands. I have no patch, no territory, and no language either. What I do have is a motorbike, and therefore, it would seem, some new friends. Yes, camping is probably OK; however this is not the last dregs going home, this is the early arrivals for a night of festivities. The president will cast his judgement when he arrives. Well, I'm committed now; I've just asked for and accepted their hospitality, I think the early night option disappeared when I did my U-turn. They all look over my bike. The mole grips are a winner, so are the stickers; war wounds say more than I can, although I can back up my bike's credibility. Not a single word of each other's language, but we can laugh, a universal language, and it seems to be flowing from both sides quite effortlessly. I'm given a beer, turn down schnapps, and pull up a seat.

The president arrives; a man of ample proportions but with a kind face. He seems accepting of me; they all do. The fire is in a fabricated barbeque enclosure; there is a spit of large pig proportions. I would fit on it perfectly. I hope I'm the only one thinking this. There are no threats or prospects out to prove themselves; in fact, I think they all proved themselves long ago. This is a club of maturity, and I may well be the youngest one here. More bikes arrive; there are about fifteen of them now, all with smiles. One of the guys takes off a leather bracelet and gives it to me. It's a really cool leather plait; I'll not wear it out of obligation alone.

A car pulls up, and a girl gets out, alone. She approaches the throng; what is she, a stripper? The club whore? One by one she goes round the men; they hold her hand too long, pull her close, kiss her cheek, and whisper in her ear. She clearly knows them all. She doesn't miss out a single one of them, and then she comes to me.

"Hi how are you?" "You speak English?"

"Yes, they called me and said an Englishman had arrived. I'm here to translate for you." Wow, what an honour, what privilege, what hospitality, what a pretty girl.

The various members ask their questions; it's hard to know who to look at when I reply—my translator or the person asking the question. Once their curiosity has been satisfied, the conversation between my translator and I becomes more personal. We laugh and flirt; she is single. I say she must be very picky when she clearly has so many admirers. Annoyingly, her sister is visiting and brought her kids too, so I can't stay at her place. It's not very often English is a secret language, but unless the fifteen club members are faking it, with our indecipherable babblings we seem to have rather quickly got into some true confessions. There is nothing superficial about this meeting. I'm obliged to have a shot with the president; corn on the cob is brought from the barbeque to the table.

Two things are made very clear; one is that I will be staying in the club house tonight, not camping outside it. The other is that I must turn the kettle off manually, or else it will burn the entire place down; wouldn't that be awkward? I'm given a tour; the shower is more of a storage area, the meeting area comprises the typical things—pool table, big TV, bar, ice machine—and the walls are covered with memorabilia. I'm told to help myself to anything from the fridge or liquor shelf. The tour concludes back in the shower room, which has now been cleared and cleaned. I'm given the key, and when I ask where to leave it, the president points under the door mat. Really? Thankfully this is not an all-nighter; they are all off to an event tomorrow, so the evening is dying down.

Do I want to go for a ride out with them?

"Now? Yeah, why not?" So I ride with the gang, not to do a drug run, not to torch a rival clubhouse or rap bike chains round the necks of some grasses or mutineers. No, we go to the ice cream parlour. We park our bikes outside. Some tables are pulled together by the waiter who speaks English and knows all their names. Earlier this evening I was trying to find a spot in a mozzie-infested forest to spend the night, now I'm eating ice-cream with a Croatian motorcycle club.

The president goes to another table where he has some lady friends to entertain. The supper is their pleasure. I say goodnight, show I still have the keys to the clubhouse, and ride back alone to let myself in. I'm told I will be met in the morning; my breakfast will be brought.

So there I am riding back to the clubhouse, unlocking it, and rolling out my sleeping bag on one of the tables. I'm so tired, so dehydrated; I think I'll just have a cuppa before I go to bed, what could possibly go wrong?

DAY 90

VIENNA, AUSTRIA, 227 MILES

At 6.30AM I hear a bike. I'm lying on top of my sleeping bag. I put on my combats and take off my T-shirt—"style darling . . . style." I think combats and a tribal back piece are a better look when answering the door than underwear and T-shirt. Warm pastries have been brought for me. I remember the guy from last night, but we can't communicate at all. He turns on the big TV; the morning news is on. The subject seems to be the sunny weather and the hoards heading for the beach.

I'm glad the responsibility of locking up is not mine. I'm back on the road bright and early and looking for somewhere to stop. The Hungarian border seems as good a place as any. The customs man says, "Old Kawasaki," when he looks at my bike. That, my friend, depends on your basis for comparison. Some people would never entertain the thought of riding something only seventeen years old.

I pull over, check my oil, and look at my map; I think the green routes will dictate the way home. Is the trip over now? I thought it was yesterday, but not yet, not if I don't want it to be, and I don't. I have a little plan, and I'm not sure how sensible it is. Actually, it's not sensible, I know that much; what I'm really trying to work out is how feasible it is. It's all feeling very European now; I see an old Russian truck and hang on the sight because it's the only really foreign thing around. My iPod is all charged up, so I listen to it and let my mind wander. My first taste of Hungary was three months ago, and it was about as exciting as tofu. A summer of marinating has done nothing to improve it.

Randomly, Dave Lee Roth sings *Good Times*. I'm not sure if it's making my mood or enhancing it; my mind wanders off to the late '80s when this song was our anthem, our orders, and became a self-fulfilling prophecy. They were

326

damn good times; better than this? Just different; these are damn good times too. Looking back on the old days is fine, but one day this will be the old days, and actually this is the best of times. When I do look back I will do so in the knowledge that I knew they were good times as I was living them. Time to live a little more.

I pass a Tesco; this is undeniably the road home. I go through villages where fêtes, festivals, and summer fun runs are taking place. I can see the delight in the preparation and anticipation of the day's annual event. People are up early preparing their stalls, hanging bunting, marking out car parks. Kids are bursting with excitement. A community is coming together, and I feel so alienated from it all. Where is my community? It's spread across the planet, too worldly to congregate in one place. We have fates, that's how we met; we just don't celebrate them with bunting and a tombola.

I'm heading for Lake Balaton, but I'm not sure why. Plastic chairs and flotation devices are evident before the water is. The traffic becomes heavier, the lake is surrounded by caravan sites, and I recall this morning's news reports and realise this place is not for me. I head away to the north, past lines of oncoming stationary traffic, impatient overheated kids in the back seats, uncool parents in the front. This must be their fate; I'm off to go and meet mine. This green road status was a token gesture from the Michelin Man to a bland country.

I'm heading to Austria to prove a point; it may be pathetic but seeing as I'm passing . . . There is a constant procession of oncoming traffic vacating the crowded city and all heading for the lake. There are plenty of bikes out too; Harley riders too cool to wave, sport bikes too fast to, tourers too heavy to.

Through an unmanned border and I'm in Austria, avoiding the toll roads, but still the slowest thing on four concrete lanes of heat as I enter Vienna. I thought I knew this city pretty well, but the high-rises all look unfamiliar. It could be a different city altogether; I don't recognize any of it. I head into the centre in the hope I will get my bearings, but although I see familiar sights, I can't get my sense of direction. It's a strange phenomenon; I know the public transport system better than the roads. I've never ridden or driven here before, always flown in. This lack of navigational responsibility means not only do I not know the roads, but most of the time I was viewing the city through an alcohol haze.

This pinpointing takes more than a posh hotel city map; it requires going against all my principles into a Starbucks. I have to pay €4.20 for a weak iced coffee to get free Wi-Fi. Before I can even get that, I have to register with the multinational motherfuckers. I search my email and find a street name.

I'm losing my cool, losing my way; I take to the streets again and head between the glamorous but indistinguishable multi-storey Viennese terraces, until I finally see a sign I recognise. I do a U-turn across some tramlines and park outside a door, a door I have been presumptuously contemplating the width of since Albania. Can I get my bike through it?

I can't even get through it; I don't know the apartment number. I press bell buttons randomly until someone buzzes me in. I know the way now; up three flights of stairs, and there is the door. Of all the possible faces that could be the other side, there is only one I want to see. I don't see any; the door does not open.

Oh well, I tried. I go back to my bike; I walk round the block. I know this area quite well; I think there is a cheap hotel round here, I know there is a bar. I walk a circuit of the block and go back to my bike then, just before I throw my leg over it, I look up to a window I've only ever looked out of. There she is.

"Flid?"

"Open the door!"

"Oh, my god." I wait for the door to buzz; it doesn't. A change of heart? Then it does; through the intercom I hear "Sorry, I forgot to press the button." No change there then, nor in appearance of the girl or her apartment.

When I was a kid one of my mates parents had a porn video; they may well have had more than one, but if they did, the others were better hidden. When his parents were out, we'd watch it. I remember one scene where a bloke in a leather jacket and carrying a crash helmet is walking up a staircase. He knocks on the door of an apartment and says to the girl who opens it, "Quick, babe. My bike's doubled parked." I've always wanted to say that . . . I still do.

"What are you doing here, Flid?"

"I was just passing."

"I need to get in the shower."

"I'll go and get something to drink." This time I take a key.

Outside, three blond girls are standing round my bike. I'm barefoot; I've only got to run to Spar.

"Are you admiring my bike?"

"You've been everywhere. Why are you here?"

"Stopped in to see a friend."

My jealous ex is looking out the window again, and unbeknownst to me, taking a photo of me talking to three blond hotties. It would be a good photo too, if not for my bloody bald patch.

Just like every other visit over the last six years, the day drifts into a haze of self-indulgence, and the only responsible thing I do is squeeze my bike through the entry door into the secure courtyard, where it stays for the next four nights.

Days 91-93

Vienna, Austria, 0 Miles

A rotating fan moves hot air around the room; lying on top of the bed I feel the vibrations from the first tram of the morning, three stories below.

I dream I'm on a winding road, pushed close to the edge as it zigzags between long smooth straights; knee bends and gentle spinal curves. As I become more lucid, I realise it's the bed I'm being pushed off by long legs bent and taking all the room. The space in the curvature of her back is the only niche I can find to counter-balance my body weight to stop my overhanging limbs dragging me onto the floor. The dream is over, but the road comparisons remain.

No more evidence is needed; I've had too much of one and not enough of the other.

It takes about twelve hours for the behaviour traits that led to our break-up to resurface, then we both remember why an ex is an ex. It takes another 72 hours to do something about it. Be a whole lot easier if she wasn't so damn gorgeous.

I visited a friend in a Californian top security women's prison; our visit was between glass, and we spoke for four hours on a phone of inadequate volume pressed hard to our ears. Having told her the story of my latest disastrous relationship, she replied with an inspired nugget of wisdom: "For fucks sake, Flid, we're all psychos; just pick one." Why is everything I like either illegal, immoral, or bad for my health?

So that's my familiarity fix; a home from home, electric kettle, milk in the fridge, a tap full of water, a bathroom door I don't need to lock. A covered bike in a courtyard of bicycles, viewed from the window by the lift shaft; a window that won't open because of all the empty bottles on the ledge. In bed for breakfast, coffee for lunch, and alcohol after. Eating out, ordering in, playing

329

songs that mean something. Avoiding calls on the 'phone, knocks on the door, and reality in general.

We're like Sid Vicious and Nancy Spungen in the Chelsea hotel but without the junk. Better get out while I'm still alive. I've got to be on my way.

DAY 94

ABERSEE, AUSTRIA, 213 MILES

Independent means. It's no wonder overland motorcycle travel has such a strong appeal to me. Unreliant on flights or dates, hire cars or hotels, I have a free will and an ever-changing plan. I'm not sure it's *adventure*, that term is as over-used as *freedom*, but it is undeniably a form of travel favoured by the selfish, the non-committal, the independent, and to a degree, the antisocial. Or at least the socially fussy, who choose their company based on their requirements as opposed to the package holiday party camaraderie. It can be a lonely business; solitude is an unavoidable part of solo travel, but it's how that solitude is dealt with that determines the enjoyment of the trip. In Azerbaijan I wasn't dealing with it well. Lately I've had the best of every scenario; I've been given accommodation and gifted tyres based on my lone status, then the exhilaration of being alone in wild northern Albania. I've had the rapport of a riding buddy, gang acceptance and assistance, and now I've just had the ultimate in creature comforts, a situation that satisfied a yearning deep inside that rarely gets acknowledged. The partnership, the couple, the sharing, the familiarity of comfortable company, shortcomings forgiven, attributes appreciated. I know it was only three days, but it filled a void. Unfortunately, as I ride away it leaves one too. That's the problem with addictions; withdrawal is a painful habit. Hard hearts don't break, but they don't bounce either. I've long been exercising the sense of denial; it makes it stronger than the sense of loss. Leaving is a daily part of this lifestyle; escaping is the long term plan of the obligated. Parting is a pain; longing is the result, a feeling not associated with enjoyment of one's own company. Missing is something you leave behind and take with you; if you don't feel complete on the road then you miss what it has to offer.

I have morning city traffic to negotiate and a bike to navigate; it's a great distraction. Once I find the road west out of the city, the transition to road mode is gradual. I find myself making mental lists of requirements and supplies.

At some point during the haze of the last few days I got a message from the guy I'm going to see Iron Maiden with. He is in Zurich. "Wanna meet?"

"Maybe." I can't commit, but now I think I'm going to make that rendezvous, so the journey is still not over.

The highway is windy and turbulent. I stop at a service station and look at the map for some green road options. Soon I branch off onto one, but I can't seem to find those confounded Alps. I do eventually come to some hills. It's cloudy and cool, very different to the hot city experience I've left behind. Why are there always grey days when you most need a little lift of sunshine? I'm thinking about my garage, unpacking panniers, bike maintenance, not the twisty road I'm riding. This was always going to happen, and to be honest, I'm quite pleased it's only just occurred. I've heard of people who race through Europe on their return in an uncontrollable urge to get home. I've managed to maintain some control over my urges, I'm not sure if my prolonged stop in Vienna smothered them or inflamed them; probably best not to try and figure that one out, anyway. There's more logic in a Ducati wiring diagram than in an animated emotion, which could well be the reason I'm attracted to the raw red beauty without a thought for the dodgy connections.

I stop for some supplies; €8 just for my staples? I'm beginning to see the reason people race back through Europe. I stop by a river to have some lunch, but a fat ugly woman shouts abusively at me to move on. Good old Austria, keeping the hate alive. I think this is my first really negative encounter the entire trip. I've been refused entry to places, like in Iraq, but not with hysterical yelling, I'm glad that one wasn't carrying a gun. Green roads and grey skies are such a mismatch; I might as well be on a motorway in these conditions. Nasty woman notwithstanding, it's actually a very biker friendly area: biker hotels, biker restaurants, biker bike parks. Shame the weather isn't biker friendly.

It's all very picturesque; neat and quaint, pretty churches, castles and houses. It's twee and tame, but I want wild and rugged. I don't expect to find that here though. I'm sure it's idyllic from the seat of a tour bus, but from my three month perspective it has little impact. My mood and thoughts today, if not my riding, have left me exhausted; I don't want to go any further. I text my lack of progress to my riding buddy to be, "Maybe tomorrow, eh?"

I come to a lake with campground signs, but it's caravan hell, not a single tent. Overweight Dutch and Germans with socks and sandals sitting in plastic chairs looking over the tops of their newspapers. I find a quieter site, ride to the far corner, and pitch my tent. I wander to a restaurant for a €10 salad that I reluctantly have to afford. I haven't really ridden my side of the bargain, and I didn't expect him to, but Quentin has decided to make up the difference in the dark whilst I've been wistfully looking at the view, watching the sun set behind the mountains, listening to my iPod in my tent, and unsuccessfully trying not to miss Vienna.

He arrives on a Transalp with a very large aluminium box on the back. On it are the obligatory stickers; Horizons Unlimited, *Overland Magazine*, Motorcycle Outreach, but from inside he produces Jagermeister, beer, and Pringles. He says he doesn't want to intrude upon my trip, but with those ingredients, mate, consider yourself fully invited.

Day 95

Kaunertal, Austria, 227 Miles

There is a strip of cloud that sits above the chalets and the tree line but below the peaks of the mountains. It looks like a big fat vapour trail; either side of it are the two halves of the same morning view. I'm not sure if I want company all the way back, but we do have the same destination, and scenes like this are better when they are shared.

Annoyingly, Quentin doesn't pronounce his name the way it's spelt. Why can't I get a riding buddy with a name I can actually say? He's got a very good map, and we take a route that isn't even marked on mine. As soon as we branch off the main road the scenery intensifies. When we pull over, Q tells me what his various hand signals mean, so if three languages isn't enough, he does semaphore too. I'm going to have to start writing this stuff down, along with a phonetic spelling of his name. He asks if I have any hand signals, but I only really have one, sometimes I stretch my left arm out horizontally, the palm at a 45 degree angle, my fingers splayed and tremoring slightly from a pivoting elbow movement. It means "What the fuck?" I generally use this when I'm exasperated beyond words or use of horn. So now we've cleared that up we can think about breakfast, or at least I can watch for a hand signal that means "Shall we think about breakfast?"

It's bright, sunny, and chilly. The smell of pine trees is on the clear mountain air, and if we weren't riding through the Alps, I'd assume we were passing an air freshener factory. We pass a waterfall and follow a river to a toll booth. Oh right, we have to pay for this scenery, do we? That puts a little blot on the landscape. We ride up to a vista point and discover there is a restaurant right at the top. It's just about open, so we sit up on the veranda and have a full continental breakfast with diluted orange juice and concentrated scenery. The day is already a winner, regardless of the cost.

It's cold up here when we are riding in the shadows and shade; I put on my heated grip, so at least one hand remains warm. I hadn't really realised how many faults my bike has; its decline has been a gradual process, but Q keeps pointing them out. In the more stringent West its dilapidated state is beginning to stick out amongst the two week tourers; maybe I should avoid Germany.

Q lives in London, even if I didn't know this, I could guess, because he is slowing down to look at cows. The distant mountains still have snow on them, and today is the first day of August. It might be a date that denotes an action; everyone seems to be out mowing, and there is a lot to mow. We are surrounded by hillsides of bright green, tall, swaying grass. In one such meadow a man is mowing the entire hillside with a petrol mower; he is leaving lines like contours around the hill as he spirals down. His dog lies watching him; it must have taken him days to do this much. The sight puts an annoying song in my head, "One man went to mow . . . " It has all the irritation qualities of hay fever.

We continue through pretty valleys and mountain views that are different again to any others I've seen on this trip. Still dramatic and striking, but with the chocolate box charm of the villages beneath, somehow it takes the edge off uninhabited nature. None of us have ever improved the wild with civilization.

Q thinks it's a lot further back to the UK than I do. He should know; he just came that way. We are riding very slowly; the scenery is much too pretty to race through. It's just so green, hills like turf farms; don't they have weeds here? There are steam trains and more waterfalls, dry ski jumps that launch into flowery pastures, wooden chalets with colourful window boxes, and so many bikes on the road. There are even bike parks with lockers for helmets and the like. It's clearly a very popular route, capitalized upon by all the bloody toll booths. These mountain views don't come for free and obviously have to be maintained; we have no choice but to contribute towards their upkeep. Eventually we wind down innumerable hairpins into a hot valley; the going is slow due to an inconsiderate idiot in a hired campervan who leads a parade of frustrated motorists, all of whom are affected by his oblivious or bloody-minded nature, but that's holiday traffic for you. Annoyingly, this hot crawling blandness has come at the most tiring part of the day; we just ride on through it. We stop at a service area; the campervan is parked up. I consider having a word, but it won't change anything; might as well keep the vibe positive.

When I was in Vienna I noticed on Facebook that a guy I worked with at a motorcycle show is also in Austria. We formulated a vague plan to meet up; it looks like this might happen tonight; we are only an hour away now. I'm failing to see how we are going to be able to head south off this highway when we are running alongside a solid wall of mountain. Ah, a tunnel. A very long, very hot, black, polluted tunnel; even a pearl diver on a Hayabusa couldn't get through without inhaling the humid exhaust fumes. Those not asphyxiated as they ride through the mountain are rewarded with access to a beautiful valley that weaves towards the grandest peak of the day.

We are on the lookout for camping opportunities, because I think this hotel we are going to is way out of our league. The receptionist certainly is; she is a perfect ten with the push-up Bavarian style dress, which is the uniform of the hotel. No point in describing her; she is visually flawless, from cheekbones to calves, all perfect. The alpine scenery pales into insignificance by comparison. She says we can camp in the children's play area. So having got accommodation sorted, we hang out with Dave and Abbie.

We are joined by an older GS-riding couple, and although I would never have thought it, the six of us create an entertaining chemistry. We bounce off each other, making for an evening of quips, witticisms, and the kind of laughing that makes beer come out of your nose and will leave stomach muscles aching. It's a credit card evening; sometimes you just have to say, "Sod it, I'm treating myself, taking advantage of what's on offer, and I'm going to enjoy it." It's too expensive to drink too much, so this is not beer-swilling banter, we must really be funny. We all seem to be bringing out the best in each other. I haven't laughed so much in ages. My slow speed is the topic of many of the jokes. I don't wear ear plugs when I ride. I don't need to; the road and wind noise are not significant at such low speeds. I do, however, wear them at night. It's suggested it's because I dream of riding fast.

This trip won't stop happening; it keeps reaching new peaks. From my tent, under a starlit sky, down the bottom of the valley is yet another one of those peaks. I wonder if it's the last one.

DAY 96

PLAINFAING, FRANCE, 174 MILES

The only thing that is on my mind are the two long days of riding that lay between here and Iron Maiden. Outside my tent is, I suppose, the last mountain view; it's time to run from the hills. It will be a long time before the sun shines into this valley, so I may as well roll up the dewy tent now.

I've put "home" into my sat nav to get an actual figure. It never occurred to me to do it before, however, it can't seem to grasp the concept, so I'm none the wiser.

I need oil desperately. I have been pushing the bike much harder than usual, and that extra 10 to 15 mph has had a dramatic affect on my oil consumption. We stop at the first petrol station we come to; they want €23 for a litre of oil, bastards. I really need it though; in fact, once I've poured it in I see the bike needs more than a litre; it's not going to get it though. I can just about see the oil level at the bottom of the viewing glass. With all the optimism I can muster, it isn't even close to half full. In addition to the bill for last night's food and camping, it makes for a very strong urge to get away from this area. My wallet is haemorrhaging money, and my credit card can't stem the flow. Now I know why people whizz back through Europe; it's so hard to come to terms with the cost of basic needs compared to the prices in far flung places that came before. Whilst we are having a little snack and doing some bike maintenance, the sun comes up and out come the bikes; they are swarming into the petrol station like mozzies. They outnumber the cars and are a pain in the arse, blocking exits and thoughtlessly congesting junctions. All of this adds to the desire to leave.

Back on the highway I feel like a tube train driver. There are constant tunnels; I get a thirty second glimpse of day lit stationary scenery before plunging back into darkness for another five minutes. You could ride this route on a rainy day and not even get wet. I've enjoyed the tunnels this trip, but these fast motorway ones are getting tiresome, especially knowing the scenery we are missing. I just can't get enough of mountains; I'm still thrilled by them, even after all I've seen. Austria takes the opportunity to extract more money from us before we leave, not charging for scenery this time but for the deprivation of it. We keep getting hit with tunnel tolls.

After my night in Croatia I spent maybe three hours in Hungary on my way to Austria, and somehow a whole week has passed in this county. I'm ready to leave, which is why I am riding faster than I would usually, and Q is riding slower, I'm quite concerned about my oil consumption; he's very impressed at his fuel consumption; slow riding has its rewards.

We enter Switzerland, a country I've never been to before, usually put off by its reputation for being so expensive, although I was under the impression from the world fuel price site in my favourite list that petrol here was only €1 per litre. But I think I must have been looking at Swaziland.

We leave the motorway to ride along the side of a lake. On the one hand, I would like to get my head down and just ride, but my bike is missing, cutting out; it seems to prefer the throttle twisting to the constant cursing speed. Ironically, in expensive Switzerland I manage to get oil for a third of the price I paid in Austria. I'm topped up and have some in reserve too. The other irony is that I have continually this trip seen sights I considered to be Swiss-like, and now I'm here I seem to have found the dullest, flattest, least stimulating scenery that Switzerland has to offer. This lakeside isn't much better than the shopping centre by the M25. That may be a bit harsh; but it's no *Ski Sunday* scenery, that's for sure.

With no more altitude and still being a long way inland the temperatures have risen to a tiring and uncomfortable level. The only escape from it now will be rain, a sea breeze, or a more northerly location like England, for example, where we will have all three no doubt.

We neatly bypass Zurich. The next big city is Basel, and the motorway splits and weaves; slip roads, underpasses, and flyovers. Lane changing, merging, and filtering; it requires a lot of concentration, but the signposts are logical and the traffic considerate. It's fast, thrilling, metropolis riding, nowhere to stop; I just keep my eyes open and my speed compatible with the other traffic. I exit a tunnel, cross a bridge over the Rhine, then into another tunnel. I pop out the other side like I'm the chosen lottery ball and discover my prize is . . . I've just entered France. I see a signpost for Paris, just in case I was in any doubt. I've just entered my twenty third country.

As I queue in a service station to pay for my over-priced fuel, I see a weather forecast on the TV; there are a lot of thunder storms about, but before I can figure out my location on the map, or even which day they are forecasting, the subject has changed. We head toward Nancy and into the hills; its good clear winding road, and with my new found speed I get into some pannier scraping cornering. When we stop, Q remarks on my riding style and says it's like when you discover that your dad is actually pretty cool. Is that supposed to be a compliment? Back-handed if ever I heard one.

There are a few campsites, but they have no appeal at all. We pass a pub that has a little grassy area at the side of the car park. I mention the possibility to Q, and we go back to ask. A strange thing happens; obviously I'm fully aware he is French, but I've never heard him speak it. Instantly, as if it's the most natural thing in the world for him, he strikes up a conversation with the owner and his wife in French. I feel like I should be able to understand; I recognize his voice and his accent, but all of a sudden the words coming out of his mouth make no sense at all. Along with his French language, he has also turned on the charm. As I watch, it very soon becomes obvious that we will be camping for free under the shady trees at the side of a river in the convenience of this pub car park. When the conversation is translated to me, I discover we will also be eating here. Two big fat beers arrive, and I can't think of any reason not to drink fast and have another one. The tent is pitched, and this morning's dew is drying off in the evening breeze. We go into the restaurant for a three course meal. It's art on a plate. Q explains to me exactly what the various creations are. It's the best food I've had . . . maybe ever. Everything about it; the situation, the company, the convenience, the aesthetics, the love and skill it was clearly made with, and ultimately the taste. You gotta give it to the French; they really know how to cook. It's no wonder they adopted ownership of the fries.

We are told (but only Q understands) that there is an event going on down in the village; we would be mad not to attend. By the time we have walked down it seems what was a day of market stalls of arts and crafts has become an evening of rock 'n' roll. A band with bigger egos than back catalogue are amplifying their covered songs from a scaffold stage. The guitarist has more testosterone than talent; he's taken off his top. I'm not sure if it's sweat or body oil that glows under the disco lights. With mirror practiced poses, he stands at the edge of the stage wanking the neck of his Stratocaster copy over the heads of the local girls, and they lap it up. The bar is out of beer, and without alcohol'd enhancement, the only impression the band will make is a bad one of the songs they are crucifying. To my surprise the next song is introduced in English; it's called *Bastard* and is about when the band's van got vandalized with crowbars at a festival they were playing. It's not mentioned in the lyrics, but I can just imagine that "tossers" was probably carved into the bonnet too. "I thought they were better before they made it big," is a phrase that will never be used in reference to this band. And after that brutal review, along with the other critics we go and find a bar. A comatose girl is lying in the shadows on the grass. I'm not sure if she fainted due to her proximity to her heroes, passed out trying to drink herself to a level at which they could be considered enjoyable, or just fell asleep out of pure boredom.

The last sound I hear when I'm lying on the ground in my tent is of a running river and crickets; the soothing harmonies are an instrumental lullaby. It's not very rock 'n' roll, but I like it. I just can't seem to stop wringing pleasure out of this trip.

DAY 97

LONDON, ENGLAND, 273 MILES

I hear raindrops on the tent and thunder in the distance; is this the storm I saw on the TV yesterday? I ignore it and hope it goes away, and it does. When I get up, the tent is dry, and I pack it up like Christmas lights, because the next time it comes out will be a first day, not a last. We are given complimentary coffee, cake, and jam. Q charms them, and I smile with appreciation, like I have been for months now.

We ride down past the now empty scaffold stage; the comatose girl has gone too. We pass a proper campground, but we absolutely made the right choice last night. We need to be very disciplined today. Q calculates that if we ride in one hour sessions and then have fifteen minute breaks we will be back at 2AM. I think we'll be back way before that, although the only fact I have to back this up is that I saw a signpost for Paris. The sat nav has completely died again, but this time it can't be reset. From the day it introduced itself to me in German I have hated it, and the thought of abandoning it in France meets little resistance. I'm still riding faster than I would like to, but it's steady and progressive. Q says we are still only doing 55 mph, but I'm sure it's faster than that. The cloud cover makes for cooler riding, then when we are having a break, the rain comes along. It's not too bad; we ride out of it, then into a rainbow and then more rain, but before we are soaked through, we are out the other side. We stop for lunch and congratulate ourselves at our discipline and progress. Q recalculates the ETA.

My bike is missing again, and when we slow down for a péage it backfires twice and dies. I've been through quite a lot of places in the last three months where a backfire like that would have attracted the wrong sort of attention. It would have been a very unfortunate way to end the trip if it had done that approaching a road block in Iraq.

The bike is hard to start, and when it does fire up again it jerks and backfires its way to the next rest area, where it dies as soon as I throttle back. It won't start again. I would rather be in a proper service area, but there you go; nothing left to do but deal with the problem. Our wonderful momentum has all gone up in flames, in the form of a fire ball out of my exhaust pipe. I get out my tools and spare parts, duct tape to stick the loose things, WD40 to loosen the stuck things. I'm not going to eliminate one component at a time; taking off the tank is a big deal. When it's off, I clean the air filter, change the spark plug, and replace the CDI with my spare one. Before I dig for my spare regulator rectifier, I press the start button, and the bike fires up on what fuel is left in the carb. Fixed without frustration, methodical and patient, very Zen-like.

Q has been very helpful and attentive; the scenario was not one of helmet throwing and foot stomping but a good example of dealing with a situation with a level head. The bike is running like a dream. I bet it was the sparkplug; it does have nearly 15,000 miles on it and has been subject to excessive oil burning over the last few days. One more stop, one more toll, and we start the countdown to Calais. I try and get my iPod to play something relevant, but it won't. Perhaps it's missing the sat nav.

We get to the port at 7PM. The ferry price is way higher than we expected; we've been looking online for the last two days but didn't book anything. The price we have to pay for not having had the constrictions of time limits is quite high. That's the down side of living on an island; it takes all your independence away. We can reduce the cost of passage by 20 euros by getting a ticket for tomorrow morning's 6AM sailing. Q thinks with this ticket we can say we arrived early and get on a boat tonight. So all we have to do is wait for this evening's sailing.

Up in the restaurant is a nasty looking self-service cafeteria, where I load up my plate. It takes about half an hour before the food reveals just how rancid it is. We should be leaving for the ferry, but I can't leave the toilet. In the space of 24 hours I've had the best and worst of French cuisine. That stuff must have been on display all day. I don't do French, and Q doesn't do confrontation, so they get away with serving such shit.

We head for the ferry; the UK customs is on this side of the channel. For the first time since I left, I speak to an official I can actually understand. However, we aren't allowed on the ship; with all his charm, Q just can't get us past the gate. I'm happy to just camp out on the dockside until the 6AM sailing, especially with my dodgy tummy, but Q has not given up. We ride back to the ticket office. I'm not sure what he does, but back at the loading barrier we are granted permission to board, and at 10.30PM we ride onto the ferry. It's full of scruffy English passengers. I've just ridden 15,000 miles; what's their excuse?

When we dock at Dover, I have to put on my fleece and big gloves. I get more petrol and oil and then head for the capital. At 2AM, as Q predicted, we pull up in Greenwich. On Q's door mat is an envelope containing the Iron Maiden tickets for tomorrow night. The journey is just not quite over yet. Looks like I'll be spending some time in Greenwich; no point in being mean now.

DAY 98

GREENWICH, LONDON, ENGLAND, 0 MILES

What am I going to do all day? I need adventure; I at least need Wi-Fi. I've got neither; do I have to admit I'm home now? No, I'm not home; I'm just back in Britain. I walk to the petrol station to get some supplies. I can read what the headlines on the Sunday papers say; I just don't care to. I can chat with the cashier; he just doesn't want to. I can use my debit card without incurring exchange rate fees; because of the price I bloody have to. As I walk back to the flat, a maintenance man sees my cup of coffee and says something along the lines of "I could do with one of those." I can fully understand every word he says; I just don't have a reply,

"I could have filled my tank in Iraq for the cost of this" doesn't seem like an appropriate response, so I just do that smile I've been doing. I've lost my ability to make a spontaneous comeback.

This happened when I lived in the States. If I replied to a stranger's comment, they wouldn't hear what I said, only the accent I spoke with. And after 30 years of prolonged visits, hearing "where are you from" every time I opened my mouth, I just stopped speaking. At lunch we go to a pub, mainly for Wi-Fi, as I have to buy some road tax for the KLR. I photocopied my last tax disc, put the copy in my tax disc holder, then sent off the original to get a refund. It's a requirement only for British roads, and I've not been on one of those for a while.

I'm at 0.00° longitude; it's the furthest west I've been this trip; the furthest east was Baku at 49.88°, which isn't that impressive really; it's not even a quarter of the way round the world. It would be a good location to recalibrate my sat nav, but its second death seems terminal.

There are some world class views from this south bank of the Thames. I can see Canary Wharf and the City of London, and of course, the O2 where Iron

Maiden are playing tonight. Q says we can walk there. Walk to a gig at a major venue? What a novelty, but how do we cross the river? He says we don't; it's on the south side. I argue that it's not. I only have the beginning of *Eastenders* to base my case on, but of course, that starts upside down. I'm beginning to get the feeling I am wrong and don't push it any further. We have an afternoon to kill; what do overlanders do when they get back? Watch overland DVDs, that's what. We watch one by a British guy who cycled to Armenia. It may have been because I've just come back from there, or perhaps because of my end of trip frame of mind, but I really enjoyed it.

All trips are the same, apart from the differences. We all have changed plans; all have lonely times, battle emotions, good ones and bad ones. We face challenges; sometimes we succeed, sometimes we fail, and sometimes we succeed by turning our backs on challenges. It's not an obstacle course with a clear finish line; we don't get penalty points for missing a bit out or doing some bits twice. After all, surely the ultimate point of independent overland travel is the freedom of it. Imposing rules upon yourself is a bit of a contradiction to the very reason for going away. Most of us aren't out to break records, be the fastest, furthest, coldest, or do the mostest. We just want to have some new experiences, the thrill of all the unexpected sights that are waiting around the corner for our entertainment, and consideration. Being a stranger in a strange land inevitably increases our ever-growing world view from tunnel vision to funnel vision as our horizons expand. It's what makes us better people; not necessarily better than other people, just better than we were when we left. We learn more and more about ourselves with every person we meet and situation we find ourselves in, and we continue to learn when we are not in company.

I like to think that when I go away next time I will be better equipped to decide what is right and wrong for me. The agony of making the U-turn decision, regardless of it being right or wrong, was an exercise in making the best of the decision I made. The most important decisions I have made in life have never been easy ones. Unmistakably, everything fell into place the second that decision was made. Contentment is our goal; it's sold to us through the idea of consumption; bigger TVs, newer cars, age reducing cosmetics, every sale, every action, and transaction is done in the hope of gaining contentment. With knowledge and experience comes a little wisdom. I know contentment doesn't come with materialism; if it did the owners of big TVs wouldn't go out and get bigger ones. It's an addiction that will never satisfy. I know a little more now of what works for me, and I think I know what will work better for me; that's what drives me. I'm not sitting back, complete and fulfilled. I still have ambition. But I seem to have found a pleasurable road to ride on the way to my goals; it's not an easy road, but the hardships make the rewards all the more pleasurable. The journey is the desire and, therefore, brings contentment.

DAY 99

HOME, ENGLAND, 63 MILES

And it was morning. Maiden's temporary tinnitus is ringing like an alarm clock. It's 7AM. There is nothing to wait for; I have a journey to complete. I've been sleeping on the floor, surrounded by the scattered contents of my panniers. I go and fetch my bike from the car park to bring it closer to the flat for loading. After all, this is England; I don't trust anyone. I left my ignorant bliss the other side of the channel. People are walking to work, going about their day, as I am mine. I go into the flat one last time to leave a note for Q and retrieve my tank box; when I come out, there is a flyer on my bike. It's advertising a motorcycle travel book; that's bloody weird. It's one thing to have lost my romantic status of long distance foreign motorcycle rider, but before I'm even home the direct competition is advertising their product on my bike. My god, is the country that full of adventure writers you can't park your bike without someone using it to pimp their product at "Will"? Anyway, I've already bought his bloody book.

I ride past the O2 and then through the Blackwell tunnel. I concede, it is definitely on the south side of the river; must try to remember that. I filter through the unforgiving traffic, stupid drivers on smart phones, and timid scooter commuters. I try not to hold up the dispatch riders; we look so similar to the untrained eye, but there is quite literally a world of difference. I know; I've lived in both of them. Once I get out onto the A13 I'm heading east again, against the flow, not to Istanbul this time, but into Essex.

Past Lakeside, which I realise now is not as nice as the one in Switzerland. As I head down the A12, I start to think of all the things that I need to do. I'm not even back yet. The journey started with the end of a list and ends with the start of one. I can feel the free time and the free thinking slipping away already.

346

I muse over the cost of the huge 4x4s that pass me; if they are owned outright, the owner could go away for years for the sale price of it. People say I'm lucky, but for the cost of a year's insurance, a service, and four new tyres for one of those vehicles, I have just been away for a quarter of the year. It's simply a choice. If my lifestyle is envied, it's only because the opportunities to do something similar are seldom taken. Maybe a great big car gives the same feeling of reward to the driver that my £700 KLR gives me.

I want to empty my panniers slowly, making a note of everything I took with me, but I think they are just going to be tipped out so I can do an Asda run. Already, life is becoming too fast to do what I'd planned to, but I'm hungry, and I don't want to eat any more meals that someone else has cooked for me.

Actually, I do. I pull off to a burger van in an industrial estate for a sausage and egg baguette.

A factory worker, whose coronary may come before his retirement, is standing at the van, his stomach overhanging his jeans. The lady serving says in all seriousness, "No, Trevor, you have to have your bacon and egg in a bap; you can have it in a baguette at lunch time; ya gotta have some variety in ya diet."

Reprimanded, but seeing the logic, he looks over to my bike, "Looks like ya loaded up there. Where ya been?"

"Azerbaijan."

"Where's that?" I should have said France; why didn't I say France?

"I bet you had a few experiences there."

"Yeah," is all I can say. Shut up, Flid; don't be a travel bore.

"Read the book. Actually here's a flyer; read this book," I want to say. I think it was easier when I didn't speak the language. Small worlds, small minds; mine has just exploded, and a fragment is stuck in my throat. I should have just talked about the weather; I assume they have been having some whilst I was away.

I think about the police and military interactions in Iraq; the welcome, the hospitality, the inquisitive smiles. I go and eat my baguette with my travel companion, our last meal of the trip together. I leave cup rings and yoke drips on its top box.

I ride the back roads to my house, past a dog walker chatting to a neighbour who is gardening. It all seems so mundane; vegetables for sale on a table top at the end of a driveway, chalked prices on a blackboard and a tin to put the money in, village commerce and trust.

I try not to ride too fast on the road I know so well. Don't screw it up here, not this close to home. My house is empty. The melting driveway is summer soft; I have the perfect solution. Out of my tank box I get the sat nav and put it under the side stand; the screen splinters in a rainbow of ruin. You have just reached your termination, I think to myself.

The spare key is still in its hiding place. I unlock the garage, pull out my mattress, and put my bike in the space it creates. I drag the mattress into a familiar house with strange smells, lay it on the bedroom floor, and fall onto it.

No doors slam, no dogs bark, no horns honk, and no one talks in corridors. I stare at the ceiling; my mind races round road memories as distorted as my sat nav screen. In my eyes I still see it, on my wind-dried skin I feel it, and on my lips I can taste it from the big fat soggy kiss I just gave my KLR.

This is where the journey ends; this is where new dreams begin. I'm not thinking there's something better around the corner; I'm just thinking about a lot more corners.

EPILOGUE

When I stopped staring at my bedroom ceiling and picked myself up off the floor, I picked up some boxes from my mum's. Last and first minute essentials and the leftovers, the items I didn't take with me: waterproofs, spare brake and clutch levers, the folder my log book was in, the crossed-off list that included my log book, and the envelope that contained my new speedo drive. It didn't take long to fit it, and just out of interest, I got up to my usual cruising rev range, and sure enough, I was doing 45 mph and had been for the last two months.

Also in the box were route plans. Place names that were nothing more than mileage markers now have a sense of identity; they evoke memories, stir feelings. A little more worldly-wise for the experience, I drew my route on my world map in the garage with a black marker pen. It doesn't look like much; the journey cost £4,564, and I rode 14,713 miles. That's only 131 miles less than my trip to South Korea but isn't nearly as impressive on the map. I should have used a thicker marker pen; too late now. That's hindsight for you. Unfortunately, hindsight lives in the future, which is why experience is something you don't get until just after you need it.

I suppose I should take these mole grips off before the MOT. They are knackered.

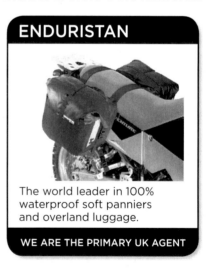

Other Books from Road Dog Publications

Also from Graham Field

In Search of Greener Grass
With game show winnings and his KLR 650, Graham sets out solo for Mongolia and beyond. Foreword by Ted Simon

Different Natures
The story of two early journeys Graham made while living in the US, one north to Alaska and the other south through Mexico. Follow along as Graham tells the stories in his own unique way.

Other Authors

Motorcycles, Life, and . . .   *by Brent Allen*
Sit down at a table and talk motorcycles, life and . . . (fill in the blank) with award winning riding instructor and creator of the popular "Howzit Done?" video series, Brent "Capt. Crash" Allen. Here are his thoughts about riding and life and how they combine told in a lighthearted tone.

The Elemental Motorcyclist   *by Brent Allen*
Brent's second book offers more insights into life and riding and how they go together. This volume, while still told in the author's typical easy-going tone, gets down to more specifics about being a better rider.

A Tale of Two Dusters & Other Stories   *by Kirk Swanick*
In this collection of tales, Kirk Swanick tells of growing up a gear head behind both the wheels of muscle cars and the handlebars of motorcycles and describes the joys and trials of riding

Thoughts on the Road   *by Michael Fitterling*
The founder of Road Dog Publications and Editor of *Vintage Japanese Motorcycle Magazine*, ponders his experience with motorcycles & riding, and how those two things intersect and influence his life.

Northeast by Northwest   *by Michael Fitterling*
The author finds two motorcycle journeys of immense help staving off depression and the other effects of stress. Along the way, he discovers the beauty of North America and the kindness of its people.
. . . makes you feel that you are on the journey yourself. The book shows how inexpensively a rider can tour America! Buy it, read it, and you will not be disappointed.—(★★★★ Amazon Review)

Beads in the Headlight   *by Isabel Dyson*
A British couple tackle riding from Alaska to Tierra del Fuego two-up on a 31 year-old BMW "airhead." Join them on this epic journey across two continents.
A great blend of travel, motorcycling, determination, and humor. —Dee (★★★★ Amazon Review)

A Short Ride in the Jungle   *by Antonia Bolingbroke-Kent*
A young woman tackles the famed Ho Chi Minh Trail alone on a diminutive pink Honda Cub armed only with her love of Southeast Asia, and its people, and her wits.

Asphalt & Dirt   *by Aaron Heinrich*
A compilation of profiles of both famous and reltively unkown people who ride dispelling the myth of the stereotypical "biker" image.